THE ABUSE OF INNOCENCE

"Remedial institutions are apt to fall under the control of the enemy, and to become the instruments of oppression."
Louis D. Brandeis
U.S. Supreme Court Justice 1916-1939

"The great masses of the people . . . will more easily fall victims to a big lie than to a small one."
Adolf Hitler (1933)

THE ABUSE OF INNOCENCE

THE McMARTIN PRESCHOOL TRIAL

PAUL AND SHIRLEY EBERLE

Prometheus Books
59 John Glenn Drive
Amherst, New York 14228-2119

Published 2003 by Prometheus Books

The Abuse of Innocence: The McMartin Preschool Trial. Copyright © 1993 by Paul Eberle and Shirley Eberle. All rights reserved. No part of this publication may be reproduced, stored in a retrieval system, or transmitted in any form or by any means, digital, electronic, mechanical, photocopying, recording, or otherwise, or conveyed via the Internet or a Web site without prior written permission of the publisher, except in the case of brief quotations embodied in critical articles and reviews.

Inquiries should be addressed to
Prometheus Books
59 John Glenn Drive
Amherst, New York 14228-2119
VOICE: 716-691-0133, ext. 210
FAX: 716-691-0137
WWW.PROMETHEUSBOOKS.COM

13   12   11   5

Library of Congress Cataloging-in-Publication Data

Eberle, Paul, 1928–
    The abuse of innocence : the McMartin Preschool trial / by Paul Eberle and Shirley Eberle.
       p. cm.
    Includes bibliographical references.
    Originally published in hardcover.
    ISBN 13: 978-1-59102-165-0
    ISBN 10: 1-59102-165-0

    1. Buckey, Ray—Trials, litigation, etc. 2. Buckey, Peggy McMartin—Trials, litigation, etc. 3. Trials (Child molesting)—California—Los Angeles. I. Eberle, Shirley, 1929–   . II. Title.

KF224.M215E23   1993
345.73'025554—dc20
[347.30525554]   92-40489

Dedication

For Walter Urban, Forest Latiner, Glenn Stevens, John Wagner, Eli Guana, Dr. Lee Coleman, Dr. William McIver, Ken Morrow, Bud and Judy Byers, and Carl Marks—the good guys who cared and dared to stand, and to do battle with evil.

For Allen McMahon, attorney, whose uncanny insight pierced the massive deception and fraud and got to the simple truth at the center of a very complicated event;

and for Ray and Peggy Buckey, who faced and endured their ordeal with courage and dignity;

and for Peggy Ann Buckey, Babette Spitler, Betty Raidor, and Virginia McMartin for the same reasons;

but most of all for Virginia, a very classy lady who stood tall and unafraid and spoke her mind when most would have sat in trembling, cringing silence.

Acknowledgment

The authors would like to express their gratitude to Mr. John Earl, a fine journalist who gave us invaluable assistance in the preparation of this book.

List of Participants

Defendants in the preliminary hearing

Raymond Buckey, 28, grandson of Virginia McMartin and son of Peggy McMartin Buckey

Peggy McMartin Buckey, 60, daughter of Virginia McMartin, mother of Ray and Peggy Ann Buckey

Virginia McMartin, 80, founder of the McMartin Preschool, mother of Peggy Buckey, grandmother of Ray and Peggy Ann

Peggy Ann Buckey, 29, granddaughter of Virginia McMartin, daughter of Peggy Buckey. Has an M.A. in special education and teaches handicapped children

Mary Ann Jackson, 60, a teacher at the preschool

Babette Spitler, 37, a teacher at the preschool

Betty Raidor, 67, a teacher at the preschool

Attorneys in the preliminary hearing

Daniel G. Davis, representing Raymond Buckey
Dean R. Gits, representing Peggy Buckey
Bradley Brunon, representing Virginia McMartin
Forrest Latiner, representing Peggy Ann Buckey
Barbara Aichele and William Powell, representing Mary Ann Jackson
Eli Gauna, representing Babette Spitler
Walter Urgan, representing Betty Raidor

Prosecutors in the preliminary hearing

Lael Rubin, chief prosecutor
Christine Johnston, who later asked to be taken off the case

Glenn Stevens, who resigned and was of the belief that all seven defendants were innocent
Robert Philibosian, district attorney when the case began
Ira Reiner, successor to Philibosian after defeating him in a 1984 election

Defendants in the trial

Raymond Buckey, 30
Peggy Buckey, 62, his mother

Attorneys in the trial

Daniel G. Davis, representing Raymond Buckey
Dean R. Gits, representing Peggy Buckey

Prosecutors in the trial

Leal Rubin
Roger Gunson

Defendant in the retrial

Ray Buckey, 37

Prosecutors in the retrial

Pam Ferraro
Joseph Martinez

Children's Institute International (CII)

Kee MacFarlane, director of CII's Child Sexual Abuse Diagnostic Center, the interviewer who questioned most of the McMartin children
Sandra Krebs, a CII interviewer trained by MacFarlane who questioned McMartin children
Shawn Connerly, a CII interviewer trained by MacFarlane who questioned McMartin children
Dr. Astrid Heger, the staff physician who examined the McMartin children
Dr. Cheryl Kent, a psychologist with close ties to CII

Police figures

Det. Jane Hoag, Manhattan Police detective who worked the case before it was turned over to the district attorney
Augusta "Gusty" Bell, an investigator for the district attorney's office who assisted Rubin

Contents

Dedication 5

Acknowledgment 7

List of Participants 9

One: The Hysteria 13

Two: The Trial 37

Three: The Closing Arguments 323

Four: The Retrial 357

Bibliography 415

One

The Hysteria

A father arrived early to pick up his little daughter at the McMartin Preschool. Walking to the front office, he heard the dissonant voices of children singing: "Ring around the rosie. . . ."

Raymond (Ray) Buckey was in the yard with his group of children. For Ray it was just another day. He could not have known that in a very short time he would be one of the most famous, or, more correctly, notorious men in the world, his name printed in newspaper articles and spoken on the electronic media almost everywhere.

A fat man with a moustache watched from across the street. The preschool was surrounded by three real estate offices. It was situated on an extremely valuable corner lot facing Manhattan Beach Boulevard, the city's main artery. The fat man with the moustache watched as Ray herded his group of three-year-olds into the classroom. Ray was a rather odd-looking young man. His drab, plaid shirt had faded from too many launderings. His thick, steel-framed eyeglasses appeared to be almost too heavy to be supported by his nose and ears. He was not a rakish young *bon vivant*. He was rather quiet and introverted. The fat man with the moustache watched. And smiled.

Ray Buckey sat at the table, leaning on his elbows in Room D, surrounded by the commotion of children's voices and the debris of art—collage and painting projects, crayons, paste, paper, watercolors. The multicolored wooden toys, shelves, and the little tables and chairs built to fit three-year-old bodies were highlighted by the bright southern California sun streaming in the windows. All of these artifacts were made by his father, Chuck, an experimental test engineer at Hughes Aircraft.

Ray was twenty-five. He liked the beach, and volleyball. And he liked his cat. There was an unspoken bond between them, and she accepted him as he was, with or without an advanced degree.

His parents, Chuck and Peggy, had given him an ultimatum: "Go to college or get a job." He had tried three colleges but was homesick and dropped out. He wanted to go home and work at the family's preschool. His job, teaching at McMartin, was an easy one. He liked the children. They liked him. They climbed on him, pulled on him, followed him, and called out to get his attention.

Some of the mothers were pleased to see a male teaching there because of the absence of any male influence in the home. Many of them were single mothers, separated or divorced, and their children had little or no contact with their fathers. Others thought it strange that a young adult male should be teaching preschoolers. There was also the fact that his hair was longish, as was *au courant* in the seventies and early eighties. And he was casually dressed; he did not wear the stiff, formal suit and tie in which some of them expected to see a teacher attired. But he was, after all, the son of its director, Peggy Buckey, and the grandson of its founder, Virginia McMartin. He would, in time, be their heir and successor. He was, like thousands of other young men and women, working in the family business.

Ray's grandmother, Virginia, was sitting in her car at the front of the little schoolhouse. Crippled by arthritis and unable to walk without crutches, she had turned over management of the preschool to her daughter, Peggy. But she still wanted to know every child who attended her school. Babs, Betty, and Mary-Ann, the other teachers, were in Rooms A, B, and C with the children. Ray's mother, Peggy, was in the office talking to a mother who wanted to place her child in the preschool.

Ray disentangled himself from a boy who was climbing the back of his chair and pulling his hair, placed the child back on the floor with the others and told him to "take it easy." He looked forward to the evening when he would be playing volleyball on the beach as he usually did with his sister and their friends.

Manhattan Beach is one in a string of small, densely populated cities in the affluent South Bay suburb of Los Angeles, tightly squeezed together in a row extending up and down the coast where the outer edge of southern California meets the Pacific Ocean. It is only four square miles, two miles fronting on the beach, occupied by about forty thousand people. The median age is thirty-five, and the average value of the homes is $200,000. Owing to its density and the close proximity in which its occupants live, the people in Manhattan Beach tend to know a lot about each other's lives. Even when they don't, they talk. The beach is kept remarkably clean. The sand is almost white. There are volleyball nets at intervals of about three hundred feet, up and down the beach as far as the eye can see. Unhurried shopkeepers sit in the sun outside their shops. Men and women, mostly under forty, jog and ride bicycles in shorts or sweat suits on the pavement adjacent to the beach. There are always people on the beach, even in November and December. A sign atop a bar on the beachfront announces that the establishment offers its clientele "turtle racing" on certain evenings. The homes and other structures are also spotlessly clean, newly painted and stuccoed, mostly white and light shades of brown and beige. Everything moves more slowly down at the beach. There is a leisurely, seashore ambience, a warm breeze and a sense of being far removed from the urban battlefields of downtown Los Angeles and New York.

Virginia McMartin's preschool had by far the best reputation of any in the South Bay. There was a long waiting list. Couples whose children had not yet been born were on the waiting list. Virginia McMartin was given the "Rose and Scroll" award by the Chamber of Commerce, commending her as the "Citizen of the Year." She and her daughter, Peggy, had been honored with many other community awards. They had operated the preschool for nearly three decades. They had cared for the children of most of the community's most respected families and were definitely prominent citizens themselves. Peggy belonged to all of the most prestigious community clubs and lunched with the civic leaders of Manhattan Beach.

The tiny preschool was an L-shaped, wooden structure with four little rooms and a play yard, with a slide, a swing, and other playthings made by Peggy's talented husband, Chuck. It was a cheerful, multicolored environment for children. Virginia's daughter, Peggy, had two children: Peggy Ann, twenty-seven, and Ray, two years younger.

It was almost noon. Parents began arriving to pick up their children. Ray and the other teachers brought them to the front of the school to wait for the mothers and fathers to arrive in their cars and open the doors. When nearly all of the children were gone, Ray sat down and rested. A woman's voice called out, "Ray? Your mother wants to see you in the office."

Ray had never seen his mother looking quite the way she looked when he entered her office. She was visibly dazed and astonished. And frightened.

"Doris just called me and she said, 'Peggy, what's going on?' She told me that Det. Jane Hoag at the police department has been calling our parents all over town and telling them that a parent has accused you of molesting her child, and saying, 'I want you to ask your children if Ray Buckey touched your child in the butt or in the vagina.' I was so shocked I could not get it in my head what she was talking about. So she repeated it to me."

Peggy paused.

"Did anything happen that I should know about so I could call the parent? Is there anything you haven't told me about?" Stunned, he thought about it for a moment.

"Annette grabbed me in the crotch once, through my pants," Ray recalled.

"What did you do?" his mother asked.

"I grabbed her hand and took it away and told her, 'You don't do that.' "

"I wish you had told me," Peggy said. Peggy called the police department and was told that Det. Hoag wasn't there. The next day she saw Doris, the woman who had called to ask her about Hoag's allegations, passing in front of a bank.

"Well, Peggy, everybody knows about it," the woman said.

Peggy returned to her house. She had been there only a few minutes when she heard a loud banging on her front door, so violent that she was afraid the door would be ripped from its hinges. She opened the door and was confronted by the police, one of whom was the father of a child enrolled in her preschool, a longtime acquaintance. He announced that they had a search warrant. They began their search of her home. Then they searched Virginia McMartin's home. Virginia kept a box of three-by-five-inch cards in her desk with the names and addresses of all the families of children who had attended her preschool, past and present. When she saw, in the newspapers, that a member of one of these families had died or married she always sent them a note of condolence or congratulation. The police took the box of file cards. Virginia vehemently and loudly objected to this seizure of her private papers but was ignored. Then, they searched the school.

In the afternoon Ray walked to the school. His father was standing there. And two policemen.

"Are you Ray Buckey?" one of them asked.

"Yes."

"You're under arrest."

When Ray walked into the house after being bailed out, he went to his mother.

"Mom, why are they doing this to me?"

"Ray, I don't know."

The police were told by the district attorney's office that there was not sufficient evidence to go forward with the case. Buckey's bail was refunded.

The next day, using Virginia's card file containing the names and addresses of children who were attending the McMartin Preschool or had attended in the past, the police sent out a letter to two hundred families:

Dear Parent,

This department is conducting a criminal investigation involving child molestation (288 P.C.). Ray Buckey, an employee of Virginia McMartin's Preschool was arrested September 7, 1983, by this department. The following procedure is obviously an unpleasant one, but to protect the rights of your children as well as the rights of the accused, this inquiry is necessary for a complete investigation. Records indicate that your child has been or is currently a student at the preschool. We are asking your assistance in this continuing investigation. Please question your child to see if he or she has been a witness to any crime or if he or she has been a victim. Our investigation indicates that possible criminal acts include oral sex, fondling of genitals, buttocks or chest area, and sodomy, possibly committed under the pretense of taking the child's temperature. Also, photos may have been taken of children without their clothing. Any information from your child regarding having ever observed Ray Buckey to leave a classroom alone with a child during a nap period or if they have ever observed Ray Buckey tie up a child is important. Please complete the enclosed information form and return it to this department in the enclosed stamped envelope as soon as possible. We will contact you if circumstances dictate same. We ask you to keep this information strictly confidential because of the nature of the charges and the highly emotional effect it could have on our community. Please do not discuss this investigation with anyone outside your immediate family. Do not contact or discuss this investigation with Raymond Buckey or any member of the accused defendant's family or employees connected with the McMartin Preschool. THERE IS NO EVIDENCE TO INDICATE THAT THE MANAGEMENT OF VIRGINIA McMARTIN'S PRESCHOOL HAD ANY KNOWLEDGE OF THIS SITUATION AND NO DETRIMENTAL INFORMATION CONCERNING THE OPERATION OF THE SCHOOL HAS BEEN DISCOVERED DURING THIS INVESTIGATION FOR ANY CRIMINAL ACT. Your prompt attention to this matter and reply no later than September 16, 1983, will be appreciated.

Harry L. Kuhimeyer, Jr.
Chief of Police

John Wenner, Captain

The result was mass hysteria. There was a meeting attended by hundreds of Manhattan Beach parents. A spokesman from the district attorney's office was there. The parents began taking their children out of the preschool.

Anonymous death threats began. Peggy Buckey closed her school for the last time. The Buckeys sued the police department, charging libel and false arrest. The district attorney's office began sending the parents and their children to Children's Institute International (CII), a private clinic in downtown Los Angeles, for evaluation. Kee MacFarlane, director of CII's Child Sexual Abuse Diagnostic Center, was a friend of Deputy District Attorney Jean Matusinka, the prosecutor. At first the parents were reluctant to put their children into a process they knew nothing about, one with rather embarrassing overtones. The prosecutor and Kee MacFarlane organized meetings in Manhattan Beach to persuade the parents to bring their children to CII. There, they were interviewed by Kee MacFarlane and her two assistants, Sandra Krebs and Shawn Connerly, who videotaped the interviews. Then the children were given physical examinations at CII by Dr. Astrid Heger, a staff pediatrician.

Parents were told at CII that every child who had attended the McMartin Preschool had been sexually abused. The police letter of September 7 caused pandemonium in the community but the statements of Kee MacFarlane and others at CII magnified it tenfold. Suddenly, tales of blood-drinking, satanic cults perpetrating "ritual sexual abuse" of children were exchanged everywhere in public in private homes. By this time the case had no further need of Det. Jane Hoag. It had taken on a life of its own.

A group of local residents began roaming the streets at night, searching for child molesters and "pornography." They torched Virginia McMartin's preschool and, using a spray can, painted their message on the wall: "ONLY THE BEGINNING" and "RAY MUST DIE."

One of these was the fat man. He had frequently visited Peggy at the preschool and unctuously tried to persuade her to sell it to him. He came to visit her again and told her that he had just come from a meeting of local residents, and that they were planning to "take away everything you have."

"Oh, they wouldn't do that," Peggy said.

According to a newspaper story, Dr. Cheryl Kent, a psychologist with close ties to CII, publicly announced that about one hundred preschoolers at a tiny, neighboring preschool in Manhattan Beach had been sexually abused.

In the wake of all this, seven preschools in the surrounding South Bay suburb of Los Angeles were closed, some voluntarily, some by order of the state. A Department of Social Services attorney, Daniel Lewis, stated that children had been swapped between McMartin and another Manhattan Beach preschool for the purpose of molestation.

The American Martyrs Catholic Church in Manhattan Beach invited a priest from San Francisco, Rev. Michael Harriman, reputed to be an expert on satanic cults, to come to the church. He addressed an audience of about four hundred parents and told them that, "This group . . . is trying to let people know that (evil) exists," by performing such horrifying acts as child sexual abuse and animal sacrifices.

The district attorney's office asked Kee MacFarlane to select the children who would make the most viable witnesses, those who would not crumble under the ordeal of cross-examination. She selected twenty-five.

On February 2, 1984, reporter Wayne Satz broke the story on KABC-TV, Channel 7, on the five o'clock news, scooping everybody at a time when ratings sweeps were being taken. He was literally killing the other media who, in a desperate effort to compete, came up with even more horrifying stories of satanic ritual abuse and the slaughter of animals.

Wayne Satz was not only a newsman; he was also a lawyer. He knew where the line was drawn between libel and reporting allegations. Some of the others did not. He was careful to use qualifiers like "alleged," and "accused." Some of the others did not. Wayne Satz had many admirers. For years, he had specialized in stories of police malpractice and brutality, a very bold and dangerous thing to do. Satz had won a Peabody Award for his reportage of police shootings of civilians. He won two "Golden Mike" awards for his McMartin reportage. Each evening he scooped everybody, broadcasting reports of new, horrifying allegations of child abuse at McMartin: charges that children had been filmed in child pornography, that they had been forced to witness the slaughter of animals to frighten them into silence; that they had been forced to drink blood in satanic rituals; and that a live baby had been sacrificed.

Deputy District Attorney Eleanor Barrett was reported to have announced that millions of pornographic photographs had been taken. District Attorney Robert Philibosian stated on television that he had just cracked the biggest case of organized crime and child pornography in American history.

In March, a grand jury was convened and indicted not only Ray Buckey but also his mother; his grandmother, Virginia; his sister, Peggy Ann; and three teachers, Mary Ann Jackson, Betty Raidor, and Babette Spitler. Ray Buckey's attorney asked to be allowed to surrender his client inconspicuously to the authorities. The district attorney's office notified KABC-TV, and arrested Ray and his mother before the cameras of Channel 7, for millions to see. Peggy fainted. All but Virginia and Mary Ann Jackson were held without bail.

The shocking accusations spread in waves across the country and around the world. On ABC-TV's "20-20," Tom Jarriel referred to the preschool as "a sexual house of horrors." He went on to say that the parents now hoped to prevent this type of tragedy from happening again. *People* magazine published a story on the case, referring to Virginia McMartin's Preschool as "California's Nightmare Nursery." *Time* magazine ran a piece on the case under the one-word headline: "Brutalized." KABC-TV bought a full-page ad in the *Los Angeles Herald-Examiner* showing a ravaged, ripped teddy bear. The ad told of the "McMartin Preschool horror," and concluded with: "This is a sick, sick story." On ABC News "Nightline," a substitute anchor declared, "All of those accused have pleaded not guilty but there is no question in the minds of the investigators that children were abused over a period off many years. How could it have gone undetected?"

The *Los Angeles Times* proclaimed, "They have told their secrets, the little ones and the adolescents, of rape and sodomy, oral copulation and fondling, slaughtering of animals to scare them into silence, and threats against them and their parents." The media reported that about four hundred children had been evaluated at CII, that nearly all of them had been molested, and that physicians had found solid medical evidence of sexual abuse.

A newspaper columnist wrote, "The truth must be faced that beyond any reasonable doubt, the molestations did occur."

At a posh bar near the Criminal Courts Building where prosecutors and other lawyers congregate, the five o'clock news began. Most of the conversation stopped as a disembodied voice coming from the television set told of the allegations of satanic, ritual molestations, butchery of animals, and the rape of two- and three-year-old children. Russell, a street-wise, black attorney, stared intensely and said without looking at anybody, "Those people are cooked."

Ray Buckey was driven to Los Angeles and escorted into the county jail. Virtually every time a law enforcement officer passed Buckey's cell, he opened the door and said with loathing, "Child molester! You're a dead man."

Ray and his mother, Peggy, were driven to the courthouse and taken into the courtroom each day for the preliminary hearing. It lasted for eighteen months, the longest preliminary hearing in history.

In the courtroom, the seven defendants sat in a row behind their attorneys. All of them were indigent, having signed over their life savings, their homes, and other assets to their lawyers. They were charged with 207 counts of child sexual abuse and one count of conspiracy. They were: Virginia McMartin, seventy-nine; Mary Ann Jackson, fifty-nine; Babette Spitler, thirty-seven; Peggy Ann Buckey, twenty-nine, Betty Raidor, sixty-five; Raymond Buckey, now twenty-seven; and his mother, Peggy, fifty-nine. An out-of-town reporter commented, during a recess, that they looked surprisingly benign, gentle, and respectable, that they looked in every way like your average, white, middle-class Americans. He was told that it was precisely such respectable, "solid citizens" who are often the perpetrators in such cases.

We still had absolutely no sense of who these people were, or what they would be capable of, having never even heard them speak. It wasn't until a little later that we came to know them and understand exactly who they were.

Journalists and spectators witnessed the strange spectacle of a tiny girl, sitting at the witness stand, beginning to answer a question with seven lawyers barking objections at her. She looked bewildered and stopped. Another girl, five years old, sat at the witness stand eating a large cookie. The lawyer cross-examining her complained that he could not compete with the cookie for her attention. The cookies were seized and carried away.

There was a sense of chaos and unreality in the hearing, even among the attorneys. A reporter asked about this and was told, "None of them have ever been in a case as weird as this."

One child told of watching Ray Buckey demolish a large horse with a baseball bat. Another small boy told of being taken to a cemetery where he and other preschoolers unearthed coffins and watched as the teachers hacked up the dead bodies, which bled. On cross-examination, he was shown a photo lineup and asked if he recognized anyone in the photographs as being among those who molested him in the cemetery. He pointed to a photograph of Chuck Norris, the actor; James Kenneth Hahn, the newly elected city attorney, and four nuns in a photograph taken about forty years ago.

Children told of being sodomized and photographed while nude, of being forced to drink blood, and of witnessing the butchery of animals while being told that their parents would suffer the same fate if the children disclosed the secrets of molestation.

The children, on cross-examination, contradicted their earlier statements and several recanted. The prosecutors and their expert witnesses stated that it is typical for a sexually abused child to recant.

An ex-convict who had shared a jail cell with Ray Buckey testified that Buckey had confessed everything to him, that he had told of raping a two-year-old boy and of having an incestuous relationship with his sister.

To almost everybody, the prosecution's case was extremely convincing. The media and spectators were told that the examining physicians said it happened, that the children and therapists said it happened, and that children never lie about sexual abuse, even though they contradict themselves or recant. In the face of many inconsistencies, denials, and recantations by the children, the prosecutors relied on their bottom-line assertion: that they had solid medical evidence.

The district attorney's office named forty-two children as victims and complaining witnesses slated to testify. The judge, Aviva K. Bobb, stated that there remained thirty uncharged suspects in the case. The group of militant Manhattan Beach residents organized to support the prosecution told the D.A.'s office that there were at least two hundred more uncharged perpetrators engaging in a mass molestation conspiracy involving satanic rituals and human sacrifice, centered at McMartin, and began pressuring the authorities to arrest them.

None of the seven defendants, after sitting for months in the longest preliminary hearing in history, indicated the slightest interest in abandoning the others and testifying against them in exchange for immunity or lenience, although such an offer was reportedly made by the prosecution.

A new California statute provides payments of up to $23,000 for crime victims. More than two hundred claims had been filed by parents of McMartin pupils. Gov. Deukmejian's chief of staff stated that, "We will do everything we can to see that the claims filed by the victims of this tragedy are expeditiously considered by the State Board of Control."

Kee MacFarlane, director of CII's Child Sexual Abuse Diagnostic Center, who interviewed most of the children, stated in a televised U.S. congressional committee hearing, "I believe that we're dealing with an organized operation of child predators designed to prevent detection. The preschool, in such a case, serves as a ruse for a larger, unthinkable network of crimes against children. If such an operation involves child pornography or the selling of children, as is frequently alleged, it may have greater financial, legal, and community resources than those attempting to expose it."

After the lunch recess, as reporters and spectators waited in the hallway for the bailiff to unlock the courtroom, there was a crowd of people with placards which read: "WE BELIEVE THE CHILDREN." A stout man, about fifty, said, puffing angrily on his cigarette, "If I had my way we'd just take those people out, one by one, and nobody'd ever see 'em again." He told the reporters that the defendants had been killing babies and secretly cremating them, and that they had been flying about the country, acting as consultants, teaching satanic ritual molestation to other preschool teachers, and that they were part of an international child pornography ring. We listened to his fulminations as we sat and waited for the door to open.

For eighteen months Raymond Buckey and the others sat there, mute while the lawyers argued and the witnesses testified. Ray Buckey is over six feet tall and slender. But his drab clothes and Coke-bottle glasses gave him a nerdy appearance.

The attorneys were an interesting mix. Bradley Brunon represented Virginia McMartin. Brunon is a very accomplished trial lawyer who lectures on cross-examination at the University of Southern California and other law schools.

Eli Gauna represented Babette Spitler. He is former professional boxer who now does combat in the courtroom. He specializes in first-degree murder cases and has never lost one.

Peggy Ann was represented by Forrest Latiner, a senior public defender and a veteran of thirty years in the courtroom. Latiner is a classy man, good enough to make it in private practice, but he has spent his entire career defending the poor and the dispossessed. Very unfashionable.

Walter Urban represented Betty Raidor. Urban is exceptionally bright and puts words together with wit, grace, and impact. He was designated as the one to deal with the media.

Barbara Aichele represented Mary Ann Jackson.

Dean Gits represented Peggy Buckey and Daniel Davis represented her son, Ray. These were the two principal players in this game since their clients faced by far the most counts. Paradoxically they were the youngest of the lawyers. Both were about thirty-eight. Both are short. Davis was impeccably groomed, wearing a dark, three-piece suit. His hair alone was a *tour de force*, assiduously coifed, blow-dried, and sprayed. Gits, too, was impeccably groomed, wearing a dark, expensive, three-piece suit. His hair, too, was a *coup de maitre*, meticulously barbered and sprayed. There was never a hair out of place. His tie and collar were never one millimeter askew. Aside from that, the two men are opposites. Davis was intractably verbose. His voice rang out like a Texas football coach. He was obdurate and defiant, which did not endear him to judges. He also put pompous, endlessly convoluted questions to witnesses, which nobody seemed to comprehend. Not much is known about Davis. Even the mighty *Los Angeles Times*, with its formidable information-gathering resources, described him as "an unknown."

Gits's style was very different. When he spoke there was an abrupt contrast: his voice was barely more than a whisper.

The lead prosecutor was Lael Rubin, a short, dark-haired woman. She was forty-seven. Rubin hadn't been a deputy district attorney for long, but had risen rapidly and was getting some big cases. It was she who prosecuted the high-publicity "Black Cathy" Wilson, getting her a long prison term for selling magazines containing sexual images. Glenn Stevens was only thirty-three and had previously prosecuted L.A. gangs. The third member of the prosecution team was Christine Johnson, a tall, young woman, about thirty.

The judge was Aviva K. Bobb. She was only thirty-nine but her short, gray hair and black robes gave her the appearance of a much older person.

Her past judicial experience was negligible. She was a traffic judge, doing mostly arraignments, and one of the last appointments of former governor Jerry Brown. She appeared to have some familiarity with the evidence code but frequently found it necessary to stop and ponder for a long time before ruling on an objection or an offer of proof. In the early months of the preliminary hearing she was having difficulty controlling her courtroom.

Most of the reporters assigned to the preliminary hearing knew nothing about the case. One of them, a middle-aged man from one of the large news services, misspelled Bradley Brunon's name: "Bunion." He also misspelled Eli Gauna's name: "Guano." Eli Gauna was not amused.

Much of the preliminary hearing was taken up not only with the children's testimony but with a debate over how the forty-two children would testify. The district attorney's office asserted that the children would suffer severe psychological harm if forced to testify in open court in the presence of the defendants.

Prosecutor Rubin had announced that forty-one child witnesses would testify but after the thirteenth, she conditionally rested her case when the judge denied her motion to allow five children to testify over closed-circuit television from another room. A new state law, P.C. 1347, gave judges the power to allow children under ten to testify over closed-circuit television from outside the courtroom if the judge found that the child would be unable to testify in open court because he or she had been threatened or intimidated. But Judge Bobb ruled that the new law could not be applied retroactively in a case that was already in progress when it was enacted. Rubin told the judge that the remaining child witnesses would not testify.

Judge Bobb dismissed sixty-four counts for which the prosecution had not called any witnesses. The next day, she dismissed an additional 145 counts. The angry parents from Manhattan Beach swarmed in the courtroom with bumperstickers that read: "I BELIEVE THE CHILDREN." The defense contended that having witnesses testify from outside the courtroom would violate the defendants' Sixth Amendment right to be confronted by their accusers.

A number of psychologists testified in support of the prosecution's motion to have the next witness, an eight-year-old boy, testify from outside the courtroom. For weeks they told of his nightmares, terror, and insomnia, and told the court that, after interviewing him, they believed he would be unable to face the defendants in open court. The mother of the boy testified at great length that her son was afraid of Ray Buckey, that he had sleep disturbances and that he sweats. Kee MacFarlane was one of those who testified. She and the others told the court that the boy could not endure the ordeal of being in the same room with Ray Buckey. Buckey laughed silently as he listened to this. Kee MacFarlane stated that all of the children reported having been terrified into silence and remained deathly afraid of the defendants. Ray Buckey smiled with a look of incredulity. He had been sitting there, month after month, inscrutable and expressionless but surprisingly, when he smiled, it was an extremely engaging smile. He really did look like the wholesome, all-American young man. Most of the time, he looked bored. He was sitting there for nearly a year and a half. He is still in custody.

We were told that the next child, if he testified, would be the last complaining witness. What happened to the other twenty-eight? Nobody seemed to know. The prosecutors said they were withdrawn by the parents. The parents said they were withdrawn by the prosecution.

September 26, 1985: Kee MacFarlane was on the stand again. Blonde, thirty-eight, and stylishly coifed, she looked angry and stressed.

"Did he say that he didn't want to testify in open court before the defendants?" defense attorney Davis asked.

"Yes," she answered, with a look of profound anger at the lawyer.

"What was it he told you about not wanting to testify before the defendants?"

"He told us he would not go in there if the defendants were present. We had to assure him that the defendants would not be there." MacFarlane's demeanor was hostile and sarcastic when she answered the lawyer's questions. She glanced at Lael Rubin, the prosecutor, with a look of exasperation, rolling her eyes upward.

When court was recessed, Betty Raidor was interviewed by a television news crew in the hallway. The hot, white lights were on her. She smiled sadly. She looked like a gentle, kindly grandmother in bright sunlight.

"Do you feel this is unfair to you?" a young reporter asked.

"Well, my home is gone. My savings are gone. All the things I put away for my old age are gone. And I didn't do anything."

They turned off the lights and thanked her, then did the cutaway. Paul discovered that he was standing next to Virginia McMartin. As usual Virginia was sitting in her wheelchair, holding her crutches. Paul, too, was using crutches, having broken a bone in his foot. She stared with great curiosity and asked Paul, "What happened to your foot?" Paul told her the dismal story. She listened with great interest. We had something in common. Crutches.

We sat down on the bench next to her and said, "We don't know anything about Ray. What did he do before all this happened? Did he go to college? Did he get married?"

"Well, he went to El Camino College. He wanted to work with children."

Mary Ann Jackson and Peggy Ann Buckey were there, waiting. They smiled and then left. Peggy Ann, as always, was pushing her grandmother's wheelchair.

On Monday, September 30, Judge Bobb announced that she would allow the boy to testify over closed-circuit television from an adjoining room, over the vigorous protests of the defense lawyers, who contended that even the most sophisticated technology could not accurately simulate the attorney-witness confrontation.

Tuesday morning, October 1. The monitors were set up in the courtroom. Three nineteen-inch screens, two for the boy and one for his "support person," in this case his mother, who was to take turns with the father. The cameras and the monitors were turned on but there was no boy on the screen. Just an empty chair and a blue wall behind it.

The courtroom and the hallway were packed with reporters and television crews and their cameras. All of those present had dressed themselves in their best clothes for the big media event. Even Judge Bobb had put on lipstick. For half an hour the reporters and spectators waited. Then, the judge came in and the bailiff called the court to order. The boy, dressed in a blue and white shirt, walked on camera and sat down, his brown hair neatly combed. He was eight years old and surprisingly small. He put his hands to his face apprehensively, wringing them together as one might do in cold weather. He leaned forward over the table.

"Good morning, James," the judge greeted him. "Can you hear me?"

"Yes," a tiny voice answered. His mouth twitched.

Lael Rubin began the direct examination.

"When you were little did you go to the McMartin School?"

"Yes."

Rubin asked him to point his finger at the defendants, the former teachers sitting behind the defense table, and recount his allegations against them. The boy said that the defendants had touched his anus and his penis, and that he had been ordered to participate in a naked game.

"When you played the 'naked movie star' game did Ray ever put any part of his body in your mouth?"

"Yes.... His penis."

The boy also testified that he was taken away to a house where children were photographed playing the "naked movie star game," in which they were told to disrobe and pose.

"Was there anything scary at the house?"

"Yes.... Ray would open this door in the floor and there would be lions."

"What would they do?"

"They would run around and roar."

"What did Ray tell you?"

"That the lions would jump up and get us if we told."

"Did you go to a mortuary with anyone from the school?"

"Yes."

"Would you tell us what you saw at the mortuary?"

"Well, he opened up some coffins and we saw some dead bodies." The boy smiled easily and did not look frightened. At this point he appeared to be amused.

During the noon recess, in the hallway outside the courtroom, seventy-nine-year-old Virginia McMartin slowly got out of her wheelchair on crutches and sat on a bench. Suddenly she found herself surrounded by television cameras, lights, microphones, and questions.

"That little boy used to sit on my lap!" she exclaimed. "Can you believe it? They can't take anything away from me. I'm seventy-nine years old. But the lies he's telling about my daughter and my grandson! Father forgive them for they know not what they do."

Cross-examination began. Bradley Brunon, Virginia's lawyer, stood behind Virginia McMartin and asked, "You're not afraid of Virginia, are you?"

"No."

"You don't think she would hurt you, do you?"

"No."

During the lunch recess, in the cafeteria, Babette Spitler and Betty Raidor came to our table. Both had gentle, kindly faces.

"What do you think of this?" Babette Spitler asked. "What do you think of that kid's story?"

"I don't know what to think. Lions? Devils? What was all that about?"

"Have you seen the school?" she asked. "It's a very small place. If you go down to Manhattan Beach and look at the school you'll see that all those things the kids said would have been impossible. That judge, she's been down to see the school and she knows that."

Lael Rubin, the chief prosecutor, walked past our table, turning her face in the other direction. When the teachers saw or spoke of her they called her "the evil witch," and "the spider woman."

Virginia McMartin joined us. I asked her about Judy Johnson, the mother whose complaint to the police started all of this. "I was working out in the yard," she said, "and I saw this lady and this strange little boy standing there and I wondered whom she was waiting for. And then I looked up again and she was gone! And there stood this little boy. She left this little boy! He was two years old and and we didn't know who he was or anything about him. The mother just left him there and didn't tell anybody. Not a soul. Well, that was enough for me. And that's when I told Peggy [that] the way she acted, I didn't want him. And Peggy felt sorry for them and said, 'Mom, we could be compassionate.' So this little boy was at our school for only six or seven weeks, two days a week. He couldn't even talk. He ran around a lot. Then she quit bringing him."

When the courtroom was unlocked at one-thirty and we sat waiting for the judge to enter, a young reporter walked over and spoke to us. He was a pale-faced kid, not more than twenty-one or twenty-two. He looked at us in shocked horror and whispered, "Do you know who those people were that you were talking to? Those were the defendants!"

In the afternoon a crowd of people from Manhattan Beach, after swarming at the district attorney's office, descended on the preliminary hearing courtroom with their placards: "I BELIEVE THE CHILDREN." They were expensively dressed and appeared to be mostly in their thirties and forties.

After the holidays, in January, three physicians were called to testify in the preliminary hearing as expert witnesses. They were reputed to be experts in the detection of child sexual abuse. They were shown four photographs: two anuses and two vaginas. Their answers were equivocal and they did not agree. One said he could not say whether there was evidence of molestation without the history of the child.

On January 9, 1986, after nineteen months of testimony, over 143,000 pages of transcript, and four million dollars spent, the preliminary hearing finally came to an end. The courtroom was packed with reporters and the angry crowd of parents. All of the television stations had their camera crews there. Judge Aviva Bobb walked in and the bailiff called the courtroom to order.

Judge Bobb ordered each of the defendants to stand, as she read off the counts. She bound them all over for trial.

She held Ray Buckey on fifty of the original counts and added thirty-one additional counts based on new accusations made during the preliminary hearing. She handed down eight existing counts and fifteen new counts against his mother, Peggy; two existing counts and one new count against Babette Spitler; two existing counts and seven additional counts against Betty Raidor; one existing count and seven additional counts against Peggy Ann Buckey; two existing counts and and three new counts against Mary Ann Jackson. She let stand the one count of "conspiracy" against Virginia McMartin and each of the others.

As she read the counts to each of the defendants she smiled sweetly. It was strangely inappropriate. She spoke with the face of a woman greeting guests at a garden party. The defendants looked weary and profoundly depressed. Virginia slumped against the wall.

"This is the biggest pack of lies I have ever seen!" she told the reporters. "This is exactly like a Nazi prison camp. I don't think there's such a thing as a truthful judge. There is no justice or honesty. The day I stepped into this court I knew that judge was against us. The D.A. came in here and lied and lied!"

A young reporter asked Virginia, "You're seventy-nine years old. Do you think you'll survive this?"

Virginia answered simply. "I'll survive it. I'm tougher than they are."

Out in the hallway Deputy District Attorney Lael Rubin, flushed with victory, faced a battalion of reporters, television cameras, lights, and microphones, telling the newspeople, "It was a victory for the children and the parents."

Kee MacFarlane was there with her communicants, grinning. The television cameras converged on her, too.

Back in the courtroom Virginia was standing next to her wheelchair, leaning on her crutches. "Well," she said. "I guess I'll keep on taking care of Peggy's dog and Ray's cat."

A week later the district attorney's office announced that it was dropping the charges on all but two of the defendants. We were speaking with one of the defense lawyers when he received the news. Within minutes it was on all the television and radio stations. In the afternoon there were banner headlines on all the newspapers. Even foreign language periodicals had the word, "McMartin," on their front pages. The five o'clock news television stations showed the Manhattan Beach parents angrily speaking of "child molesters going scot free." Ira Reiner, the district attorney, said, "The evidence against those defendants was so flimsy it was nonexistent." Then, there was Peggy Ann on Channel 2, saying, "If there's no evidence against me there's no evidence against my mother and my brother because it's the same kids telling the same stories." On another channel Reiner was asked about this but refused to comment. Then, on Channel 4 there was Danny Davis, Ray Buckey's lawyer, saying, "There is no difference in the evidence against these defendants that were dismissed and the evidence against the remaining two."

We changed channels and there was Walter Urban, Betty Raidor's attorney, saying, "They had no case. There is no case. There never was."

Ray and Peggy Buckey were bound over for trial, a victory for the prosecution. Although the Manhattan Beach parents were enraged by the dismissals of the other five defendants, this had the effect of trimming down the case and making it more likely to result in guilty verdicts on at least some of the counts.

On Thursday morning, January 23, 1987, Ray and Peggy appeared for arraignment in Los Angeles Superior Court.

"How do you plead?" Judge Aurelio Munoz asked.

"Not guilty," Peggy said softly.

"Not guilty," Ray answered.

It was the first time Ray had spoken in court after sitting, silent and inscrutable, for eighteen months in the preliminary hearing. What we heard was a surprise. In contrast with his lean, spare frame and seedy appearance he had an extremely deep, crisp, masculine voice, like a television announcer. A bass-baritone. Ray and Peggy were ordered to return on February 20 for a pretrial hearing. Judge Munoz was told that the mother and son were indigent. He asked their lawyers, Davis and Gits, whether they would be willing to represent their clients as court-appointed attorneys.

"I would be honored to represent Mr. Buckey," Davis's voice rang out. Gits quietly said that he, too, would be willing, and they were then appointed by the court. Ray Buckey had been in custody for almost three years. His face had taken on the pallor of library paste. He was still being held without bail. His mother was also still in custody, on $500,000 bail. She faced twenty counts of child molestation and one count of conspiracy. Ray faced seventy-nine counts of molestation and one count of conspiracy.

On March 23 Peggy was bailed out. Friends and family members put up several pieces of real estate to satisfy the $500,000 bail. The next morning she sat on a bench out in the hallway for the first time. Until then she had been brought into the courtroom from an adjacent holding cell. We were introduced to her and spoke with her briefly. She told us cheerfully that she had read our book, *The Politics of Child Abuse.*

Shortly after the preliminary hearing ended, one of the prosecutors, Glenn Stevens, resigned. Faced with a confluence of reporters, microphones, and television cameras, he was asked, "Why did you quit?"

"I didn't want to send seven innocent people to prison when there was no evidence," he answered. He went on to say that the D.A.'s office had kept innocent people in jail long after they knew there was no evidence on which to hold them. Stevens said the chief prosecutor, Lael Rubin, was very much aware that Judy Johnson, the woman who made the original police report, was unstable, and that the complaint that started the whole thing was fallacious.

"Without Judy Johnson the letter from the police would never have gone out and the CII would never have gotten into it. The case involved a lot of looking with no finding. Leads turned to leads and everything turned out to be dead ends. . . . There was absolutely no corroboration."

Several weeks were spent selecting a judge. Dozens were rejected by the prosecution; as many were rejected by the defense. Finally, the case was assigned to Superior Court Judge William Pounders. But before the trial could begin, Pounders was faced with defense motions to disqualify the district attorney from prosecuting the case, a motion to have the charges dismissed, a motion to exclude the prosecution's medical evidence on the ground that there was no consensus in the medical profession as to what constitutes proof of child sexual abuse.

Dean Gits, Peggy Buckey's attorney, asserted that scientific studies indicating what is a normal hymen in a child do not exist and that even the prosecution's medical expert witnesses had acknowledged that there is no such medical knowledge. An evidentiary hearing on this motion could last for weeks. There was also a pretrial motion challenging the admissibility of testimony by prosecution witness George Freeman, who testified in the preliminary hearing that Ray Buckey had confessed to him while they briefly shared a cell in county jail. Davis, Ray's attorney, stated that Freeman was a known informant with a history of concocting confessions for the district attorney in exchange for leniency and witness relocation money.

On December 19 a bail hearing for Ray Buckey ended with Judge Pounders denying bail. Ray's attorney assured the judge that Buckey would not and could not flee if he were freed on bail. He also told the judge that if Buckey were released, defense investigators would guard him twenty-four hours a day at no public expense.

Gregory Mooney, an attorney, speaking for the pro-prosecution parents' group, read excerpts from letters purportedly written by children expressing their fear that Buckey would kill them if he were set free. Mooney is the husband of Colleen Mooney, director of the South Bay Counseling Center, where many of the McMartin children were sent by MacFarlane and her colleagues after visiting Children's Institute International. She opened a preschool close to the time when the other seven were closed.

Buckey said to the judge, "I have never in my life harmed a child, nor can I comprehend how anyone would, or could, harm a child.... This case is my life. My future is in this case. There is one thing I do not fear and that is the truth, the truth of my innocence and my mother's innocence.... The truth will set me free.... I have never in my life threatened a child or harmed an animal."

Pounders denied Buckey's motion for bail on the ground that past testimony by alleged victims accused Buckey of threatening to kill them or their parents if they spoke of the alleged molestations. He said he was keeping Buckey in jail in the interest of public safety because a man facing eighty felony counts and a lifetime behind bars might have an incentive to flee. However, he also said that Buckey's freedom "could be just around the corner," and that if Buckey were acquitted after spending five years in jail, it would be "a shocking result." Deputy District Attorney Lael Rubin, the prosecutor, argued that Buckey was still a danger to the community and should remain in custody without bail throughout the trial.

On the same day, Judy Johnson, the woman whose complaint to the police launched the case, was found dead in her apartment. Defense attorneys Gits and Davis moved that the case be dismissed on the ground that her mental condition and her bizarre allegations were concealed from the defense throughout the preliminary hearing and the ensuing months. A hearing on that motion was set for January 5. Prosecutors strongly asserted that Judy Johnson's mental instability was caused by the stress of the case, but the defense attorneys told the court that documented evidence proved she was mentally deranged long before the case began. In a statement published by local newspapers Johnson had said, "I may be crazy but I listen to my children."

In the hearing, the defense claimed that crucial evidence was withheld intentionally from the court, evidence which, they asserted, might have exonerated Buckey and his mother. Some of Johnson's statements were not given to the defense until June 1986, almost three years later, and the statements were in the form of police reports that excluded the more bizarre statements of Judy Johnson. The police report surfaced with a typewritten note attached to it which read, "Confidential information. Not to be related to defense in McMartin Seven trial, per D.A. Lael Rubin."

Glenn Stevens, one of the original prosecutors, testified in the hearing that although the prosecutors were under a court order to turn over all evidence they had to the defense, they told police to withhold evidence they did not want the defense to have. One piece of evidence that surfaced during the hearing was some notes of Anthony Brunetti, a district attorney's investigator, which said that Judy Johnson's son was unable to identify Raymond Buckey from photographs shown to him.

The defense attorneys accused prosecutor Rubin of lying to the judge and to District Attorney Ira Reiner in order to keep Peggy Buckey in jail for twenty months, as well as withholding evidence of the mental illness of Judy Johnson.

Parents of twelve of the complaining child witnesses asked the state attorney general's office to request the California bar to disbar Stevens for turning over prosecution information to the defense. According to the Los Angeles *Daily News,* the request was made by attorney Gregory Mooney.

Stevens accused Deputy District Attorney Lael Rubin of lying to the court, the defense attorneys, the parents, and Reiner in order to keep the Buckeys in jail. He also accused Rubin of withholding evidence that could exonerate the Buckeys and of overstating the number of witnesses who could or would testify.

Seeking to block the hearing on defense allegations of prosecutorial misconduct, Deputy District Attorney Harry B. Sondheim accused Stevens of "having every motive to deceive and mislead." Sondheim conceded that the D.A.'s office withheld two important documents pertaining to the mental illness of Judy Johnson, handwritten notes and an investigator's notes of an interview with her, which were in the hands of the prosecution in early 1984. One of these documents was not turned over to the defense attorneys until June 1986. Rubin said she knew the defense was entitled to receive this information immediately in 1984 but decided to wait. Defense attorney Davis said the admission revealed a pattern of hiding information that would exonerate the defendants. Davis said he had read notes of an interview quoting former prosecutor Christine Johnson as saying, "Lael felt the defense shouldn't have it." Peggy's attorney, Dean Gits, commented later, outside the courtroom, "If we had had this in 1984 there wouldn't have been a preliminary hearing."

Stevens testified that the prosecutors lied to the judge in the preliminary hearing and overfiled charges to keep the defendants from being granted bail. He contradicted Rubin's statements that she was unaware of Judy Johnson's mental illness. "It was pretty much believed by both of us that the woman was crazy," he said.

When the hearing was recessed at the end of the day, Rubin told reporters she had "a lot of reaction to Stevens' testimony but I'll wait until the testimony is concluded and we hear all of Mr. Stevens's lies."

The hearing lasted for six weeks. Toward the end, Stevens declared that both Ray Buckey and his mother, Peggy, were innocent and that all three of the original prosecutors in the case were responsible for the failure to turn over evidence to the defense. Stevens's apostasy infuriated the Manhattan Beach lynch mob, who sat and listened with their bumperstickers: "I BELIEVE THE CHILDREN." One man put his fist close to Stevens's face and shouted obscenities. The hearing had begun over the suppression of only two documents but it disclosed several other pieces of evidence Gits and Davis said they never received. During this hearing, Stevens stated that he had seen his two coprosecutors holding a letter written by Judy Johnson in which she said she could not distinguish between fantasy and reality.

On February 2, Judge Pounders recessed the hearing for one week before deciding whether the charges against Ray and Peggy should be dismissed for prosecutorial misconduct. He was confronted with 148,000 pages of record and hundreds of hours of videotapes.

On February 5, Ray Buckey's attorney, Daniel Davis, filed a motion for a change of venue. Included in his motion was a survey of potential jurors in Los Angeles County, 97.5 percent of whom believed Ray Buckey was guilty. The pollster, John B. McConahay, a Duke University professor, said, "This is the highest percentage of prejudging guilt I have ever encountered in over thirty years of surveys of this sort across the country."

On February 11, Judge Pounders stated that the accusations against Ray and Peggy Buckey by at least four of the child witnesses appeared to be spontaneous and truthful, based on his observation of the videotaped interviews made at CII.

That evening Peggy Buckey told us, "Two of those children went to the school when Ray wasn't even there. One of them wasn't even born yet when Ray was at the school."

The defense attorneys provided the judge with written arguments stating that the evidence against their clients was in no way different from the evidence against the five former defendants whose charges had been dismissed. Dean Gits, Peggy Buckey's attorney, asserted that the twenty counts against her were made by the same seven children who accused the five dismissed defendants.

On February 12, Det. Jane Hoag testified that she had ordered police to withhold evidence from defense attorneys in 1983. This was the information that Judy Johnson had told of her son being taken by teachers to a church where he witnessed a baby being beheaded and was forced to drink the blood.

A week later, the judge ruled that the district attorney had acted appropriately in going forward with the prosecution of the two remaining defendants, Raymond and Peggy Buckey. He rejected the defense assertion that the D.A. had discriminated against them when he kept them in the case after dismissing charges against the others. "These defendants are in a distinctly different position," Pounders said. "I am saying there is credible evidence."

Defense attorneys Gits and Davis stated to reporters outside the courtroom that D.A. Reiner was taking the Buckeys to trial to avoid the political embarrassments of dropping the $5 million case.

Jury selection began on Monday, April 20. Pounders had ordered five hundred prospective jurors, and they were brought into the courtroom in groups of eighty. The jury selection process was expected to take weeks, or possibly months. In the courtroom were a group of the parents with their placards: "I BELIEVE THE CHILDREN." Attorney Walter Urban smiled and said to us, "By the time this is over they'll be saying, 'I believe the adults.' "

When the judge ordered a short recess, Lael Rubin walked out into the hallway and was confronted with the television cameras. There were many questions.

"It's been a long time coming," she said, looking weary. It had been a year and three months since the end of the preliminary hearing.

On Thursday, April 30, jury selection was interrupted by a hearing on a discovery motion by the defense concerning approximately two hundred videotaped interviews of McMartin children by CII. According to defense attorneys, the tapes were still at CII, and CII had persuaded the parents of these children not to give their consent for the defense to see the tapes, or, if they already had, to withdraw their consent. The defense wanted to see the tapes.

Davis told the judge, "I would like an inventory of all tapes and the names of all children on videotapes. What were the tapes and who were the children. Serious evidence exonerating my client is hidden at CII because CII does not want us to see them."

The judge replied, "I am not eager to look at one hundred hours of these tapes." He agreed to review four of the tapes. Davis cited one pair of siblings who were interviewed by Kee MacFarlane and stated that MacFarlane told the older one that the younger sibling said she saw the older sister being molested. "This was a lie," Davis asserted. "There was nothing on the tape of the younger sibling that says that. All this was false! Not one of these statements in the tape of the other sibling said that. All of this was false. The older sibling cried and swore at Kee."

Gits stated that Dr. Astrid Heger of CII pressured one little girl who clearly said she was not molested. "A whole body of information is available that has been hidden from the defense," he said.

The judge replied, "If there is exonerating evidence and the court cannot see it, it is a travesty of justice."

Gits said, "At least fifty children said nothing happened, according to Kee MacFarlane. The CII interfered with the court."

But later on, the judge said, "This has not particularized the need of the defense to see these tapes. I don't want to spend hundreds of hours viewing the tapes."

Davis responded: "I think I should have a reviewing of all the tapes. When the prosecution attempts to prevent us from having that information it constitutes a denial of due process. There will be a denial of due process if the defense is denied all evidence that would exonerate our clients."

Judge Pounders replied, "I'm not sure that parents' refusal constitutes suppression of evidence." He then announced that, "Every Monday we will take up the question of discovery."

A week later, during another discovery hearing on the two hundred videotapes still at CII, one of the parents, a father, testified that he did not want the tape of his child's interview seen by anybody. He was a short man with a bushy little black moustache. He spoke in an angry tone.

The judge told him, "These people are here on charges that could send them to prison for two hundred years. We cannot try them on anything less than full and complete information." The man was not moved by that statement. Recess was called and he muttered angrily to his companions. When Davis approached him during the recess he hotly told Davis, "If you got anything to say to me, say it in front of that judge," and he turned his back.

It would be several weeks, perhaps months, we were told, before a jury would be ready.

All of the defense motions were denied. After weeks of examination twelve jurors and six alternates were selected. The jury consisted of seven men and five women. Most of them worked for the government or for large corporations. Four appeared to be in their twenties, six in their thirties, and one in his fifties. One was seventy-three. Seven were Caucasians; three were black; one was Asian, and one was Filipino. Eight of the jurors were parents.

Faced with one hundred counts of child sexual abuse, Ray Buckey and his mother, Peggy, sat at the defense table and waited.

Two

The Trial

The courtroom was packed and the hallway crowded with television crews and their cameras, lights, cables, microphones, and various other gear. The bailiff called the court to order as the judge in his black robe entered and sat down.

"We are back in *People* v. *Buckey*," he said, "and all defendants and counsel are present." He admonished the media photographers against taking close-up pictures of the jurors or of the children who would be witnesses and ordered the newspeople not to publish the true names of the child witnesses. He then explained to the jurors that the opening statements they were about to hear "are not evidence but rather a forecast of the evidence." Each juror was given a printed statement of the charges. Deputy District Attorney Lael Rubin rose to speak.

"Your honor, ladies and gentlemen, this is a case about trust and betrayal of trust . . . trust placed in the hands of Ray Buckey and Peggy Buckey. Parents who will testify will tell you . . . they didn't ask about activities that were going on at the preschool. They didn't piece together the clues they were getting from their children. These parents will tell you they now understand the importance of listening. The case contains one hundred felony counts of Section 288-A and B, and one count of conspiracy."

Rubin said the teachers had photographed the children while nude, "played naked games and did transport these children away from McMartin." She further stated that they had threatened the children with great bodily harm if they told of the alleged molestations, and that the teachers engaged in "lewd and lascivious acts including oral copulation. All these acts," she said, "were committed with the intent to sexually arouse these children." She told the jurors that "trees along the property may have obscured what was really going on." She told them that on March 27, 1984, a convicted felon was placed in Ray Buckey's cell. "He will tell you that Ray Buckey made devastatingly incriminating statements, that Ray Buckey admitted sodomizing a two-year-old boy, had sex with children, that photographs and films were taken."

She told the jury that the children who would be testifying showed scarring of the anus, and that doctors "found evidence consistent with sexual abuse. You will learn that there is a body of knowledge . . . about child sexual abuse. These doctors ruled out trauma other than sexual abuse."

She told the jurors that "Ray and Peggy played, among other games, 'the Naked Movie Star,' where children were photographed in the nude. They will tell you in their own words that Ray placed his penis in their vaginas and rectums." She also told them that animal remains were recovered in a search of the schoolyard.

"Betrayal! These innocent children placed their trust in these two teachers and the teachers betrayed them. . . . One mother observed her two daughters performing oral copulation on each other. Another mother saw a sore rectum in her child. She will tell you she did not want to go to school, did not want to sit on her father's lap and that she ran through the house singing. 'What you see is what you are/ You're a naked movie star.'

"One mother will tell you that she saw her daughter masturbating with a wooden pole. One mother will tell you that her children had nightmares. One mother will tell you that her child had a rectal fissure. Another mother will tell you she saw bloody stools when her child went to the bathroom. Then, the people will ask you to bring back verdicts on all one hundred counts."

Rubin said a few words of flattery to the jurors, telling them they had been chosen as being the "best" of a pool of five hundred, and with that she ended her opening statement. She had told the judge she might take a full day for her opening. It was scarcely more than twenty minutes. Court was adjourned until the next morning at ten-thirty.

The television crews surrounded Danny Davis and a reporter asked him, "Do you believe that none of these children was molested or that they were not molested by your client?" Davis replied that Judy Johnson had accused her son's father. "She also accused Ray Buckey of molesting her child at a time when Ray Buckey was in jail."

A lawyer peripherally involved in the case was engaged in conversation with a group of reporters. One of them asked him, "What do you think of this, so far?"

"It reminds me a lot of Joe McCarthy," he answered.

"Who was Joe McCarthy?" she asked. "I never did know what that was all about." She was working for one of California's largest daily newspapers. The lawyer spoke with another reporter who was with one of the big, network television stations. She, too, knew nothing of Joe McCarthy nor the seventeenth-century witch trials. These are the elite of the Los Angeles press corps, the ones who get the big stories.

Tuesday morning, July 14. The courtroom was packed again. Judge Pounders entered and there was silence. "For the record in *People v. Buckey*," he said, "defendants and all counsel are present."

Dean Gits, Peggy Buckey's lawyer, rose to begin his opening statement. He told the court he intended to show excerpts of four CII videotapes which, he said, would demonstrate that the child witnesses were led, manipulated, and coached by interviewers at CII, and then again by prosecutors. "A visual presentation is absolutely necessary," he explained, and cited two cases in support of his proposed viewing of the tapes. "There is judicial authority for me to do this. I'd ask the court's indulgence."

Prosecutor Lael Rubin objected vociferously and there ensued a long argument. The judge allowed Gits to show the tapes with the jury still absent from the courtroom. The videotapes were perplexing. Rather than encouraging the children to talk spontaneously, it seemed to us that the evaluators did virtually all the talking and told the children very forcefully what answers they wanted from them.

The judge ruled against Gits and refused to let him show the tapes to the jury, saying they did not belong in an opening statement. The jurors were brought in and when they were seated, Gits began.

"Ladies and gentlemen, yesterday, Miss Rubin told you this is a case about trust. I'm here to outline Mrs. Buckey's defense. This is not a case about trust. This is a case about victims. It is your job to decide who are the victims, and what I call 'the enemy.' " He placed a large sheet of posterboard on an easel, listing under the heading, "VICTIMS," the following:

Mrs. Buckey
Teachers
The children
The parents
Manhattan Beach Police Department
CII

"It is the theory of the defense that all these people are victims," he said. "There is one more victim I will not name, but before this case is over you will know who he is." On the other side of the posterboard he had written just one word: "ENEMY."

"You will come to know Mrs. Buckey," he continued. "You will find out she is not a perfect person. Some say she talks too much, that she is nosy. But under all of it you will see a warm and kind heart. You will come to know that Mrs. Buckey does not molest children. She loves children. You will come to know that Mrs. Buckey does not slaughter animals. The D.A. seems to talk about games and mentions that someone dug up a lot, and someone left the school with a bunch of boxes, suggesting that pornography was somehow secreted. You will come to know exactly what was taken out. Also, you will come to know the money that was spent and the people utilized. It's what I call the nonevidence in this case." Again, he placed a large sheet of posterboard on an easel facing the jury, which read:

INVESTIGATION

PEOPLE EMPLOYED:

Three D.A.s full time
Five D.A. investigators, and as many as 14
Two full-time CII employees, and as many as 20
Twenty-two Sheriff's Task Force investigators who investigated 695 families about McMartin and four other pre-schools
One full-time Manhattan Beach Police Department detective and four others involved
Two full-time FBI agents and seven others

SEARCHES:

Twenty-one residences
Seven businesses
Thirty-seven cars
Three motorcycles
One farm

SEARCHED FOR:

Child pornography
Nude pictures
Records, diaries
Evidence of mutilated animals
Bank account records . . .
[a long list followed]

"The people interviewed," Gits said, "included 450 children and 150 adults. Also, forty-nine photo lineups were prepared, bank account records were seized and examined. Eighty-two locations were photographed, one church was investigated. Three churches were implicated, two food markets, two car washes, two airports, and one national park. Thousands of pornographic photographs and movies, confiscated by police, were examined in a search for pictures of the McMartin children. Laboratory tests were conducted of twenty blankets from the school, children's clothing, sheets, rags, and a long list of other items, including mops, kitchen rags, notebooks, soil samples, sponges, animal bones, quilts, underwear, and an archeological dig was conducted.

"All of these investigations came up negative," he said. "They were looking for secret tunnels, trap doors. They conducted surveillance of Ray Buckey, his family, and friends, which consumed 135 hours. They consulted with a satanic expert, U.S. Customs agents. They contacted pedophiles; they checked real estate records, utilities records, relatives, friends, associates of the Buckey family, other possible offenders, vehicles, uncharged suspects.

"They attempted a pornography buy. All of this cost more than one million dollars. The results? Zero! We believe the money was well spent. It was well worth it. Everything they investigated[—]and found nothing[—]is defense evidence! It was well worth it.

"Between August 17 and September 7, 1983 . . . Det. Hoag will tell you she contacted twelve families, and you can imagine what impact that would have. But the result of the investigation was zero molestation. Peggy's name was never mentioned. So, as of September 7, 1983, there was no molestation. There was a search, and the purpose of the search was to find pornography. So she executed a search warrant. A letter was sent out stating that Ray Buckey was arrested for child abuse. It told the parents 'ask your child. . . .' As of that date, nobody indicated any molestation was going on at that school.

"Within the CII structure, many things happened that you have to know. . . . And when Kee MacFarlane said a child had been molested, the mother would talk to another mother. . . . The interviewers gave the parent a nine-page questionnaire, and while the parent was filling out the questionnaire, they took the child into a separate room and interviewed the child for an hour, or two hours!

"You need to look at that tape carefully. . . . Why did the parents take their children there? They were told that they were experts. They had an impressive building. They had a separate unit called 'Child Abuse Diagnostic Center.' These people must know what's going on. The parents were told and believed they were experts.

"The interviewer in every case walks in the door and says, 'Mr. and Mrs. [parent], I have some bad news for you. Your child has been molested.' You will see the tape. Each and every parent was told, 'You have to be supportive of the child.' It is hard to disagree with that, but the result is that it reinforces the child.

"And they wouldn't look at the whole tape. They would fast-forward so that the parents never saw the denials . . . the parents were convinced that it happened. . . . The child gets love and affection. You will see that they were referred to a therapist. One of those people was an employee of the very agency that did the evaluation, connected ideologically. . . .

"The involvement of the CII didn't end there. They brought in an employee of CII, Dr. Heger. She will testify her findings. She will conclude [that] they are consistent with sexual abuse. She will testify the children were molested."

Gits said that the "medical evidence does not exist."

"You will find further reinforcement of the child. . . . It provides a bonding with other families. They have been told and they believe their children were molested in these cases.

"You will see from the tape how [a child] testified in the preliminary hearing that she was locked in a closet. There are no closets in the preschool!"

Gits cited another example, a small girl who testified of molestations and then retracted and said it didn't happen. When asked which story was true, she said she was telling the truth when she said it didn't happen. Gits cited this as an example of sibling rivalry. She went to CII with her parents and her sister. "And . . . she felt jealous and when the family went home she noticed that the family paid more attention to her sister and figured out that if she told the story at CII her family would love her more.

"You will see how easy it is to think that constitutes evidence of molestation. So simple. So easy. You will hear of trips away from the school and the problem of maintaining the school while all the teachers are away molesting entire classes. The parents did come and go, and yet you will hear of entire classes molested. The 'Naked Movie Star' game. Each of thirteen children spoke of this and not one played the game the same way."

Again Gits listed the victims: Mrs. Buckey, the parents, the children, the teachers, the Manhattan Beach Police, and the CII. "Why were the Manhattan Beach Police, and CII victims? Because they believed in what they were doing. They were not entirely victims, because they should have known better.

"There is one more victim, and that last victim is the same as the enemy. And when you get to know this person you will have solved this case." With that Gits concluded his opening statement. Court was recessed until Monday morning. The jurors moved indifferently toward the door and left.

Monday, July 20: Davis began his opening statement. "Good morning, ladies and gentlemen. As you might expect, I might take a full two days or even a third." The jurors frowned.

"I have heard negative things about betrayal of trust. There was something very, very wrong about what happened. The truth never really had a chance," he said, because children were artificially traumatized by interviewers into falsely believing they were molested.

"The evidence itself will be a source for you to decide. There are people who are primarily responsible for what is very wrong in this case. . . . What is the effect of telling parents that their child has been molested? If the child has not been molested, could you ever convince the parents thereafter that the child was not molested? Can winning a trial at all costs be consistent with justice?"

This brought a quick, shrill "Objection!" from prosecutor Lael Rubin.

"The evidence . . . will tell you that Ray Buckey was not at the school at the critical times." One of the child witnesses, Davis said, was interviewed at CII and shown a photograph of Ray Buckey and could not identify him. Then, after being interviewed at CII, the child went into the preliminary hearing as a witness and did identify Ray Buckey.

"Ray Buckey was not even there at the school when the boy was there.

The teachers who have died were not accused. Those who are living were all accused.

"There were good reasons for people putting their trust in the school. There will be testimony that naked games were played. The children played good, wholesome, healthy games. The children went on field trips. Parents came along. . . . Songs were sung. There was a music environment. No guns were permitted. . . . There were projects. Individual pieces were put up on the bulletin board. There were drawings and paintings these children did. . . . There were pets. Turtles, rabbits, guinea pigs, dogs, bird feeders. It was a happy environment.

"The D.A. sent [the families] to CII. CII said they were molested and referred them to therapists. . . . They were directed to Manhattan Beach Police Department and made statements . . . and parents were told to go to an agency that provides funds for victims. That led to payments to CII and therapists. . . . Witnesses were generated. The D.A. is putting on his case with witnesses almost entirely from CII. CII provided the witnesses."

"Ray Buckey is twenty-nine. He was born in 1958 in Hawthorne. He attended the Virginia McMartin Preschool. He is an athletic person. You will find that he has been active in a number of sports. He attended El Camino College for two years. He has coached a variety of sports.

"When he was at home he kept a number of pets. He is not a person who could likely harm an animal. They secretly taped conversations between Ray and his mother for hundreds of hours, hoping to hear conversations of crimes. Instead, they talked about animals. He began as a teacher at McMartin Preschool in 1981, took classes at UCLA. He became a teacher in 1981 until he was arrested. He was living with his parents. The house he lived in was searched. Ray Buckey rushed to a hiding location and pulled out some pornography and attempted to flush it down the toilet. It was not child pornography. It was pictures of nude adults. He was caught trying to flush it. Nude adults.

"I am Ray Buckey's attorney and I do speak for him, so I would like to tell you that I will be testifying in this case. He will be testifying. And we ask that you keep an open mind and that you await all the evidence in this case, and that he fully intends to reveal all he knows about the case, and that there may be victims on both sides."

Davis stated that he intended to call as a witness the son of the woman whose allegations triggered that case. The judge has ordered that the media not publish the true names of the children, so we will call him Peter. The child's father, according to the *Los Angeles Times* has stated that the boy will testify "over my dead body." Davis said he would call the father, who had been accused of being the perpetrator, as a witness. Davis stated that while an actual molestation may have occurred, Ray Buckey was falsely accused of the crime by a mother who may have been trying "to protect a guilty father."

"Mrs. Johnson told authorities that Peter was molested at a time when Ray Buckey was in jail," Davis said. "He gave no testimony at the preliminary hearing. He was interviewed on videotape by Dr. Gloria Powell. That videotape has disappeared."

Addressing CII again, the Davis said, "We were told that they were experts, that they had expert credentials. . . . Kee MacFarlane's only credentials were a driver's license and a welder's license." Dr. Astrid Heger did have an M.D., but, Davis said, there is no medical knowledge that enables a physician to determine whether a five-year-old blemish on the tissue of a child's genitals is proof of molestation."

Davis stated that the parents did not look at their children's videotaped interviews, and that the children were praised when they made accusations and criticized when they didn't. He also stated that he intended to call Glenn Stevens and Lael Rubin as witnesses for the defense. He excoriated CII, the police, the news media, and former D.A. Philibosian for combining to create mass hysteria. "McMartin," he said, "was not a Harvard for preschoolers. It was a fun school." And that was it.

"We will be in recess until tomorrow morning at ten-thirty," the judge said.

"The first prosecution witness will testify tomorrow," we were told outside the courtroom by defense lawyers Davis and Gits, who also said that four of the children on the prosecution's witness list were at the school during a period when Ray was not there. "They are going to ask us to believe that somehow he was able to be in San Diego, a hundred miles away, going to college, and also be in Manhattan Beach at the same time."

The eleven children scheduled to testify were all in the preliminary hearing. The boy who told of the cemetery and Chuck Norris and of being molested by four dead nuns was dropped, as was the boy who told of the lions and the mortuary, and then recanted. The boy who told of drinking blood in satanic rituals was still slated to testify.

The defense would not be allowed to tell the jurors of the bizarre allegations and insanity of the mother who started the whole thing, the woman who said that Ray Buckey flew in the air like a bird.

Forrest Latiner, Peggy Ann's lawyer, no longer in the case, was in the hallway talking with lawyers and spectators. "Their chances of getting a not-guilty verdict are almost nonexistent," he said. "Ninety-eight percent of the public believes they did it. And if they're convicted, their chances of getting it overturned on appeal are just about zero. All of the appellate judges are [Governor] Deukmejian appointees. Ultraconservative. And they know that Deukmejian wants a conviction in this case. I'm afraid they're going to do a lot of time."

The state's first witness, Dr. William E. Gordon, was called to the stand by the prosecution. He was being presented as an expert to corroborate Dr.

Astrid Heger's findings that the children were molested. There are about a dozen physicians in California who, like Gordon, have frequently testified for the prosecution in molestation cases. Several of them were on the prosecution's witness list and would be coming in to testify, as well as the CII evaluators who interviewed the children. These were the people whom the defense attorneys refer to as "the Child Abuse Industry."

Gordon is sixty-six but looks older. He has had a series of heart attacks and open-heart, bypass surgery. He spent most of the day recounting his career, beginning with his graduation from a medical school in Missouri. He spent another day explaining in minute detail how he examines children for sexual abuse. By the end of the week he had not yet discussed any of the fourteen children in the case.

Deputy District Attorney Roger Gunson was asking the questions. He was the other half of the two-prosecutor team, with Lael Rubin. He is extremely small, scarcely over five feet tall and very thin. He appears to weigh about one hundred pounds. He looks pale and tired. Like Davis and Gits, he is impeccably attired in his three-piece suit, and his graying blond hair is so heavily sprayed it looks like a hat. It is combed forward and then back again in a horseshoe curve, covering the encroaching pattern baldness of middle age. Gunson is soft-spoken, sometimes barely audible.

"Are you a certified pediatrician?" Davis asked on cross-examination.

"No. I have taught pediatrics and sexually transmitted diseases."

"Did you have a formal education in diagnosis for children in molest[ation]?"

"No sir. No such courses did exist at that time." He said that he taught law enforcement groups on exhibitionism, incest, and child molestation. There was a long series of questions and answers on the colposcope, an instrument with a magnifying glass used to examine and photograph the anus and genitalia, with variable magnification from 5- to 25-power. In 1969, Gordon testified, he was chief psychiatrist at California Men's Colony, a state prison.

"Is it fair to say that during most of your career you worked closely with law enforcement?" Davis asked.

"No," the doctor answered, but later acknowledged that he had testified for the defense in only three cases, and that he had not been paid privately for examining a child but had always been paid by the government.

"Is there any difference between looking at a slide and looking at a child? Any distortion?" Davis asked.

"Color distortion and depth of field. I can show slides here but there's no way I can examine a child's genitals in front of a jury." This brought a chorus of laughter.

"Have you ever found that a child was not molested?" Davis asked.

"I saw fifty to seventy-five children this year. Two or three were not molested."

"Did anyone give you formal training in the colposcope?"

"Yes. They, too, had not had training."

Outside the courtroom during recess, Davis asked us, "Were you impressed with this guy?"

"Not really," we said. "He's been doing all these evaluations without any body of scientific medical knowledge to support them. But the jury doesn't seem to dislike him. He comes on like a kindly, craggy old country doctor."

"He's a cop!" Davis said. "He's a prison doctor. He's been working for law enforcement and the prosecution from day one."

Back in the courtroom they were talking about the prosecution having hundreds of slides of children's anuses and vaginas. A young lawyer sitting next to us said, "I wonder who are the real pornographers in this thing."

We received a tip from Victims of Child Abuse Laws (VOCAL), an organization for persons falsely accused of child sexual abuse, about Dr. Gordon, along with a list of sources and and their telephone numbers. We passed this information along to a reporter. In the morning, there it was on every newsstand, on the front page of the *Herald-Examiner*. The story explained that Dr. Gordon had recently been banned from examining children for sexual abuse in his own county because of complaints by other professionals that his interviewing techniques were harmful. San Luis Obispo County Health Agency director Dr. George Rowland said he had ordered Dr. Gordon to cease evaluating children as part of the Sexual Assault Response Team (SART). He said his decision resulted from criticism against Gordon from the social services department, prosecutors, judges, and defense attorneys. "Those who process the information didn't appreciate his methods," Rowland was quoted as saying. There were complaints that Gordon was conducting exams that were excessively long. There was also displeasure on the part of prosecutors who said that he was "blowing" cases because of his apparent bias in favor of the prosecution.

But the largest issue was that in one case, a Superior Court judge instructed a jury that Dr. Gordon had "willfully discarded" a tape recording in which a child victim denied being molested, in order to keep it out of the hands of the defense. The judge was not impressed with Dr. Gordon's explanation that he "did not find the information relevant." Defense attorneys, according to the newspaper story, accused Gordon of being a "zealot" who would go to any length to establish that molestation had occurred. Even a San Luis Obispo prosecutor criticized Gordon and said he had been in the system long enough to know that he should have preserved the tape. A defense attorney from the same county said, "I can't think of anything better to happen for the defense (in McMartin) than for the prosecution to call him as their first witness." None of the other media reported this story, and the McMartin jurors were never informed of any of this. But Dr. Gordon did not return the next day. Prosecutor Lael Rubin's explanation to the judge was that the parents did not want to take their children out of school in the autumn, so the prosecution was going to try to put on as many of the children as possible in July and August, and then bring back Dr. Gordon to complete his testimony later on.

The next witness was the father of the first child scheduled to testify, the alleged victim in counts number 63 and 64. We will call her Cathy. The father stated that he had taken his daughter to the McMartin Preschool and that he had received a copy of the letter from the police implicating Buckey. He said that Cathy had denied any knowledge of molestation at the school, and that she was taken to CII after talking to other parents who had taken their children there.

"It was a modern facility which was able to get kids to admit to certain things others were not able to get out of kids," he said.

"Prior to CII, had Cathy talked about being molested?" he was asked.

"Bob Currie said his kids had been molested and probably Cathy had been molested. . . . She had a talk with a little boy about going to CII. The little boy said he told secrets and felt better. She wanted to tell secrets and feel better, too. . . . She did not remember. It was triggered at CII Institute."

On cross-examination he was asked, "Did you ever see anything suspicious at the school?" He said no.

"Did you see Ray Buckey at the school?"

"No."

"Do you feel that Ray Buckey molested Cathy?" Davis asked.

"I'm convinced of it," the father replied.

"I'd like you to identify the people who believed their children were molested before Cathy went to CII."

"The first statement was Bob Currie," the father said. "Bob Currie came to me and said he had been to CII, said his kids had been molested and that my kids probably had been."

"You went to CII with the objective to find out whether she was molested?" asked Davis.

"They were experts who get out of her the truth."

"You felt they were competent?"

"Yes."

"You didn't make any inquiry into their credentials?"

"I felt they were qualified at the time."

"What made you think they were qualified? Was it because they were selected by the District Attorney?"

"No."

"Was your choice of CII based on statements of other parents?" Davis asked.

"I thought it was logical."

"Did you ever, any time, independently interview your daughter?"

"Cheryl Kent, a therapist, did."

"Recommended by CII?"

"I don't know."

"Did Cheryl Kent give a finding of her [Cathy] being molested?" Davis asked.

"Yes."

"Did you go to other therapists?"

"No. I believe she was molested."

"Did you get a second opinion after what Astrid Heger told you?"

"No."

"Were you satisfied with Dr. Heger?"

"Yes. She's an expert in her field."

"On the day Shawn Connerly said she'd been molested, did anybody tell you about her denial on the tape?" Davis asked.

"I don't doubt it."

"Did your daughter deny molestation?"

"Yes . . . she denied it."

"Did you see how Cathy was pressured on the tape?"

"I saw leading questions. It's the only way to get this out of children, the only way kids could admit that it happened."

"Has Cathy seen any other therapist? Cheryl Kent?" Davis asked.

"Two to four months."

"Any other?"

"The D.A. There were a series of meetings. . . ."

"How many?"

"Three or four times with Christine Johnson. Six or seven times with Lael Rubin."

"Did you send either daughter to South Bay Counseling Center?"

"She may have had one session there with Cheryl Kent."

"Did you try to get Cathy to remember?" Davis asked.

"In one session she disclosed everything at the preschool. We were devastated. It was like an atom bomb fell on our house."

"Did you file claims for compensation? You got help during the process at CII?"

"Yes. The victims assistance agency. My wife filed a police report."

"You were convinced that Cathy was molested?" Davis asked.

"There was physical evidence. Scarring."

"When Rubin and Det. Bell came and talked to your daughter six or seven times, do you remember, were they taking notes?"

"Yes."

"How long did they stay?"

"In the beginning half an hour. Later, an hour and a half or two hours."

"Do you recall a meeting in which Kee MacFarlane was participating?" Davis asked.

"Yes."

"What was the purpose of the meeting?"

"To discuss the McMartin molestations. . . . There were a large group of people . . . a room as large as this, full of people."

"Did Kee MacFarlane get up and speak?"

"Yes."

"Did she say the preschool was involved in mass molestations?"

"She did, yes."

"In the carpool, did the kids change their stories?" Davis asked.

"Somewhat."

"Before CII did she ever tell you anything[,] that she might have been molested?"

"No."

"You told her the teachers at the preschool did bad things to children?"

"Yes."

"And that was based on what you heard from other parents?"

"Yes."

"We will be in recess until tomorrow morning at ten-thirty," the judge said. Lawyers and spectators moved slowly toward the door and out into the hallway. In the men's lavatory someone had written on the wall in large black letters, "NO D.A. ARRESTED THIS WEEK. A FIRST!"

This was an anonymous comment on the fact that several prosecutors had recently been charged with serious crimes, including sexual molestation of children.

An eager young reporter standing next to us approached Davis and asked him a question about the proceeding. Davis demanded to know who the young man was and asked him, "Do you have a card?" He gave Davis his card with his name and address on it and the title of his newspaper. He then asked for Davis's card. Davis tilted his head back, looking down his nose at the reporter, turned and walked away, throwing the young man's card into the wastebasket.

Shirley and I joined a group of reporters and lawyers at a restaurant across the street where most of the attorneys and media people go for lunch. As we waited for our sandwiches a middle-aged man covering the trial for a magazine told us, "They've only scratched the surface of this thing. Ninety-five percent of the molesters are still out there. Hundreds of thousands of kids are being sexually abused in satanic rituals. And it's still going on, secretly. The prosecution has bungled this thing so badly there's no way it can be rehabilitated."

Monday, August 3, 1987. Cathy is brought into the courtroom and seated at the witness stand. She is a very pretty young girl with blond hair and a pink, satin bow toward the back of her head. She is wearing a print party dress, pastel blue, green, and pink. The judge told her, "You can cover the mike and talk to me. I want to make sure you're all right. Each child has the right to have someone in the room to make them feel better. In this case, the parents." Cathy's parents were seated behind the prosecutor, Lael Rubin, who spoke to Cathy from a lectern fifteen or twenty feet away from the witness stand. Cathy was sworn in and Rubin began her direct examination.

"How old are you today?"

"Twelve."

"Do you live in Manhattan Beach?"

"Yes."

Rubin showed Cathy a photograph taken in 1986.

"Yeah. That's me."

"What school do you go to?"

"American Martyrs."

Rubin showed her photographs of the preschool, the teachers, and her contemporaries there. She asked Cathy to circle, with a pen, certain people and rooms.

"Did you go to the McMartin Preschool?"

"Yes."

Rubin asked the girl to name the teachers she remembered at McMartin. She named Miss Lo, Peggy, Betty Raidor, and Mary Ann Jackson. Davis and Gits sat at the defense table in their dark, three-piece litigation suits with a look of magisterial solemnity.

"You said Ray was at the school. Can you tell us what Ray did?"

"Kind of a helper."

"What was his relationship to Peggy?"

"Ray is Peggy's son."

"Can you look around and see Ray?" The girl pointed out both Ray and Peggy.

"I'd like to talk to you about McMartin. Did you stay all day or half a day?"

"Sometime half a day. Sometimes I'd stay for lunch and a nap."

"Did you tell your parents you didn't like to stay for a nap?"

"Yes."

"Your honor, I ask that this exhibit be made number twelve," Rubin said. It was a small diagram of the preschool. "When you were at the McMartin Preschool how many rooms did you see?"

"Four." She was asked to label them A, B, C, and D.

"There is a little yard. Can you tell us what was in the little yard?"

"Tricycles and things like that."

"If you look again at the photo of the school do you see a squiggly line between the rooms? Can you tell us what that is?"

"I think it's like an accordion divider."

"Did you play, and you had to take your clothes off?"

"Yes."
"What was the name of the game?"
"The 'Naked Movie Star.' "
"Did someone tell you to take your clothes off?"
"Yes."
"Who?"
"Ray."
"In what room was Ray in?"
"Room A."
"Did somebody say something to you?"
"Yes."
"What?"
" 'We're gonna play naked movie star.' "
"Who was the person who said that?"
"I'm not sure. Ray or Peggy."
"And when Ray or Peggy said, 'Time to play naked movie star,' was that in a classroom full of children?"
"I'm not sure."
"When Ray said, 'We're gonna play the "naked movie star game," ' what did you do?"
"Just stand or do something."

Cathy went on to say that the children were told to take off their clothes, put them in a pile and "like, pose."

"Did you hear anybody taking pictures?"
"Yes. I heard clicking."
"Did you ever see a person taking pictures?"
"No. I could see the lens sometimes."
"Where was the click coming from?"
"The accordion divider."
"When you played 'naked movie star' did Ray or Peggy have their clothes off?"
"Sometimes."
"When you finished modeling or posing, did you put your clothes back on?"
"Yes."
"What did you do then?"
"Went back outside and played with the kids."
"During the 'naked movie star' did you ever see another adult in the room?"
"Miss Peggy . . . Virginia. . ."
"Where?"
"In the doorway of Room A."
"How many times did you play 'naked movie star' at the school?"

"I don't remember."
"When you played 'naked movie star' was there any music?"
"I don't remember."
"Was anything covering the windows?"
"Curtains at each end of the window."
"At any time you played 'naked movie star' did anyone have an animal they showed to you?"
"Yes."

Cathy told that, after the game, a cat was put on the table and, "He cut it on the side and told us if we told anybody he would do the same to our parents."

"Was the cat dead when he brought it in?"
"Yes."

Cathy said she was taken to a reddish house where Ray and Peggy and some children were present and the 'naked movie star' was played. She said there were adults there who were not the same adults as those at the school, and that the strangers took pictures.

"When you were at the house where you played 'naked movie star' did you get undressed?"
"Yes." She said the adults also disrobed.
"Do you remember when you were going to the McMartin school, waking up in the middle of the night shaking or having nightmares?"
"Yes."
"Do you remember going to CII?"
"Yes."
"On March 14 you went to CII and talked to a woman named Shawn. Did she ask you what happened at McMartin?"
"I told her I didn't know anything."
"During and right after the 'naked movie star' did anybody touch you?"
"Ray and Peggy."
"Tell us what Ray did—how he touched you. You said Ray and Peggy touched you. Describe to us what Ray did to you. Did Ray touch you in some part of your body? Tell us as best you can. . . ."
"He touched my vagina."
"Did Ray put anything inside your vagina?"
"Yes."
"One time or more than one time?"
"I don't remember."
"Did Peggy touch you in some part of your body?"
"Yes."
"Outside or inside?"
"Outside."
"One or more times?"

"I don't remember."
"You remember one time—right?"
"Yes."
"You're not sure?"
"No."
"When Ray touched you with his finger in your vagina were his clothes on or off?"
"Off."
"When Peggy touched your vagina with her finger were her clothes on or off?"
"Off."
"Can you tell us when was the first time you told anybody that Ray and Peggy touched you?"
"July 3 of this year."
"Before you told your mom in July did you tell anyone else?"
"Sometime before July 3 I tried to tell somebody."
"Who?"
"You."
"Why didn't you tell me?"
"I was embarrassed. I started to cry."
"Any reason you just told your mom about Ray and Peggy touching your vagina?"
"I couldn't even admit it to myself."
"No further questions, your honor."
Time for cross-examination.
Our lawyer friend, Irene, leaned over and asked, "Do you think the jury is buying this?"
"We can't read them at all," we said.
"That girl is one of the kids who attended the school when Ray wasn't even there. He was a hundred miles away. She is extremely well rehearsed. She's almost too slick. They have one big problem. The 'naked movie star game.' Can you imagine a spectacle like that going on in such a tiny, little schoolhouse crowded with children? And parents coming and going all the time? And another thing. She just doesn't look like a pitiful victim. She looks like a girl who's been chosen to be queen of the Rose Parade. She's the star of the show. Newsmen from all over the world. And she'll be in the news. She's radiant! Just look at her smile. Do you remember anything that happened when you were three years old?"
"Not a thing."
"Neither does she."
The girl was sitting with her mother and both were laughing. Dean Gits began the cross-examination. "Cathy, I'd like to ask you some questions. If they seem too hard, stop me."

Cathy smiled.

"Cathy, when you went to McMartin you went for about three years. Is that correct?"

"Yes."

"And what grade are you in?"

"Sixth grade."

Cathy said she remembered having a good time at the preschool, that she arrived at nine in the morning and was picked up at noon.

"As you think about it now, can you remember how long you were in class?"

"About forty-five minutes."

"What happened when your mom and dad picked you up?"

"They just came to the gate."

"Where would you be?"

"Outside in the yard."

A photograph was passed from Gits to the clerk to the judge and then to the girl. "Cathy, if you would have a look at that, do you remember whether that picture was taken during your second year at the school?"

"Yes."

"You said Miss Lo taught in Room B, right?"

"Yes."

"When the 'naked movie star' was played was Miss Peggy your teacher?"

"Yes."

"When you started at the preschool Miss Lo was your teacher, right?"

"Yes."

"And in the third year was Miss Peggy your teacher?"

"Yes."

"You talk about going to see Shawn at CII. . . . Do you think your memory is better today than when you went to CII?"

"I don't know."

"Do you think your memory was better with Shawn at CII than at the preliminary hearing?"

"Well, it wasn't a better memory."

"Do you think your memory is better today?"

"Yes."

"Why?"

"Because I've thought about it."

"Going back to McMartin, were you afraid?"

"Sometimes."

"You talked about the 'naked movie star' game. Did that happen in the morning?"

"I'm not sure."

"Before noon?"

"Yes."
"So it was not at naptime?"
"No."
"You told us you were not sure how many times you played the 'naked movie star' game. What would be your best ballpark figure?"
"I don't want to say because I'm not sure."
"Can you tell us when it was you were afraid to go to school?"
"A couple of months after something happened at the school."
"You talk about times you stayed during naptime. Did anything bad happen during naptime?"
"Yes . . . that's when I went to the house."
"Did you ever go to the house in the morning?"
"I don't remember."
"Cathy, when you talked about the time you were taken to the house during naptime, did that happen more than one time?"
"Yes."

Cathy said she did not remember how many times. She also did not remember how many children were taken to the house, whose car was used to take them there, or how she entered the house.

"Do you remember how many grownups were there?"
"No."
"Did you take your clothes off and put them in a pile?"
"Yes."
"Did Peggy have her clothes off?"
"No."
"Was she touching anybody?"
"No."
"Did Ray take his clothes off?"
"Yes."
"Did he touch anybody?"
"I don't know. He didn't touch me."
"You said Ray brought in a cat and it was dead."
"Yes."
"Was that the first time you played 'naked movie star'?"
"Yes."
"Do you remember you played the second time at school?"
"No."
"So you eventually forgot what happened at the preschool?"
"Until I went and saw Shawn. I put it back in my mind."
"You had friends at American Martyrs who went to CII?"
"Yes."
"And they told you about yucky secrets. . . ."
"Yes."

"You told your parents you didn't remember anything bad happened at the preschool and one time they offered to take you to CII and you said there was no need to because nothing happened."

"Maybe. I don't remember."

"Did you tell anybody in the world about this before CII?"

"I don't know."

"Some of your best friends and classmates had been at CII?"

"Yes."

"Did your parents tell you something bad happened at the school?"

"Yes."

"Did you believe something bad happened at McMartin? You got a sense of that from your parents and CII?"

"Yes."

"You had a sense that something bad happened at McMartin but you couldn't remember until Shawn told you about the 'naked movie star?'"

"Yes."

"Were you told that this was being videotaped?"

"After we were done my parents came in. We looked at the tape, and they talked while I was out of the room."

"Do you remember Shawn telling your parents you were molested at the preschool?"

"I'm not sure what she said because I wasn't there."

"You were shown portions of the videotape? Did you see bits and pieces?"

"Yes."

"Did Kee tell you that Ray had threatened children?"

"I don't remember."

"Do you remember testifying at the preliminary hearing that Kee told you that Ray had touched children?"

"I don't remember."

"Do you remember testifying at the preliminary hearing that Kee told you Ray forced children to play the 'naked movie star' game?"

"I don't remember."

"And you told Cheryl Kent, right?"

"Yes."

"Do you remember Deputy District Attorney Christine Johnson?"

"Yes."

"How many times did you talk to Christine Johnson about the case?"

"I don't know. A lot."

"After the preliminary hearing you talked to Lael Rubin six or seven times about the case?"

"Yes. . . . Her and Roger came to see me."

"Six or seven times?"

"Yes."

"Was Gusty Bell with her each time?"
"Yes."
"All the times you were talking about the case, were they taking notes?"
"Yes."
"Did the talks get longer and longer?"
"They were usually close to an hour and then they got longer."
"Did Lael Rubin give you transcripts of the preliminary hearing?"
"Yes."
"Do you remember telling at the preliminary hearing that somebody gave the kids a pink medicine?"
"No."
"Today you're not sure you were given any medicine by the teachers at the school?"
"I didn't want to tell something I was not sure."
"Do you think your memory about the 'naked movie star' game was better at the preliminary hearing than today?"
"No. My memory is about the same on that issue."
"Are you aware of a song, 'The Naked Movie Star'?"
"Yes."
"Did you ever hear that at the preschool, Cathy?"
"I'm not sure."
"Do you remember testifying at the preliminary hearing that you don't remember in what room you played the 'naked movie star'?"
"I don't know."
"Do you remember testifying that the 'naked movie star' game was played in Miss Lo's class?"
"I don't remember."
"Why is it today you say you weren't in Miss Lo's class?"
"I thought a lot about what happened."
"Do you remember telling us at the preliminary hearing that the cat was not cut until about four months after you played the 'naked movie star' game?"
"I don't remember."
"Did Lael Rubin or Gusty say it's rather strange that the cat was cut four months later?"
"I don't know."
"Cathy, if you can, tell us why you're sure now that the cat was cut the first time you played the 'naked movie star' game. Do you feel the cat was cut the first time you played the 'naked movie star' game?"
"I'm positive."
"Was your testimony wrong in the preliminary hearing?"
"I thought about it."
"Did you ever see any one of the teachers give you shots at the school?"

There followed a long sidebar conference on an objection. The jurors were yawning. It was four-thirty and the judge recessed the court until morning.

Outside the courtroom the television crews were waiting. Lael Rubin came out first. The lights came on. The cameras moved in closer. A television reporter spoke first. "There seem to be a lot of contradictions and changes in this child's testimony."

Lael Rubin replied, "I think it shows what magnificent courage this child has. She wasn't afraid to admit her past mistakes and correct them."

The astonished reporter asked, "You mean to say you think her contradictions are a positive thing for the prosecution?"

"Yes," Rubin said with a forced smile. "It shows what magnificent courage this child has." It was not a convincing performance. Like Cathy she sounded perfunctory, tired and unable to get any sense of conviction into her statement. She spoke so softly we could barely hear her, only three feet away. It appeared that she really did not want to be heard but she was surrounded by microphones, cameras, lights, and reporters and she had no choice.

Tuesday, August 4, 1987. It was the second day of Cathy's testimony. Unlike the previous day's bright colors and loosely combed hair, Cathy was now wearing a dark green dress, the color of a Girl Scout uniform. Her hair was severely pinned close to her head and fastened at the back. Cathy's mother and father were there. Her father is a large man who affects a tough, macho demeanor. His wife is short, blonde, and looks fragile and passive.

"Your honor," Gits asked, "I have in my hand fifty-two mug photos. May I enter them in evidence?"

"Yes."

Gits asked Cathy about many people shown in the mug photos whom she had identified to Kee MacFarlane as being present during the 'naked movie star' game. Her answers to all the questions were "I don't remember."

"Cathy, did you talk yesterday about nightmares at the time you were going to the preschool?"

"Yes."

"Do you recall what they were about?"

"Dragons. Alligators. I was afraid to get up and go to the bathroom so I wet my bed."

"Did you have any redness or soreness in the vaginal area?"

"I don't remember."

"Did the district attorney ever show you a transcript of the videotape at CII?"

"Yes."

"Did they read portions of it to you?"

"Yes . . . last week."

"Did Lael and Gusty do that?"

"Yes."
"Did Lael come to visit you Saturday?"
"Yes."
"How long?"
"Two hours. Sometimes longer."
"What do you think was the longest?"
"Four hours."
"Did she go over what you're going to testify in this case?"
"She went over her outline."
"You told us the 'naked movie star' game was played before lunch, right?"
"Yes."

Gits asked several questions about parents coming to visit or to pick up their children. All her answers were "I don't know" and "I don't remember."

"When it was all over was the recess still going on?"
"Yes."
"I think you told us that the 'naked movie star' was played during recess."
"Yes."
"Was Peggy in the classroom when Ray came in and announced the 'naked movie star' game?"
"I'm pretty sure she was inside."
"Was anyone else there?"
"I don't remember."
"Is there any one child you can recall now that was present when you played the 'naked movie star'?"
"No."
"Going back to your first year at the preschool, was Ray there in Miss Lo's class?" Gits asked.
"I don't remember."
"Do you remember testifying in the preliminary hearing that Ray was in Miss Lo's class?"
"I don't remember."
"After your testimony in the preliminary hearing did anybody tell you maybe Ray wasn't there at the school when you were in Miss Lo's class?"
"I don't remember."
"Did anybody tell you that Ray was not at the school when you were in Mary Ann's class?"
"I don't remember."
"Was there any music during the 'naked movie star' [game]?"
"I don't remember."
"You said when you went to the house you were walking around in a circle holding hands?"
"I'm not sure."
"Would you stop and pose or keep walking?"

"I'm not sure."
"After the curtains were put up, was it dark?"
"Yes."
"Did you see a flash from a camera?"
"I don't remember."
"Did children cry during the 'naked movie star' [game]?"
"No."
"When you were touched by Ray did you cry?"
"I don't remember."
"Was the recess still going on?"
"Yes."
"Did any of the other kids come in?"
"I don't remember."
"When Ray came in with the dead cat did he have the cat in a bag or a box?" Gits asked.
"It was like a mashed paper bag with a cat on top."
"Did he cut it first or did he say something first?"
"I don't remember."
"Did blood go all over?"
"Just on the paper."
"Do you remember telling us at the preliminary hearing that blood got all over?"
"Yes."
"Do you think your memory is better now than at the preliminary?"
"Maybe."
"Was there a lot of blood that came out of the cat?"
"Yes."
"And did Ray say this will happen to your parents if you tell?"
"Yes."
"Up until Ray cut the cat were you horrified?"
"Not really."
"So it was Ray cutting the cat that really made you afraid?"
"Yes."
"Did you get sick and throw up?"
"I don't remember."

"We will be in recess for fifteen minutes," the judge announced, and the girl rose and walked casually over to where her parents were seated. She was smiling. In the hallway, Peggy Buckey whispered to us, "Did you ever see such a little liar?" A paralegal asked us, "Do you think anybody really believes this? There's not a word of truth to it! Ray wasn't even there!"

"Do you think it's at all possible that she's actually come to believe this really happened?" we asked.

"No!"

After recess, Gits continued to cross-examine: "Going back to the school, Cathy, do you remember Miss Betty?"

"Yes."

"Was she your teacher during your last year there?"

"Yes."

"Was she there at naptime?"

"I don't remember."

"You told us after the morning session a lot of moms came and picked up children and other children stayed during naptime."

"Yes."

"Were the teachers in A and B rooms watching the kids?"

"Yes."

"Did they tell you they were taking you to a house?"

"No."

"Did they say, 'Come with us'?"

"Yes."

"Who?"

"Ray or Peggy."

Providing her with transcripts from the preliminary hearing, Gits asked her many questions about the details of her alleged abduction to the house. Almost all of her answers were "I don't know" and "I don't remember." He asked her about the many changes and contradictions among her statements at CII, at the preliminary hearing, and at the trial.

"Go to page 43, line 6. When Kee talked to you at CII did Kee tell you Ray touched children in their private parts?"

"I don't remember."

"Do you recall being taken to the house where the 'naked movie star' game was played, in the morning?"

"Yes."

"Then Ray said, 'Come with me'?"

"No, it was at recess."

"Do you know who was watching Peggy's kids while Peggy was at the house playing 'naked movie star'?"

"It wasn't recess and the other teachers were watching them."

Gits ended his cross-examination and Ray's lawyer, Davis, began.

"Cathy, it's been a little over two years. . . . Has anything come to mind . . . if you think of anything you didn't say, please tell us now so we can get to the final truth about this. Do you think there's anything you haven't told us?"

"Not right now."

"Back in the preliminary [hearing] you said, 'I think' and 'kind of.' Does that mean you're not sure?"

"Yes."

"Did you learn that Bob Currie told your father that children were molested at McMartin?"

"No."

"When you went to CII did you have a feeling that something might have happened to you?"

"Yes. Sort of."

"But you said, 'Dad, it didn't happen to me'?"

"I don't know."

"By the time you talked to Kee you had a strong feeling Ray had been molesting children?"

"Yes."

"When you went to the preschool you had a good time, right?"

"Yes."

"From what you saw at American Martyrs did everybody say there was an investigation going on at the preschool?"

"Yes."

"That was the hot topic? That was the thing you heard people talking about?"

"Yes."

"Did you ever see Ray Buckey's picture on TV?"

"Yes . . . it seemed like every day, and what was going on."

The judge recessed the trial until morning and admonished the jurors not to discuss the case with anyone, not to read any news reports on the case, and "not to form any opinion until the case is submitted to you." He also instructed the newspeople not to publish the names of any of the child witnesses.

Wednesday, August 5, 1987. Cathy is back on the stand and Davis is asking questions about "naked games." Almost all of her answers were "I don't remember" and "I don't know."

"You told Shawn about a lot of naked games, and now at the trial only one naked game. Did you believe, when you told Shawn, that there were other naked games?"

"I don't remember."

"The house you talked about in the interview with Shawn, was it a brown house?"

"Yes."

"But you didn't say brown. Do you recall saying brown?"

"Not really."

"I want to get to the people you had discussions with before the preliminary hearing. Christine Johnson. You had three meetings with her before the preliminary hearing and you talked about statements on the videotape."

"Something or other."

"Didn't you do questions and answers you would be testifying in the preliminary hearing?"

"Yes."

"And you were preparing for your testimony so you would know what to say. Didn't you prepare so you would know what to say in court?"

"I don't know. It was more like I knew what was going on."

"Did you do the same with Lael Rubin?"

"She asked me things I wasn't too sure about. She said names and I didn't even know who the person was."

"Did you go over questions and answers for the trial?"

"Yes."

"Shawn told you all the other kids were molested?"

"Yes."

"Did you know Lael Rubin during the preliminary?"

"I'm not sure."

"Did you come to know her better when you came to the meeting with her to prepare for the trial?"

"Yes . . . I met Roger, too."

"You read the notebook. Did you ever discuss the notebook with your parents?"

"We read transcripts from the preliminary hearing."

"You opened your notebook and Lael opened hers?"

"Well, she would just, like, if there was a hard answer, how to answer. . . ."

"She would say, 'Answer like that' and it would be okay?" asked Davis.

"Yes."

"I have some pictures here. Take a little time. . . . Do you still have the feeling that a child could fit in the cupboard?"

"No."

"Do you remember anything bad that happened in the bathrooms at the school?

"I don't remember."

"Did you ever tell one person that the house you were taken to was one of the teachers' houses?"

"I don't remember."

"Do you remember anything about the house?"

"There were wooden animals. The mailbox is like an animal."

"You've been to Peggy's house many times. You know there are wooden animals there."

"I was talking to Lael. She brought pictures and showed it to me.

"So today you don't know whether the house was Peggy's house?"

"No. Kee said it was Peggy's house."

"Do you remember you said it was a white house when you talked to the police department?"

"No. I don't remember. . . ."
"Do you remember anything that happened at the white house?"
"No."
"Do you know the name of any other child that was with you when the cat was killed?"
"No. I don't remember."
"Do you know the name of one single child who was present when you were touched?"
"No."
"Do you remember one child who was present when you played the 'naked movie star' game?"
"No."
"When you say you were taken to Peggy's house, is that a guess?"
"No. Kee said. . . ."
"At the preliminary hearing you said the cat was cut six months after the 'naked movie star' [game] was played the first time. Today you said it was cut the same day. . . . Is this something you were telling Lael Rubin . . . did she tell you that it didn't make sense for you to say six months and not be frightened about it? And not to tell your parents? Can you tell me anything that would contribute to the change that you haven't thought about?"
"No."
"You described touching and changed your testimony. Is that correct?"
"Yes."
"What caused you to change?"
"I'm not sure what happened."
"You testified of a grownup that drugged little boys and girls. That's a very serious thing."
"Yes."
"And you were saying that?"
"It was the truth to me at the time."
"When the truth came to you what happened?"
"I just saw Pepto-Bismol in the refrigerator."
"In the preliminary hearing testimony you told Dr. Heger cats, turtles, and rabbits were cut up."
"Not that I remember."
"Did you ever see anything like that?"
"Not turtles and rabbits."
"We will be in recess until ten o'clock tomorrow morning," Judge Pounders announced.

Thursday morning, August 6, 1987. Cathy is beginning to fade. It is her third day on the stand and she is visibly fatigued. She is wearing a flowered jacket and white pants. Davis entered into evidence a group of seventy-six photographs and a transcript from her CII interview. There followed a long series of questions and answers about cats, particularly the one alleged to have been killed by Ray Buckey. Most of her answers were "I don't know" and "I don't remember." She said she did not remember ever seeing Ray Buckey at the preschool. She also said she did not remember playing the 'naked movie star' game.

"Did Shawn tell you that 110 children had already been interviewed at CII . . . and every one of them had something happen to them at the preschool? Did she tell you that?"

"Yes. I don't think she would lie to me."

"When the police were following Ray around did that make you think Ray Buckey did bad things?"

"I don't know."

"When you talked to Shawn [at CII] you said you were touched on the vagina by teachers at the school."

"Yes."

"Did it hurt?"

"Not specifically."

"Is it true today that it did hurt?"

"Yes."

"Are both of these statements true?"

"I don't know. What is the question?"

"Two answers being true. Did you bleed?"

"No."

Davis reminded her that she had told Shawn, at CII, that there were no strangers at the house when the "naked movie star" game was played. Now, at the trial, she was saying that there were strangers there.

"Do you feel your memory was better when you talked to Shawn and at the preliminary?"

"I don't know."

"Did teachers actually touch private parts of children?"

"I don't know."

"Did you ever see Ray Buckey?"

"No."

The questions go on for hours, focusing mostly on the changes in Cathy's testimony from the CII to the preliminary hearing to the trial.

"When did Ray touch you?"

"I don't remember."

"What part of his body did he touch you with?"

"His fingers."

Finally, Judge Pounders asked the girl, "In what position was his body and your body? Standing, sitting, or lying down?"

"I don't remember," she answered. Pounders did not appear to be satisfied with her answer. There followed a long series of questions about pictures of houses Cathy had been shown at CII. Her answers were vague and sometimes inconsistent. A more interesting exchange occurred when Gits asked the girl, "When you got the transcript from Lael did she tell you how to answer questions with the tabs? What were the tabs for?"

"They pointed out some things," she said. "Like a smart answer."

"Tabs to look at to understand smart answers at the preliminary hearing?" Gits asked.

"Yes."

"Rubin gave you some smart answers?"

"We went through the answers and looked at them."

"Was Lael going over the transcript, telling you how to answer?"

"Sort of."

Many of the questions focused on the excessive coaching the girl had with Lael Rubin and her colleagues from the district attorney's office. As the cross-examination continued, Cathy said that she had been visited by Rubin six or seven times for as long as four hours. Later, outside the courtroom, Davis told the newspeople, "What we have got is a district attorney training children to get ready for court with what she calls smart answers. That is not straight." Gits told the microphones that the lack of detail in the child's testimony confirmed the defense's theory that those who convinced the McMartin children that they had been molested neglected to provide them with the details of the alleged molestations. The defense attorneys' statements were not reported in the media. Throughout the day and most of the week, the fat man with the moustache sat in the audience section toward the rear of the room, smiling.

Monday, August 10, 1987. The witness is a woman whose two children account for over one-third of the prosecution's case, thirty-seven of the one hundred counts.

"Do you have anything to discuss before the jury is brought in?" the judge asks.

"Yes," Daniel Davis replies. "I think we may have a problem with the jurors sleeping during the proceedings. Enough people have brought this information to me that I felt it necessary to bring it to your attention." The jury is brought in and the judge asks them, politely, to try to remain awake during the trial.

The witness is about forty, short, slender, pretty, and fashionably dressed. Her daughter is eleven years old. Her son is ten. They attended McMartin Preschool between the ages of two and five. The eldest, Melinda, graduated in 1978. The woman's son left in 1980. He attended two days a week at first, then began going three days a week. The children usually were picked up at noon, she testified, but sometimes were left there in the afternoon when she had errands. They went back to visit at Christmas and on other occasions, she said. She was told, she testified, that parents were not permitted to pick up their children between 1:00 P.M. and 2:30 P.M., so as not to disturb their naps. She was shown a number of photographs and asked, by Rubin, about the details of how and where she brought and retrieved her children while they attended the preschool.

The woman testified that her daughter had bladder infections when she attended the McMartin Preschool and that the infections disappeared when she left the school and then returned when she revisited the school. She also testified that her daughter suffered from nightmares about five times a week during this period, and that her vaginal area had been "red and sore."

"Did you notice any other behavior in the evenings?" prosecutor Rubin asked.

"She masturbated a lot," the woman said. "And we noticed, that she danced a lot, scantily clad. We discouraged this."

"Did you notice any strange behavior in James?" Rubin asked.

"He looked extremely pale."

"Did he ever come home with clothing that didn't belong to him?"

"Yes, he came home wearing somebody else's clothing, with his own clothes in a bag. We were told that he had had an accident."

The mother was asked if she had received the letter from the police department. She did, she said, and had asked her children if they had been touched. They said no, she told the prosecutor. She said she continued to question them during the ensuing months because she had close friends who told her that children had been molested at McMartin. She said her daughter told her she had seen Ray Buckey put his hands inside a little girl's trousers.

"I have no further questions, your honor," Rubin said.

Dean Gits, Peggy's lawyer, rose to cross-examine.

"Taking you back to the time when you took your children to McMartin, what was the reputation of the school?"

"The reputation was excellent. I checked it out myself." She said she had been permitted to sit in on one of the classes.

"Would it be fair to say you were satisfied that it was a good preschool?"

"Yes. I was very close to Virginia."

"During the four years your children attended the preschool did you observe anything improper at the school?"

"I wondered why a twenty-year-old male was there with these children."

"Did you know he was the son of Peggy and the grandson of Virginia?"

"Yes, I did."

"And you were concerned about the fact that a twenty-year-old male was a teacher?"

"Yes, it was of some concern to me."

"Did Melinda have any terrible reaction to the school?"
"Not at that time."
"On a number of occasions James was pale. When was that?"
"Toward the last year he was there."
"Did you take him to a doctor?"
"He was always taken to a doctor for regular checkups."
"Were you told that everything was okay?"
"Fine."
"During the time Melinda attended the school, did she ever say anything bad about the teachers?"
"I can't remember."
"You received a telephone call from a friend whose children attended McMartin?" Gits asked.
"She told me she got a letter from the Manhattan Beach Police Department."
"After hearing that, did you believe Ray Buckey could have touched kids?"
"I thought it was a definite possibility."
"You didn't question the kids?"
"No. We talked to each of them and the responses were all negative."
"Did you notice any anxiety or fear?"
"I don't remember."
"You told us [that] after talking to them you were satisfied that nothing happened?"
"Yes."

Gits then asked the woman a number of questions about the proliferation of hysterical gossip during the four or five months subsequent to the sending out of the letter from the police.

"Did Melinda indicate to you that kids were being molested?"
"No."
"Did Melinda ever indicate to you that kids played naked games?"
"No."
"Did you believe kids were molested by Ray Buckey?"
"Yes."
"Did you believe that the CII had the power to determine whether children had been molested?"
"Yes." She said that when she questioned her children again separately, they both replied, "Nothing happened, Mom."
"You spent the whole day at CII?"
"Yes."
"And when Kee came out she told you that Melinda had been molested?"
"I don't know if that was the word she used but the sense of what she said was that they had been molested."
"Did Kee tell you that it was important to be supportive of Melinda?"

"Yes."
"How long was James with Kee?"
"An hour and a half."
"After an hour and a half Kee came in and told you the same thing she told you about Melinda?"
"Yes."
"And she told you to be supportive, same as Melinda?"
"Yes."
"You and your husband watched James's tape?"
"Yes."
"You took the children to Dr. Cheryl Kent?"
"Yes."
"How long?"
"About a year."
"Did you attend meetings at community churches?"
"Yes."
"How many times?"
"Maybe ten."
"And you had conversations with parents after CII?"
"Yes."
"It was the talk of the town, right?"
"Yes."
"As you walked out of CII you were absolutely convinced that your children were molested?"
"Yes."

There were many questions about the woman's involvement in groups formed around the belief that their children had been molested, about forty families.

"Did you see Ray and Peggy arrested on television?"
"Yes."
"And you all got together, and would it be fair to say that the occasion was a party to celebrate the arrest of Ray and Peggy?"
"Yes."
"Were refreshments offered to the kids?"
"There was food for everybody."
"Were you present at home when Lael Rubin and Gusty Bell talked to Melinda on two occasions?"
"Yes."
"Was the purpose to go over Melinda's testimony for answers in court?"
"Yes."
"What was the length of time of these meetings?"
"Two or three hours."
"Were transcripts provided?"

"Yes."

The mother also told of her involvement in the "Telephone Tree," a group organized to inform all of the people in this movement whenever there was a meeting or some kind of gathering. Each member was to call four people and each of the four people called was to call four more. She also told about the dig, in a vacant lot next to the school, for the purpose of finding animal bones as evidence that animals had been mutilated. She said the men, including her husband, were there, all day, digging, and there were thirty or forty families.

Gits concluded his cross-examination and Davis began. "If you would, tracing the things most affecting your state of mind as to the belief that your children were molested, can you remember anything before the letter of 1983?"

"It caused me to start asking questions I should have started asking long ago."

"Did anything occur before you received the letter that led you to believe that molestation had occurred?"

"I did not think of sexual abuse." The mother said she did not remember seeing Ray Buckey, and that Melinda went back to visit many times after graduating from the preschool.

"Do you feel that Melinda was molested at that preschool when she went back to visit in 1982?"

"I definitely feel she was molested. Not necessarily in 1982."

"Was it because of anything you saw at the preschool?"

"No."

"And you definitely feel that James was molested?"

"Yes."

"Anything you saw at the preschool that indicated that?"

"No."

"What made you feel that James was molested?"

"He told me."

"What did you observe that was out of the ordinary at the preschool?"

"I noticed he was a male. . . . It seemed strange someone his age would want to be working with children."

The witness spent most of the next day telling of her daughter's masturbation, bladder infections, constipation, and bed wetting and her belief that there was some causal relationship between these and molestation.

"Did you ask doctors about it?" Davis asked.

"I don't remember."

The questions went on for hours, concerning the girl's health and urinary problems, one of which was her propensity for "holding off" and postponing urination and defecation. These problems, she said, occurred only when the child attended or visited the school.

"Melinda was interviewed in February 1984?" Davis asked.

"Yes."

"And she had a medical examination by Dr. Astrid Heger?"
"Yes."
"And she was interviewed by Lael Rubin and Det. Bell on May 8, 1985, and testified in the preliminary hearing in May and June 1985?"
"Yes."
"The investigation focused on Ray Buckey?"
"Yes."
"And the police were asking parents to make inquiry of the children?"
"Probably."
"No one else was named?"
"Correct."
"And you began to believe . . ."
"Yes."
"After CII, were more people than Ray Buckey implicated?" Davis asked.
"I don't remember."
"From the time Melinda went to McMartin to the time she was interviewed by CII was about a six-year lapse?"
"Yes."
"Did the kids tell you what they noticed at the school?"
"They didn't notice anything out of the ordinary. Ray liked the children."
"Did you feel, when you saw the [CII] video, that you saw evidence of molestation?"
"I believe so."
"Little dolls made you feel . . ."
"It wasn't dolls. It's things she said. Body language. She became frightened."
"Do you recall the Ray doll?" Davis asked.
"Yes."
"Was it a large, black doll?"
"I don't remember."
"Were you convinced of molestation?"
"I was convinced both were molested. Everything fell into place."
"You did not see the entire tape. . . ."
"That's correct."
"You saw excerpts queued up, the latter part of the video?"
"I don't recall."
"Did you see your daughter and son explain on other portions of the tapes that they heard about it from parents and others?"
"I don't remember."
"Did Kee suggest that all the kids interviewed had been molested?" Davis asked.
"They did tell us that the kids have been molested."
"When you picked up your preschoolers in the afternoon, did you ever see the 'lookout' game played?"

"I wasn't aware of it."

"Your daughter told you about the 'lookout' game. What recollection do you have about that?"

"She told me the kids had to play and let Ray know, run in and tell Ray when children were picked up."

"When you picked up your kids, were there some adults there?"

"Yes."

"Was Ray Buckey there?"

"Different places at different times."

"When you picked up your children, were other teachers there?"

"Ray, and Betty was there, too."

"Did you see Virginia?"

"Yes."

"In what particular locations did Virginia locate herself?"

"In front of the school, usually in her wheelchair."

There were more questions about the urinary problems of her children, and about the party held to celebrate Ray's arrest.

"Was there a time when special prayers were made at a community church for the children involved in this?"

"Yes."

"Did you also attend meetings at your church?"

"Yes."

"Who was there?"

"Families of the children attending the preschool."

Davis then questioned the mother about her attendance at a large number of meetings organized to plan action to be taken against the Buckeys and other defendants. She said she saw representatives of the district attorney's office there, as well as Kee MacFarlane. She also stated that she believed the school's prohibition of parents picking up their children during naptime could have been a cover for molestation.

"You indicated that sometimes you were late and sometimes you would come early. Did you see anything that looked like molestation?"

"No."

"Would it be fair to say that your belief in molestation is based just on things you heard?"

"No. It was based on what my children told me."

"Did you ever go there and find out that you were locked out?"

"No."

"Did you ever see any evidence that children were being molested?"

"No."

"When you went to CII, did you do anything to inquire into the credentials of the people?"

"Objection."

"Sustained."
"And Dr. Heger found that she had been molested?" Davis asked.
"Yes, she did."
"At the time you took your children to Cheryl Kent, who was the director there at South Bay Counseling Center?"
"Colleen Mooney."
"Mr. Gregory Mooney's wife?"
"Yes." Mooney was an attorney who stated that he represented children in this case. He frequently attended the trial.
"It was CII that referred you to Cheryl Kent, wasn't it?"
"Yes."
"When did you see blankets on the classroom windows?" Davis asked.
"In the afternoon when I picked up the children."
"Did you think there was anything unusual about that?"
"No, I thought it was for nap purposes."
"You indicated that your children went back to the school together . . . times when you were shopping?"
"Yes."
"You believe they were molested during those times?"
"Yes."

There were more questions about Melinda's bladder infection. The woman stuck to her assertion: "Because she developed a bladder infection at that time, I do believe that molestation occurred on that day, yes."

Thursday, August 13, 1987. This is the day Melinda is to testify. She is wearing a flowered print dress with a large, lace collar. She is a round-faced, chubby little girl, eleven and a half years old. Like Cathy, she does not look like a victim of unspeakable crimes, but looks vaguely amused, smiling as she sits above the assembled lawyers and spectators, on the witness stand. Deputy District Attorney Lael Rubin puts her through the same opening litany as the others. She is sworn in, asked to give her name and age. She is shown photographs of herself, the preschool, and of her teachers, and asked to identify them. She does not look, or sound, stressed. But her testimony was hair-raising!

"Your honor," Rubin addressed the judge, "I have two exhibits. I ask that they be marked 25 and 26, a boy on a swing and a girl on a swing. Melinda, do you recognize who that is?"

"Yes, that's me." Melinda testified that when she was at the preschool she played "lookout," a game in which "Ray would pick me and tell me to go to the swing and whenever I saw a mom coming I would go in and tell Ray." She said that Ray was inside, touching and hurting kids.

"What was he doing?" Rubin asked.

"With the girls he put his finger and his penis in their vagina and their bottom. With the boys he put his finger and his penis in their bottom." After that, she said, "Ray poked his head out and said, 'Here's your child,' and they left."

"How many times?"

"I don't remember."

"Was there anything covering the windows?"

"Blankets."

Rubin brought out two more photographs, exhibits 27 and 28, and asked the girl to identify the swings and the room.

"When you were going to the McMartin Preschool did you ever leave the school grounds?" she asked the child.

"Yes."

"Where did you go?"

"Two houses, a farm, a car wash, a market."

"When you went to the green house, who did you go with?"

"Ray and his friends."

"Did you walk or go in a car?"

"In a car . . . a blue car that was Peggy's. Sometimes a van."

"Did you go to the green house more than one time?"

"I don't remember."

"Were there any other adults there?"

"Yes."

"How many?"

"I don't remember."

"How many times did you go there?"

"I don't remember."

"Ray's friends . . . did they have cameras?"

"Yes."

"And when you went to the green house, what did you do?"

"The 'naked movie star.' "

"The same way as at school?"

"Yes, but Ray touched me."

"Were there people taking pictures?"

"Yes."

"Will you tell us what Ray did in the green house?"

"He put his finger and his penis in my vagina and my bottom." She continued to repeat her account of this assault throughout her testimony.

"Did he put his penis in your mouth?"

"No."

"Did Peggy touch you in the green house?"

"Yes. She put her finger in my vagina and my bottom."

"At some point after CII did your mom and James drive around looking for the house?"

"Yes."

Rubin brought out more photographs, Exhibits 30, 31, and 32, and asked, "Do you recognize what's in these photographs?"

"I don't understand."

"Is this the house you believe you were taken to?"

"Yes."

"Did you go to a farm?"

"Yes."

"Who with?"

Melinda replied that she had gone to a farm with Ray, Peggy, and some children in a van. "It was Ray's," she said.

"What did you do?"

"We went in the barn and played 'naked movie star.' "

"Did you take your clothes off?"

"Yes."

"Did Ray and Peggy take their clothes off also?"

"Yes."

"Did Ray and Peggy touch you in the barn?"

"Yes."

"Tell us what Ray did."

"Ray put his finger in my bottom and my vagina, and he put his penis in my bottom and vagina. Peggy put her finger in my vagina and my bottom, and she touched her vagina to my vagina."

As Melinda said these things we had expected to see some expression of stress, fear, or revulsion on her face, but her face and voice were devoid of emotion. She told of this gross, four-way assault with all the conviction of a child reciting a nursery rhyme, or a mantra.

"After the 'naked movie star' [game], what did you do?" Rubin asked.

"We went and played."

"Did you go there many times?"

"Yes."

"How many times?"

"I don't remember."

"Did you go to other places with Ray?"

"Yes."

"Where?"

"A car wash."

"Do you remember the name of the car wash?" Rubin asked.

"The Red Carpet Car Wash."

"Did any other people go with you?"

"Ray and the children."

"How many times did you go to the car wash?"

"I don't remember."

"When you went to the car wash with Ray and the kids, what did you do?"

"He took me in the bathroom and took his clothes off."
"What about the other kids?"
"They stayed outside."
"What did he tell you to do?" Rubin asked.
"He told me to take my clothes off."
"Then what happened?"
"He put his penis and finger in my bottom. With the girls he put his penis and finger in their vagina."
"Then did you put your clothes on?"
"Yes."
"What happened then?"
"He told me to go out again."
"Did you see Ray with the other kids?"
"Yes."
"What did he do with them?"
"He took them to the bathroom."
"All of them or one at a time?"
"One at a time."
"Thank you. I have no further questions."
Dean Gits rose to cross-examine the witness.
"Melinda, when you went to the McMartin Preschool you were about two years old, right?"
"Yes."
"And you went there for about three years?"
"I don't remember."
"Do you remember having a teacher named Miss Lo?"
"No."
"When you went to CII did you talk to a person named Kee?"
"Yes."
"When you talked to Kee, did you remember the preschool and what happened?"
"Yes."
"Did you tell her the truth?"
"Yes."
"Did you also talk to the grand jury?"
"Yes."
"And did you tell them the truth?"
"Yes."
"You told your parents what you talked to Kee about, what happened at McMartin?" Gits asked.
"Yes."
"And you saw the video . . . at least parts of it, right?"
"Yes."

"Before the preliminary hearing, Lael and Gusty came out and talked to you?"
"Yes."
"At the preliminary [hearing], were you telling the truth?"
"Yes."
"Melinda, I'm going to show you a photograph marked Number 16 for identification. I'd like you to have a look and see if there's anybody you recognize." Gits said.
"I see myself, my brother. . . ." Melinda named several other children, plus Peggy and Virginia.
"Melinda, does that look like a class photograph?"
"Yes."
"Do you see any teachers you recognize? Take your time, please."
"No."
"As you look at that picture, can you tell us if those were some of your classmates when you were at the preschool?"
"I don't remember."
Gits asked her a long series of questions about the preschool, what happened there on a typical day, and at what time. The answer to almost all of the questions was, "I don't remember."
"Do you remember who your first teacher was?"
"No."
"Do you remember who your second teacher was?"
"No."
"Do you remember who your third teacher was?"
"No."
"Were there any closets in the classrooms?"
"Yes."
"Could you get down and show us where?" She got down from the stand and pointed to a door in the photograph.
"Were there any other closets?"
"Yes, but I can't remember where."
"Do you see another closet in the photograph?"
"Yes."
"Is that the closet?" he asked, pointing to the photograph.
"Yes."
"Melinda, there's another picture of a closet, right?"
"Yes."
"I'd like to talk to you about the 'lookout' game, okay? Was it played in the afternoon or the morning?"
"Only in the afternoon."
"You said Ray was there, right?"
"Yes."

"Was he babysitting kids?"
"Yes."
"In the afternoon at naptime?"
"Yes."
"At naptime kids got on cots? Each kid got on his own cot?" Gits asked.
"Yes."
"When the 'lookout' game was played, you wanted to be lookout?"
"Yes."
"When you first played, you got to be lookout, right?"
"No."
"Did Ray say, 'We're gonna play the "lookout" game'?"
"I don't remember how he said it."
"When you played 'lookout' and you learned you were going to be lookout did he tell you to swing high?"
"Yes."
"Why?"
"He said, 'Swing high so you can see the moms.'"
"When he told you to do that you did it, right?"
"Yes."
"The windows were covered up, right?"
"Yes."
"You went on the swing?"
"Yes."
"There weren't any other kids in the yard?"
"No."
"Were you looking for moms driving or walking?"
"Walking."
"What did you do?"
"Go in and tell Ray."
"Was the door in the classroom locked?"
"No."
"You opened the door and went in the classroom?"
"Yes."
"Did Ray give you a password?"
"No."
"You'd just go in and tell him?"
"Yes."
"And Ray had his clothes off?"
"Yes."
"And all the kids had their clothes off?"
"Yes."
"And you saw Ray doing things to kids?" Gits asked.

"With the girls he was putting his finger and his penis in their vaginas. With the boys he was putting his finger and penis in their bottom."

"Did you see any of the kids run out of the classroom?"

"No."

"Did you see any of the kids crying?"

"No."

"Did you see any of the kids screaming?"

"No."

"When you went in to tell Ray and he was molesting the kids you didn't hear Ray or the kids shouting or saying anything?"

"Right."

"What did Ray say?"

"I didn't see Ray. He ran into the bathroom and put his clothes on."

"What did he do with the kids?"

"He just told them to get dressed."

"And you went back and closed the door, right?"

"Yes."

"Sometimes, when a mom came, did you see kids come running to tell Ray?"

"Yes."

"What did Ray do?"

"He ran in the bathroom and got dressed."

"Do you remember testifying in the grand jury hearing . . . you testified that Ray put all the kids in the closet?"

"Yes."

"At the time you told the grand jury did you think the rooms had closets in them and that the kids could be shoved in?"

"I don't understand the question."

"Is that what you thought happened?"

The girl sat there, silent, for a long time, blankly, and then said, "I don't understand your question."

"At that time, you thought there were closets, right? Later, you found out there weren't any closets in the school, right?"

"Right."

"Do you remember your testimony at the preliminary hearing that when the kids came to tell Ray, he shoved the kids in the bathroom?"

"I don't remember."

"You told the judge Ray shoved all the kids in the bathroom. Is that what happened?"

"No."

"Were you telling the truth?"

"Yes."

"Can you tell us why both these stories are true?" Gits asked.

"Because when I told it at the preliminary [hearing] that's the way I remembered it." A smart answer.

"You say Ray went into the bathroom and put his clothes on. Did he close the door?"

"Yes."

"Did a mom ever say anything to you?"

"No."

"When you went in to tell Ray a mom is coming did you yell out?"

"I don't remember."

"Did the kid look scared?"

"I don't remember."

"After you closed the door and got back on the swing did you start swinging again?" Gits asked.

"Yes."

"You told Lael that a mom knocked on the door, right?"

"Yes."

"Ray opened the door?"

"Yes."

"What did the mom say to Ray?"

"I don't remember."

"Did the mom say anything to Ray?"

"No."

"There were times when you were in the classroom when a mom came, right?"

"Yes."

"What did Ray say?"

"He said, 'Go to the little yard. That's where your child is.' "

"Did you ever hear a mom say, 'Why didn't you tell me my child was in this room?' "

"No."

"Did Ray leave his clothes in the bathroom?"

"Yes."

"And did all the kids take their clothes off?"

"Yes."

"He came out with his clothes on?"

"Yes."

"Not only he but all the kids had their clothes on, right?"

"Yes."

"When he heard a knock, did Ray say, 'Go to the little yard'?"

"Yes."

"And by the time the mom walked to the little yard and back again, the kid had his clothes on?"

"Yes."

"And what did Ray do?"

"He put his finger in the kids' vagina and bottom and he put his penis in their vagina and bottom."

"Did you ever hear a mom say, 'Why didn't you tell me my kid was in the classroom?'"

"I don't remember."

"Melinda, you told us you went to a car wash," Gits said.

"Yes."

"How many kids were there in the van?"

"I don't remember."

"Enough so all the kids could fit in the van, right?"

"Right."

". . . and all the kids got out?"

"Yes."

"One by one he took the kids into the bathroom?"

"Yes."

"He took you into the bathroom and took your clothes off, right?"

"Yes."

"And then he'd take another kid to the bathroom, right?"

"Yes."

"Did you hear any screaming or crying?"

"No."

"Then he took another kid in the bathroom, right?"

"Yes."

"And you would be waiting outside?"

"Yes."

"And did Ray take all his clothes off in the bathroom?"

"Yes."

"This happened to every child that went to the car wash?"

"Yes."

"Did anybody ever walk by and ask, 'What are you kids doing here?' or 'That van's been sitting here for a long time'?"

"I don't remember."

"Did anybody ever come into the bathroom?"

"No."

"And after that you'd all just walk out and go back to school?"

"Yes."

"We will be in recess until tomorrow morning," the judge said. As everybody began moving toward the door, an elderly reporter from out of town asked us, "Are we supposed to believe this guy is standing in a public lavatory, stark naked, buggering three-year-old kids, and nobody walked in?"

"Yes," we said. "The busiest car wash in town." The man shook his head and walked toward the elevators.

* * *

In the morning Gits continued his cross-examination. Ray Buckey was sitting next to his attorney, Daniel Davis. Ray was wearing a dark blue suit. His eyeglasses had been replaced by contact lenses, and he had been given a very good haircut. The change in his appearance since the preliminary hearing was striking. He looked as dapper as the lawyers flanking him at the defense table.

Gits entered Melinda's preliminary hearing testimony into the record as evidence of her inconsistency. There were also many inconsistencies with her testimony before the grand jury and CII.

"Were you taken to the farm at a time when Betty went along with you?" Gits asked Melinda.

"No."

"Did you testify at the preliminary hearing that Betty took children to the farm?"

"Yes."

"Was your memory better at the preliminary hearing?"

"I don't know."

"How many kids went to the farm with you?"

"I don't remember."

"Do you remember testifying at the preliminary hearing that about eight kids went to the farm?"

"Yes."

"Do you think your memory was better at the preliminary?"

"I don't know."

Gits asked dozens of questions about the visits to the farm. Again and again, Gits brought out Melinda's testimony from the transcript of the preliminary hearing and her answers to the questions were not the same.

Finally, he asked her, "As you think about it now, can you name just one child who went to the farm with you?"

"No. I don't remember."

"As you think about it today, can you name one child who you played 'naked movie star' with at the school?"

"No."

"Can you remember one child who played 'naked movie star' with you at the house?"

"I don't remember."

"You talk about threats made to you . . . that your parents would be killed. Can you remember that?"

"Yes."

"When you talked to Kee, you had forgotten the threats?"

"I don't know."

"When you talked to Kee you said you weren't afraid that Ray would hurt you. . . ."

There was a long silence as she sat there, blank-faced.

"Can you remember the name of one child who was present at any of the houses you were taken to where naked games were played?"

"No. I don't remember."

"You said that at the green house the 'naked movie star' [game] was played. Can you tell us what happened?"

"Ray went into the bedroom and got undressed, and he told us to get undressed."

"What about Peggy?"

"She went in the bedroom and took off her clothes."

"When it was played, what did you do?"

"Run, skip, and hop."

"What did Peggy do?"

"The same."

"After the dancing, did anything happen?"

"Ray and Peggy touched me."

"What did Ray and Peggy do when they touched you?"

"She put her finger in my vagina and Ray put his finger in my vagina."

"How long was the 'naked movie star' [game] played at the house?"

"I don't know."

Tuesday morning. Judge Pounders admonished the jurors once again for sleeping during the testimony. Gits's cross-examination focused again on the contradictions between what Melinda said in the preliminary hearing and what she was saying in the trial. In the afternoon he finished, and Davis rose to cross-examine.

"Well, Melinda, some of the changes you've gone through, like closets and children being put in the bathroom, came from information Kee told you, right?"

"No."

"You told the grand jury [that] kids were put in closets . . . that wasn't true, was it?"

"I don't understand."

"Well, you never saw any closets because there aren't any closets in the preschool, are there?"

"No, there aren't."

"How long ago did you go to the preschool?"

"Seven years ago."

"And the closets were happyface cupboards, right?"

The girl was silent for a long time. Finally, she said, "Well, at the time I knew Ray put the children somewhere but I didn't remember."

"Do you remember testifying at the preliminary hearing about Peggy putting her vagina inside your vagina?"
"Yes."
"And that never happened, correct?"
"Yes."
"And you talked it over with some adults and they explained. . . . Did your mother tell you that you can't put a vagina inside of another vagina?"
"I don't know whether it was my mother or Lael."
"And because of what you were told you changed your testimony."
"Yes."
"Do you remember you said that not only Peggy but also Betty put her vagina inside your vagina?"
"I don't know."
"How old were you when you were last molested?"
"I don't remember."
"How old do you think you were when you were first molested?"
"Two years old."
"Tell us what happened?"
"I remember Peggy putting her finger in my bottom and her finger in my vagina and put her vagina together with my vagina."
"Where?"
"At the school."
"Where at the school?" Davis asked.
"I don't remember."
"What time of day?"
"I don't remember."
"Did she have her clothes on?"
"I don't remember."
"What position was your body in?"
"I don't remember."
"This was the first time in your life, the one time you'll never forget, right?"
"I don't remember."
"When you went to talk to the puppet lady [Kee MacFarlane] you forgot that any of this happened, right?"
"I didn't forget. I just didn't tell her."
"When you talked to Dr. Heger about what happened at the preschool . . . were you sometimes guessing?"
"Yes."
"Doesn't that mean you were guessing and not sure?"
"Yes."
"Who told you that animals were killed at the preschool?"
"I don't know who told me. I just heard of it."
"Did you ever see a cat at the school?"

"Yes, but it didn't belong there. It just walked in. . . . It just walked around and then it left."

"In the preliminary hearing you said you didn't remember that it hurt when you peed. Now you say you do remember. Is there anything you can tell us about the thought process . . . did you talk to anybody about this?"

"No."

Asked about her testimony that Buckey put his penis in her mouth, she described it in such a way that it was virtually certain, at least to us, that she had neither seen nor experienced such an event.

Davis asked many questions about the prosecutor, Lael Rubin, practicing with Melinda at great length, rehearsing questions and answers with her for the trial and the preliminary hearing, coaching and shaping her testimony. Most of the answers were "I don't know," and "I don't remember."

The next day of the trial brought a surprise. Virginia McMartin told her family and attorneys at her eightieth birthday party that she doubted she would live long enough to testify at the trial, which could last another year or more. She said she wanted the people to hear what really happened at the school. Because of the possibility of her death or inability to testify after the prosecution rested, which might not be for months, she asked the judge to allow her to come in and testify "out of order" on videotape with the media and the public excluded from the courtroom. He agreed, but called it a "conditional deposition," meaning it would be shown to the jury during the defense portion of the trial only if she is unable to testify at that time.

Attorneys from newspapers joined with the defense lawyers to protest the exclusion of the public and media, and Pounders then agreed to let them in because the attorneys showed that the statute Pounders cited had been overturned by decisions in recent cases. The first morning Gits focused mostly on Virginia's training and experience in child care, and the many courses she had taken at various universities. "I'm one of those unusual people who loves to study," she said. "I worked with children most of my life."

Virginia said that when she was working at a nursery school in Manhattan Beach her employer asked her, "Why don't you have a school of your own?" When she learned that the school was for sale she offered to buy it, and the owner was delighted, she said.

Virginia operated the school until 1984 "when we were threatened."

"Did you ever see Peggy Buckey touch the genitals of a child?"

"No."

"Did you ever see Ray Buckey touch the genitals of a child?"

"No. Never."

"How did you help the teachers?"

"I would watch the children. Sometimes I would organize a little game."

"During the morning, did the parents come and go?"

"All day."
"When you arrived after lunch, did you stay in your car?"
"Yes. . . . Right in front of the school."
"Did you ever see a child alone on the bench?"
"Never."
"Did you ever see a child alone on the swing?"
"Never."
"Was there some kind of a consent form signed by parents for children to be taken off the grounds?"
"They signed that when they enrolled. If a child needed first aid we could take him to a doctor without consent of the parents."
"Were there rabbits at the school?"
"Yes."
"Did anything happen to them?"
"They were stolen. The birds were, too."
"Did you ever see anyone harm animals at the school?"
"Never."
"Were there any closets at the preschool?"
"There were no closets at the preschool. We had cupboards but there were shelves. There's no way we could stand a child inside."
"Did [the school photographer] ever photograph children who were not fully clothed?"
"No. There's no way he could do that."
"Did you ever see anyone kill a turtle?"
"No. In my opinion turtles belong out on the desert. . . ."
"Were cats kept at the school?"
"No. There was a neighbor cat that came around."
"Did you ever see a dead cat there?"
"No."
"What kind of a relationship did Ray have with the children?"
"Just marvelous. The children loved him."
"Did you ever see any child molested?"
"No. I've never seen so many evil-minded people!"
"Objection! [nonresponsive]"
"Sustained."

Gits brought out the box of file cards and asked if Virginia had had an opportunity to look at them.

"No. Not since they were stolen from me."
"Objection!" Rubin's voice rang out.
"Sustained. The last half of the answer is stricken."
"Can you tell us when you were last in possession of these?"
"The police department stole it, and they used it to send out that filthy letter!"

"Objection!" Rubin interrupted.

"Sustained. The answer is stricken."

Virginia testified that children never were taken off the premises except for the annual Halloween parade and field trips to the police and fire departments. Asked if she ever molested a child she replied, "Never. To be perfectly frank with you, I'm not sure what any of you mean by 'molest.' Until this case I had never heard of it."

Asked if she had ever seen Ray or Peggy do anything that might even be misconstrued as molestation, she answered, "You'd have to be awfully evil-minded."

"Objection!" Rubin called out.

"Sustained," the judge ruled. "The answer is stricken. It will be edited out of the tape."

When she was asked about a teacher named Maxine, she said, "Maxine? She's dead. This trial killed her."

"Objection!" Rubin objected to almost every answer that was more detailed than a simple yes or no. By insisting that the answers were nonresponsive she could restrict Virginia's statements as much as possible.

"Sustained. The answer is stricken."

Virginia forcefully stated that no pornographic pictures were ever taken at the school, and that it was very seldom that there were not parents and other adults coming and going at the preschool.

Virginia was generally calm and restrained during the first day of her direct examination, but when prosecutor Rubin objected to some of her answers on the ground that they were hearsay, she angrily retorted, "It is not hearsay! I was there!" Again, her answer was stricken and was to be edited from the tape. Asked if she went to the police department to discuss the allegations when they first surfaced, she said, "They told me I had no rights whatsoever. They wouldn't even tell me who the child was."

She appeared old and tired, as you would expect an eighty-year-old to look, but she was clear-eyed, extremely lucid, and remembered the dates of significant events without referring to any notes or written records. Her face disclosed a gentle strength and dignity, and some anger. Her answers were simple and direct.

Asked about the school's prohibition on picking up children during naptime, she replied, "They were asked not to pick up pupils during that period because it was disruptive, but they did it anyway. I don't know if you've ever had the experience of a whole room full of children being awakened."

Asked about the allegations that guns and knives were seen on the premises, she said, "We didn't allow anything that suggested violence." Toy guns and knives were not allowed to be brought into the school. She characterized claims that Buckey killed and mutilated animals to frighten children into silence as "the most ridiculous thing I've ever heard. . . . He's very indulgent of animals.

Same of her [Peggy]. She's loved animals all her life. We always had them." Asked about the allegations that children were taken to a farm, car wash, and strangers' houses, she said, "In two hours and forty-five minutes you don't do a great deal of running around."

Virginia also said that Ray was not even there at the school during the time period indicated in many of the allegations against him. She said he was exceptionally good with children. "Just marvelous. The children loved him. I've never seen so many evil-minded people."

"Objection!"

"Sustained."

From the stand, Virginia waved to her grandson. "I miss him," she said during a brief recess. "Imagine! Three and a half years in jail and you've never done anything wrong."

Outside the courtroom, Lael Rubin told reporters, "There are greater areas of inquiry that have not been gone into." She said she intended to address these issues in the morning.

The relative tranquility of the preceding day was shattered the next morning when Rubin began her cross-examination of Virginia McMartin. She hurled her accusations like a warrior, her voice ringing out in self-righteous condemnation. She was clearly baiting Virginia, trying to shake her composure and bring the wrath of the judge down upon her.

"On occasion you saw Raymond's penis hanging out of his shorts, didn't you?"

"No. I don't look at people that way."

"You saw Raymond Buckey touch children's genitals, and your daughter, Peggy, told you children touched his genitals, didn't she?"

"That was one time," Virginia replied. "A little girl had a habit of doing that to her father, and she grabbed Raymond's. And so Peggy told the mother immediately and the mother said the father allowed it, and she apologized."

"In fact, Mrs. McMartin, you knew Raymond Buckey had a problem with touching children's genitals, didn't you?" Rubin charged. That did it.

"No, I didn't!" Virginia exploded. "And don't try to put words in my mouth! I did not. You are lying!"

Judge Pounders instructed Virginia to "respond only to the questions."

"Then you speak to her!" she demanded. "I want you to know I was brought up a lady. I've been one all my life and I expect to spend my senior years as a lady. You can speak to me respectfully or not at all! And that goes for you, too," she said, looking at the judge.

"Mrs. McMartin," the judge told her, "I want to remind you that at your age, if sent to jail, it will be difficult, and I'm not at all reluctant to send you to jail in the event that you do not respond to my orders . . . to the orders of this court."

"I've already been in your jail and seen the horrible way you treat people,"

The Trial 91

she raised her voice, undaunted by the judge's warning. It was noon and the judge told her to "think about it over the noon hour or expect to go to jail on a contempt citation." Then he hurried out of the courtroom.

"I will not think about it!" she shouted after him. Her daughter, Peggy, helped her down off the witness stand and into her wheelchair. "She's not going to say dirty, filthy things to me and get away with it," Virginia went on, enraged. Apparently her daughter, her lawyer, and friends managed to cool Virginia down during the lunch break. After the recess, Rubin continued her onslaught but Virginia was calm and restrained.

"You knew your grandson had a problem about touching the genitals of children, didn't you?" Rubin charged.

"I did not," Virginia answered.

"You knew Raymond was seeing Dr. Richelieu for that problem, didn't you?" Rubin's voice rang out sharply.

"I didn't know why he was seeing Dr. Richelieu," Virginia said.

"If there were notations in your diary about Raymond seeing Dr. Richelieu on a regular basis, those notations would be correct, wouldn't they?" Rubin continued to batter Virginia with her questions worded as statements of fact, fast and stridently. "You knew your grandson was interested in pornography, didn't you?" An elderly lawyer whispered to us, "I've never seen anything like this since the McCarthy hearings."

At recess, reporters gathered around Rubin as she left the courtroom. One of them asked: "Do Virginia McMartin's journals say that Ray was seeing Dr. Richelieu for problems related to child abuse?"

Rubin replied that he was seeing the doctor "for problems."

"Do you have evidence that the problem dealt with child molestation?" the reporter asked.

"Yes," she replied.

Dr. Richelieu is a Protestant minister, Peggy told us in the hallway. "I'll tell you what that was about. He went to Dr. Richelieu for counseling about his drinking! Lael Rubin made that up. It was a pure lie!"

But the *Los Angeles Times* trumpeted to its 1,100,000 readers the next day, a headline which read: "BUCKEY KNOWN AS MOLESTER, D.A. SAYS." The same day, Richelieu told a reporter in a telephone interview, "I never counseled Raymond Buckey for child abuse nor molestation. I counseled him for matters dealing with himself. He was drinking. We never discussed sexual molestation at all. I read the *L.A. Times* article and it was ridiculous. I don't know what they were basing it on." Dr. Richelieu also noted that if the counseling had been about child abuse, he would have been compelled to report it to law enforcement officials under the child abuse reporting law.

Despite all this, the *Los Angeles Times,* the next week, published a story about the incident, falsely reporting that, "Church officials have declined to comment." We showed this to the young reporter who had interviewed Richelieu and he said, "I saw that. I couldn't believe they would do that."

When Rubin was asked about Richelieu's denial that he had ever counseled Buckey about sexual molestation her answer was evasive: "Why don't you wait and hear the evidence?"

In the hallway, two women approached Davis and asked, "Weren't those questions Lael Rubin asked somewhat unethical? Is she really allowed to do that?"

"It's just Lael Rubin's style of cross-examination," he said. "It's insinuation. And insinuation does not go beyond reasonable doubt."

"Who's going to be the next witness?" we asked.

"Another doctor," Davis said. "I think his name is Simpson."

"They're not going to bring back Dr. Gordon?"

"Would you?" he smiled.

Back in the courtroom, Rubin continued to hammer Virginia. "Mrs. McMartin, isn't it true that between October 1983 and June 1984 you tore up and threw out records pertinent to the McMartin school?"

"The police took everything. I could not have thrown out anything."

"Did you tear up pictures . . . did you tear up proofs prior to that?"

"We always did. You can't operate a school for twenty-eight years and keep everything."

"Would you please turn to the entry for June 9. . . . Do you see anything about people throwing out materials from the school?"

"The police had been to my house four times and took everything they wanted. There was not much left."

"Didn't Peggy tell you that one of the parents complained that Raymond was not wearing underwear?"

"I don't remember."

"Wouldn't you think there was something peculiar about a young man not wearing underwear?"

"No I wouldn't. I'm not that narrow-minded."

Outside the courtroom during recess, reporters surrounded Rubin with questions. She told them: "We are seeing someone who is very evasive, someone who has a convenient memory loss about important dates in this case. One ought to be very suspicious about her hiding or covering up evidence."

Asked what evidence was being hidden, Rubin answered, "I can only speculate what she's covering up and I think all of you can, too." The housebroken reporters did not interview Virginia or the lawyers.

On redirect, Gits asked Virginia about an entry in her diary that referred to a "witch lady." Virginia replied, "I probably was referring to some part of the prosecution. As far as I'm concerned they're all witch ladies."

Two physicians testified briefly for the prosecution, about the child of Judy Johnson, the woman who made the original complaint. One, Dr. Scott

McGeary, M.D., said he examined the boy for possible sexual abuse and found everything to be healthy and normal except for a "band of redness around the anus," and said he believed the examination suggested he might have been penetrated by some object in the rectum. He told Davis that, "The mother would not allow a rectal examination."

"Would it be fair to say, from what you heard from the mother, that she was intentionally concealing the identity of someone?"

"Yes. Her first statement was that she wasn't going to allow any questions about the perpetrator," the doctor said.

"When you filed your report," Davis asked, "you weren't certain the child was molested, were you?"

"No," the doctor replied.

"And you aren't today?"

"No."

Dr. Jean Simpson-Savary, who examined the boy a week after McGeary had examined him, at Harbor-UCLA Medical Center, said she felt the boy had been sodomized. She also said this was the first and only case of suspected sodomy she had ever diagnosed. There were some inconsistencies between her findings and those of McGeary. Simpson-Savary said the boy was circumcised and Dr. McGeary said he was uncircumcised. McGeary said the excoriation (redness) was in the peri-anal area at "three o'clock and nine o'clock." Simpson-Savary said the redness was at "six o'clock."

One more physician, Dr. Richard Shearer, testified briefly. Davis showed him a report he had prepared three months after Ray Buckey's arrest. He asked Shearer if the boy had accused his father of molesting him.

"That is what is reflected in the report," the doctor said. He had written in his report that, according to the mother, "Eight days ago child reported that father poked him in anus."

The next witness, officer John Dye of the Manhattan Beach Police Department, provided nothing of any significance and, in fact, his testimony was exculpatory. Asked what was seized in a search of the school in which he participated, he reported having taken some shoelaces, group photographs of children sitting with teachers, a filing cabinet, some children's underwear, masking tape, and a bag with some yarn and wooden sticks in it.

He was asked if he found any evidence of pedophilia in the search of Ray Buckey's living quarters; he said, "I didn't see any at all." When Davis asked him if any pornography had been found in Ray's apartment, he responded, "*Playboy* and girlie magazines." He also testified that the shorts Buckey wore "came about halfway down the leg."

We had a lengthy conversation with Virginia after court was recessed for the day. Sitting in her wheelchair, she told us, "You'd be surprised how many people didn't believe a bit of this until Kee MacFarlane got a hold of them. Then the district attorney sent all the children down to the CII and that Kee MacFarlane. They have made so much money off of this and she has made a big name for herself. They got one little girl down there and she said she was never molested and they said, 'That's very normal for a molested child.' That's Roland Summit's theory. But if you could see those tapes and see how they manipulated those kids. They only showed the parents bits of it. Just the parts they wanted them to see. But can you believe that prosecutor, Lael Rubin? She went on TV and said I founded the school for the purpose of pornography! The FBI went all over the United States. They even went to Europe. They went to South Dakota and dug up the national park! And they never found one thing. And I spoke right up in court and said, 'Why you dirty sneaks!'

"And every time a little kid got caught in a lie Judge Bobb would give them a recess and then the D.A. would take the kid out and talk to him and then he'd come back in and tell a completely different story. One little girl said Peggy put a lighted candle up her vagina. And nobody heard anything. If that really happened you'd hear that kid scream for a mile. I'd be embarrassed to tell a story like that because it would make you look like an imbecile."

Virginia suffers from severe arthritis and cannot walk without crutches. She is always in great pain. She told us that when she was arrested and taken to the county jail the police who fingerprinted her pushed her arthritic hands down with greatly excessive force and grinned with sadistic pleasure as she cried out, and that they then taunted and mocked her. She told us that when the police searched her home they threw all of her things on the floor and appeared to be enjoying it.

We spoke with one of the lawyers who specializes in this type of case; he frequently sat in the courtroom listening to the trial. We became somewhat friendly.

As we sat in the deserted hallway, he told us, "What she just told you goes to the heart of the matter. At first, most of the parents and other residents of Manhattan Beach didn't believe any of it and rallied behind the McMartin Preschool teachers—until they were told by their lawyers that the school was required by law to carry liability insurance. One million dollars per kid. And they were told that if any of the defendants got convicted they would have grounds to sue and collect very substantial damages. Big bucks. And so now they 'believe the children.' It's big bucks and fame and fortune and better days ahead—for everybody except the Buckeys. They lost everything. About two million And the other five lost everything. It's an uneven struggle. The prosecutors don't have to sell their houses and give up their life savings to stay in this poker game. They just collect their salaries and bask in the credibility of the government. And the support of those dippy media reporters."

In the morning we sat in the courtroom and waited until the judge finally came in.

"We are back in *People* v. *Buckey,* and all counsel and defendants are present," he said. "Anything to take up before the jury is brought in?"

There was indeed. There were lengthy arguments concerning the next prosecution witness—George Freeman, the jailhouse informant, or "snitch," as the defense attorneys called him. The judge allowed no television or still photographs of Freeman because, according to Freeman, there were contracts on his life as a result of his having given information and testimony for law enforcement and prosecutors in prior cases.

Freeman was brought into the courtroom and directed to sit at the witness stand. His appearance was a surprise. We had expected to see a raunchy, abject figure, but Freeman was about six feet tall, square-faced, square-shouldered, and looking very much like a cop. He wore a full moustache of the style and shape worn by television cops. His hair was stylishly coifed and blow-dried. They had dressed him up in a natty beige suit with a silk tie and an expensive dress shirt. Lael Rubin began by asking him to give his name.

"George Homer Freeman," he answered.

"Mr. Freeman, are you known by any other names?" Rubin asked.

Freeman gave a list of aliases he had used.

"Mr. Freeman, have you been convicted of any felonies?"

"Yes, I have."

"How many?"

"Five felonies." He said these included robbery and burglary.

"Are you on parole?"

"Yes, I am."

"Were you recently arrested?"

"Yes, I was."

"When?"

"November 10, 1987." The arrest was for assault.

"Have any promises been made to you in order to get you to testify in this case?"

"No promises whatever." He went on to testify that he was housed in the 7000 section of the county jail, a special module for "keepaways," prisoners charged with particularly odious crimes, high-publicity cases, ex-cops, and other prisoners who would have a high probability of being put to death if they were placed with the general prison population—particularly informers.

Freeman said that when he was moved into Ray Buckey's cell he told Buckey that he, too, was charged with child molestation "in order to make him feel comfortable."

"Did Ray tell you he left town?" Rubin asked.

"Yes he did."

"Why?"

"He said he was told to leave town and took the pictures and films to South Dakota. He was told to burn them but he buried them."

"Did Ray Buckey say that molestations actually occurred in the preschool?"
"Yes, he did."
"When?"
"At naptime."
"Did he tell you he used anything to help him molest children?"
"Yes, he did." Freeman never answered with a simple "Yes," or "No." He always gave a three-word answer: "Yes, I did," "Yes, he was," or "Yes, there was."

"What did he use to help him molest children?" Rubin asked.

"KY and baby oil." He quoted Buckey as having said that the pictures and films showed children engaged in sexual acts, and that he had had incestuous sex with his sister since he was six years old. Freeman told a similar story in the preliminary hearing.

He went on to say that he relayed all of this to law enforcement and was told to keep written notes on everything Ray Buckey told him. It was subsequent to his statements about Buckey taking child pornography to South Dakota that law enforcement began digging up the Wind Cave National Park.

The questions went on for hours.

"You told Ray Buckey you had molested children in order to make him comfortable. Why is it you wanted to make him comfortable?"

"I was curious. . . . I have kids," he said piously. He went on to to say that Ray Buckey had told him of having molested other children at the preschool and in a van.

"What did he tell you?"
"He said he fucked a two-year-old boy in the butt. . . ."
"Did Ray Buckey tell you he took pictures to South Dakota?"
"Yes, he did."
"Did he tell you what was on the pictures and films?"
"Kids in sex acts."
"Did he tell you what was done with any other pictures?"
"Yes, he did. He said some of them were in Denmark."
"Did you talk to Ray Buckey about church?"
"Yes, he did. He said he belonged to a church I couldn't get into—like a cult."
"Did Ray Buckey say anything about hurting animals?"
"Yes, he did."
"What did he say?"
"If the kids told on him. . . . He slaughtered a cow at a ranch."
"Were there kids present?"
"Yes, there were."
"How did you get to know Sgt. Dvorak?"
"I met him in 1983."
"Was this in another case?"

"Yes, it was."

"Did he help you out on your case?"

"Yes, he did. . . . He went and talked to the judge in San Fernando and instead of three years in prison I got one year in county jail."

"On March 28, did a sheriff come and take you to see an attorney?"

"Yes, he did."

"When you got to the attorney room did you see any person you see here today?"

"Yes, I did."

"Who did you see?"

"Danny Davis and Ray Buckey."

"And what was said?"

"He said the Aryan Brotherhood want my ass and two Mexicans in San Fernando and the BGF in Soledad wanted to get me and he said he would put me on TV and the newspapers where everybody could see what I look like. He told me to get my ass out of Ray Buckey's room. He said there would be two men waiting for me on the day of my release."

"Did you tell Sgt. Dvorak about your meeting with Mr. Davis?"

"Yes, I did."

"Did he look at your notes?"

"Yes, he did. . . . He said he couldn't read 'em."

During a brief recess, a cable television reporter confronted Lael Rubin and asked, "Miss Rubin, this witness has had five felony convictions! Do you really think he's believable?"

"This testimony is so powerful!" she said, her eyes wide with fervor.

"But this man has five felony convictions!" the newswoman replied.

"This testimony is so powerful!" Rubin repeated. "Because it shows how desperate Mr. Davis must be if he would do that. It shows how worried he was about the weakness of his case!"

After recess, back in the courtroom, Rubin continued, "Has anyone in law enforcement told you that because of your testimony in this case, the murder case will not ever be refiled?"

"No, they haven't."

"Did someone suggest that you move out of L.A.?"

"Yes, they did."

"And did anyone give you assistance?"

"Yes, they did. Mr. Gil Brunetti of the D.A.'s office paid the first month's rent, approximately one thousand dollars."

"Did you contact a TV station?"

"Yes, I did." Freeman said that after being released from county jail he had contacted Dan Leighton, an investigator for Wayne Satz.

"What did Dan Leighton tell you?"

"He told me I could make a lot of money from a movie or a book."

Freeman said that, after meeting with Leighton, "I thought he was pulling my leg." He said he then called someone from Channel 2, "a oriental lady. . . . She told me Dan Leighton was full of baloney. . . . She said they don't buy information."

"Did you talk to reporter Wayne Satz at Channel 7?"

"Yes, I did. . . . Satz wanted to put me on TV." He said he was televised as a silhouette so that his face could not be seen as he told his story.

In the hallway during recess we asked Peggy's lawyer, Gits, "Isn't it a bit irregular that a man is out on parole for a major felony and he gets arrested for assault and battery and he is not returned to prison for a parole violation?"

"Yes, it is," Gits replied. "I've seen people returned to prison on parole violation for as little as getting a traffic ticket, and I've seen it happen for things even more trivial than that."

"Then why is this guy still walking the streets?" we asked.

"I'd like to know the answer to that myself," he said.

Further down the hallway was Ray's lawyer, Davis, standing with a group of attorneys and investigators. I asked them the same question.

"How about murder," Davis answered. "He was charged with strangling a woman and raping her while she died. He was put through a preliminary hearing and bound over for trial, which means the judge found that the preponderance of the evidence was that he was guilty. But he was never prosecuted."

"What does that mean?" I asked.

"He works for the D.A."

"There is no statute of limitations on murder," one of the investigators told me. "That means they can refile on the murder charge at any time. He will say anything they tell him to say. This guy has spent most of his life behind bars, and he has a long history of giving false testimony under oath. He's made the circuit of every high-publicity case in the state. They use him whenever they want a conviction and don't have the evidence."

"Freeman is building up IOUs with the D.A.'s office," Davis said.

"Did you really threaten George Freeman?" a reporter asked.

"If I had done that, I would have been charged with threatening a witness long ago," Davis answered.

The next morning, things got even stranger. The prosecutors told Judge Pounders that Freeman had admitted committing perjury in three prior cases and would invoke the Fifth Amendment and refuse to testify about those perjuries. Judge Pounders asked if the prosecution would request that Freeman be given immunity from prosecution to compel his testimony. Prosecutor Roger Gunson indicated a reluctance to do so and the judge stated that the only alternative would be to declare a mistrial.

Defense attorney Davis angrily charged that this information of Freeman's previous perjuries was deliberately withheld so that his extremely damaging testimony could be heard by the jury, and that Rubin's strategy was to deprive the defense of their right to cross-examine Freeman and attack the credibility of his statements. Rubin suggested that excerpts from Freeman's testimony in the preliminary hearing be substituted for cross-examination.

According to Davis, Freeman concocted the murder confession of a cellmate in another case and was never prosecuted for perjury even though he admitted to having lied under oath in prior cases.

"The ethical questions are most profound," Davis said, "when the prosecution uses someone with a history of lying under oath as a key witness! They're willing to go ahead with a perjurer!"

A long chambers conference took up most of the morning. Based on courtroom discussion after the conference and on interviews the attorneys participated in, we surmised that Rubin suggested that Freeman should be represented by a lawyer for the rest of his testimony. Meanwhile, George Freeman sat in the courtroom, waiting, his head hanging down, looking extremely despondent, like a man whose plans have gone badly awry.

Asked by reporters outside the courtroom why she had waited until after Freeman had completed two days of testimony before advising him to retain an attorney, Rubin answered that it had suddenly occurred to her that she was going to go into that area in her questioning. "It kind of hit me over the head. I realized he might want to consult an attorney."

Freeman, however, said, "I told her I wanted an attorney. She said I didn't need one." He said he had asked Rubin for an attorney three times before testifying. He also said Rubin urged him to testify without taking the Fifth Amendment. The judge appointed an attorney for Freeman. Asked about his lying under oath in the earlier cases, Freeman invoked the Fifth Amendment fifteen times. Judge Pounders noted that, "The witness here has testified to acts of molestation, death threats, and acts of incest by the defendants. I don't believe this could be struck . . . so the only alternative would be a mistrial if that is requested." He asked Rubin if the prosecution wanted to request immunity for Freeman. Rubin asked for a recess.

When she returned, she said to the judge, "Rather than starting a new trial all over again we have decided to ask for immunity."

"I think it is most appropriate that he be granted immunity," Pounders said, but made it clear that the immunity applied only to charges of past perjury, and not to the murder case in which Freeman remains a suspect. "I don't think anyone wants to immunize him on a homicide," Pounders said.

Davis, Ray Buckey's attorney, confronted by reporters outside the courtroom, spoke out angrily, "If you lie under oath in the McMartin case as George Freeman has done, do it with wild abandon because it is sanctioned by Ira Reiner himself."

Prosecutor Rubin asserted that, in spite of Freeman's long history of lying under oath, his testimony in this trial was truthful.

The next morning brought another surprise. Rubin had said that she needed only a few minutes more to complete her examination of George Freeman, but when the judge arrived, Rubin informed him that Freeman had failed to appear and had gone, instead, to a hospital complaining of chest pains and coughing blood. He had been diagnosed as having bronchitis, she reported. Pounders told the jurors they could go home and that, "Mr. Freeman has sought medical attention and our best information is that he will be here tomorrow."

Thursday morning brought still another surprise. Again, Freeman did not show. Rubin told the judge that Freeman's daughter said she had driven him to a hospital, but investigators who went to the hospital were told that there was no record of his being admitted to the hospital that day and that his whereabouts were unknown. Rubin said she had received a call from Freeman and that the call had been disconnected before she could find out where he was calling from. According to Rubin, Freeman was frightened and needed "a few days to think."

Judge Pounders was angered. "I'm not going to give him time to think. It's not his option." Pounders issued a bench warrant for Freeman's arrest.

Davis said he suspected Freeman would flee the country, as he had done during the preliminary hearing. "He has good reasons never to come back," Davis said. "I fully intend to convict him of murder." Davis typically made statements like this. He was not a prosecutor and had no authority to "convict" Freeman. Davis just wanted to emphasize that Freeman had an open murder charge and would be motivated to give testimony supportive of the prosecution.

A mistrial was virtually certain if Freeman was not apprehended. Chief Deputy District Attorney Gilbert Garcetti publicly criticized Rubin for failing to obtain an attorney for a prosecution witness who had admitted perjury in prior cases.

Freeman was found and arrested early Friday morning and taken before Judge Pounders, who ordered him held on one million dollars bail.

There was, once again, a debate over the prosecution's failure to provide the defense with discovery—in other words, all evidence it possessed to support its charge—as required by law. "If Mr. Freeman committed perjury, I am entitled to know in what proceedings and on what dates . . . the specific case numbers and titles. I believe that Miss Rubin knows that. I do not have that information," Davis protested. When the judge asked her about this, Rubin handed him a sheet of paper.

"This is unreadable," the judge said, "These are not complete sentences, and it's written in pencil."

Outside the courtroom, Gits asked reporters, "Why don't you ask Ira Reiner if it's more politically expedient to grant immunity to a perjurer than to see justice done in this case?"

* * *

Tuesday, October 13, 1987. Freeman was waiting in a holding cell next to the courtroom. The prosecution requested that he be allowed to shower, shave, and change into clean clothes.

"I have no concern for Mr. Freeman after wasting $2,700 a day for two days, waiting for him to come in," the judge said. "As far as I'm concerned, he's the last one on my list. The jury knows he's a five-time loser and has committed almost every felony in the book. I don't see how his mode of dress is going to change that whatsoever." Pounders also refused to rule on a defense motion to dismiss and a motion for a mistrial.

George Freeman was brought into the courtroom, escorted by a man from the district attorney's office. His appearance was very different from what we had seen the previous week. He was wearing a dirty, short-sleeved, dark blue t-shirt, revealing immensely muscular arms covered with tattoos. He had spent twenty-five years in prisons and jails, lifting weights. He could bench press 440 pounds. His hair, which had been stylishly blow-dried the last time he was in court, was now greasy and sloppily combed straight back. He had not shaved for four days.

Davis, on cross-examination, spent most of the day going over Freeman's past perjuries, in which he lied under oath, and occasions when he made false statements to law enforcement while in custody. During his questioning, Davis elicited the fact that Freeman had falsely testified for the prosecution throughout his criminal career in exchange for favorable treatment from prosecutors in the 1979 murder case and other proceedings in which he was a defendant, and that he had several times concocted "confessions" of other defendants. Freeman admitted providing "information" that was not truthful to get favors from law enforcement. On one occasion when he was charged with burglary and assault, officers of the Los Angeles Police and the L.A. County Sheriff's Office urged a judge to "go easy" on him. His sentence was reduced from three years in prison to one year in county jail.

"Mr. Freeman, are you a rat?" Davis asked.

"They say I am in different places," he answered.

Freeman was never charged for the lies he told law enforcement and under oath in court proceedings. He admitted he was placed in twelve different cells and had informed on six fellow inmates to a Sgt. Dvorak, who was allegedly known among inmates as the "snitch liaison." When Freeman was released in 1984 he was provided with a home, a job, and a new identity by the district attorney's office. The prosecutors apparently needed Freeman because months of investigation had failed to produce any adult witnesses, "pornographic" photographs, or any corroborating evidence to support the stories the children told after visiting CII.

Now, under the protection of immunity, Freeman slouched in his chair at the witness stand, smiling with scornful amusement as he casually admitted to the past perjuries and to the fact that law enforcement officers repaid him for his services by persuading judges to reduce his sentences or drop charges pending against him.

Freeman also testified that the district attorney's office had placed him in the witness protection program, which paid his living expenses, and then placed him in Buckey's cell in violation of Buckey's Fifth Amendment right against self-incrimination and his Sixth Amendment right to counsel; Freeman then fabricated Buckey's "confession." During a brief recess, a young woman with bleached blonde hair who appeared to be one of Freeman's friends, said impatiently, "Why don't they just send 'um to the joint and get it over with?"

After recess Davis continued, "Mr. Freeman, how would anybody in the world know how many lies you told in the preliminary?"

"Only God," he answered.

"And you're a strong-arm robber, aren't you?"

"Depends."

"Depends on what?"

"If I'm drunk enough."

"You were an informant in the Bailey case?"

"Yeah."

"And you lied in front of the jury."

"One thing, I believe."

"Did you consider that a serious lie?"

"I had my reasons."

"Those reasons you carried throughout your criminal career, right?"

"Right."

Davis tried to go into the 1979 murder charge still pending aqainst Freeman and was quickly cut off by Rubin's objection. But the jury heard it, loud and clear. Throughout the cross-examination Freeman maintained that he had lied in court to protect his family. He said he was afraid they would be killed in retaliation for his prosecution testimony. Davis asked him, "When was the last time you lived with your wife and children?"

"Nineteen sixty-nine." he said.

"I'm going to list cases in which you committed perjury," Davis said, and he proceeded to do so. "Is there any case in which you didn't perjure yourself?"

"I don't know."

"Was there any case where the D.A. didn't know you were lying under oath?"

"I don't know."

"The D.A., Watts, used you as a witness after he knew you lied."

"Yes, he did."

"He wrote a letter for you after you told him you lied to him?"

"Yes, he did."

"In Bailey did you get up and say he made a confession . . . like you did in this case?"

"Yeah."

"I'd like to talk about what you did with some sheep." Nearly everyone in the courtroom gaped and then burst into laughter.

"Objection! Assumes facts not in evidence," Rubin cried out, and there was another lengthy sidebar while the jurors yawned. When it was over, Freeman said that he had stolen some sheep and then offered to inform on his accomplices to get another pending criminal charge against him dropped.

"You said you had only five felony convictions. Isn't it the truth that you've had nine felony convictions?"

"Yeah, maybe . . . the way you calculate, yeah."

"Have you ever said that a man committed murder when he did not?"

"That goes back to Soledad. I didn't see him stab anybody."

Freeman was confronted with his answers in the McMartin preliminary hearing and his answers to the same questions he was asked in the trial—they were not the same. In the preliminary he said he told the police that Ray Buckey had denied any wrongdoing.

"You were afraid [that] being seen in newspapers and television would endanger you, right?"

"Yes."

"Two days after you got out of county jail, whom did you call?"

"Channel 7 Eyewitness News."

"And that interview was broadcast on TV, right?"

"Yes."

"You were under a court order not to have any interview with news media."

"Yes."

"And you deliberately disobeyed that order."

"Yes."

"And you had a relationship with Sgt. Dvorak and that's the reason you weren't afraid of disobeying an order from a judge?"

Freeman's answer was an inaudible mumble.

Davis's questioning lasted for three weeks.

Finally, at a noon recess, the judge exploded at Davis. "You told me that you needed two or three hours to cross-examine Mr. Freeman, and he's been up there for three weeks! At some point you've got to sit down and shut up."

"I trust the court is not angry with counsel," Davis said.

"Yes, I am!" the judge raised his voice angrily. "I do not want to spend the rest of my life sitting here. . . . I have never seen anything like this!"

"You and I have never seen a case like this before, your honor."

Lael Rubin asked a few final questions on redirect but Davis dropped one last bomb on Freeman before he was excused.

"You say you were concerned for the safety of your family and that was why you committed your perjuries. Would that be principally your mother and sister?"

"Yes, it was."

"And isn't it true that in 1983 you tied up your mother and your sister and robbed them and burglarized their home?"

Freeman equivocated. Court was recessed for the day and Davis told a couple of reporters, "Until now I planned my strategy on the assumption that I was dealing with an intelligent, competent prosecution. The fact that Roger Gunson would put on a doctor who said Peter was poked by his father and then this guy, tells me I can no longer assume I am dealing with an intelligent, competent prosecution."

The jurors laughed frequently during the last two days of Freeman's appearance on the stand, but did not seem to be taking him seriously. He seemed to have done the prosecution more harm than good. When Lael Rubin left the courtroom and was confronted by reporters questioning her about Freeman's history of perjury, she said that his testimony in this case was truthful. "If he was not a credible witness we would not have put him on the stand."

Although it angered the judge, Davis's strategy of keeping Freeman on the stand for such a long time was a good one. It gave the jurors a long look at the kind of man the prosecution was using as its star witness, on whom they were building their case.

Not long after that, there was a plethora of news stories that appeared in nearly every California newspaper about Leslie White, a jailhouse informant who told reporters that, like Freeman, he had been used by prosecutors to falsely testify in criminal trials against fellow inmates when the evidence against them was weak, saying they had confessed their alleged crimes to him. White reportedly explained and demonstrated to reporters how this was done. He claimed to have been doing this for prosecutors for eleven years. For several days there were newspaper stories telling how prevalent this practice is. A prominent defense lawyer was quoted as saying that prosecutors use these professional perjurers "in every high-publicity case where the evidence is weak."

The newspaper stories made no mention of the McMartin/Buckey trial—in spite of the fact that it was George Freeman's testimony that blew the cover off of this scandal and that it was a reporter covering the trial who, after hearing Freeman's statements, began investigating, interviewed other jailhouse snitches in the county jail, and disclosed the practice to the public.

"Why did they blank out the McMartin connection?" we asked one of the reporters.

"I don't know," he said. "There's something very strange going on here."

As Freeman was taken back to a holding cell and the spectators and lawyers shuffled out of the courtroom, a high-ranking deputy district attorney stood at the back of the room, smiling, a corpulent man with a moustache. A female reporter with her spiral notepad and pen in hand approached him and asked, "This witness by his own admission is a liar and a perjurer. Isn't it a prosecutor's obligation to see that justice is done rather than win at any cost?" The man grinned.

Freeman was excused, but the story did not go away. Newspaper stories on prosecutors' use of these jailhouse snitches, trading leniency for perjury, continued to appear in the daily press. It was not that it was anything new. But the McMartin trial was the first occasion when the inner workings of the legal system were so openly exposed to public scrutiny.

As the others moved toward the elevators, a lawyer who was in the preliminary hearing went to the snack bar and ordered coffee. He was asked by a friend of the Buckeys: "They're putting on witnesses who they know are lying. They concealed exonerating evidence. Don't we have enough criminal conduct by the prosecutors to put them behind bars?"

"It doesn't work that way," the lawyer laughed. "The law is just for the little people. When we break the rules we go to jail. When they break the rules they go to lunch. And maybe get a promotion if they do it right."

"But what about the law?" the woman gasped. "What about the Constitution?"

"I'm afraid that's just one of those nice, comforting fantasies like the tooth fairy. There are only two classes of people. Those who hold power and those who do not. And in any dispute the guys who hold power will decide which way it's going to go. And if there's any problem the rules go out the window. I hope you understand that this is not about child abuse, just as McCarthyism was not about Communists."

Walter Urban, Betty Raidor's lawyer in the preliminary hearing, was in the hallway. He was now defending a man accused of first degree murder in another courtroom on the same floor. A death penalty case. He asked me how McMartin was progressing. I told him of the bizarre events I had witnessed.

"They dug a hole and they don't know how to get out of it," he laughed.

Officer Jim Noble of the Manhattan Beach Police Department testified briefly. He said that after October 1983, he spent most of his time working the McMartin case, planning and executing search warrants, and that he had received a call from a deputy sheriff at county jail who "advised me that an individual had been a cellmate of Ray Buckey and that Buckey had given him some information." It was George Freeman. An interview was arranged and Freeman told him that Ray Buckey had flown child pornography to Wind Caves National Park in South Dakota. The officer did not bother to make any studied assessment of Freeman's reliability as an informant but flew to Wind Caves, where he found nothing but several hundred acres of rock.

Noble said he told Freeman to tell Buckey that he had people who were willing to pay money for the pornography. Again, they came up with nothing.

On the way home we passed a newsstand and saw a newspaper headline which read: COST OF McMARTIN CASE: $6.7 MILLION AND RISING.

In the morning, the witness was Dr. William Gordon, brought back to continue the testimony that was interrupted in July! A slide projector and a large screen were set up to show slides taken by Dr. Astrid Heger, the CII physician who said that all of the McMartin children had been molested. The slides were of the children's anuses and vaginas. Gordon had not examined the children himself. He was brought in to corroborate Heger's findings. One by one, Gordon was shown the slides and pointed to what he described as thickening and scarring of tissues as indicative of sexual abuse. Deputy D.A. Gunson showed one of the slides and asked the doctor if an injury had been the result of penetration by an adult penis. The doctor admitted he could not tell. More slides were projected on the screen. They were identified as those of one of the girls slated to be a witness for the prosecution. Gordon pointed to what he described as "abnormalities," but admitted that some of the abnormality was congenital. The rest, he said, was caused by some kind of trauma. After a few hours of this, the jurors were noticeably tired. On the next three slides, Gordon stated that the anal opening was abnormal in appearance. Court was recessed for lunch.

After the recess, Gordon was shown exhibits 100a, b, c, d, e, f, and g. He said he saw abnormalities in the child's vaginal opening and ruled out the possibility of causes other than molestation. He remarked that it was "a beautiful slide." He stated that he possessed the largest collection of photographs of children's anuses in the state of California.

Prosecutor Gunson showed forty-seven slides of the genital and anal areas of eleven children. Dr. Gordon said the children's history and the slides convinced him that there was a "high degree of probability" that ten of the children had been sexually abused and that "marginal" evidence of sodomy was present on the slide of the eleventh child. Even though the slides were greatly magnified, most of the spectators we spoke to or overheard in the halls said they saw what appeared to them to be normal anuses and vaginas.

Dean Gits, Peggy Buckey's attorney, began his cross-examination by questioning Gordon about the slide of a boy who was a complaining witness in eight counts against Raymond Buckey. Gits asked if the slide alone was sufficient evidence for a doctor to conclude that the boy had been molested. Dr. Gordon replied, "I would certainly be suspect." After Gits pressed him for a more precise answer, Gordon said he could be 80 percent certain, from viewing the slide, that the boy had been sodomized. Gits then reminded him that when Roger Gunson showed him the same slide four days earlier he had said that the slide showed "marginal" evidence of molestation. When Gits asked him if he would have testified that the ten other children had been molested if he had not been given the "histories" from CII, he said, "I can't tell you what I might have done without the histories."

Gordon was asked whether he was familiar with a study that concluded that a hymenal opening of more than four millimeters in a young girl was evidence of molestation. He said he was, but that the study was no longer thought to be accurate. When Gits asked Gordon how many criminal cases he had testified in during which he had said, under oath, that a hymenal opening of more than four millimeters indicated a high probability of sexual abuse, Gordon was unable to answer. He had stated earlier that he had testified for the prosecution in as many as three hundred molestation trials.

"Have you done anything to try to go back and rectify your testimony in those proceedings?" Gits asked. Judge Pounders sustained Gunson's objection to the question.

Then Gits asked Gordon if he was aware of a study conducted in the period 1984–86 at Harvard Medical School, titled: "General Findings In Sexually Abused, Symptomatic and Asymptomatic Girls," a study that concluded that the symptoms in sexually abused girls and the symptoms seen in girls with vaginal complaints who were not abused were indistinguishable—in other words, symptoms that prosecution doctors like Gordon were pointing to as evidence of molestation were actually nonspecific. Gordon said he had a copy of the study but that it was "flawed."

At the end of the day we called Dr. Lee Coleman and told him of Gordon's testimony. "He's making claims that are not medical evidence!" Coleman said. "I just finished a case where there was an acquittal where we had a tape recording of what Gordon did, with a police officer, in manipulating a child. It was a total outrage. It's not just that he gives unfounded opinions, but he also contaminates witnesses by horrible interview methods, and that's why they stopped him from doing what he was doing because he was manipulating the kids."

Then, it was Davis's turn to cross-examine the doctor, and reporters grumbled that this could go on for days. Altogether, Gordon was on the stand for three weeks. During this time, we were confronted with a barrage of anuses, glaring from the large screen as Davis asked him, with each new slide, "Doctor, isn't this a perfectly normal little anus?" The doctor replied, "No, counselor, I see something that troubles me, in the upper right corner, a thickening of the tissue. . . ." It seemed to us that his answers were lengthy yet evasive. When Davis asked him, "Do you have specialized training in the anus?" he answered, "When I was a student in medical school I was the only student who had a permanent cadaver. The cadaver was kept in a cement vault. I have always been interested in anatomy especially."

Gordon responded to Davis's questions with a plethora of Latin medical terms like, "synechiae," "condyloma accuminata," and "agglutination of the labia minora," and "vicularis." From our observations, he almost never gave a simple, forthright answer. Having testified in hundreds of molestation trials, he had become extremely adept at dealing with defense attorneys' questions. He projected the image of a kindly old country doctor. He was only sixty-six but appeared to be considerably older. He walked in a stooped posture. The jury still had not been told that he destroyed crucial evidence in another trial, nor that he was banned from examining children for molestation in his own county. After a number of chamber conferences on this issue the judge had not allowed the defense to disclose these facts to the jurors.

"Have you read any studies comparing children molested in the anal area to children who were not?" Davis asked.

"No."

"You're not certain that any of these children were molested, are you, doctor?"

"No, not 100 percent, but I believe from what I see that they may have been molested. It is consistent with molestation."

"Did you get medical records? Did you consider the possibility of constipation? Did you see any report indicating constipation in this child?"

Gordon fumbled through his notes and records. "Well, there's one entry here. It says the child is very tired and constipated.... I considered it but I did not consider it significant."

"Do you have an opinion that there is a high probability that this child was molested?"

"I have an opinion that the history and the physical findings are consistent."

"Do you consider that they could be 'not consistent with sodomy'? Looking at this child, isn't that perfectly healthy, normal tissue?"

"No, it is not. The history and clinical findings are consistent."

Another slide. "Isn't this a perfectly normal anus?"

"I'm concerned about something in the right hand corner," the doctor said. Even under great magnification, we could see nothing.

"Dr. Heger looked at the slides of Cathy and called the hairs scars, didn't she?"

"I don't know."

"Do you see any scars on the photographs of Cathy?"

"No."

Another slide. "Do you see anything unhealthy in this child?"

"Yes, there appears to be a thickening of the tissue, very much like the tissues on the hand or the sole of the foot." He called it "corrugation," and said he thought it was thicker than normal.

"Isn't this a perfectly normal child?"

"No, I think if I examined this child in a clinic I would think something might have happened . . . something inappropriate."

"You cannot conclude that a scar is the result of molestation, can you?"

"I cannot."

"Have you read any of the literature on false allegations in child abuse and the psychological process in producing false allegations in child abuse?" Davis asked. Gordon replied that he had read the work of Dr. Heger and seen a video on the subject.

"Are you aware that the issue of false allegations in child abuse is a large issue in medical debate? Is it possible that a child might delay disclosure because he was not molested?"

"I think that could be possible but . . . does not seem reasonable."

"Have you had occasions when children told you they were not molested and you testified [that] you believed the child was molested?"

The doctor's answer was long and vague. He also admitted that he had not seen the CII videos nor read the children's testimony.

"The history you relied on was primarily the history of Dr. Heger?"

"Yes."

"And she found evidence of sexual abuse in all of the children?"

"Yes, that's correct."

"And her opinion did affect your opinion, correct?"

"Yes."

"And in none of these did she find that children were not molested?"

"That's correct."

"We will be in recess until one-thirty," the judge said. We found ourselves next to Peggy, walking toward the elevators.

"How do you like looking at that all day?" she asked.

"Looking at colossal, blazing anuses, day after day, is not particularly entertaining," we said.

"I don't even look at them any more," she said sadly.

One of the slides projected on the screen showed a child's anus with a rectangular indentation on one of his buttocks. Gordon had testified more than once that the edge of the rectangle was a scar, but the line was so straight and the rectangle so perfect that it was almost certainly a plastic ruler or some other object pressed against the soft tissue of the child's buttock, or the remaining impression from one recently removed.

"You said you sometimes use a clear, plastic ruler when you examine children," Davis said. "I'd like your opinion if what we're looking at in the picture may not be skin at all." Dr. Gordon had even shown the court the ruler. But he denied the mark seen on the child was a ruler or any other tool. On the slide there appeared to be no doubt that it was a clear, plastic ruler, but on a print made from the slide by the prosecution, it appeared to be a permanent condition of the child's skin.

Gordon had testified that each of the forty-seven slides was proof of rape, even after admitting that some of them appeared to be "within the normal range." The slide show went on for days as Davis challenged Gordon's findings in great detail, much of which was not visible even though the anuses were immensely magnified. Several of the jurors appeared to be drifting off during this long, often tedious testimony.

What Davis sought to establish in his marathon cross-examination was that Gordon's analysis of the prosecution's "medical evidence" was more fabrication than science. Gordon admitted that there is not one published, scientific study on the use of the colposcope, or on the significance of asymmetrical hymenal openings, thickening of the genital or perianal tissue, corrugation of the skin surrounding the anus, or scarring, all of which, Gordon had said, were evidence of sexual abuse. At the beginning of his testimony he said there was a "high probability"—80 percent—that ten of the children whose slides he was shown were molested. As Davis's cross-examination progressed, Gordon revised his assessment from "high probability" to "possibility." When asked by Davis to translate "probability" into more precise terms he said he could not quantify his opinion. What Davis accomplished, if nothing else, was to raise serious doubts as to the credibility of child abuse "experts." Gordon had asserted that the slides showed scars and other abnormalities "consistent with molestation" where other child abuse "experts" found none, or saw evidence of molestation that Gordon did not see. Whether the jurors got the message is another question.

During his questioning, Davis asked Gordon about Melinda, the girl who had already testified. Gordon said she had had problems with toilet training and that according to her medical history there was a very pronounced lack of affection between the girl and her mother. A pediatrician had examined her and found nothing abnormal. The mother had found her uncooperative and said she did not measure up to expectations.

"Is it possible the child may have agreed with the mother and gone along with the mother's (accusations of molestation) to get affection?"

"I don't know if that happened," Gordon answered.

"Isn't everything you've told us just guesses?" Davis asked. Gordon replied that it was not.

There were a number of questions about "white tissue," which, it turned out, were reflections of light!

After three weeks, the defense was finished. Prosecutor Gunson asked a number of questions on redirect to establish that Gordon had conferred with other doctors on his findings, and that the other physicians were reputable doctors who had been published in medical journals. The doctors were the same well-known, well-paid prosecution witnesses.

Gits questioned the doctor again on recross. This consumed most of the day. The questions were about several children who had urinary and genital complaints before thay attended the McMartin Preschool. Melinda's mother, according to these records, had complained of her habitual lying and wetting herself during the day. Gits asked if another child's fever and vomiting could be manifestations of molestation. Gordon said they both could be. Gits then asked him if middle-ear infection could be indicative of sexual abuse. His answer was ambiguous.

"We will be in recess until one-thirty," the judge announced. We walked out into the hallway and heard someone call out softly, "Shirley?" It was Peggy. She was, as always, sitting on the bench next to the door.

"How did you like looking at those slides?" she asked us. We smiled and shook our heads with a look of despair.

"I don't even look at them," Peggy said.

"You've got to look at them!" Shirley said. "You've got to look at everything! Your life is at stake here!" Peggy seemed to like me, or, at the very least, felt comfortable with me. We came from the same ethnic and cultural background and are approximately the same age group. We are both WASPs, both women, both mothers. Davis and Gits were sitting only four feet away on the next bench, listening intently with extremely angry, acerbic faces, watching through narrowed eyelids, catching every word. Finally, Gits spoke to me in a harsh assaultive tone:

"I don't want anyone interviewing my client!"

Shirley quietly explained to him that it was the legitimate function of journalists to watch and report what the government and the legal system was doing, and that this was precisely the function we were intended to perform by those who wrote the First Amendment to our Constitution. She was quoting from an article by Supreme Court Justice Potter Stewart that she had read the night before. Gits looked further angered and frustrated by the discovery that he was not dealing with some ignorant, frightened woman who could be bullied and intimidated. He angrily disposed of his cigarette and left, walking down the hall with Davis, who was whispering something to him. What really angered them the most was when Shirley accompanied Peggy into the ladies room where they could not follow and listen. She did not understand why it was so important to them to listen to two women talking about food, children, cats, clothing, and the witnesses.

"Lawyers," Peggy said. "They think they're little gods."

On the way home, we stopped at several bookstores. We had been reading everything we could find on the subject of witchcraft and satanic cults because the prosecution had made this a part of the allegations. We wanted to find out what their sources were. We discovered that there had been a great volume of literature published on this subject, some of it by legitimate scholars, and some authored by genuine, orthodox lunatics, many of whom have Ph.D.s and other advanced degrees. One of these is a man who has authored literature on the subject and goes to conferences and seminars where he expounds his belief that hundreds of infants are being murdered by satanic cultists. When he is asked, "Where are the bodies?" and "Why is it none of the bodies has been found?" his reply is that the satanic cultists eat them. This man is a board-certified psychiatrist with an M.D.

There has also been a great volume of paperbacks published by those who wish to turn a quick profit on the current wave of demonomania. What we learned is that the similarities between the current molestation witch hunt and the seventeenth-century witch trials were much more striking than we had imagined. In a large, second-hand bookstore the owner asked, "How is your McMartin book coming along? Do you think they're guilty?"

"What do you think?" we asked.

"I think Ray Buckey is probably guilty," she said.

"Which of the witnesses did you think was the most convincing?" we asked.

"I don't know anything about the case."

The general public still did not understand anything about the case, but the county had spent millions on it and was apparently prepared to spend millions more until it could finally be disposed of in some way that would not trash the careers of prominent public officials. A conviction would cut through all of their problems.

Tuesday, November 24, 1987. The witness is the mother of the next child slated to testify. She said she recalled making an entry in her diary that her son "liked the school," and "couldn't wait to get to the school." Even after the police department sent out its famous letter, she said, he told her that "nothing happened," and that "Ray wasn't a bad guy. He was a good guy." She denied having seen anything suspicious at the preschool during the three years her son was there.

Then, she testified, she received the celebrated letter from the police and discussed it at great length with her friend, Ann Currie, the wife of Bob Currie. She said she also attended several meetings at which Kee MacFarlane and representatives of the district attorney's office spoke. Then, on January 17, after being told that many other children had been identified as victims of molestation at the preschool, she called CII and made an appointment for an interview for her son. Following a lengthy interview, she and her husband were told that their son had been molested. She also testified that ten of the fourteen children who were prosecution witnesses were are now attending the same elementary school as her child.

The mother stated that "the thing that really bothered me" was that on graduation day she saw her son and another boy sitting on Ray Buckey's lap, one on each knee. After seeing this, she said, she would not send her other child to the preschool despite its excellent reputation.

"Did you have a conversation with Ann Currie about the lookout game?" Gits asked.

"I did because we were close friends."

"Your son talked to Mr. Currie?"

"He did not!" she exploded.

"Were you present at a conversation when he claimed what happened to his boy?"

"We didn't ask him."

"Bob Currie said you wouldn't even want to know some of the things that happened to him?"

"I'm not sure."

"The time your son came home dirty, did you think that was a sign of molestation?"

"I do now."

"What was it about the dirt?"

"His whole body was dirty. . . . He was always a clean little boy."

In the morning before the jury was brought in, Gits and Davis demanded to know the name of the second therapist the boy had been taken to for six weeks after the CII interview. "We are entitled to know the identity of the therapist, his credentials. We may subpoena him. . . ."

"Your request is denied," Judge Pounders replied.

Prosecutor Rubin told the judge, "[The boy] has requested that Mr. Currie be allowed to be in the courtroom during his testimony."

"I would object to Mr. Currie's presence," Gits responded. "He offered a reward for evidence against Mr. Buckey. He has been continually and actively involved in objecting to the five defendants being dismissed. He has had continuous contact with the children's families. He has been doing his independent investigation—including his arrest for carrying a loaded firearm. He has been the most outspoken pipeline between the parents. So there is a great danger that other parents may be cued to match up with his testimony. Currie is an outspoken advocate of the prosecution. He is a potential witness in the clearest terms. For him to be here as a third support person, that's inherently improper. We are looking at a potential pipeline. They have disparate accounts in the tapes. You have different positions."

"Your request to exclude him is denied."

It was also on this day that Deputy D.A. Gunson notified the court that George Freeman, the prosecution's principal witness, had just been arrested for armed robbery.

Monday, November 30, 1987. The prosecution called Charles, the son of the woman who testified the previous week. Also present in the courtroom were his parents and Bob Currie. Currie had been described in newspaper stories as a "mortgage banker." He was one of the men who spoke to us during recesses in the preliminary hearing and told us the defendants were part of an international conspiracy of satanic cultists engaging in "mass molestations" and murdering children. Square-faced, wearing a moustache, he was always flawlessly dressed in an expensive suit and tie and stands very straight and somewhat stiff, like a military man.

Charles was eleven years old, almost twelve. He was seated at the witness stand, elevated above the jurors and lawyers. Leal Rubin's questions began. Much had been said about his "terrible nightmares" during the three years he attended the preschool, but when asked by Rubin about this he said the nightmares were "not of the school . . . but of a gorilla chasing me."

He testified that he was molested and forced to play naked games. On cross-examination Davis asked him why he had said, at the grand jury hearing, that he was photographed in a red convertible, and now he was saying that it was a green van. Davis showed him a copy of the transcript of the preliminary hearing in which he said that during the "naked movie star" game, children undressed, one at a time, and now, in the trial, he said they all undressed at the same time. He answered, "That's how I remembered it then. This is how I remember it now." Like the other children, he gave that same answer, over and over again during his testimony.

Asked if he remembered the names of any of the children who played "naked movie star," he said he did not. In the preliminary hearing he gave the names of several children who, he said, played naked games with him.

"Can you think of any reason why you told the grand jury you saw Miss Betty's boobs?" Davis asked.

"That's how I remembered it then. I remember it differently now," he answered. At times the boy babbled incoherently, breaking off in the middle of a sentence and then starting in the middle of another. He appeared to be having some difficulty remembering.

The hard-faced parents were there, mostly middle-aged women and a few men. They were whispering and glancing at us and I could hear our names and the title of our book (*The Politics of Child Abuse*) being muttered.

Davis asked the boy several questions as to what time of day the "naked movie star" game was played. He said he did not remember. In the preliminary hearing he testified that the game was played after lunch.

"Did you see Miss Betty's boobs?" Davis asked.

"No."

"Did you tell the grand jury you did?"

"I could have."

"And it never happened?"

"That's how I remembered it then. I remember it differently now."

"Did Lael ever tell you some of the things you told at the preliminary were different from what you said at the grand jury?"

"I don't remember."

"You told the grand jury about a movie camera and you said you knew it was a movie camera, and you say you didn't know what a movie camera was and nobody told you. Is that something Kee MacFarlane talked about to you?"

"Yes, it was."

"Do you remember testifying in the preliminary hearing that you lied when you told that Ray Buckey photographed you? Do you feel you were under pressure when you told the grand jury [that] he took pictures of naked children? Were you under pressure?"

"They kept asking the same question over and over. . . ."

At the grand jury you said the kids were naked. Now you say Ray Buckey was sometimes naked. What was Ray doing in the 'horsey' game when it was a naked game?"

"Ray would crawl around and the other kids would be running around trying not to get tagged by the kid riding on Ray. . . ."

Davis asked a long series of questions about the details of the alleged molestations. Charles's answers to all the questions were, "I don't remember" and "I don't know."

"Did he ever put his finger in the hole in your bottom?"

"No."

"So when you talked to Kee, she was using little dolls . . . do you think today using little dolls helped you to understand?"

"No."

"You told the grand jury [that] Ray put his finger in your butt and put his wiener in your butt?"

"I don't remember."

Davis recited a list of sexual acts of which the boy had accused Ray in the preliminary hearing. "These things didn't happen, did they?"

"Not that I remember," the boy answered.

"You told us one thing at the grand jury and something very different here. Can you tell us which is the truth?"

"Objection!"

"Sustained."

"The answers you gave at the grand jury, the preliminary [hearing] and the trial are very different. In the 'horsey' game did the children take their clothes off?"

"I'm not really sure."

"Didn't you tell us that [that] happened two or three times a week at the preschool?"

"Well, it's not true. I don't know how many times."

"How were you positioned when Ray put his penis in your mouth?"

"I don't remember."

"Did your parents ever tell you at any time before you testified that they believed Ray had touched the private parts of children?"

"Yes."

Ray Buckey sat impassively listening to the child. He never looked at the spectators. He watched the witness and the lawyers. Sometimes he looked at the jurors. During the trial and the preliminary hearing we never made eye contact with him. We talked to his mother, Peggy, every day. She was free on bail and sat out in the hallway during recess, knitting. Ray was brought in from a holding cell. He had no contact with the outside world except that of sitting there at the defense table as a mute spectator. They could as easily have put a photograph of him there, mounted on posterboard.

During the noon recess, Peggy told us that all three of the children who had testified for the prosecution so far were children who attended the preschool at a time when "Ray was not even there! He was going to college in San Diego. Also, two others who will be testifying were at the school when Ray wasn't even there!"

We asked Peggy about the parents from Manhattan Beach who had gathered in the courtroom and were now strolling out toward the elevators and lunch.

"Don't you have a gang?" we asked. "A group of people who believe in your innocence?"

"There are lots of people who've told us they believe we're innocent," she said. "But they're not coming in."

"Why not?" we asked.

"They're afraid."

"Afraid of what?"

"The police. And the Catholic community."

"Manhattan Beach is a very dense little community," a lawyer sitting with Peggy told us. "They all live right on top of each other. They all know each other. Anybody who expresses disbelief of the wacko stories the media have been pumping out becomes an outcast, and may be targeted by the mob and be in danger of violence and vandalism."

Back in the courtroom, Davis asked the boy, "Do you remember testifying in the preliminary that you were never touched by Ray with anything but his hand?"

"I'm not sure."

"Do you remember testifying that nobody put anything inside your bottom?"

"I don't remember."

Davis read from the transcript of the preliminary hearing.

"Now, you told some things that didn't happen. Do you remember?"

"Yes."

"Weren't you at one time telling that Ray threatened to kill your parents?"

"I'm not sure."

"Do you remember changing your testimony?"

"Objection."

"Sustained."

Davis concluded his cross-examination and Gits began. "Your honor, I have in my hands a card. May this be marked 558 for identification?" He showed the boy the card with photographs of children on it, and asked the boy if he saw any children who were in the naked games. He didn't.

"Charles, I want to focus on individual games you talked about and how your testimony changed over time. At the grand jury, did you tell them that Babs, Betty, and Peggy were watching naked games?"

"Well, I read it."

"You said at the grand jury that Babs, Betty, Peggy, and Virginia watched?"

"Well, I said that at the grand jury but I don't think that way now."

Gits went on and on, referring to transcripts of the grand jury hearing and the preliminary hearing, showing the contradictions between Charles's statements in the various proceedings. "Were you lying to the grand jury?" he asked. "I don't know," the boy answered.

Paul had lunch with his old friend, Mort, a very accomplished criminal defense lawyer. "You know," Mort said, "you've been giving me a running account of the McMartin trial, and it's so different from what we've been getting from the media. It's like two entirely different cases. The media give you only the prosecution's version of the case. There's something very weird going on here," he said. "I'd like to find out what it is. How do you get along with the prosecutors?"

"I don't," Paul said. "They don't talk to me. They just squint at me and then whisper to each other."

"You're playing a very dangerous game," Mort said. "Look out for new friends who want to hang out with you, or people who claim to be old acquaintances from way back, or distant relatives. Don't be predictable. Don't drive the same car every day. Don't park in the same parking lot every day. Take the bus sometimes. Don't eat lunch at the same place. This thing is a hot potato."

Mort had been practicing law for about thirty years. He was a Republican and a Shriner. "When are you going to become a judge?" Paul asked. "You know all the Republican bigwigs. You should be in line for appointment to the bench."

"Not a chance," he said. "I'm a defense lawyer. Gov. Deukmejian wants only prosecutors for judges."

The next prosecution witness was a woman who testified that she had brought her child to the preschool to look at it and possibly enroll her little boy there but never did. She recalled that she was troubled by her observation that the children there were exceptionally well-behaved and quiet. Instead, she placed her child in the Trinity Lutheran Preschool. There, she met Judy Johnson, who called her one evening and warned her that her child was being molested at the Trinity Lutheran Preschool. She spoke with the director of the preschool, who convinced her that the allegation was false. During her testimony she also spoke of the police letter of September 8, 1983, its accusations about the McMartin Preschool, and the explosive effect it had on the community. "It was the topic of discussion among all the parents."

The overdressed young reporters sat in the press section and exchanged vapid smiles. They obediently scribbled prosecutor Rubin's accusing questions and her prepared statements outside the courtroom during recess. In the afternoon, when the defense lawyers cross-examine the witness, they are gone.

In the morning Rubin announced to the judge, "We call Paul Bynum." Bynum is a former police lieutenant who was retained as an investigator for Ray Buckey and his attorney, Davis, at the beginning of the case. Davis objected to Bynum's testimony as a violation of the attorney-client privilege, because he had been employed by the defense, but his motion was denied. According to the prosecutors, Bynum was to testify that he had found tortoise shells buried in a vacant lot adjacent to the school. Davis asserted that a veterinary forensic pathologist had examined the turtle's remains and had determined that the turtle died of natural, not traumatic causes. At 2 P.M., after lengthy arguments, Bynum was called to the witness stand and testified for about forty-five minutes with the jurors absent from the courtroom. His testimony was part of an "offer of proof" by the prosecutors that his statements were relevant. In response to Rubin's questions Bynum stated that he had given the evidence he found to law enforcement and members of the district attorney's office, failing to remember at the time that it was subject to attorney-client confidentiality. He was asked whether he had an attorney and replied that he had consulted one and had been advised not to testify at all. Judge Pounders, after listening to Bynum's testimony, ruled it admissible.

In the morning we arrived early to hear Bynum's testimony and instead we heard Judge Pounders tell the jurors, "The witness is dead." He instructed them that "it was not due to any criminal cause" and that they were not to draw any inference from it. The jury was excused until the next morning. I asked a woman employed by the district attorney's office, as everyone was leaving, "Was it Paul Bynum who died?"

"Yes," she answered.

"But he looked so young and healthy yesterday!" we said. "He looked like he was only about thirty years old. What was the cause of death?"

"I guess he just died in his sleep," she said, closing the door and quickly vanishing.

On the way home we heard on the car radio a news report that Bynum had been found with a .38 caliber hole in his head and a .38 caliber revolver nearby. According to the radio station, police had called it an "apparent suicide." We went home and called everyone we knew who had known Bynum or knew anything about him. None of them believed he had committed suicide.

One attorney told us, "I just don't buy it. Four hours before he's to testify, he's found dead. Why? I think we may never get the answer to that question."

Davis faced a large group of reporters in the hallway and declared that the prosecution had called Bynum in order to diminish the impact of evidence Rubin knew the defense was going to present. "I do know [Bynum] was concerned that [his call to testify] was designed to distort the truth." Davis stated that Bynum had preserved evidence that supported the defense and that he could not yet assess the damage done to the defense as a result of his death. He said he believed that pressure had been applied to Bynum "to modify his state of mind." None of his statements were broadcast or printed in the media.

Of all the people who knew Bynum, none could offer a plausible reason why he would commit suicide. The official explanations were extremely unconvincing. According to his friends, he was happily married and had a new daughter whom he adored. He had just completed a remodeling project on his home and was extremely pleased with it. He was employed as an investigator for the bar association. He was an exceptionally handsome man. Everything in his life appeared to be going well. One of the strangest scraps of information that surfaced after Bynum's death was the report from law enforcement officers involved in the case that two of Bynum's police citation books had been found in Buckey's apartment when he was first arrested. This was five months before Bynum became involved in the case. Bynum told a reporter that he didn't know how the citation books got there. Why would Bynum have been in Buckey's apartment, and why would he have left the books there? And if he did not, who did?

A reporter asked him about this the day before his death. Bynum replied, "They wouldn't dare ask me about [the books] . . . because the prosecution would be cutting its own throat." He refused to say anything more, except to tell the reporter, "I hate this case."

During a recess the next day, we asked Peggy, "Why would they call a defense investigator as a prosecution witness?"

"They were blackmailing him," she said.

"What were they blackmailing him about?" we asked her.

"I can't tell you." She turned and walked away.

This was the third important witness to be found dead under suspicious circumstances. The first was Judy Johnson, the woman who reported to authorities that Ray Buckey flew in the air like a bird. The official report that she died of acute alcoholism was extremely unconvincing. She was only forty and did not have the ravaged skin of a chronic alcoholic and she did not look unhealthy. There was no hard evidence that she was murdered, but her appearance on the witness stand would have been disastrous for the prosecution and those who stood to benefit from a conviction in this case, so it was a possibility that could not be ignored. An investigator told us that the court file on Judy Johnson's divorce case had been cleaned out. To remove documents from a court file and not return them is a felony and one cannot but wonder who would take such a risk and for what reason.

The second important witness to die under suspicious circumstances was a man named Winkler, a machinist. Both the police and the prosecution named him as an "uncharged suspect." He was disabled and earned money occasionally as a babysitter. He was found dead November 7, 1985. Police stated tentatively that the cause of death was a drug overdose, but his friends and acquaintances denied it. Peter's older brother, also accused of molesting him, recently died.

Greg Latimer, a photographer, was called by the prosecution and testified, briefly, that he had been hired by Bynum to photograph a dig in the vacant lot adjacent to the McMartin Preschool. Rubin brought out a sheet of posterboard with forty-nine photographs of the yard pasted on it and questioned him about each of them. Latimer's answers offered little or nothing of value to either side. Rubin asked Latimer to unseal and open a box and remove its contents. He took out two large tortoise shells. Presumably this was to corroborate the allegations that Ray Buckey had smashed turtles and then told children their parents would suffer the same fate if they told the "secrets of molestation."

But the tortoise shells were intact, except for a few small fragments that were also in the box. Latimer stated that when he first saw the shells exhumed, they were even more intact. Certainly they had not been smashed. Rubin asked him to unseal and open another box, which he did. When she asked him to remove the contents there was nothing but some coarse soil and a few small bones of unknown origin.

When court was recessed at the end of the day we walked with Peggy toward the elevators and told her we wanted to know more about Bynum and what he was being threatened with. She declined to discuss it but told us that it was her understanding that someone in the district attorney's office had threatened the parents of several children who attended the preschool, and had warned one mother, "If you testify for the defense, I'll see to it that your son gets in a lot of trouble."

Up until this time the media had reported almost exclusively the statements of the prosecutors and ignored the defense. The first to knock a large hole in this wall of silence was Mike Wallace on CBS's "60 Minutes." Wallace interviewed District Attorney Ira Reiner, who stated that his predecessor, Robert Philibosian, had "charged these people without any investigation whatever." Virginia McMartin, who has always been a conservative, appeared on the screen and declared, "We have the rottenest justice system in the world. Don't talk to me about Russia or South Africa. We have it right here! You are guilty and God help you if you try to prove you're innocent. That's the way we've been treated since the first day."

"You're charging the former D.A. with an unprofessional, miserable job," Wallace asked District Attorney Ira Reiner.

"That hardly begins to describe it," Reiner replied.

Wallace asked Mary Emmons, director of CII, if she believed that corpses were dug up and animals slaughtered, and whether there were satanic rituals and pornography.

"I know of none," she admitted. "But there's very, very convincing medical evidence that backs up what the children are saying."

"Meanwhile," Wallace continued, "the prosecution tried to corroborate the children's stories and they failed despite a worldwide search, aided by the FBI. Nothing was found."

Ray Buckey made his first appearance before any of the media in which he actually spoke. He looked like the all-American boy. Wallace asked him if he had ever molested a child."

"Never," he answered simply.

"You know what's going to happen if you're found guilty by a jury. You're going to prison for a long time."

"If I survive in there."

"What do you mean?" Wallace asked.

"They've marked me. They've marked me if I'm in prison. They've marked me if I'm free."

"If you're in prison you're afraid something could happen to you at the hands of the prison population?"

"Not afraid . . . I'm aware of the reality of prison."

"And if you go free?"

"I've watched them ruin my family. I've watched them ruin my mother and grandmother's lives. I've watched them ruin my sister's career. I was just starting at that school. I hadn't made up my mind what I wanted to do in life. But they've burned a scarlet letter on me that I can never get rid of. I don't know what kind of life I would have. I can't trust people anymore."

Then, Peggy Ann, his sister, appeared and said, "I think people have to know what happened here. I think people need to know this was a witch hunt, that nothing happened at the school, and that it could happen to anyone. Because it has been! It's been happening all over the country."

The *Los Angeles Herald-Examiner* published an eloquent editorial by Ben Stein who wrote, "In the name of justice, District Attorney Ira Reiner, if you believe in the law, let Peggy and Ray Buckey go free." He stated that the charges against them were "as false as anything can be. . . . There has been a stunning violation of civil rights in this case. Seven people's lives have been ruined. A whole nation was hoodwinked."

The proprosecution parents and their supporters were struck dumb with anger by these heresies. Until then they had had every reason to believe they had the mass media in their pocket and that any exonerating information would be blacked out. Newspapers were inundated with irate letters to the editor and talk shows were flooded with babble concerning this outrage.

During this period our book *The Politics of Child Abuse* had been published. We appeared on many talk shows. On a Los Angeles TV talk show, we began to explain the intricacies of the McMartin case, the unanswered questions, and the enigma of so many almost identical cases across the country. The hostess, a woman who looked like a younger Nancy Reagan, interrupted us and blurted out, "Mr. Eberle, this is shocking! We want to hear that they did it! We want to hear that they're guilty!"

"You mean you'd be happier to hear that children were harmed, and distressed than to hear that they were not?" Paul asked incredulously. She went blank. The director quickly went to a commercial for cat litter.

When we appeared on another TV talk show the producer approached us after it was over and said, "You don't believe those people are innocent, do you?"

"Have you formed a belief that they're guilty?"

"Yes. I think they're guilty."

"You must have spent an awful lot of time reviewing the evidence. Which of the witnesses did you think was most convincing?"

"I don't know anything about the case," she shrugged.

Thursday, December 17, 1987. The courtroom was crowded because this was the day of Ray Buckey's bail hearing, after the noon recess. The morning was spent finishing up with the cross-examination of Latimer, the photographer. The jurors looked bored. Two were yawning. One appeared to be sleeping peacefully.

At 1:30 P.M. court was reconvened with the jury absent. The gallery was filled with friends and supporters of the Buckey family.

The judge began speaking. "If Mr. Buckey is not granted bail and if he is in jail for five years without bail and he is acquitted, that is going to be a shocking result. I know a lot more about this case than I did a year ago." He said Rubin's position that Buckey might carry out threats against children "is a great burden for the prosecution to establish."

Davis made a brief statement on Buckey's behalf, telling the judge that he would have Ray Buckey living in his home with an electronic device locked onto his arm so that if he left Davis's home at any time, five law enforcement agencies and Davis's office would be immediately notified.

"There is no evidence that he made threats," Davis said. "He was under surveillance for five months, and if he had any intent to carry out threats, it would have been at that time. . . . Ray Buckey and his attorney, from the first day of this case, have said, 'We are going to come to the legal system and face this.' You can adduce from the evidence that he is not a violent individual who hurts people. He has been an ideal defendant."

"He has!" the judge agreed emphatically. "I agree. He has been a model defendant."

"He intends to tell all he knows," Davis continued, "and stand up to these charges. What I am offering the court . . . is that Mr. Buckey be placed in a quasicustodial situation. I would provide a twenty-four-hour security guard. . . . I am willing to have Mr. Buckey reside with me. He will fail to come to court only if I fail to come to court. I would also urge that the court give some consideration to the nature of the Buckey family. . . . If he fled it would remove him from the last social contacts he has. All he has left is in this room. He was arrested late in March 1984, after five months of listening to Wayne Satz, realizing he was the focus of all this. He did not flee. He would have less reason to flee now. If he was going to flee, he would have fled long ago. All he has left is his family in this courtroom. If he flees he has nothing. He went with me to surrender himself. I can only argue that when he was out he didn't run. I am willing to have him live with me."

The judge said, "I need twenty minutes to decide." He declared a twenty-minute recess which, typically, lengthened to about forty-five minutes before the bailiff called us back into the courtroom. Then, Judge Pounders returned to a hushed courtroom and said, "I have decided to grant bail to Mr. Buckey." The spectators broke into a long, loud, wild applause. Judge Pounders appeared shaken and unnerved by the noisy demonstration. Like nearly everyone else, he apparently believed that the Buckeys' supporters were so few in number as to be virtually nonexistent. But they were there, all over the country. The media had blacked them out and had shunned even the national conferences of Victims of Child Abuse Law (VOCAL), the organization for people falsely accused of child abuse.

When the room was quiet again the judge asked if either side had any proposals as to the amount of bail that should be set. Lael Rubin stated that Buckey's bail should be no less than five million dollars. "It's a very real risk," she said, "that if this defendant were granted bail or made bail . . . there would be other children that would be molested." Davis asserted that anything over one million dollars would be the same as no bail. After listening to brief arguments from both sides, Judge Pounders announced that Buckey's bail would be three million dollars. Court was recessed. In the hallway, the Buckey family, friends, and supporters were discussing various ways to try to raise the bail. Our friend, Irene, a lawyer, came over to say hello. She had been sitting inconspicuously in the audience during the bail hearing.

"Well, what do you think of all this?" she smiled.

"It's unreal."

"You still can't quite believe. . . . You think this is some kind of anomaly, some rare malfunction of the judicial system. It's not. McMartin *is* the judicial system. The child abuse witch hunt has simply added more bodies to process, more cash flow, careers, fame, and fortune. They know the Buckeys didn't do it. They couldn't care less."

We reflected on the broader implications of what she had said.

124   The Abuse of Innocence

* * *

Monday, January 4, 1988. The prosecution called Mrs. Katherine McCleish, a woman who had lived in a house next to the McMartin Preschool. She testified that she had never observed anything that led her to believe children were being molested, that she had never seen a child get into a car with Ray, and that she had never heard anything that sounded like animals being hurt. Her testimony was exculpatory. Apparently the prosecutors were filling time until one of their heavy-duty witnesses was available to come in and testify.

The next day Norma, the mother of Alice, the next child slated to testify, was called to the witness stand. She was a plump, brown-haired woman wearing a blue and black dress. This witness was significant because she owned a local beauty shop. Beauty shops are meeting places and provide a hospitable environment for the proliferation of gossip. The mother testified that her child, Alice, cried and did not want to go to school, hardly unusual behavior. District Attorney Rubin asked her whether her daughter had had any vaginal or urinary problems. She said she had seen some redness in Alice's vaginal area, that she had taken her to a physician who advised her not to give the girl bubble baths and to keep the vaginal area clean. Rubin, again, asked if the child had had nightmares. The mother answered that she had. Although nightmares are a perfectly normal occurrence in childhood, and adulthood as well, Rubin continued to raise this insinuation that the child experienced some unspeakable horror at the nursery school.

The mother also stated that she had seen Alice masturbating by inserting a tinkertoy stick into her vagina "more than seven or eight times," and that she had walked into the girl's bedroom and observed Alice and her sister "in the sixty-nine position," touching and licking each other's vaginas, in the summer of 1981, after she attended the McMartin Preschool. Suddenly, the jury was wide awake, watching and listening attentively. How this testimony incriminated Ray and Peggy was not explained but apparently the prosecutor, because of the lack of any corroborating evidence, was insinuating that the child was eroticized beyond what would be normal for her age, based on the popular but absurd belief that children are naturally asexual.

The woman testified that she had received a telephone call from the police in the late summer of 1983 that sent her into "total shock." She said the police officer told her there was suspicion of "improper conduct" at the school, that it was "not public knowledge," and ordered her not to discuss it or "spread it" or mention it to the teachers at the preschool. Naturally, she went directly to the telephone, called the school and asked Peggy Buckey, "What is going on? What are they talking about?" She said that Peggy thanked her for calling and said she would find out what was happening.

On cross-examination Norma stated again that she was in shock when she received the call from the police. She was very dramatic, and used the word "shock" many times.

"Did you see anything suspicious?" Gits asked.

"No." She went on to say that the parents, at that time, did not believe anything improper had happened, but that there were fewer and fewer children attending the school. She testified that neither of her daughters said any such thing was going on. She said her daughters were interviewed at CII and that Kee MacFarlane "didn't say 'molested.' She said something drastic had happened."

"Do you now think in your mind that she was molested?" Gits asked.

"Yes," she answered.

"Did you see the video?"

"Not the whole thing." She said that after they left CII her daughter talked continuously about McMartin, and that when Alice was interviewed by Sandi Krebs at CII the family sat down to watch the video and Krebs selectively fast-forwarded the tape to the parts she wanted them to see. She said Alice was crying.

Gits asked her if, after the visit to CII, she had attended meetings in the community. She said yes, she had attended meetings at a community church, in which the district attorney spoke. She said there were meetings "going on all the time." She said that Kee MacFarlane also spoke.

"At CII, did Astrid Heger tell you that Alice was molested?"

"Yes. . . . I was already angry. I knew she was." Alice's mother also acknowledged that she had attended the party to celebrate the arrest of Ray Buckey, and that she had been involved in lobbying for tougher laws pertaining to child molestation, and was also involved in "the telephone tree," calling other parents when the district attorney was speaking in the community. The mother also acknowledged that she had received several visits from Lael Rubin and was given transcripts of her preliminary hearing testimony, and Alice's.

Gits brought up the fact that Alice had recanted in the preliminary hearing. Rubin objected and was sustained.

"Did you discuss with Alice the fact that she denied she was molested at the preliminary hearing?" Gits asked.

"Yes."

"Would it be fair to say that she changed her position?"

"Yes."

"Did you discuss it with Alice?"

"No."

"Alice's answers at the preliminary hearing were entirely different. . . . Were you convinced that she was molested at the preschool?" Davis asked.

"Yes."

"Before you went to CII, did you form an opinion that Alice was molested?"

"No."

"When you filled out the form you [wrote] 'Not showing any signs.' Did you make a statement [that] you believe[d] Alice was molested?"

"I never said it up to that point."

"Did anybody? Even a doctor?" Davis asked.

"No," Norma answered.

"There was redness in the vagina and she was poking tinkertoy sticks in her vagina . . . and you saw a doctor . . . and he said it was a normal act for a child of that age?"

"Yes."

"Did Alice come back to visit the preschool?"

"Yes. When she was at American Martyrs, on a holiday."

"Do you believe that for some five years your children were molested at McMartin?"

"Yes."

"Did you read news reports about Ray?"

"Yes."

"Did you view the reports by Wayne Satz on Channel 7?"

"Yes I did."

Judge Pounders called a brief recess at 2:45. As we sat with Peggy on a bench in the hallway she told us, "That woman is lying." Peggy sat there every day during recess and ate her lunch out of a brown bag, sliced apples and celery stalks. She smiled and offered people some of her sliced apple. She always invited you to share her meager lunch and she looked genuinely pleased to see us enjoy the apple slices.

What she endured in the county jail for nearly two years borders on the wanton cruelty of the Spanish Inquisition. We have met several people who were in the county jail with her and they recalled that her life was threatened two or three times every day. She was handcuffed when the other prisoners were not.

"I can't begin to describe to anybody . . . I can't even put into words what they did to me," she told us. "They tried every way to break me. My life was threatened all the time. I saw the other women with cuts and bruises from the brutal beatings by the sheriffs. And for no reason. They couldn't do that to me because I was in a high-publicity case, but I saw what they did to the other women who were just unknown people. The girls showed me their backs where they had been beaten. Everything there is designed to break you. That's the way the system is. But the rapes that go on! Constantly!" She recalled seeing a group of inmates pinning a girl down on the floor and then gang-raping her while law enforcement officers watched indifferently and walked away. She told us that the sheriffs in the jail put handcuffs on her so tightly that she now suffers from arthritis in her hands as a result of the loss of circulation.

Peggy said that the female prisoners were regularly forced to strip, open their vaginas and cough. When she asked the guards what they were looking for they replied, "guns." She went on to say that she had befriended many women in the jail who had committed major felonies but that it was her perception that, in many cases, "once you get to know them you find out it's their background. They can't help what they've become." She said that the inmates she met in the county jail were generally less evil than the prosecutors and judges with whom she had had to cope in the legal system. She described her two years in the county jail as "a trip back into the eighteenth century." The fear still showed on her face as she recalled that her claustrophobia and the constant death threats made her life almost unbearable, and the only things that sustained her were her letters from her son, Ray, and her Bible. The cops entered her cell, took these things away and threw them into the trash. When she entered the jail she was wearing two expensive diamond rings given to her by her late father. They were taken from her when she was booked and never returned.

An older woman, a friend and supporter of the Buckeys, told us that just before Peggy was arrested a man came to her house, hid in waiting for her near her back door, grabbed her from behind, then stabbed and cut her several times with a pair of scissors. When her husband, Chuck, called the police they refused to come, and no action was taken to find her assailant. The woman also told us that a day or two later, a large group of people, after attending mass at the local Catholic church, agreed to place a bomb in Peggy's car. These Christians, she said, had actually found a man who was able and willing to do the job.

"When all of this is over with I would like to go away somewhere and take care of animals. I thought I would be a nursery school teacher for the rest of my life, like my mother. But now all that's gone. I would like to have a house."

After the recess Davis resumed his cross-examination of Norma.

"When you saw your daughters in the sixty-nine position was that when Alice was enrolled at the McMartin Preschool?"

"No," Norma said.

"Did she suffer rashes?"

"Diaper rash . . . yeast infection when she was born."

"Continual rash in the vaginal area?"

"Yes."

"Did you take Alice by a house to see if it was the one [where the 'naked movie star' game is allegedly played]?"

"Yes. One at a time."

"What prompted you to go to the house?"

"The police department gave me the address."

"Did you see harmful things at the preschool?"

"No."

"Did you go to meetings when Kee MacFarlane was there?" Davis asked.
"Yes."
"She appears to have made the statement that one hundred kids were molested there.... Did these statements add to your belief?"
"I know what my kids told me.... I heard people.... They told me."
"Only after CII?"
"Yes."
"Kee MacFarlane talked about young children molested?"
"Prominent people reinforced my feelings."

Toward the end of the day there was an angry outburst from Norma. Davis was conducting his cross-examination from the defense table, while seated next to Ray. The woman suddenly shouted harshly, "Do you mind coming over here and talking to me? I don't like looking at Ray.... He molested my child."

Davis remained sitting coolly at the table. "Did you file lawsuits?" he asked.

"I hope he goes to jail forever."
"Why didn't [Alice's sister] testify?"
"She can't cope."
"Alice can cope?"
"We weren't given the option to be here today. If I had my way I wouldn't be here."

Norma was not the only witness to make that statement. Other parents and children said that, if given a choice, they would not have come in to testify. Virginia told us, that night, that some of the defense witnesses had told of being threatened.

"We will be in recess until tomorrow morning at ten-thirty," Judge Pounders said, concluding the day's proceedings.

Irene was standing at the rear of the courtroom, smiling as we left. She handed us two magazines containing reviews of our newly published book.

"Your book is having a big impact on the public perception of this thing," she said. "Did you know it's being read as expert testimony in courtrooms all over the country?"

"How can that be?" we asked, astounded. "We're not doctors. We're not priests or shrinks. How can it be expert testimony?"

"When it's being read aloud by a doctor who's being paid two thousand dollars a day it becomes expert testimony," she laughed. "But you were the first to break the silence. The lawyers must be very grateful."

"No," we said. "Whenever they see us they look angry."

Peggy sat on a bench in the hallway with her knitting, waiting for her ride home. We talked. She said, "Jane Hoag and the D.A. were at the bottom of all this, but there's something more to it. Something very mysterious."

"What about the fat man with the moustache?" we asked.

"Well," Peggy said, "back about the time all this started happening he kept coming over and trying to buy the school from us. And one day he came over and said, 'You are going to lose everything you have.' And it came true! He's the one who goes around talking about all that satanic stuff."

Monday, February 1, 1988. The witness is Alice, daughter of the previous witness. She is eleven years old but rather small for her age, with brown hair and a round face like her mother's.

Almost all of her answers were "I don't remember," and "I don't know." She denied her mother's statement about the tinkertoy incident and the "sixty-nine" event with her sister. In fact, she denied many of her mother's statements and contradicted many of her own prior statements. She misidentified teachers from the preschool and did not recognize children in her class photographs from McMartin—except for those who were still her classmates in elementary school. It had been almost eight years since she had attended the preschool. She remembered little or nothing about the McMartin Preschool but she nevertheless recited the same litany of sexual abuse allegations as the others, saying she had been touched in the anus and vagina. She made the statements perfunctorily, like an arithmetic lesson, and did not appear to be at all enthusiastic about being there and testifying.

"Did Peggy put any part of her body inside you?" Rubin asked.

"She put her finger inside my virginia [*sic*] . . . and put her finger in my butt."

"In a classroom?"

"Yes."

"Did Peggy have her clothes on?"

"I don't know."

She testified that Ray had cut a rabbit's ears off with a knife. Rabbit remains were found in the school yard but a veterinary forensic pathologist examined them and found they had died of natural, nontraumatic causes.

On cross-examination by Gits, Alice said she was there only from nine to noon and did not stay for lunch or naps. Alice said she did not remember being afraid of the teachers, did not remember having nightmares, and did not remember the children in her class.

"Was some part of your body hurt at the preschool?" Gits asked.

"My virginia."

"Your virginia? Any other part of your body?"

"I don't remember."

"Did Peggy go in the bathroom before touching you?"

"I don't remember."

"Did she take off her clothes?"

"I don't remember."

"Did you have your clothes on?"

"Yes."
"And she had her clothes on?"
"Yes."
"Did she touch you on the virginia?"
"Yes." Asked what position she was in, and where else she was touched, Alice said she did not remember.
"Did you have panties on over your virginia?"
"I don't remember."
"What happened when Peggy touched you?"
"I would leave the classroom."
"Did you tell other kids?"
"No."

Alice also said she did not remember the "naked movie star" game or any other naked games, or any nude photographs being taken. She testified that before going to CII she had never told her mother that she disliked Peggy, Ray, Babs, or Betty.

"Have you heard that Ray touched you?"
"Yes."
"You heard that children had been touched at the preschool?"
"Yes."
"Do you remember [your sister] talked about being touched at the preschool?"
"No."

Alice answered the same question with a "yes" in the preliminary hearing.

"After [your sister] went to CII, did she get more love from your mother than you?"
"No."

In the preliminary hearing Alice had said the opposite.

"After you talked to CII and you told your folks you had been touched, did you seem to get more love?"
"No."

Again, this is the opposite of what she had said in reply to the same question in the preliminary hearing.

"Before you went to CII you never told your mom and dad that Ray or Peggy touched you?"
"No."
"Each time [your parents] asked you if you were touched at the preschool you said no, didn't you?"
"Yes."

Alice said her father stated that he believed the teachers "touched" children, that the "puppet lady" and others helped her to remember. There were many questions about Lael Rubin's visits to Alice's home to prepare her and her mother for their testimony at the trial. Alice's answers were vague and equivocal.

She said she knew her mother did not like Ray and Peggy, and, once again, denied seeing any naked games.

Rubin asked for a sidebar conference. She was visibly displeased with the direction the cross-examination was taking. She called for sidebar conferences repeatedly throughout the day.

The questions went on and on. Alice denied having gone to a car wash or a farm with Ray and denied seeing Ray bring in a dead cat. She acknowledged that she had been taken to the party held to celebrate Ray Buckey's arrest.

"Did you see kids taken away from the school by Ray?" Gits asked.

"No."

Earlier, Alice had said Ray took her to a house in a van.

"Before you went to CII did your mom and dad talk to other moms and dads?"

"No."

According to her CII transcript, Alice had said that her parents did talk to other parents about allegations of molestation at McMartin before visiting CII.

"Alice, did you ever see any kids naked?" Gits asked.

"Yes."

When she was asked the same question at the preliminary hearing, Alice had said no. She also said, at the preliminary, that she could not remember Peggy touching her.

Gits finished his cross-examination and Davis began.

"Alice, do you feel afraid because Ray is here in court?"

"No."

"Your parents said bad things happened at McMartin?"

"Yes."

"After going to CII you had new pictures in your mind . . . did that make your mom and dad happy?"

"Yes."

"Did you tell that turtles were hurt at the school?"

"Yes."

"Did you see turtles stabbed?"

"No."

"Did you see Ray do bad things to you?"

"No."

"Was there a time you believed woman teachers touched children at the school?"

"Yes."

"Some grown-ups took their clothes off? Which one?"

"Peggy."

"Can you describe what you remember seeing?"

"No."

"Do you remember testifying in the preliminary hearing that you never saw any child naked?"
"No."
"Did anybody put any part of his body in your mouth?"
"Ray."
"What part?"
"His penis."
In the preliminary hearing Alice had denied this.
"Did you practice questions with Lael Rubin?" Davis asked.
"Yes."
"Did someone put his penis in your mouth?"
"Yes."
"What position were you in?"
"I don't remember."
"Do you believe teachers took pictures of children naked?"
"No."
"Before court, did your dad tell you you had been molested?"
"Yes."
"Alice, did your parents hug your sister to get the words out of her?"
"I don't remember."
In the preliminary hearing Alice had answered the same question affirmatively. One exchange at the preliminary hearing was particularly exculpatory.

Q: Alice, did Ray threaten to shoot your mom and dad?
A: No.
Q: Did you hear that any other little girl was touched on the bottom?
A: No.
Q: Did you hear that Ray took pictures of kids naked?
A: No.
Q: Did Ray ever tell anybody to take their clothes off in the bathroom?
A: No.
Q: Did you see Ray naked at any time?
A: No.

At the trial, Alice testified that Ray touched her while playing "horsey," but when asked, could not provide any of the details, such as whether she or Ray was dressed, or what position she was in.
"Do you remember [that] in the preliminary [hearing] you were afraid?" Davis asked.
"Yes."
"You went back to the witness room and you cried."
"Yes."
"You were afraid because the parents and Lael Rubin were unhappy with your answers?"

"No."
"Do you remember you started crying when Lael Rubin came in the room?"
"No."
"Did anybody scare you at the preschool?"
"Yes . . . he [Ray] said he would hurt my parents."

As related in the testimony in the preliminary hearing, Alice had said that Ray did not threaten to hurt her parents.

"Before Ray came into the courtroom you didn't know what he looked like [did you?]" Davis asked.

"No."

After hours of questions, answers and sidebar conferences, Davis ended the day with an extremely strong finish. He read from Alice's testimony at the preliminary hearing in May 1985:

Q: Who told you about the "horsey game"?
A: I don't know.
Q: Was "horsey game" ever used at school?
A: I don't remember.
Q: Before the puppet lady?
A: I don't remember.
Q: Before you talked to Lael at home?
A: I don't remember.
Q: Did you ever see Ray without clothing on?
A: I don't remember.
Q: Did you ever see Ray with his pants down?
A: I don't remember.
Q: Did you ever see Ray with his pants unzipped?
A: I don't remember.
Q: Did you ever see Ray's penis?
A: I don't remember.
Q: Did you ever play the "horsey game"?
A: I don't remember.
Q: Did you ever play a game where you sat on him?
A: I don't remember.
Q: Did any of the teachers play the horsey game with you?
A: I don't remember.

Alice was excused. Her testimony had taken a full week. The judge said, "We will be in recess until Monday at one-thirty."

Monday, February 8, 1988. It portended to be a dull and predictable day. Instead, it turned out to be an explosive one. It had come out during the last day of Alice's testimony on Friday that she had cried in the witness room after she had finished her testimony in the preliminary hearing in 1985. It was the position of the defense that she had cried because her parents and Rubin were angry and disappointed with her performance on the witness stand and felt that she had let them down. The prosecutors' position, of course, was that she had cried because she was terrified of Ray Buckey and the other teachers present in the courtroom.

The prosecution called Gloria Belmontes, an employee of the district attorney's victim-witness program. She walked to the stand and was sworn in.

"Was there a time," Rubin asked, "when Alice was testifying in the preliminary hearing that you observed her crying in the witness room?"

"Yes, I did."

"Would you tell us what you observed there?"

"When I came into the room her mother asked her, 'How're you doing?' and she started crying and she said she was afraid of Ray and we tried to console her."

"When you entered the room, was I in the room?" Rubin asked.

"No, you weren't."

Belmontes went on to say that during Alice's testimony, she sat in an adjacent room watching Alice on a television monitor.

"What, if anything, did you observe about Alice?"

"Observing the monitor and observing her behavior, she appeared to be very frightened. . . . It appeared she was looking in a direction where Ray was sitting at."

"And when Alice came back into the witness room, did you write any note?" Rubin asked.

"Yes." Rubin produced a piece of paper and asked that it be marked as a prosecution exhibit. She showed it to Belmontes and asked her if she recognized the handwriting. Belmontes said it was her handwriting and signature.

"Did it say that Alice was scared to talk?"

"Yes."

"And at the time did you hear me give any explanation why Alice was crying?"

"No."

"No further questions."

Davis began questioning Belmontes.

"Have you read the transcript of the proceedings?"

"Yes."

"Do you have a personal belief that molestation occurred at the preschool?"

"Yes."

"Do you have training in child abuse?"

"No."

"Were you an eyewitness in Manhattan Beach?"

"No."

Belmontes explained that based on Alice's crying she believed the girl had been molested because she had seen other children who had been molested who cried.

"Would it be fair to say you have a biased opinion?"

"No."

" 'She won't admit the truth' was your comment?"

The note Belmontes had written said that Alice was "afraid to tell the truth."

"Yes."

"Did you see Ray Buckey on the screen?"

"No."

"You didn't see what she could see?"

"Yes."

"What did you see of Ray Buckey on the screen?"

"I'm not sure . . . the back of his head."

"Do you know whether Alice could see Ray?"

"I don't know."

"What was she looking at?"

"I'm not sure."

"Was she crying?"

"I'm not sure."

"Did Alice say anything in the courtroom about being afraid?"

"No, sir."

Gits asked her, "Did Alice appear upset?"

"Yes."

After a brief recess Davis and Gits brought in a television monitor with a videocassette player and placed it before the jury. On the screen we saw Alice, three years younger and smaller, sitting at the witness stand in the preliminary hearing. We saw only Alice. The defense attorney questioning her is not seen. He asked her if she was molested in various ways at the school, running through the entire repertoire of molestation. To each question she answered, "No," or "I don't know."

This is the tape of her recantation! And the defense managed to get it in front of the jury! Not only does Alice not appear to be frightened, but she is smiling! Then, she yawned.

"Terrified people do not yawn," Gits observed.

It was a stunning coup for the defense. The child denied all of the prosecution's allegations and was very quick and definite in saying "No."

Now that Ray Buckey had been granted bail, albeit an almost impossible amount, his lawyer allowed the media to interview him. We saw him on several television stations. On each of them he was asked, "Did you molest children at the preschool?"

"Never," he answered.

"But the children are saying you raped and sodomized them."

"People don't stop to think . . . with two-year-old children that would be like putting a camel through the eye of a needle," Buckey responded. "There is no fact-finding process in that courtroom. They just want to get a conviction."

"The prosecution is making a big issue of the fact that you did not wear underwear," Mr. Deepvoice says. "Don't you think that's rather unusual?"

"You've got to remember that Manhattan Beach is a beach town," Buckey responds. "Three-fourths of the population there went around without underwear. There were mothers who came into the school who were not wearing bras. Does that make them some kind of sex criminal?"

"What do you think will happen if you are released on bail? Would your life be in danger?"

"I don't know. There are crazy people in here and there are crazy people out there, too."

"What about the allegations? They are pretty serious."

"I intend to face them—and make them face it, the lies, the blindness, the ignorance, the malice, the corruption."

"They have a very strong case against you," said one speaker, a nasty little man, smiling down at Ray with the expression of someone gloating over the predicament of a person less fortunate than himself.

"The kids are all telling the same story!" he added.

"No two kids told the same story," Ray replied.

"What if you're convicted?" another television voice asked.

"I'll have to face whatever life holds for me."

"What is the worst part of this thing?" the announcer asked. We had watched Ray Buckey for over three years as he sat, barely twenty feet away from us, inscrutable and expressionless. This was the first time we saw the full depth of his agony reflected on his face. With his elbow on the table and his face resting on his hand, his knuckles covering half of his mouth, Ray sat there, silently, for a long time, then finally said, almost inaudibly, "I don't know."

He had been held in a jail cell for four years, although he had never been convicted of any crime. "I've been here so long I've forgotten what it's like to be free," he told one television newsman.

While Shirley and I were having dinner the telephone rang. I picked it up.

"Hello. Is this Paul Eberle?"

"Yes. Who are you?"

"I'm Glenn Stevens." Glenn Stevens is the prosecutor who resigned after the preliminary hearing and said all seven defendants were innocent.

"Glenn Stevens? I didn't think you even knew who I was."

"Didn't know who you were? I just read your book."

"You certainly did a very courageous thing. Not very many people would do that," I told Stevens.

"Well, everything was coming up nothing. It all boiled down to zero. Everybody used this case for their own personal gain. I was no different in those days. McMartin was my ticket to something bigger and better. But the prosecution's case has got to show that the defendant is guilty as charged. And we could not do that. None of the kids was traumatized by seeing Ray again. None of this happened to the kids. Let's say that Ray did all the terrifying things they said he did. If you looked at his picture and you were about six years old, what would be your reaction? You'd go absolutely bananas. It would trigger all these terrible things in your subconscious. It would be visible on your face. But you look at the tape and some of the kids didn't even remember who 'Mr. Ray' was. None of them showed any emotion telling about this. It was just a game! None of them suffered a trauma from seeing Ray again.

"For CII to tell a kid, 'We talked to your friends and they all told us you were touched,' that's so powerful! Because it turns into a game and peer pressure and they ended up trapping a lot of people into making allegations which weren't true. But once she started, the case really became astronomical in its proportions and there was no way she could back down. . . . Once the kids were pulled into this process it was very difficult for them to back down. There was a reward system for answering the questions affirmatively. Every time we did a search warrant we came up empty. We searched just about the entire South Bay and came up empty, and when the investigation was finished you could boil it all down to one number. And that number was zero."

"What about Judy Johnson?" I asked. "Did the prosecution know she was crazy? Did Lael Rubin?"

"They knew it from day one," he laughed.,

"What about Judy Johnson's story that her dog was sodomized?" I asked. "Did she tell that to Jane Hoag?"

"She told that to me," Stevens said. "Remember, the child was nonverbal. He never said anything. All this came from Judy Johnson."

"To whom did she make the statement that her son saw animals being chopped up, and that he rode on a lion?"

"Those were just written notes that she turned over. She also said that somebody killed a baby and made him drink the blood, and he had to stick his finger up the anus of a goat, and Ray chopped off a baby's head. All the stuff that usually goes on every day at preschools. And she said there were witches and a goatman there."

"What, exactly, was the goatman?" I asked.

"Oh, it was not descriptive. I figured it was just the usual goatman."

"Was it a four-legged animal with a man's head?"

"It was either that or a two-legged man with a goat's head. It could be either. There are so many of each, it's hard to tell. These are Judy Johnson's handwritten notes, turned over to the D.A. in 1984 in February. Millions of dollars were spent on an investigation and the investigation kept coming up empty, empty, empty, empty. And that's when I started changing my mind."

"And yet Lael Rubin, of all the people in the D.A.'s office, was the one who wanted most tenaciously to hang on to the case," I said.

"Yeah. All these women conspiring to molest children. It happens all the time, right? You know, people who are real experts in the field of sexuality will tell you that being a homosexual or a pedophile is something you have in you for a long time. It doesn't just suddenly happen one day. So will somebody explain to me why Virginia McMartin would suddenly become a pedophile at age eighty?"

"Lael Rubin and Philibosian were telling the world that those women were running that preschool for twenty-eight years and chopping up animals and babies and producing child pornography," I said.

"And not one of these kids came forward and said anything," Stevens responded. "And better yet, one of the parents who goes around with that sign that says 'I believe the children'—his kid didn't even know who Ray Buckey was. 'I believe the children.' How much do we believe the children? Do we believe they were flown around in hot air balloons? Do we believe they were forced to shoot elephants? Where do we draw the line in what we believe? Do we believe there were naked nuns and priests running around drinking blood? Do we believe that 1,200 kids were molested and nobody knew until Judy Johnson blew the whistle? And it started eating at me and eating at me."

"How was Kee MacFarlane able to get the kids to say all these things?" I asked.

"It was a game! They were just going along with the game! Like, 'If Ray touched you where would he have touched you?' And once they said it happened they got rewarded for it. And then their parents are praising them for it. And they can't back off and admit they lied."

"Kee MacFarlane seemed to be able to get anything she wanted from the parents," I observed.

"Exactly. She'd say, 'Well, today I need more on Peggy Ann. And then it would come back. I mean is it just a coincidence that the first ten kids only talked about Ray? And when they just pick out another doll and say, 'Let's make this the Peggy doll.' "

"Another thing that puzzled me," I said, "Kee and Cheryl Kent said the last kids in the preliminary hearing were too terrified of the defendants to testify in the same room, and that they'd have to have closed-circuit TV. I didn't see any evidence of that."

"I didn't see any evidence that any of them were terrified of Ray at the preliminary hearing," Stevens said. "Most of them didn't remember Ray."

"No two kids described the same event," I recalled.

"Each of them was doing his own mental confabulation of what Kee MacFarlane wanted to hear. She would reward them for the basics. Just the touching. 'You're such a good boy! You're so brave! Your parents will be so proud! And now show us how this game was played.' And they start fantasizing. Kids like to play. But once they've said these things they're stuck with it. They can't back out and admit they lied. Then when they get to the grand jury or the preliminary hearing they don't remember what they said last time. They just remember the basic skeleton and they just improvise on the rest of the details."

"You would think the judge would look at this with some measure of skepticism," I reflected. "Has he actually read the record? All 100,000 pages?"

"He's just going to lay it off on twelve jurors. That's the way it's going to have to end, you know, Paul. He's not going to take the heat. Nobody's going to take the heat."

"But don't those judges realize that Jane Hoag took something very insubstantial and created a colossal circus out of nothing? And started calling everybody in town. Virginia told me she called some people as many as five times a day."

"Plus, she sent the letter," Stevens added.

"I thought it was Capt. John Wenner who sent the letter."

"She was the one who wrote it. It was signed by Wenner but she wrote it."

"At first most of the people in Manhattan Beach looked at this with skepticism," I said. "And then all of a sudden they believe their kids were molested. How did that happen?"

"At first they said, 'No. It's impossible. It couldn't have happened. And then the letter went out and everybody started talking and once they went to see Kee MacFarlane and MacFarlane says, 'Yes, your child was molested.' And they're told that she's an expert. That's it. The only license she has is a New York State welder's license."

"I find it difficult to imagine sixty-year-old Peggy Buckey raping a baby," I said.

"I find it difficult to imagine any of them doing that, although I suppose it's easier to imagine Ray doing it because he's a male. Also, there's another thing, Paul, and that is that we as citizens like to believe that all this is not for naught. There has to be something there. And it's so easy to pin it on the guy. Nobody likes to believe that so many authorities could have been bushwacked."

"And the general public, too," I said.

"Okay, generally kids don't lie about sexual abuse if it's under the right circumstances. If a child comes up to you and says, 'Mommy, a man touched me on the penis,' you have to give that some credibility. But if the interviewer says, 'If a man came up and touched you on the penis how would he have done it?' that has less credibility. And when the kids are being praised for giving affirmative answers and scolded for giving negative answers, then kids do lie because kids are human beings and human beings do lie and kids are no different from adults."

"There's nothing more frightening to a kid than ostracism," I remarked. "To be told that he's the only kid that's dumb. The only one who's a rotten kid. The only one nobody likes."

"Yep."

We were told that Officer Jane Hoag would be testifying soon. We looked forward to that with great interest. What the police seized from the Buckey residence is worth mentioning. From Peggy's living quarters they seized a rubber duck that they entered into evidence as "proof" of an "interest in children." How this could be construed as perverse or criminal was never explained so far as we know. From the home of Peggy's daughter, Peggy Ann, they seized a black garment which, they boldly asserted, was a satanic robe. It was Peggy Ann's graduation gown. From Ray Buckey's room they seized a copy of *Playboy* magazine as evidence that he was a man of weird cravings, depraved desires, and maniacal longings. We wondered how this would play before the jury. Surely some of the jurors looked at *Playboy* occasionally, as do some thirty million people in America alone. And there are certainly no pictures of children.

Suffering from a severe case of writer's cramp, and hoping to get a more accurate and complete record of the proceeding, we filled out the forms requesting the court's permission to bring in a small tape recorder. The bailiff handed it to the judge who showed it to Lael Rubin. She said something to the judge that we were unable to hear. The judge looked at us and said, "We will have to have a hearing on this tomorrow because the District Attorney has the right to state any objections they might have."

"What time do you want to have the hearing?" we asked the judge.

"Tomorrow morning at ten-thirty," he said. "We'll do it first thing tomorrow."

We arrived early the next morning in our best clothes. The judge came in and the bailiff called the court to order.

"First, we have the matter of Mr. Eberle's request to bring in a tape recorder," the judge announced. "Do the People have anything to say on this matter?"

Lael Rubin objected loudly and vociferously, insinuating that our real purpose in requesting permission to bring in a tape recorder was not really for the purpose of writing a book, but for some more sinister, nefarious purpose. The judge listened and then spoke. His tone was skeptical and impatient. "I have seen Mr. Eberle's book. He *has* written a book, and he has been here almost every day, taking notes. My only concern would be that it not be given to the media. I do not want it played on any radio station, and I do not want any of the children taped." There was another strident outburst from Rubin, but the judge said, "I see no reason to believe that Mr. Eberle wants the tape recorder for any other purpose than note-taking. Permission is granted."

Our friend, Irene, the attorney, was in the courtroom. She came over to say hello. "Somehow I almost get the impression that Lael Rubin doesn't like you," she grinned.

"I don't know why we're getting so much heat. We just tried to write an honest, factual book," Paul told her.

"That's not what they want," she smiled sagely. "This whole thing is an immense fraud and an outrageous deception, and a lot of careers are going to go down and a lot of funding is going to dry up if they don't get a conviction. They've read your book and they know what your position is. They're not going to make it easier for you. I also get the perception that Gits and Davis also intensely dislike you."

"Me, too," Paul agreed. "No question about it. I don't understand that. We were the first writers in the world to break the silence and tell their side of the story. And we took a lot of heat for that. And they make no effort to hide their dislike for us. I don't understand."

"If you think about it for a while you will," she smiled. "You two are the only writers here who are not owned by anybody and have no sticky relationship with either side, so nobody trusts you. They know you're going to tell the whole world what happened here, but they don't have the slightest idea what you're going to say about it. Everybody in that room wants you kicked out. And because you're strictly on your own, they think they have no reason to fear the consequences of trying to grind you under. If you were someone with very visible and powerful clout behind you, like Jack Anderson or Dan Rather, they would come up to you with greasy smiles and try to assimilate you into their camp. They think you're alone. Isolated. Like Ray. And they feel that they should be in front of the television cameras rather than you."

"We call Dr. Astrid Heger." Heger is the CII physician who conducted the physical examinations of the McMartin children and took the photographic slides of the children's anuses and genitalia. Slender, blonde, and fashionably dressed in a beige suit, she sat at the witness stand. Deputy D.A. Roger Gunson asked the questions on direct examination. He examined the doctors; Lael Rubin did the children and the parents. Heger testified that she was licensed to practice medicine in California and Oregon, that she was director of the child abuse unit at the University of Southern California Medical Center, that she had taken an M.A. in librarianship in 1968 and then entered medical school and graduated in 1972, and after a residency in pediatrics, joined the staff of CII in 1982 with a "central focus" on abused children. She stated that she was a member of an evaluating panel for Superior Court and offered "expert opinion" to people referred to her clinic by district attorneys, physicians, and law enforcement and that she was a member of Alpha Omega Alpha, an honor society.

Again the giant anuses and genitals blazed from the slide projector screen, high above us, day after day. In spite of the great magnification there appeared to be nothing there other than perfectly normal orifices, so far as anyone could tell. "It was a deception presented with total solemnity," one of the lawyers commented. Each time Gunson named one of the children in the case and questioned Heger, the doctor's conclusion was that the child had been sexually abused. When she examined over one hundred children who attended the McMartin Preschool she stated that all of them had been molested. As the slides were projected onto the screen, she described symptoms of what she termed "blunt force trauma." She used that phrase repeatedly throughout her testimony. It is one of those phrases whose ambiguity makes it safe. On some of the children she could find no signs of trauma, but these children, too, she said, had been sexually abused. Oddly, Heger's examinations of these children were done, and the photographs taken, as much as five years after the children had last attended McMartin. Nevertheless she said it was a "medical certainty" that these children had been sexually abused.

Heger's testimony frequently contradicted that of the parents, Dr. Gordon, and even her own prior statements. She testified that she had been trained by Dr. Bruce Woodling and had worked under his supervision when she performed the physical examinations in 1984. Woodling is a well-known prosecution witness. He, too, would be testifying. He once stated at a conference, "It is imperative that an examiner of children never make a diagnosis, 'No evidence of sexual abuse,' which is probably the single worst thing a medical examiner can do, because if you make that conclusion, the case will never go forward."

On cross-examination, the questions focused on the fact that at the time Heger examined the children her experience in the sexual abuse of children was minimal, next to nothing. She was a new doctor and had examined less than a dozen children for sexual abuse prior to the McMartin case. The defense attorneys also asserted that the entire medical profession had absolutely no body of scientific medical knowledge that would enable them to conclude that a child had been sexually abused years before.

Dean Gits read from a book Heger had co-authored: "Any conclusion should validate the child's story and state clearly that the presence, or absence, of physical findings is consistent with the history of sexual abuse."

Asked if she believed that, Heger stated, evasively, that the absence of physical evidence does not mean that the child was not molested."

"Then what good is a medical exam?" Gits asked.

"It's tremendously important," she answered.

"To whom?" Gits asked.

"To the child," Heger replied.

Gits asked her the central question: "Is there any medical evidence that is clearly inconsistent with child molestation?"

"No," she answered.

Heger was cross-examined for three weeks. The defense attorneys did their best to make the jurors understand that physicians' ability to diagnose distant past sexual abuse simply did not exist, and that Heger was biased because her reputation rested solely on the McMartin case, and that reputation was now in jeopardy. They also endeavored to show that when she diagnosed the McMartin children, Heger was acting as an agent of the district attorney's office, in the service of the prosecution, not as part of a neutral, objective, fact-finding process. Heger stated that the most important part of a medical examination was "the history," and that the actual physical exam was secondary. "But what if the history is the product of mob hysteria and fraud?" one of the attorneys commented.

Heger also made the remarkable assertion that "a child cannot be led to disclose having been sexually abused if it didn't happen." Even the most obtuse, prosecution-oriented reporters raised their eyebrows at that one. Heger was asked about a child who recanted in the preliminary hearing and denied that anyone molested him.

"That is very common for a child who has been molested," she said.

Davis presented her with a hypothetical situation. "Assuming a child lied, how would you know if the child lied?"

"I don't know."

"How do you know whether a child told the truth in this case?"

"I believe the child," she answered.

The questions went on, hour after hour, day after day. Heger was extremely facile and answered the questions with medical jargon. When she was stuck for an answer she smiled charmingly at the jurors.

"She comes on as a sweet, little girl," Peggy told me during the lunch recess. "But we have a videotape of her being really mean to kids and trying to bully them into saying they were molested." After the recess, Davis asked the court's permission to show the jury the tape of a child being interviewed by Heger at CII. Judge Pounders denied Davis's request. According to a transcript prepared by Davis's office, Heger told the child that, "[Another child] told us all about the stuff that happened to you." The child continued to deny it, and Heger told the child, "I don't want to hear any more 'nos'!" and "Every little boy and girl in that school got touched. . . ." According to the defense Heger told the child she would be permitted to go and be with her parents on the condition that she "disclosed." In denying the motion, Judge Pounders described Heger's interview as "an attempt to use all her skills to communicate with the child. . . . This was a child who would not cooperate."

There were many questions about the colposcope, a magnifying lens outfitted for taking photographs of the anus and vagina.

"Before you examined the McMartin children, what experience did you have in the colposcope?" Davis asked.

"None," she answered.

Davis projected on the screen the slides of the anuses and vaginas of the children and asked Heger what her findings were. In almost every case she ruled out congenital defects, straddle injuries, or any other possible cause and stated her finding was "blunt force trauma." She said she made no inquiry into the possibility that the alleged abuse could have occurred within the family or at any place other than the McMartin Preschool.

Toward the end of her three weeks on the stand, Heger asserted, once again, that it was impossible to lead a child to make false "disclosure," to disclose something that didn't happen. Davis asked her to explain this theory.

"It's the basis of my professional life and shared experience with other professionals in the field," she said.

"Do you think it may be possible to encourage a child to make allegations of molestation that didn't occur?"

"Objection."

"Sustained."

"Don't you feel that as an interviewer you may have induced a child to make claims that didn't happen?"

"Objection. Assumes facts not in evidence."

"Sustained."

"Was there a child who said he didn't want to talk about it?"

"There was one child who didn't want to talk about it because he didn't want to be separated from his mother."

"Where are the records or notes from this interview?"

"In a garbage fill somewhere in L.A. County."

"Do you think a garbage fill is a good place to put evidence?"

"It wasn't evidence."

"You said every boy and girl who attended McMartin was molested. Do you still believe that?"

"I no longer believe every boy and girl at McMartin was molested."

"When you saw John's anus, it was a perfectly normal anus, right?"

"Most children who report sexual abuse have normal exams."

"If a child was perfectly normal, would you conclude she could have been a victim of sexual abuse?"

"If it is consistent with the history of sexual abuse."

"Do you have a memory of an opinion you uniformly gave in response to prosecutors' questions?" Davis asked.

"They asked, 'Is it consistent with penetration by an erect penis?' And my answer was yes, 'Consistent with blunt force trauma' is a better way of answering that question," Heger answered.

"Do you have an opinion now about what you observed?"

"An object the size and consistency of an adult erect penis. I believe all the findings we testified to, both vaginal and anal findings, are consistent with blunt force trauma, and I believe now they are consistent with penetration."

"Dr. Heger, I am posing to you a hypothesis. Do you believe a child denying molestation is a typical molested child?"

"It's classic for a sexually abused child to delay disclosure."

On one of the examinations there were no photographs taken. Davis asked Heger, "Without taking any history at all, could you conclude he was a victim of sexual abuse?"

"Based on that alone, I could not. No evidence of trauma that I could document." Asked why the child was not photographed, Heger said the camera was not functioning. When she was asked the same question in the preliminary hearing, she had said she did not photograph him because he was "too anxious."

There were questions about the Harvard study that concluded that physical findings in sexually abused girls and another group of girls with vaginal complaints who had not been molested were indistinguishable. Heger said she did not agree with the study.

There was also much discussion of recent and old signs of trauma to the anus and genitalia, since most of the child witnesses examined by Heger had attended McMartin Preschool five or six years before the examinations were performed. The defense lawyers raised the possibility of old scars having been the result of any number of other causes. Heger stuck to her assertion that the physical findings were "consistent with blunt force trauma," and "consistent with sexual abuse."

On the last day of her cross-examination, Davis asked Heger, "Were you a victim of child molestation?"

She declined to answer.

"Did the experience affect your objectivity?"

"No," she answered.

Expecting to hear of some shattering trauma, we waited for the news. Heger said that when she was three and a half years old, a teenager had put his hand up her skirt, and that her brother was present when it happened. She also told that when she was sixteen, a man had "flashed" her from inside a car. They were hardly cases of "blunt force trauma." Judge Pounders expressed concern that one of the attorneys might provide this information to the *Herald-Examiner* or to Lois Timnick of the *Los Angeles Times*. Davis replied that he would never call Lois Timnick under any circumstances. In fact, he had complained repeatedly of what he considered a proprosecution bias in her reportage of the case.

After Heger was excused, Gits stated that, "It would be a tragedy if these two defendants were convicted based on medical evidence that may some day prove to be worthless. . . . I think we've established that she owes her reputation as a leader in the field of child sexual abuse to McMartin and that she has a lot at stake."

That evening we spoke with Dr. Lee Coleman, who had testified in many of these molestation trials as an expert witness. He was worried about the way the trial was going and told us he had heard that the defense was not going to use him as an expert witness. He felt that Gordon and Heger had done "a great deal of damage."

"I could be of great assistance to [the defense]," he said, "if they would just call me. I could be of great assistance in their cross-examinations. The county has already paid me for all the work I did for them and they might as well make use of it." We told him we would relay this message to Davis and Gits, since we were in the courtroom every day and Coleman lived in Berkeley. The next day, during recess, we approached Davis and told him what Coleman had said the evening before.

"What's his problem?" Davis asked belligerently.

"He's worried. He wants you to win. He wants to help," we said. Davis's mouth twisted with contempt, and he walked away, his face and neck red with anger.

That evening we attended the dinner meeting of an organization of publishers, editors, and writers. A woman sitting at our table who was an editor at a large national magazine asked us, "Do you still think those people are innocent? After the kids and doctors said it happened?"

"There is absolutely no scientific, medical knowledge that would make it possible for a doctor to look at a kid and make an accurate finding that he or she was or was not molested five years ago," we told her. "As for the kids, you can get a kid to say anything and believe it. You can do that with most adults."

She looked at us and her eyes seemed to say, "You have reached a number that is not working and has been disconnected."

Another woman at our table asked, "But if nothing happened, why would they be in court all these years? Why would it be on TV every night?" As we explained the case to her, the absence of any medical evidence, the absence of any corroborating evidence, the inconclusive interviews, her eyes darted back and forth, scanning the room. She found an acquaintance and quickly moved away and started a conversation with him.

In the morning we sat in the courtroom and waited. Judge Pounders appeared and sat down.

"Please remain seated and come to order," the bailiff chanted.

"We are back in *People* v. *Buckey* and all counsel are present," Pounders began perfunctorily. The prosecutor called Mrs. Greco, the mother of Arthur, the fifth child witness who would be testifying as soon as the mother was excused. There was a problem. The defense attorneys asserted that Greco was a therapist at the South Bay Counseling Center, an organization with close ties to CII, and that she provided therapy to other McMartin children, some of whom were complaining witnesses in this trial. She has been an outspoken advocate of the prosecution and of the Buckeys' conviction. "She has a very strong conflict of interest," Davis argued. "We have a right to know who these children are [that she had interviewed]. We do not have this information."

The director of South Bay Counseling Center, Colleen Mooney, had also been an active supporter of the prosecution and both she and Greco were part of what the defense attorneys called "the child abuse industry," those who derived personal gain from the current epidemic of child abuse cases.

Gregory Mooney, the attorney husband of Colleen Mooney, argued that the court could not override her privilege without violating her constitutional rights and those of her clients. Gregory Mooney also had been a vociferous supporter of the prosecution and had appeared on television talk shows speaking in support of the accusations.

The defense lawyers argued that Greco's position as a therapist whose clients included child witnesses in the McMartin case created a "cross-contamination" of gossip that reinforced the community's belief in the accusations. It was ironic to note that the South Bay Counseling Center also operated a preschool that had had problems similar to those of the McMartin Preschool. A teacher's aide employed there had recently been arrested and charged with "fondling" a child. After lengthy arguments flowed from the mouths of all four attorneys the judge stated, "I think the privilege does exist. . . . Your request for that information is denied." But Greco was allowed to testify only as a mother; the defense was not allowed to ask questions about her communications as a therapist.

Greco walked to the stand and was sworn in. She testified that at the time her son, Arthur, attended McMartin, when he was two years old, he frequently became angry at his mother, opened his trousers and pulled out his penis, pointing it at her. She further stated that during this time he drew pictures of men with extremely large penises. One of them, she said, was a self-portrait drawn with a penis "as large as his legs." Greco also testified that Arthur refused to wear underwear. All this, of course, was insinuation that Buckey somehow eroticized the child, based, again, on the prevalent belief that if a child manifests any interest in sex it is proof that he has been corrupted by an adult. There were hours of questions about the drawings, the underwear, and Arthur's habit of pulling out his penis when he was angry at his mother. Greco acknowledged that the teachers laughed when they looked at Arthur's drawings.

"Do you think the pictures could be indications of molestation?" Davis asked.

"No. Symptoms," she answered.

"Do you have a personal belief that some of the women teachers molested Arthur at the preschool?"

"I don't know. There is no doubt in my mind that Ray Buckey molested my child. Peggy knew." Rubin asked for a sidebar conference and all the lawyers from both sides approached the bench. After a few minutes they returned to their tables. Rubin was smirking over some small victory, as she frequently did after a bench conference.

"Is Ray a pedophile?" Davis asked.

"Yes he is," Greco answered.

"And what is your definition of a pedophile?"

"A sexual deviant who molests children."

"Did you ever see him do anything like that?"

"No, I haven't."

"You didn't see anything at all, when your boy was going to that school, that would lead you to believe today that Ray was a pedophile?"

"I did not. I'm not an eyewitness of Ray molesting any child."

"So you do allow that some people could merely be accused and not be pedophile[s]?"

"Yes."

"What do you mean when you use the word, 'disclosures'?" Davis asked.

"When referring to it, it's usually when Arthur disclosed to Kee MacFarlane at CII about sexual abuse."

". . . When you say 'disclosure,' what do you mean, relative to what's on that tape, when you describe the video of Arthur at CII?" Davis asked.

"What did I see that I considered disclosure?"

"Yes."

"What sticks in my mind vividly is when Arthur describes oral copulation with the dolls," Greco answered.

"Was that at the beginning, in the middle, or at the end of that videotape?"

"I have no idea."

"When he pulled down his pants and pointed his penis at you, did you have reason to believe that [that] had anything to do with the preschool?"

"No, I didn't."

"During [Arthur's] first year at the preschool you never saw Ray Buckey?"

"I don't recall seeing Ray Buckey."

"Now you have brought it out in trial here that [Arthur] expressed that he didn't want to take naps. Do you feel that's somehow associated with the possibility that he may have been molested?"

"I think that could possibly be a reason."

"Do you think a possible reason could be that he just liked to stay up and play?"

"No."

"Did he ever say anything negative about Ray during the three years he went to that preschool?"

"Not that I recall."

There were many questions about the rampant gossip spread by the mob, and the party held to celebrate Ray's arrest. Greco was extremely small, about five feet tall, and, like many of the other women in the proprosecution group, she spoke with a tiny, childlike voice.

Greco testified that Arthur was examined by Astrid Heger and that there were no physical findings of sexual abuse and that, nevertheless, Kee MacFarlane came out and told her that her son had been molested.

When both sides had finished redirect and recross there were several hours remaining during which Arthur could have begun his testimony, but Lael Rubin asked that the child be allowed to begin Monday instead, "so that he would not fret over the weekend." Peggy angrily told us, during recess, "They want to really work on him over the weekend and make sure he gets his answers straight."

Monday morning. Arthur looks like his mother: short, dark-skinned, and brown-haired. He does not look enthusiastic about being in the courtroom. He is eleven years and eight months old.

"We are back in *People* v. *Buckey* and all counsel [are] present," Pounders begins. Arthur is called to the stand and sworn in.

"Did Ray put anything in your mouth?" Rubin asked.

"Yes."

"Which part?"

"His penis."

"In a classroom?"

"I don't know."

"Do you remember seeing Miss Peggy without clothes on?"

"Yes. . . . I looked in the window. She had her bra on."

In the preliminary hearing Arthur identified another teacher as the one he saw "with her bra on."

"Referring the court to Exhibit 161-A, do you recognize it?"

"I drew it."

"Can you see the writing someone else made? Who was that?"

"My mom."

On the drawing is written, "mean," and "scared."

Davis rose to cross-examine. He stood at the lectern and propounded.

"Arthur, did you see a horse get killed?"

"Yeah."

"Was it a full-grown horse?"

"Yes."

"Do you know what color it was?"

"I don't know."

"How did the horse get killed?"
"Ray hit it with a bat."
"Where?"
"I don't remember."
"Did they ride the horse before it got killed?"
"I don't know."
"Were other kids there when the horse got killed?"
"I don't know."
"Who was your teacher when Ray killed the horse with the bat?"
"I don't know."
"Who was your first teacher at McMartin?"
"I don't know."
"Before today you had a meeting at your home?"
"Yeah."
"Did you go over your questions with Lael Rubin?"
"Yeah."
"Lael Rubin asked you questions and you'd practice answers?"
"Yes."
"Some of the answers you gave, you talked about with Ms. Rubin?"
"Yes."
"Did you practice the names of the teachers?"
"Yes."
"Was your mom there practicing with you?"
"Yes."

Davis went over the "naked games," one by one, asking about Rubin rehearsing him before his appearance in court.

"Did you practice with Lael?"
"Yes."
"Did you have other meetings with Lael?"
"Yes."
"You remember how far from the horse you were when it got killed?"
"No."
"Did the horse make a sound?"
"I don't know."
"Was the horse standing?"
"Laying down."
"How many times did he hit the horse?"
"I don't know."
"Did the horse jump around?"
"I don't know."
"Was there any grownup there when it happened?"
"I don't know."
"How did Ray touch you?"

"With his finger."
"Did he touch your wiener?"
"Yes."
"How long did he touch your wiener?"
"I don't know."
"Did Lael Rubin practice your testimony with you?"
"No."
"Did anybody practice your testimony with you before the trial?"
"No."
"Last Friday, Lael was at your house showing you pictures?"
"Yes."
"Did you practice questions and answers?"
"Yes."
"Was there a time you forgot about molestation?"
"I forgot everything."
"Did grownups help you remember?"
"Lael?"
"Were there other grownups that helped you remember?"
"Yes."
"How about the puppet lady? Did she help you remember?"
"Yes."
"Would it be fair to say you didn't remember anything about molestation?"
"Yes."
"Did your mother tell you you were molested at the preschool?"
"Yes."
"Did she tell you [other children] were molested at the school?"
"Yes."
"Did you believe her?"
"Yes."
Arthur did not remember who attended the preschool with him.
"Do you remember some twenty adults told you what happened?"
"Yes."

"May we approach, your honor?" Rubin called for a sidebar. The lawyers whispered to the judge. Gunson looked at the clock. Rubin slouched arrogantly against the judge's desk. There followed a long series of questions and answers that made it clear that both Lael Rubin and the mother had been coaching Arthur relentlessly before his appearance as a witness in the trial.

"Does 'bra' mean underwear to you?" Davis asked.
"No."
"What is underwear to you?"
"I don't know."
"Did you play 'naked games' outside?"
"I don't know." Arthur told the grand jury it happened in the yard.

"Do you remember talking about the 'tickle game' with Lael Rubin [while] preparing your answers?"

"Yes."

"In the 'tickle game' were you touched on your private parts?"

"Yes."

"Were you touched in the dirt?"

"I don't know."

In the preliminary hearing Arthur said he was touched while sitting in the dirt.

"Do you remember what position you were in when Ray touched you?"

"I don't know."

"Do you remember what he did with his hands?"

"Yes. He touched me with his hands."

"Could you describe how he did that?"

"No."

"Do you remember any hand touching your penis today?"

"No."

"Do you remember telling at the preliminary . . ."

"Objection."

"Sustained."

Davis asked, again, to be allowed to read from the preliminary hearing transcript. Rubin cut him off, asking, "May we approach, your honor?" Those of us observing the trial sat and waited through another long sidebar while the whispering lawyers argued and Gunson stared at the clock.

Throughout the day, Davis brought out the inconsistencies between Arthur's testimony in the trial and his statements in the preliminary hearing, the grand jury hearing, and the CII interviews. Lael Rubin repeatedly asked for sidebars to block this line of questioning.

"Arthur, did you practice with the lady D.A.?"

"I don't know."

"When you went to the preschool, Ray wasn't a teacher, was he?"

"I don't think so."

"Did you see Ray during your first year at the preschool?"

"I don't know."

"During your second year?"

"I don't know."

"During your third year?"

"I don't know."

"Do you think, when you talked to the puppet lady, that you were guessing answers?"

"I don't know."

"Back when she asked you about the 'tickle game' do you remember saying [that] Ray didn't touch you?"

The Trial   153

"No."

Davis read from the transcript of the CII interview with Kee MacFarlane.

Kee: Was the game some sort of tricky game?
Arthur: I don't think Ray did anything.
Kee: Pacman glad to remember tricky games . . .
Arthur: Not of me.
Kee: Other kids?
Arthur: I never saw that. . . . Ray never touched me.
Kee: Oh, Pacman knows all the secrets.
Arthur: I don't know any secrets.
Kee: We know the sneaky game. (She picks up the puppet and places it on top of another doll.) Can you show me the sneaky place? (Arthur points to the doll's abdomen.)
Kee: How yucky! Any place real sneaky? Some place private?
Arthur: Maybe in wiener?
Kee: How well you remember! You have done a real good job!

After recess the defense lawyers asked to be allowed to show a video in which the boy was asked to simulate oral copulation using a microphone as a penis. Rubin objected. Davis said, "The jury should have it." The judge would not allow it.

Davis asserted that in the preliminary hearing Arthur had said he was sitting in the dirt when he was molested; in the trial he said he was sitting on Ray's lap, and in the grand jury hearing he said something entirely different. Davis said "the jury should have it."

"Did you see Ray's penis?" Davis asked.
"I don't know."
"Did anybody pee in your mouth?"
"I don't know."
"Did Ray put his penis in your mouth?"
"Yes."
"Did it happen more than once?"
"I have just one picture. I see Ray."
"What is Ray doing?"
"He's sticking his penis up me."
"Did you have your clothing on?"
"I don't know."
"Did he say anything?"
"I don't know."
"When Ray did this, was it hard like a stick or limp?"
"I don't know."
"Have you seen a hard penis?"
"I don't know."

After a short recess the defense lawyers wanted to show a CII video on the ground that it showed coaching by the prosecution. The judge denied the request. Rubin smiled.

Davis read from the transcript of a CII interview.

Kee: Did anybody put something yucky in your mouth?
Arthur: (No response)
Kee: Can you remember?
Arthur: I'm not sure.
Kee: How about a finger in your hole?
Arthur: Yes.
Kee: Boy! I bet it did! We'll see how smart you are. Did anything come out of Ray's wiener?
Arthur: (No response)
Kee: What did the stuff taste like?
Arthur: He never did that.

Davis continued the cross-examination.

"You knew Ray Buckey had been accused of doing things, didn't you?"

"I don't know."

"Did the puppet lady help you remember that you were molested?"

"I think so."

"Do you believe Ray Buckey put his penis inside your bottom?"

"I don't know."

During his cross-examination, Gits brought out an interesting revelation. Arthur acknowledged that he had received gifts from the families of other prosecution witnesses during the time he was testifying at the preliminary hearing.

Near the end of the day, when Gits had finished, Lael Rubin rose to do her redirect and announced that she intended to read lengthy portions of the grand jury transcript and the preliminary hearing. The reporters and lawyers in the audience section looked surprised and whispered that they thought Rubin had "blown it" and would now incur the anger and exasperation of the judge. Instead, Judge Pounders turned toward the defense table, when they quickly objected, and vented his wrath upon Davis: "I have given the defense great latitude, and I am fed up!" he shouted. "You are abusing it, and wasting time, and from now on I am going to sit you down as fast as I can possibly do it and hold you as tight to every rule of law that I can possibly do to shut you up because there's no other way to do it. You take forever! I give you as much leeway as I can and you abuse it. Twenty minutes of direct-examination and you want several days more to counteract what they're doing!"

"It is not the defense that is wasting time," Davis countered. "It began a long time ago when too many counts and too many children were presented in this case." Referring to the brevity of Rubin's direct-examination, Davis said, "They are avoiding the depth of the evidence in this case, and I have to meet it."

The defense lawyers objected to Rubin's request on four different grounds. "We were ready to go with Arthur last Thursday, and you allowed Miss Rubin to bring in a filler witness so she could postpone Arthur until Monday. Now, she wants to read all this. It's adding another charge and the defense is entitled to cross-examine."

In the hallway, after court was recessed for the day, we sat with Peggy talking about Arthur, who had just been excused.

"What's going to happen to these kids when this is over?" we asked

"They're going to grow up to be liars. We're going to have a generation of kids trained to be liars," Peggy replied. Gits and Davis watched angrily, red-faced.

During the week of March 7 to March 11, the prosecution put on several witnesses who contributed nothing. They were witnesses to the dig at the vacant lot adjacent to the school. One said that a backhoe went back and forth across the lot, digging parallel ditches. This was done because children had told of being taken into underground caverns and molested there. The witness said that no underground caverns or rooms were found but that he still believed children had been taken into the underground rooms to be sexually abused and that satanic rituals occurred there.

Another witness testified that all of the accusing families were there, watching the dig, and that they had brought picnic tables and chairs, ice chests, food and beverages, and watched. It was a festive occasion.

Another witness, Deborah Green, employed by the Sheriff's crime lab, testified. Her testimony was nothing more than an inventory of the boxes of soil and debris taken from the lot.

During lunch in the cafeteria we asked a group of lawyers and paralegals, "Why is it that the judge boils over on Davis for wasting time but never on Rubin?"

"He's under a lot of pressure," one of them said.

When we took the elevator back to the fifteenth floor we saw Peggy sitting on a bench in the hallway, eating her sack lunch, as she did each day during the noon recess. She told us that the vacant lot had once been part of a farm and that there were almost certainly animal remains there, which the mob hoped to unearth and use as "evidence" against the Buckeys. The witnesses had stated that there were four digs but Peggy said law enforcement and the mob were digging there constantly that spring. Peggy said that it was one of the mob parents who had rented the backhoe and was bossing the operation, and that it was Bob Currie who had wanted to buy the school.

She offered to share her lunch with us. Peggy was a kind and gentle lady. Defense attorneys told us that the excessive cruelty inflicted upon her at the county jail was done in order to break her, mentally and emotionally, and thus diminish her credibility. Everything she owned—homes, savings, the school, and the land it was situated on, all of her assets—was now gone, sold to pay lawyers' fees.

"We call Dr. Bruce Woodling," prosecutor Gunson's voice announced weakly. Again we were confronted with the huge, blazing anuses on a large slide projector screen high above the assembled lawyers, jurors, and spectators. Woodling stated that he was a physician, that he received his M.D. in 1972, completed an eighteen-month internship at L.A. County-University of Southern California Medical Center, then did a family practice residency at Ventura County Medical Center between 1973 and 1975. He had also completed an internship residency in gynecology and pediatrics. He had served as director of medical examinations for the county of Ventura "and I examine children who are referred to me by either child protective services, law enforcement agencies, or the district attorney." Woodling said he had examined over 1,500 children and listed the medical associations of which he was a member.

Gunson asked Woodling what training he had received to prepare him for the examination of allegedly abused children. He answered, "I have participated in a number of training seminars that initially, in the 1970s, were gatherings of individuals who, like myself, were involved in doing sexual abuse examinations, where data was shared and where papers were presented in the work we were doing. I became very active in the area of sexual abuse evaluation and have participated extensively with the California Medical Association, the California Prosecuting Attorneys' Association. . . ."

Woodling went on to say he was appointed to the state advisory board on sexual abuse and was made chairman of the California Medical Protocol Committee for sexual abuse. "We developed the State of California protocol for examining suspected victims of sexual abuse. . . . I have participated in programs that involved the education of physicians and nurse practitioners through teaching hospitals . . . also through the California Prosecuting Attorneys' Association. In 1975, I published a protocol in the California Prosecuting Attorneys' Association guidelines for dealing with sexual abuse." Woodling went on to list the articles he had published.

What it all added up to was that Woodling had worked entirely in the service of the prosecution, rather than the accused, and was one of the leading figures in what defense attorneys dub the "child abuse industry." Woodling was called to affirm Astrid Heger's findings, which he did, as Gunson showed the slides of the children, one by one.

The jury was removed from the courtroom while the lawyers debated the admissibility of allegations of misconduct by Woodling in a case in Bakersfield in which he testified that a child's anus was greatly deformed as a consequence of sodomy. The judge wanted a second opinion and called in another doctor from U.C.L.A., who examined the same child and found that his anus was "perfectly normal." The allegation raised serious questions as to Woodling's credibility. He testified for the prosecution in several of the big, "satanic mass molestation" cases in Bakersfield, cases which later collapsed, and the charges were dismissed. Another case, the Pitts case, later crumbled and the defendants were released. Judge Pounders ruled that the accusations leveled against Woodling were not relevant. He did not allow the defense to bring them up before the jury.

The jurors were brought back into the courtroom and Davis began his cross-examination. His questions focused again on whether there was any body of medical knowledge that made it possible for a physician to determine, from a physical examination that a child had been molested in the distant past. The answers did not indicate that any such knowledge existed, but Woodling's answers were evasive. Having testified for the prosecution in over one hundred trials, Woodling used esoteric medical jargon—"squamous epithelium," and "anterior forchettes," "neovascularization," and "condyloma accuminata"—to explain how his examinations were done.

Davis asked whether Woodling had attended any conferences where blind comparisons were made, where there were no suggestions as to whether or not the photograph depicted a molested or a normal condition.

"I've never participated in those kind of conferences at any time."

"To your knowledge has any such study ever been attempted?"

"No."

"What are the necessary ingredients for rendering a competent opinion about sexual abuse in a child?" Davis asked.

"I have established for myself as a criterion that I will have a data base. I will have a history, and I will have photographs if I don't have the child."

"Isn't it true," Davis asked, "that every human being is unique and no two are exactly the same?"

The doctor acknowledged that this was true. His face reddened with anger as Davis established with question after question that what the doctor had been doing was inexact, and that there were no known criteria that could be used to determine, by a physical examination, whether a child had been molested in the distant past, five to ten years before. There were many questions about Woodling's career to communicate to the jury the fact that he had always worked in the service of the prosecution, not the defense, and that he was anything but an impartial, objective witness:

"As a result of providing testimony on behalf of the prosecutors, how were you paid?"

"Through district attorney funds."

"At what amount?"

"My time is $2,500 a day."

"You were compensated for examining McMartin children in 1984?"

"I was."

"What was your rate of compensation?"

"Two hundred fifty dollars per examination . . . conducting the examinations, meeting with Dr. Heger and Kee MacFarlane, discussing the cases, preparing the reports. . . ."

"Doctor, have you seen children who may have been molested . . . and found there were absolutely no physical symptoms of molestation?"

"I have seen cases where there were no physical findings."

"And have you ever found, after seeing a child suspected of being molested, with no symptoms at all, and found that that child was molested? You look at the child and found there was absolutely nothing wrong with it . . . and you determined that [the] child was molested?"

"As a physician who examines children for being victims of sexual abuse, what I do is collect a history which may include an allegation and the name of the perpetrator. . . ."

Woodling's answer was not responsive to the question and we wondered why the defense lawyers do not object or move to strike.

"In a court, you have actually articulated your opinion that both Donald and Veronica were sexually molested, haven't you?" Davis asked.

"I did."

"Now, in your own view, that's an incompetent finding for a doctor, isn't it?"

"No."

"Wasn't it true that that was ultimately a legal decision?"

"Objection."

"Sustained."

"Have you ever, without any physical finding, stated under oath that in your opinion, a child was molested?" Davis asked.

"I'm certain that in cases where there were no findings of molestation, what I have testified to in the past is that the lack of a physical finding does not preclude that the child was in fact either sodomized, fondled, or involved in an act of vulvar coitus," the doctor declaimed.

"Have you ever testified, when there were no physical findings, that in your opinion there was no evidence of molestation?"

"I've never used that word. . . ."

"Have you ever, in a court of law, testified that, in your opinion, a child was not molested?"

"I don't believe I ever testified about [children being] 'molested.' I talk about trauma . . . consistent with digital manipulation, penile-genital contact, an act of sodomy. . . . The fact that a physical injury is not present does not preclude that a certain act may not [sic] have occurred."

"Now when you talked to Veronica, did you find any physical evidence . . . on her anus, consistent with sodomy by a penis?"

"I saw no evidence of trauma to her perianal area whatsoever . . . but certainly the lack of signs of trauma did not preclude a finger or other object entering her rectum."

"Did you see anything that, today, would affirm that a finger was put into her anus?"

"I saw nothing."

"Now doctor, as a teacher and a lecturer, have you ever advised other physicians that their testimony should never include statements that there is no finding of sexual molestation?"

"I usually teach them . . . one of the points that I teach them is that when doing examinations as physicians we are examining children where a report is generated to be used by other persons in arriving at a determination and I suggest to all of the physicians that they should never use as part of their diagnosis that a child . . . was not raped or was not molested, rather, I say that if you have to make an opinion. . . ."

Woodling went on and on.

During a recess, Davis walked over to a man who had been sitting in the courtroom as a spectator and asked, "Well, what do you think?" The man said, "I must confess I don't understand where you're going."

"Don't you see?" Davis said. "They have no standards whatever!"

After recess, using the slide projector again, Davis showed the doctor a slide of an anus belonging to one of the children slated to testify. He asked if this was anything other than a perfectly normal anus. Woodling replied that it was "significantly deformed." In quickly canvassing those observing the proceeding, most of the spectators appeared to react with disbelief. There was nothing visible that could be identified as abnormal. Our friend Irene quietly entered the courtroom, sat down next to us, and stared at the blazing giant anus.

"I see it's Anus Awareness Week again," she said. "How long has this been going on?"

"Three weeks," we said despondently. "They're almost finished with him. It hasn't been very edifying."

After recess Davis continued, "Is it possible that a leading question might produce a false answer from a child?"

"A leading question might produce a directed answer," Woodling replied. He was tall, had a strong, resonant voice, and the jury appeared to be impressed. He had been testifying in such cases for a long time and had been instrumental in sending many people to prison.

"I have never been involved in any case where interviewers influenced children to say they were molested when in fact they were not. That has not been my experience," he expounded with a tone of finality.

But Woodling had been involved in at least three cases where an overly zealous district attorney who was determined to win by any means found it expedient to dismiss the charges.

"Did you look at the interviews of the McMartin children at CII?" Davis asked.

"I did not." Woodling said he could find scarrings and later they would not be there, ". . . so the fact that I found no findings of scarring did not mean to me that sodomy did not occur. It only means that no scarring occurred from the sodomy."

Woodling told the court that a child cannot be led to lie about sexual abuse. This is the new orthodoxy of the child abuse industry. If the child says it happened, then it happened, because children never lie. But if the child says it did not happen, that is "typical of the sexually abused child." Denial and retraction, we were told by the prosecution doctor, are part of the typical behavioral process of the sexually abused child. This new dogma is a powerful weapon in the hands of the prosecution. Heads I win; tails you lose.

"In evaluating Veronica and other children, did you hold the conviction that children do not lie about molestation?" Davis asked.

"Objection."

"Sustained."

"Do you believe, doctor, that children don't lie about something as serious as rape and sodomy?"

"Objection."

"Sustained."

"Do you feel that your belief that children don't lie about molestation may have influenced your opinion about Veronica?"

"No, I do not."

"You profess that belief, don't you?"

"Objection."

"Sustained."

"Do you believe that when children are being asked about molestation and say nothing happened, that can be a truthful statement?"

"It is my belief that sometimes children will say that nothing happened because they have a great deal of difficulty talking about the issue, and I believe a history is sometimes difficult to obtain. . . ."

"Can a child, in your experience, tell that he was not molested and be telling the truth?"

"Certainly."

"Let's take the child [who] says he hasn't been molested and then, three or four months later, says he was raped and sodomized. Can both of these statements be truthful?"

"I think that in my experience children don't give false reportings . . . and

I know of a great many children who had a great deal of difficulty in making a disclosure. . . ."

"Do you think it's possible for an adult to influence a child to believe they were molested when in fact they weren't?" Davis asked.

"That has never been my experience and it's not my belief. I have never been involved in any case where I [felt] interviewers influenced children who were not molested to say in fact they were. . . ."

"Did you look at the CII interviews of the McMartin children?"

"I did not," Woodling replied.

"If a child makes serious allegations of rape and sodomy and then time passes and the child says instead of a penis going into a vagina, says it was a pencil—she changes the facts—in these circumstances would you consider the history to be believable in terms of molest[ing]?" . . .

"Would that give you any concern about the accuracy and reliability of the child?"

"No."

"If she told you, when you examined her, that it was a pencil, and, years later, said it was a penis, would that change your opinion about what happened?"

"No."

"I'd like to talk to you about false reports. By your definition would that include a situation where a child might say that he or she was sodomized and then, later on, say it didn't happen? Is that a false report by your definition?" Davis asked.

"That would be a false report but I have never seen an allegation of something where it was proved that it did not in fact happen. I'm aware of children retracting allegations, but that's part of the process of understanding the psychological dynamic of making disclosures," Woodling said.

"So your view of a child who retracts an allegation of molestation is not a child that's engaged in false reporting?"

"I would not conclude by retraction that a false report was made."

"Do you believe a child can believe they [sic] were molested because of statements of adults?"

"I've never seen a child that, to my knowledge, wasn't molested that's been convinced that he was. I've never had that experience."

"Did your medical findings corroborate sodomy?"

"There was no evidence on my examination of scarring but . . . the fact that I found no findings, in the sense of scarring, does not mean to me that sodomy did not occur, only that no scarring did occur from the sodomy. . . ."

Woodling seemed to be leaving no room for the possibility that a child, once identified as a victim, had not been molested.

"Do you feel, as a general principle, that children don't lie about molestation, and that they should be believed?" Davis asked.

"Objection."

"Sustained."

"The exhortation that children don't lie about molestation and that you should believe them . . . is that something you say every time you speak to your peers about evaluating child molestation?" Davis asked.

"I make that statement," Woodling answered.

"When you say that, do you place any limitation on that premise?"

"I usually have explanations I give . . . but I do make that statement that children, when they make disclosures, should be believed. . . ."

"Do you think your belief that children never lie might have something to do with the low incidence of your findings of false reports?" Davis inquired.

"I don't believe so."

"You produced a videotape and you ended that videotape with the statement that children don't lie. Remember?"

"Yes. That's the last thing I said on that tape. Yes."

"Have you changed from that position any?"

"No."

"Your position on the anus of Veronica is that it's consistent with the history, right?"

"Yes."

"Without the history it would be 'no opinion,' right?"

"Without the history it would be a normal anus."

"Could a doctor then say, looking at the anus of Veronica, 'It is consistent with no molestation'?"

"It would be consistent with molestation with no trauma or no molestation."

"And that's the state of the medical evidence of Veronica today?" Davis asked.

"That's correct."

The next witness was a mother whose child was not going to testify in the trial. She filed one of the earliest complaints. She told of a telephone conversation she had with Peggy in which Peggy, naturally angered by the accusations, allegedly said her lawyer would tear her daughter's story apart. According to the woman, Peggy had said, "I would hate to put my daughter through what my lawyer would have to do to her on the witness stand." According to the woman's testimony, Peggy told her she had worked with children for twenty-eight years, and that "children do lie."

The defense attorneys objected to the mother's testimony as hearsay and, since her child was not going to testify, a denial of the right of confrontation and cross-examination.

The woman also said that when she spoke with Peggy, Peggy told her not to believe the letter from the police, that Ray was not the kind of person to hurt children, and that she would not allow such a thing to happen at her school. The woman's daughter was interviewed repeatedly by law enforcement, examined several times by physicians, and then sent to CII. According to the mother, the girl was not willing to testify at the preliminary hearing and was not willing to talk to Det. Hoag. Yet, the *Los Angeles Herald-Examiner* published a story about this witness the next morning, under the heading:

THREAT KEPT GIRL OFF STAND IN McMARTIN TRIAL

The *Los Angeles Times* published a story the next day that was equally biased and misleading, presenting the prosecution's version from beginning to end. That morning, the defense lawyers bitterly protested the prejudicial reporting of the case by the two newspapers, the largest in California. But to a considerable degree they had themselves to blame. Although the media had been astoundingly lopsided in their reporting of the case, more resourceful lawyers in similar cases have succeeded in turning the reporters around and winning them over to the defense side, and then gone on to win their clients' acquittals. Criminal cases often are won in the media, more than in the courtroom. The influence of the media on the outcome of trials is incalculably important. Davis and Gits had been generally unfriendly and unresponsive to reporters, a serious mistake.

For the next three weeks, which consumed most of the month of March, we listened to a long series of witnesses who were present at the dig on the lot adjacent to the school: parents, criminologists, law enforcement officers, and a turtle doctor who examined the turtle remains and found that they died of natural causes. There was a man from a private consulting firm who strained the soil through a screen. The trial began to take on the surreal character of a Keystone Cops movie. Ninety bags of soil were taken from the dig and stored in the district attorney's evidence room. No underground tunnels were found, no trap doors, no weapons. The witnesses did not find any evidence supportive of the prosecution. The jurors were yawning and two appeared to be asleep.

Nevertheless, Davis cross-examined each of the witnesses for hours. Reporters and spectators looked at each other in anguish at the prospect of listening, day after day, to Davis's endless questions. Many of the questions were ungrammatical and their meaning unclear. Davis's unvarying flat voice, its lack of color and modulation, did not help. He seemed to be substituting length for substance. His endlessly tiresome cross-examinations, his posturing, did not play well with the jurors. Their faces betrayed a dislike for all four lawyers. Gunson looked pale, tired, and disconsolate. He did not appear particularly happy about being in this case. All day, he looked at the clock. He was a short, extremely thin man, fifty years old, Scandinavian in appearance. Gunson was also an extremely seasoned player in this game. Although the jurors did not appear to like any of the lawyers on either side, Davis occasionally succeeded in getting a laugh out of them. Rubin did not, nor did Gunson. When Davis finished with a witness and Gits began to cross-examine, there was an abrupt contrast. Gits's tone, like Davis's was monotonous, but, unlike Davis's, Gits's voice had no harmonic resonance. Even the jurors complained that they were unable to hear Gits, although he stood less than six feet from the jury box. His dull voice and lack of fire were taking their toll on the jurors' attention span. Toward mid-afternoon there were only two or three people in the audience section and the press section was empty. We have always wondered why lawyers and politicians generally do not avail themselves of a good voice teacher who could teach them to get the best possible tonal quality out of their larynxes. Like actors and singers, they earn their living with their voices.

After a particularly boring stretch of testimony about the soil evidence, we asked one of the lawyers during recess, "Why are they wasting weeks with all this pointless testimony?" He was with a group of defense lawyers and their colleagues from the preliminary hearing.

"The [prosecution] established the chain of custody. They have to show that the evidence they took from the dig was brought in here without being tampered with. I'm afraid they botched it. Not too surprising. They botched everything else."

We went up to the fifteenth floor and sat with Peggy. She told us there was not just one dig, but that people were there digging constantly that spring. She went on to tell us that Ray's cat had just died. "We're not going to tell him. We're going to give him another cat when he gets out, from the same mother cat."

Peggy told us that law enforcement officers had called her best friend and warned her that if she testified for the defense, they would put her son in prison. The woman's son was on probation for some minor offense. The woman was not only Peggy's friend, she was a teacher at the preschool during the time period specified in the allegations. She was an extremely important witness. Peggy told us the woman was followed everywhere she went, that her telephone was tapped, and her mail intercepted and opened.

We spoke with Peggy's husband, Chuck, in the courthouse hallway. He could not go into the courtroom because he was on the witness list. He was a big, jolly man, and had not lost his good humor, despite the horror inflicted on his family. Earlier, during the preliminary hearing, police and prosecutors announced that they were going to arrest Chuck, that he was an uncharged suspect. This was broadcast on all the media. But the police discovered that he had a perfect attendance record at Hughes Aircraft and therefore could hardly have been drinking blood, dancing with naked nuns, worshipping the devil, raping babies, and at the same time be at Hughes making airplanes. So he was never arrested. Peggy and Chuck had been married for most of their adult lives. "After all that's been done to her, she still believes there's good in everybody," he shook his head sadly. "And she tries to be kind to everybody."

Peggy's daughter, Peggy Ann, told us that when Peggy was asked by a law enforcement officer if she would loan him some document so he could make a copy of it, she said, "Oh sure." Peggy Ann said, "No! Mother! That man wants to put you in prison for the rest of your life!" Peggy didn't believe it.

The mother of the next child witness, Mrs. Wood, is called to the stand. Her son's testimony was among the most bizarre offered in the case. Wood was sworn in and told that during the first grade her child had been infested with pinworms and that when she opened his buttocks, while he was sleeping, he awoke with a jolt and screamed, "What are you doing?" She found this suspicious, she said. She also testified that there were many mornings when he cried and did not want to go to school. Her voice broke; she seemed to be crying. She did this repeatedly throughout her testimony.

She stated that, like all of the others, she heard the rampant gossip of molestation at McMartin, and that, like the other parents who testified, she was visited and talked to by Bob Currie about the allegations, and then promptly took her children to CII. She testified that her son, Billy, said, "If they ask me anything about the McMartin Preschool, it's gonna be 'No, no, no!'"

"He said he didn't remember anything unusual happening but he couldn't look us in the eye," the woman said.

A group of the militant proprosecution parents were there in the audience, the hard-faced mob. They were staring at the witness. Usually they looked around and made ridiculing, demeaning remarks about the defendants and their friends and supporters, but today their attention was focused on Wood. They look worried. They appeared apprehensive about something.

Rubin asked Wood if she took Billy to CII shortly before the grand jury hearing. She answered that she did.

"Did Dr. Heger, after that examination, give you any result of the finding?"

The woman sat there, silent, for a surprisingly long time and finally said, "I don't remember." She also said she did not see any of the slides taken of Billy by Heger.

In the morning, before the jury was brought in, the judge told the lawyers, "In my view it seems that Mrs. Wood is unusually distraught over her testimony and she is very sensitive and was on the verge of tears several times . . . and consistent with her emotional state on the stand I am going to limit very severely objections to her testimony that might otherwise be valid.... I had the perception that the defense was apparently using objections to needle her."

"I had the perception that she was play-acting!" Davis demurred. "And that she was forcing emotional responses. I also had the experience of looking back on statements she made earlier and exaggerating statements she made earlier into 'terrifying' and 'hysterical.' Those kinds of words. So I have a completely different perception based on my knowledge of the record.... I am concerned about any witness who is genuinely upset. I am more concerned about this witness because they have made serious accusations against my client and he was never even at the school. He was never a teacher or an assistant. He was never even present when Billy was there. So I'm very concerned, more than [for] any other witness.... I am not as concerned about little children that believe they have been molested even if they weren't. The concern I have is about children who are consciously lying about things that didn't happen. I come with that attitude about Billy because there is too much objective evidence that at the time he attended the McMartin school, my client was never even there—more so than any other child. So my perception is that the parent is corroborating what I believe is an intentional misstatement of the facts. So I want you to understand that my reactions were that we heard someone that was play-acting, who has increased the seriousness of statements from one testimony session to another ... is not saying the truth, and is intentionally doing this, so I can accept that children may not have been molested but, by a process, have been made to believe they were, and treat them a little different than someone who comes in ... and says they believe statements that investigations have proven were not true."

"I understand your feelings about her testimony," the judge said. "It's very significant testimony, and I can understand that you want to treat it seriously ... but using objections to upset a witness is something I cannot tolerate. Go for it on your questions. That's what questions are for. Objections are not for that purpose."

On cross-examination Wood acknowledged that McMartin had the best reputation of all the preschools in the area, that she had been on friendly terms with Peggy until the tidal wave of molestation gossip swept over the community, and that she had once made a quilt for Peggy. There were many questions about her being visited by Bob Currie. As with the other parents, the lawyers' questions focused on the parents' lack of any belief that their children had been molested until Currie came to them and told them, explicitly or implicitly, that their children had been identified as victims, sending them rushing in panic to CII for evaluation by the "experts." Currie had frequently come to the trial, sitting in the audience with his entourage of women. He smiled, casually, and appeared to be amused by the proceedings. He often approached Davis in the hallway during recess and engaged him in conversation. There appeared to be no hostility between the two, and, in fact, they exchanged friendly smiles as they chatted.

Asked about Currie's allegations of satanic "mass molestation," Wood's answers were vague. Before answering one of Gits's questions she sat, silent, for a surprisingly long time, as expressionless as a wooden Indian. The judge and jury sat there, waiting uncomfortably. There was no sound in the room, except from the clock.

"Until Bob Currie came to your house and talked to you, you were not concerned about having Billy evaluated at CII, were you?"

"No."

"However, immediately after Bob Currie talked to you, you became very concerned and attempted to make an appointment, right?"

"That's correct."

"When Bob Currie talked to you, did he come over to your house?"

"Yes, he did."

"Was his wife with him? Ann Curry?"

"Yes, she was."

"And is she in the courtroom today?"

"Yes, she is."

After recess there was a discussion about the apparent fact that two of the jurors had been sleeping. The first was brought out. The judge told him, "Throughout the trial you have been one of the most attentive jurors." The man denied having any difficulty staying awake. The second, a black man, was brought out. "Are you having trouble staying awake?" the judge asked.

"Yeah."

"And what is the reason for that?" Judge Pounders asked.

"Well, to be perfectly honest, it's not exciting," the man said in a soft, deep voice. "It's like listening to the rain. It just kinda puts you to sleep." He told the judge that both Gits and the witness were soft-spoken "and the questions are not very interesting." One attorney stated that he had observed this juror sleeping on seventeen occasions since the trial began. The judge told the man he would no longer be serving as a juror.

After that, the judge told Gits, "I think a second problem is that you are very soft-spoken, and I would suggest that you use the microphone if you want to be heard. If you want to get through and make sure the jurors are listening, I would advise that you hold the microphone. I know it's difficult but it's either that or speak up and make sure you have their attention . . . it's difficult to hear. If you want to make sure the jurors are awake and listening, use the microphone."

One of the alternates was selected at random by placing the names of all six in a box and drawing one out. The one selected to replace the excused juror was a black man, which was significant because the prosecution tried very diligently to keep blacks off of the jury. It had been their experience that blacks did not have the same blind faith in law enforcement and the judicial system as middle-class whites. The blacks were very much aware of this process and commented frequently about it during jury selection.

Gits ignored the judge's advice and resumed his cross-examination without a microphone.

During the mid-afternoon recess we sat on the bench with Peggy. Gits was standing next to us. "Why don't you speak louder so they can hear you?" Peggy asked. Then she turned to us and said, "Tell him, Shirley!" I did not enjoy being pushed to the forefront of this dispute, but I looked at Gits and told him, "You should speak louder. I sit right behind you and I can't hear you. And my tape recorder doesn't even pick you up." Gits looked down at me disdainfully and said, "I don't have to talk louder just so *you* can hear."

"Even the judge told you to talk louder," Peggy protested.

"I'll take it under advisement," Gits said condescendingly and turned his back to me. Peggy and I often had lengthy conversations. Gits and Davis sat nearby on the bench and listened, looking very angry. Again, Gits said to me harshly, "I don't want anyone interviewing my client." Again, I gave him my Potter Stewart lecture. But he did not interfere when other writers approached Peggy and interviewed her. I have no idea what that was about. We often went into the ladies room and talked, which is something Paul cannot do. This seemed to infuriate Gits and Davis even more because they could not come in and listen. One time while I was sitting on the bench talking with Peggy, Gits was surrounded by a group of young lawyers peripherally involved in the case. Some of them were involved in the civil lawsuits. One of these, a thin young man with a grotesque mouth, was looking at me. I heard him say to Gits, "Get rid of her." This came as somewhat of a surprise to me since we had always been supportive of the defense and dubious about the prosecution's spectacular allegations, both on talk shows and in our book.

Back in the courtroom, Gits continued to cross-examine Wood.

"Mrs. Wood, before the break we were talking about a conversation with Bob Currie and Ann Currie. I think you said they came to your house. Is that correct?"

"That's correct."

"Did Bob Currie indicate to you that he had something important to talk to you about?"

"Yes."

"Could you tell us what it was that Mr. and Mrs. Currie talked to you about that day?"

"The part that I recall hearing . . . I recall hearing them telling my husband and myself that they had taken their children to the Children's Institute . . . and their child had disclosed some sexual abuse."

"By whom?"

"All I basically remember is them suggesting that we make an appointment at Children's Institute. . . . I remember them saying that their son had disclosed some information and my son's name was mentioned. . . ."

"Did Mr. Currie or Mrs. Currie indicate to you what kinds of things happened with respect to molestation?"

"Not that I remember. . . . I was concerned that Billy, while giving whatever responses that he gave, could not look at his father or I [sic] in the eye. That disturbed me somewhat."

"Was he confronted with that? Did you say, 'Billy, look me in the eye when you say that nothing happened'?"

"I don't think so."

"Was Billy told at the time that other kids had said they were molested at the preschool?"

"No." Like the other parents, she said that her child never said anything about being molested before his visit to CII. She said that the CII videotape was shown to her after her son's interview but that the tape was fast-forwarded and she saw only brief excerpts. Gits finished his cross-examination and Davis began.

"Mrs. Wood, do you have a personal belief that your son, Billy, was molested at the McMartin Preschool?"

"Yes, correct."

"Do you have a strong desire to convict, with your testimony, Ray Buckey of molesting your son?"

"Yes."

"Would you like to see Ray Buckey spend the rest of his life behind bars?"

"Objection. Irrelevant."

"Overruled. You may answer."

There was an extremely long silence. Finally, she answers: "Yes."

"When Billy was going to the McMartin Preschool between September 1978 and the first two weeks of June 1979, describe for us one single occasion when you can say you saw Raymond Buckey at the preschool."

"Objection. Irrelevant."

"Overruled."

"I don't remember. I don't remember if I saw him there."

"You cannot describe one time ever seeing Raymond Buckey when Billy was going to the preschool. Is that correct?"

"Objection. Irrelevant."

"Sustained."

"Do you remember any of the things that Billy talked about, about what happened at the McMartin Preschool, at home?"

Again there was a very long silence. Finally she answered, "Yes."

170   The Abuse of Innocence

"And what were they?"
"The 'naked movie star' game."
"Anything else?"
She sat there silently while we waited. And waited. Finally she said, "I can't remember anything else."
"Did any statement [by Billy] influence your belief that my client had done harm to Billy?"
"Possibly."
The woman was on the stand for five days and she wept, or appeared to be weeping, at least once on each of those days. On each of these occasions, one of the jurors was laughing. So we had at least one juror who wasn't buying it. Once, Wood wept so loudly that her sobs sounded like percussive shouts that echoed harshly, shattering the silence of the courtroom. Asked whether she had discussed the allegations of molestation with other McMartin parents, Wood said no, but later she admitted that she had attended a number of meetings with the prosecution, that she had appeared on television with them, that she had had meetings with Kee MacFarlane and Lael Rubin, and that she had participated in the dig.

Wood said that in 1978 and 1979 her son had an anal fissure, chronic diarrhea, and pinworms, but that she had failed to tell this to Dr. Heger at CII, to the grand jury, or to Billy's pediatrician. She said her son sometimes did not want to go to school, which she characterized as unusual behavior, and that he still had a pacifier when he was in the third grade. Wood said she had wanted to see the entire videotape of her son's interview at CII but was permitted to see only "bits and pieces." Her answers to questions about Bob Currie were evasive.

"How long have you known Bob Currie?"
"I don't know."
At the very end of her testimony Wood had one last, loud cry. Sobbing, she said, "I'm a Roman Catholic . . . and I'm supposed to be forgiving. I'm having difficulty. . . ."

Monday, April 18, 1988. The judge sat down and began: "We are back in *People* v. *Buckey* and all defendants and counsel are present." The prosecution called Billy to the stand. He was plump, red-haired, and very white-skinned. He had dark eyes. Answering Rubin's questions, he stated that he was thirteen years old, was in the seventh grade, and attended American Martyrs, a Catholic school.

Billy was the forty-second witness called by the prosecution. Eight counts against Ray Buckey and four against Peggy concerned Billy.
"Did you go to the McMartin Preschool?" Rubin asked.
"Yes, I did."
"Who were your teachers?"

"Peggy, Peggy Ann . . . I can't remember any more." Peggy Ann's name was frequently brought into the testimony. It seemed more than coincidence that she was, at that time, engaged in litigation to get back her teaching credentials. If she were successful it would have had the effect of diminishing the credibility of the prosecution's case.

"Were there any adults at the school that were not teachers?" Rubin asked.

"Ray."

"What did he do?"

"He helped in projects."

"Did you play any games where you had to take your clothes off?"

"Yes, I did."

"Can you tell us how the games were played?"

"We would hold hands in a circle, naked, in a secret room, and they would take pictures."

"Did somebody tell you to take your clothes off?"

"Peggy, Ray, Peggy Ann . . ."

"Did anybody touch you on your penis?"

"Ray, Peggy, Peggy Ann."

"Where?"

"In the secret room."

"Did Ray ever put any part of his body in your bottom?"

"I don't remember."

Billy went on to say that he and other children were taken to a house in a beige station wagon and told to take their clothes off. He said he was taken to a farm where Ray took a machete and chopped a pony to pieces. He said this happened more than once.

Billy told of being taken to a church that he believed was the St. Cross Episcopal Church, where strangers in black robes formed a circle around the children "and they would just moan and chant." Billy said he could not see the people's faces because they wore hoods. In Peggy Ann's hearing Billy testified that he had been molested by "atomically radiated mutants."

"Ray went outside," he said, "and brought in a rabbit and killed it on the altar." He said that Ray took the blood from the altar, put it in a cup and told him to drink it.

The prosecution was reintroducing Satan into the case. In the preliminary hearing several children told of drinking blood with naked nuns and priests, and other diabolical adventures.

In our extensive reading on satanic cults and witchcraft, we learned that the pursuit of satanic cults, like the child sexual abuse scare, had become a thriving growth industry with "satanic task forces" in law enforcement and "experts" in positions of governmental power giving seminars and lectures on the ubiquity of satanic cults engaged in sexual abuse and murder of small children.

The satanic stories we heard in the McMartin case had their origins in the Spanish Inquisition. These bizarre tales, which we had thought to be merely the discarded rubbish of a more primitive age, have been replicated and passed on with remarkable similarity between the Dominican inquisitors of the 1480s and the child abuse witch hunters and trash television of the 1980s. We learned that the two industries are very much interlaced and overlapped. Allegations of "satanic ritual abuse" have been made in molestation cases all over the country.

Weaving together the tales of satanic cults with allegations of child molestation has been an extremely clever strategy of the child abuse industry because (1) it inflamed the public's hunger to burn witches and to destroy the Buckeys and defendants in the hundreds of other bogus molestation cases across the country; (2) it helped to rally public support for the child abuse racketeers; and (3) it distracted our attention from the grotesque and hideous antics of the accusers.

Satanic investigations are one more instrument to tighten the grip of governmental power over the individual; erode our constitutional rights; and crush unorthodoxy, diversity, dissent, nonconformity, privacy, and most of all, the family.

In our research we discovered that the similarities of the sixteenth- and seventeenth-century European demonomania to the child abuse witch hunt of the 1980s was far more striking than we had expected. We really haven't changed much. The differences are trivial. In Europe "confessions" were exacted under torture and, according to Huxley, nearly a million people were burned. In America in the 1980s and 1990s convictions were obtained with false witnesses bought with plea bargains backed by the threat of long prison terms and the offer of leniency or immunity, by the testimony of corrupt doctors, mercilessly manipulated children, and massive media hype.

In America there are thousands of people in jails and prisons for molestations that never occurred (see the bibliography and references for details). In post-Reformation Europe, as in the American molestation mania, it was lawyers who profited by the fraudulent prosecutions and reaped a copious harvest of witches and demented accusers. Periodically, in times of great social change and uncertainty, we tend to focus all our punitive anger on a specific group, real or imaginary, as an alternative to facing the reality that we are all responsible for society's evils—particularly our leaders in government. We prefer to burn witches. The child sexual molestation witch hunt of the 1980s was one more manifestation of the dark, truly evil forces latent in the human mind.

"Before lunch you told us the teachers took you to a market," Gits asked Billy. "What market?"

"Harry's Market," the boy answered.

"What happened at the market?"

Billy said he and a group of about ten children were taken to the market a number of times to play the "tickle game."
"Do you know the owner of Harry's Market?"
"Ray Fadel."
Gits asked Rubin for the correct spelling of the owner's name.
"Abou Fadel," Rubin replied.

The supermarket story had problems. According to Billy, the area where the children were allegedly molested had swinging doors like a saloon and the lower edge of the doors was between two and three feet above the floor. He said the children were molested while sitting and lying on the floor. Gits showed Billy a number of photographs that clearly showed that customers and employees in the store would have been able to view this spectacle without stooping or bending over. Billy stated that this happened while the store was open for business. Why would a person desiring to molest children take them to a supermarket and do it in plain view of customers and employees?

The "secret room" also had problems. It was never found. It did not appear on any of the photographs or diagrams entered into evidence. Gits showed two drawings made by Billy for the prosecutors. One showed the secret room outside the school, adjoining the building; the other showed the secret room inside the building.

As for his allegation that Ray Buckey sliced ponies into pieces with a machete, it is hardly necessary to comment. Yet, Billy went on and on, confident, poised, and surprisingly articulate for a thirteen-year-old. None of the previous child witnesses gave similar testimony.

Outside the courtroom, Davis told reporters, "The more times he accuses my client the better, because my client was not even present at the preschool during the year the boy attended the preschool."

Gits told reporters, "The kids appear to have been so prepped for trial that their testimony has been weakened. There is no spontaneity."

In the morning we sat on a bench in the hallway reading all of the morning's newspapers while we waited for the bailiff to unlock the courtroom door. The *Los Angeles Herald-Examiner* had a story saying that the county had now spent eight million dollars on the case. Another newspaper carried a story asserting that "satanic ritual mass molestation" of children was on the rise everywhere in astronomical numbers. The paper defined it as a vestige of the counterculture of the 1960s peace movement. Another newspaper reported that dozens of bills had been introduced in the California state legislature designed to strengthen the hand of the prosecution and cripple the defense. These included a bill to allow hearsay evidence, a bill to prohibit libel or slander suits by persons falsely accused of child abuse, a bill to abrogate the Sixth Amendment right to be confronted by one's accuser, a bill to forbid the reunification of the family in cases where there is nothing more than suspicion of abuse, and a bill to add nine years to the sentences of convicted defendants in molestation cases. Several states had proposed legislation providing for the castration of sexual deviates. Everybody in government was jumping on the bandwagon, posturing for votes, including some legislators whose private sexual proclivities were, shall we say, bizarre.

The judge walked in and the bailiff called the court to order. Judge Pounders noted that the trial had been in progress for one year. It was April 20, 1988, the anniversary of the birthday of Adolf Hitler.

Billy was cross-examined for five days. Almost all of this time was spent pointing out contradictions between the boy's trial testimony and statements he made at the preliminary hearing, during the grand jury hearings, and at CII. So many were the contradictions that there were four stacks of transcripts on the judge's desk, each about a foot high.

"If a kid really had been molested, he would have told the same story every time," a lawyer told us in the cafeteria. "These kids are just improvising on a story they heard years ago and they can't remember, no matter how much the prosecutors rehearse them. Most people don't want to believe that those who are responsible for the administration of justice could be so corrupt and incompetent as to perpetuate a thing like this for five years. You'd think that somebody would call a halt to it. But those D.A.s are not inordinately gifted people. Their careers in the D.A.'s office are all they've got. They're not the kind of people who could go out and start a new career at age forty-seven and make it big. This is all they've got, and they're not gonna blow it.

"This is not some little case coming out of L.A., or Jersey City, or Medford, Oregon. It's coming out of the heart of the federal government. They have a little office in Alexandria, Virginia, attached to the National Association of District Attorneys, sort of a headquarters for all these crooked prosecutors and their crooked doctors and the whole gang of child abuse racketeers. That's who's orchestrating this thing. They have a lot of support. There were some real estate hustlers who wanted the real estate the McMartin School was situated on, and they did their best to stir up this thing so they could bankrupt the school and force them to sell it cheap. The Buckeys were really cut out for the role. They believed in the system. They believed in the government. They believed in the police. They believed in respect for authority. They believed you should obey."

The lawyer laughed.

"They trusted everybody! Peggy goes off and leaves her purse on the bench when she goes down to the snack bar. In a building full of thieves and cutthroats. This is a courthouse!

"And when all of this stuff came down, they ignored rule number one: When you're in deep trouble you shop and shop and keep on shopping until you find the best lawyer there is. The Buckeys took the first one that was offered to them. They had never been in trouble before. They're not criminals. And they didn't know about rule number one. By the way, Paul and Shirley, don't talk to anyone in that courtroom or anywhere in this building. The D.A.s have their little snitches everywhere. Everything they hear goes straight to Rubin and the judge. But between the time they hear it and the time it reaches the judge's ears the truth goes through several permutations."

The next day, the prosecution called two police officers who participated in the search of the Buckey residence in March 1984. They testified that they found "pornography" on the premises, but that it was not child pornography. On cross-examination they admitted it was nothing more than magazines containing photographs of adult women in a state of undress. What they found was *Playboy* magazine!

What all this strongly indicated was that Ray Buckey's sexual interests focused on adult women, not children. But the media scrupulously ignored that important fact and reported that "pornography" had been found, bolstering the prosecutors' endless insinuations that Ray Buckey's sexual proclivities were perverse. One of the officers testified that he had found a black robe there, another insinuation of satanic rituals. But the black robe was the gown Peggy Ann had worn at her graduation ceremony.

The officer said he had found photographs of children but the children were fully clothed, playing on the school yard. He also told the court that he had found undergarments with cartoons and humorous slogans printed on them, items found in gift shops and novelty stores everywhere. Prosecutor Gunson pinned the garments up on a bulletin board with the grave air of one who had just revealed evidence of unspeakable horrors.

The black graduation gown, the *Playboy* magazine, the photographs of children, and the undergarments added up to absolutely nothing, but Gunson blandly told reporters that, "Taken together, they point to a preoccupation with oral copulation and children."

"Do you feel that Ray Buckey molested children?" Davis asked.

"Yes," the officer answered.

"Did you ever know Ray Buckey?"

"No sir."

"Did you find any evidence of pedophilia?"

"No."

The next prosecution witness to be called was Det. Jane Hoag. She was sworn in and stated that she had been a police officer for seventeen years and was a detective in the Juvenile Division. Her countenance was grim and forbidding; we never saw her smile. Her manner was tough and tight-lipped and her voice surprisingly low. A tough cop. She told of executing her search warrant on the Buckey home where she seized knitting yarn and string, items found in almost every American home but specified in the search warrant because of allegations that children were tied up at the school. Hoag also said she found and seized two copies of *Playboy* and a book entitled *Sex-*

ual Secrets. During a brief recess one of the spectators, a psychiatrist, told us, "I have that book in my library! I hope they don't arrest me." Hoag admitted, on cross-examination, that she found no child pornography, no evidence of pedophilia, and no beige station wagon. She also said she had questioned the boy named in the original complaint and spoken with his older brother and was told that there had been some touching in the shower between the two boys, on the penis.

"Did you explore that?"

"No."

Hoag also testified that when she showed the boy a photo lineup containing a picture of Ray Buckey and several other people, he did not recognize nor identify Buckey and misidentified others in the photographs. She said that when the boy told of being molested he used the words, "private parts," rather remarkable for a two-and-a-half-year-old whom nearly everyone had described as "preverbal."

Monday, May 2. The witness was the mother of a child expected to testify the next week. The woman was about forty, overly tanned but very tastefully and expensively dressed. Her husband was a lawyer. On direct examination Rubin elicited from her the statement that her child had nightmares. More insinuation. But on cross-examination the woman said they were nightmares about monsters, not about the Buckeys. She said that when she went into Ray Buckey's classroom it was "total chaos," that children were climbing on him, sitting on him, jumping on him. She did not like what she saw, the lack of discipline, she said, and spoke to Peggy Buckey, who told her that many of the other parents liked Ray's teaching methods as much as she disliked them. She said that Ray did not look "academic" or "teacherly."

The nefarious *Playboy* was brought into the colloquy again, an extremely poor strategy of the prosecutors because, again, it showed that Buckey's sexual interests focused on adult women, not children. But the prosecutors were now using it to generate the insinuation that Buckey was showing it to children. But there was no evidence that Buckey showed the magazine to children or even had an intent to do so. In fact, no other witness corroborated the woman's statement that Buckey had been seen with a copy of *Playboy* magazine at the McMartin Preschool. She testified that she did not like Ray's teaching methods and Peggy told her the children loved Ray. She took her children, she said, to CII where she was told that they had been molested. She was then referred to a therapist, reinforcing the belief that molestation had occurred. Asked about her participation in the rampant gossip and the vigilante meetings, the woman's answers were vague and somewhat evasive.

Some of the jurors sent a note to the judge, asking where the emergency exits were, because this was the day Nostradamus had predicted there would be a disastrous earthquake. It appeared that we did have jurors who would believe anything.

On cross-examination the woman said that she was shown only brief parts of the CII video, and that in late 1983 and early 1984 the police called her a number of times and told her that her children had been molested at McMartin but would not tell her who was making the allegations. She said she had told them to stop calling her and that she believed at the time that the investigation was a "giant witch hunt." She said she came to believe the allegations only after her daughters were taken to CII, supporting the defense assertion that CII created the case out of nothing.

During recess, as we sat in the hallway, Peggy told us that this woman, like the other parents who testified against her and the others who were not witnesses but were part of the mob now screaming for her blood, was once her good friend—or so she had thought. Many of the others had also been friends. Now, they were trying to send her to prison for the rest of her life. We could see the pain in her face. She is a trusting, gentle, kind woman. She did not believe in the existence of evil—until August 1983. When we asked her if there weren't people in the community who could come in and explain the impossibility of the allegations, she told us, again, that they were not likely to come in because of their fear of reprisals by the police and the Catholic community.

The jurors came out of the courtroom on their way to lunch. They had been behaving strangely for the past two weeks. At the beginning of the trial they were serious, quiet, and reserved. Now, they were acting giddy, talking rapidly, making silly jokes. They appeared, almost, to be going through some kind of neurological breakdown, having learned that they would spend another year sitting in the courtroom listening to the trial. Almost everybody involved in the case, including the judge, had shown signs of weariness and despair—except for Davis and Rubin.

We went out for lunch. The courthouse was in the heart of the inner city where the indigent and the homeless beg for small change from passersby. They are everywhere. The affluent young lawyers in their expensive, three-piece suits never give them anything.

The next witness for the prosecution was the eleven-year-old daughter of the woman who had just testified. In response to Rubin's questions, she said perfunctorily that she was told to play the "naked movie star" game by Raymond Buckey and was photographed in the nude, and that she saw Buckey stab a rabbit.

"Was there a time someone at McMartin put something inside your vagina?" Rubin asked.

"Yes," the child answered listlessly. Reporters obediently scribbled all of this down on their spiral notepads. In the afternoon, when the defense cross-examined, they were gone. At recess the child was showered with hugs and smiles by Rubin, the mother, and her friends. The mother was grinning radiantly throughout the day, at her friends.

Davis began his cross-examination by getting the girl to admit that Lael Rubin, the prosecutor, had visited her at her home at least four times and had gone over questions and answers with her at great length, for hours. Again and again, he began each of his questions with, "When you practiced your answers with Lael Rubin," so that the jury could not fail to get the message. As with the others, he brought out endless contradictions between the girl's testimony in the trial and her statements in prior proceedings.

In the trial the girl had said Buckey killed a rabbit with a knife; in her CII interview she said he did it with his finger. On another occasion she said she didn't see it. She said she had no recollection of the "naked movie star" game and did not remember who was her teacher at the time, nor did she remember any of the children who were present when the "naked movie star" game was played. At CII she said Ray took his clothes off; in the trial she said he did not. Davis also noted that Kee MacFarlane, the CII interviewer, used a black doll to represent Ray Buckey. Three of the jurors are black. Kee MacFarlane, the girl said, told her that Ray was a bad person.

During recess the mother joined her friends, grinning exuberantly, like someone at a social event. In the hallway, a woman who was a friend of Peggy said, "If they really believed that kid was molested, they wouldn't be standing there laughing and grinning. They would be dead serious. They've got to know it never happened. Ray and Peggy were set up! There's something very mysterious about this thing. There's a lot that's being covered up. It was all too well planned, too carefully orchestrated. Everything came together, right on cue. Kids were put into that school to set them up. I can tell you who they are. But there's more. The federal government is definitely involved. Why would there be so many cases that are exact replicas of McMartin, in every state, every county?"

The cross-examination went on for four days, hundreds of questions to which most of the answers were "I don't know," and "I don't remember." This was the child who, in the preliminary hearing, said Ray touched her with his penis but, on cross-examination, said she did not know what a penis was. She also admitted she had received gifts from anti-Buckey families before testifying.

The next witness was Veronica, the younger sister of the girl who had just finished testifying. She was a bouncy little girl, all smiles, eight years old. They didn't tell why, but there were no photographic slides of this girl's anal and genital areas.

Rubin began by asking the girl if she saw Ray and Peggy Buckey in the courtroom. She answered, "No." Rubin looked as though she had suddenly been shot. We saw the hard anger in her eyes. The child did not even recognize Ray and Peggy. Her answers to Rubin's questions were vague. Her testimony was interrupted by the illness of one of the jurors, which halted the trial for several days. Then, Peggy Buckey became ill and the courtroom was dark for another four days.

We spent this time researching the child abuse industry with the help of some very resourceful researchers. We obtained stacks of documents listing the organizations and persons engaged in the child abuse witch hunt, both inside and outside of government. It was astounding. Until then we had never in our wildest speculations imagined that there was such a vast consortium of molestation hunters at all levels of the state government—and this was only California! We were confronted by a stack of paper almost two inches high, listing the commissions, committees, agencies, councils, departments, centers, task forces, programs, boards, child sexual abuse investigation units, child sexual abuse training centers, advisory committees, councils, directors, chairmen, bureau chiefs, program managers, enforcement officers, analysts, coordinators, child sexual abuse units at every level of the state government. There were endless lists of "state nonprofit agencies," in which CII was included; page after page of legislative committees, training centers, legislative subcommittees and task forces, administrators; an endless list of brochures, pamphlets, newsletters, and hotlines. There was page after page of new statutes: a statute to redefine the crime of "touching" to include physical contact through clothing; another allowing parents suspected of child abuse to be charged for costs of the investigation; another to allow a child witness to tell his story to only one interviewer, eliminating the ability of defense attorneys to impeach a witness who had told six different stories; and a statute to increase penalties. This massive consortium represented only the state of California!

Then, there is the "invisible college." The "invisible college" is a sobriquet used by the defense community to describe the nationwide network of corrupt prosecutors, physicians, psychologists, social workers, law enforcement officials, public officials, and media figures who, aside from their many lectures, conferences, seminars, and media presentations, socially and privately share their strategies and generally unfounded theories, such as the premise that "children never lie." There is also a federal molestation hierarchy, apparently orchestrated by the National Association of District Attorneys.

When Veronica returned to the witness stand, two weeks later (May 22), she was a very different witness. She now recognized Ray and Peggy in the courtroom, and testified that Ray had "peed" in her mouth, and taken nude photographs of her. Clearly, the child had been heavily coached during the previous two weeks.

Veronica stated that when she attended the preschool, Ray was wearing a beard. Peggy, and a number of other persons who were there, told us that Ray had never worn a beard at any time. The girl also told of being taken to a "costume house" where there were many bathtubs, with a group of other

180   The Abuse of Innocence

children, and given a bubble bath. She testified that she was engaged in an act of oral copulation but was unable to describe fellatio. She said she was then driven to an airport, taken on an airplane ride, and then returned to the school—all of this in less than three hours!

There was a dramatic turn of events during Veronica's cross-examination, perhaps one of the most important turning points in the trial. Jurors number two and four sent a message to the judge telling him they had observed the little girl's mother signaling to her, with her hands, when to answer yes and when to answer no. The two jurors were brought out, with the rest of the jury out of the courtroom. Rubin turned on them furiously, questioning them about their report in a very threatening manner. One of them said, "I saw the parent making, when a question is asked of the witness, you know, kind of gestures up and down, left and right."

Rubin argued that the two should not be allowed to remain on the jury and questioned whether they could be objective. She said the mother was suffering from an earache and was putting her hand to her head for that reason and not for the purpose of signaling the witness. Co-prosecutor Gunson asked that the judge instruct the jurors to disregard what they had seen and not consider it in their deliberations, nor discuss it with the other jurors. Judge Pounders responded: "I cannot believe that a jury is not entitled to believe someone may have been coaching a witness. A jury cannot and shouldn't disregard that." Rubin and Gunson counterattacked by citing cases in which judges had admonished a defendant for smiling or showing some facial expression in reaction to a witness's testimony. The judge did not appear to be impressed. It was generally believed by the courtroom "regulars" that this incident had done irreparable damage to the prosecution's credibility. The media did not report this important development.

The defense attorneys finished cross-examining the girl a day earlier than the prosecutors had expected, leaving them without an available witness to call. They filled the time by showing the videotaped interview of Veronica's CII interview in November 1983. The interview lasted for two hours, and the child disclosed no act of sexual abuse during the entire session. Veronica's manner and facial expression indicated that she did not want to be there and was annoyed. She played with the dolls. Kee MacFarlane repeatedly drew her attention to the dolls' genitalia, but got nothing from her. Finally, the girl said, "Time to go home." MacFarlane said, "No. Not now . . . I want you to help me figure things out." The girl responds, "I don't want to." At the end of the interview she is exhausted, lying on the floor.

The next witness was the mother of a boy who would be testifying the next week. She was small, blonde, and spoke in a thin little voice, like someone about to break into tears. Her husband, she said, was a real estate broker. When she was asked what signs of molestation she saw in her child, she said that he refused to take off his underwear when he took baths, that he stayed in the bathtub for as long as an hour or more, that he danced in his underwear, and that he was afraid of the dark. She also testified that she heard the boy sing the "naked movie star" chant: "What you see is what you are/You're a naked movie star."

The woman received the letter from the police department in September 1983, asking parents to question their children about molestation at the preschool. She said that both of her sons told her nothing happened to them. She said she was satisfied at the time that her son had not been touched, until he was evaluated at CII. Like the others, she said that before the trial her son was visited by Lael Rubin and Det. Bell, who brought copies of his testimony from the preliminary hearing to his home. All of the children's stories changed radically from the CII interview to the grand jury to the preliminary hearing, and again at the trial. The prosecution was apparently trying to get them to be consistent.

On cross, the mother said she did not see anything unusual at the preschool, nor did she see anything that indicated Ray Buckey was there when her son attended the school. She admitted hearing the rampant gossip of molestation in 1983-84 and said that CII told her to be supportive and referred her to a therapist, reinforcing her belief that her son had been molested. She also said that her son had complained of a sore throat and that, after CII, she viewed the sore throat as a sign of molestation. Suddenly the woman covered her face with the transcripts and began sobbing loudly, too loudly. Shouting. As her jarring shouts echoed across the room, the judge said, "We need to take a ten-minute recess."

The following Monday morning, the woman's son was on the witness stand. He was thirteen years old, almost full grown, and was taller than his parents. He told of playing the "naked movie star" game with his entire class but didn't remember how it was played, nor how many times. This was another child who attended the preschool when Ray wasn't there. Most of the boy's answers about the "naked movie star" game were "I don't remember." He was asked a number of questions about the events Billy had described, but he did not corroborate any of Billy's testimony. He told of being taken to a car wash by Ray Buckey in a van with a group of children, and said the children were undressed, molested, and then dressed again while going through the car wash, an act of preternatural stamina. This, he said, was the Red Carpet Car Wash, the same one the other car wash kid had testified about.

The car wash story had problems. They did not let you remain in the car while it was being washed—they asked people to get out so they could vacuum the rugs and upholstery. In any case, it takes only about one minute for a car to go through the car wash. Was Buckey able to undress a group of children, molest them, and then dress them in one minute?

While the boy told of being raped and sodomized, his father was nonchalantly reading the real estate section of the newspaper, showing no emotion. He looked somewhat serene and appeared to be almost smiling. It was hardly the behavior of a man who believed his son was raped and was once again hearing the sordid event retold. There were endless questions about the car wash. The jurors were yawning. Then, the mother began weeping again and we got another ten-minute break.

After the break Davis read from the transcript of the boy's CII interview, in which he said Ray did not take his clothes off during the "horsey" game. Now he said Ray was naked. There was a long series of questions, and almost all of the boy's answers were, "I don't remember."

On the last day of trial before the three-week summer vacation, Davis wanted to extend his cross-examination for another hour, or into the next day, which would have deprived everyone of one day of vacation. The jurors looked shocked.

The judge exploded at Davis, shouting, his face red with anger, "I'm not keeping this witness. Sit down and shut up!"

Davis complained that the judge was insulting him and replied, "I'm not going to shut up. I'm on to your game."

"Watch your language!" said the judge, threatening him with contempt.

"I have a constitutional record to make," Davis said. "You have never been a defense attorney."

Gits asked the boy a number of questions. His answers did not match up with his prior statements.

At 4:30 Judge Pounders announced, "We will be in recess until July 18 at 10:30." Everyone appeared greatly relieved to be, at last, on vacation from this marathon. That night we spoke with Virginia McMartin. "Danny Davis sold my house. They're demolishing it. I lived in that house for thirty years," she told us, choking back her tears.

Meanwhile, in a hearing taking place only one block from the courthouse where her mother and brother were being tried, Peggy Ann Buckey was engaged in litigation to get her teaching credentials restored. Deputy Attorney General Stephanie Wald, representing the state and the California Commission on Teacher Credentialing, brought many of the same allegations that had been made in the trial and the preliminary hearing. Two McMartin trials were now going on simultaneously, only a block apart. Peggy Ann was arrested and charged in 1984, and in January 1986, the charges against her were dismissed. But the Anaheim High School District refused to reinstate her, asserting that her "moral fitness" remained in doubt. Because her teaching credentials expired during the preliminary hearing, she was, technically, making a new application. Therefore, the burden was once again on her to disprove all of the allegations being made against her.

One of the allegations Peggy Ann had to disprove was that she had killed a horse with her bare hands. According to attendance records, several of the children on Wald's witness list were not enrolled at the preschool when Peggy Ann briefly taught there. She said she had never even met three of the children slated to testify against her. At the end of the hearing, regardless of whether or not the judge ruled in her favor, the credentialing commission had the discretion to accept or reject the judge's ruling.

One of the witnesses for the state, a mother, testified that she still believed children were molested in subterranean tunnels under the school. Four children testified. One said she was not certain she had ever seen Peggy Ann at the preschool. Another testified that he had been molested by "mutants affected by atomic radiation" and "nuclear mutations." Another child accused fifteen people and said he was molested approximately one hunderd times, although he attended the school for only five days. That would be about seven times per hour.

John Wagner, Peggy Ann's attorney, called the state's position "another example of the frightening power of mere accusations," and said that authorities had failed to turn up one shred of evidence to corroborate the accusations against Peggy Ann.

"So the D.A. has to free her, and now another instrumentality of government picks up these old, discredited, discarded accusations and tries to use them to prevent this young woman from resuming her teaching career and putting her life back together."

Deputy Attorney General Wald told reporters that Peggy Ann was "unqualified to teach children ever again."

The high school where Peggy Ann taught had received no complaints about her teaching and her evaluations had been excellent. The hearing was recessed until October because no hearing room would be available until then. At that time, Wagner said he would call 140 witnesses to refute the allegations that Peggy Ann was unfit to teach.

"It would be easier to give up and run away," Peggy Ann said. "But it's not fair to punish me now even more with my career when I didn't do anything wrong."

Monday, July 18, 1988. The vacation was over and we were back in the courtroom. There were more reporters than usual because it was expected that another child witness and her mother would be the next to testify. Insurance adjustors sat in the courtroom every day, taking notes. It was very interesting to note that both CII and the McMartin Preschool were insured by the same carrier. Also interesting was that, according to a recent newspaper story, defense attorney Davis and prosecutor Rubin belonged to the same health club.

"We are back in *People* v. *Buckey*," the judge began, "and all defendants and counsel are present.... I have a request from Mr. Davis for twenty-three items ... the problem I have with that is that we've already had the record read to impeach [the last boy to testify] forty-three times so far in cross-examination and I think that is excessive."

Davis responded, "At one time he says he wasn't sodomized. Another time he says he was. That puts in an issue that I was not able to present to the jury."

There was a problem with the nine-year-old girl who was to be the next witness. Her parents said she was unwilling to testify, and the prosecutors asked that they be allowed to show the jury a seven-and-a-half-hour videotape of the girl's testimony from the preliminary hearing. However, only a few days before, the U.S. Supreme Court ruled in *Coe* v. *Iowa*, that the use of videotaped testimony was unconstitutional because it denied the defendant's right to a face-to-face confrontation with the accuser.

The child had been served with a subpoena. The judge said, "The court can't imprison a child, but can authorize her to be escorted to the court. . . . I need to be sure she is refusing to testify on her own volition and not because of coercion by her parents or others." After two days of lengthy arguments, the child was brought in and interviewed by the judge in his chambers for about thirty minutes. At the conclusion of the interview he stated that he would not permit the prosecutors to show her 1985 videotaped testimony to the jury. The girl reportedly told the judge she wanted no part of the trial and was not willing to testify in any form. The girl's mother testified that her daughter had rashes, and that she once saw her daughter sitting on Ray Buckey's lap. But she admitted the rashes had been present before, as well as after, the girl went to the preschool. This was the girl whose anus Astrid Heger described as "totally destroyed" during the trial, but in the first examination in 1984 described as normal. The child's father testified that when he applied ointment on his daughter's rash he saw nothing that indicated her anus was damaged.

The prosecution disclosed that its next witness would be Kee MacFarlane.

Monday morning, August 8, 1988. Kee MacFarlane was called to the witness stand, sworn in, and asked to give and spell her name. Prosecutor Gunson asked, "What is your occupation?"

"I am a social worker and a director of the Child Sexual Abuse Center at Children's Institute International," she said. She said she was director of the program focusing on sexual abuse of children, that she received a bachelor's degree in fine arts in Ohio, then decided to discontinue her studies in fine arts and begin working with children. "I applied to graduate school at the University of Maryland and . . . began work with a number of organizations that were involved in services to children. I worked with groups that were studying the court system . . . just trying to get to know people and how the system worked." MacFarlane said she had received her master's degree in social work in 1947.

"I was requested by one of my professors to try my hand at writing federal grant proposals. There was a priority announcement for federal funding for child abuse centers, ten of them in the country. And various universities and other organizations were applying for them, and so I was asked to write a grant proposal which hopefully would allow the University of Maryland to be the source of one of these grants and start a child abuse program.

"The grant was awarded.... I helped to organize the people who would run that project." In 1974, MacFarlane said, she went to New Jersey to work at another child sexual abuse program, another of the ten. "It was a major grant. Two of the components of the grant were made into subcontracts of the grant which I was in charge of." She went on to recount her work in New Jersey writing reports and participating in cases with law enforcement.

"Where did you go in 1976?" Gunson asked.

"To Washington, D.C. I went to join the staff of the National Center on Child Abuse and Neglect.... I was asked to come and be a member of the staff of the national center. My job title evolved into 'child sexual abuse specialist.'

"I oversaw a number of programs that were funded by the federal government.... I was in Washington for six years. The United States Congress passed an amendment which provided special emphasis on child sexual abuse ... and they authorized separate federal funding that would be specifically targeted to child sexual abuse...."

In 1982, MacFarlane testified, she came to California, contacted CII, and was encouraged to become involved with the agency.

At the noon recess, Rubin announced to reporters that the remaining three child witnesses would not be coming in, and were unwilling to testify. A cable television newswoman asked her how important these children were to her case. Rubin replied that all of the child witnesses were equally important. The newswoman noted that the loss of the last four children constituted one-third of the case and asked if this wasn't a serious blow to the prosecutors, if they were equally important. Rubin said it was not. The prosecution's portion of the trial appeared to be almost over.

Rubin departed and the reporters converged on Davis, who was standing nearby. "The three remaining witnesss had, in my belief, a greater amount of contradictions and unbelievable accounts than those the jury has heard. They were a liability to any prosecutor," Davis said.

"Have you been forbidden by the court to contest Miss MacFarlane's credentials?" a reporter asked.

"No. She has none," Davis said. "In 1983 she came with a driver's license and a welder's license. I don't contest her credentials. They don't exist. She's a grant writer, raised to management level without having to work up. The prosecution's case is falling of its own weight."

"If all those counts are dropped," the reporter asked, "what effect does that have on the medical evidence the jury has already spent weeks looking at, the slides?"

"It would seem to me that if we start a trial by putting up slides and having three experts comment on one side of the litigation, and never bring on the child, you're either asking the jury to believe the medical evidence and discount any other type of evidence, or you're asking the jury to forget the counts. The medical evidence comes at a time when it was not even settled. The notions of normal are not even resolved by competent study. So the effect is to push on the jury an inadequate showing of proof. It was over our objection that they put on testimony in advance of the child testifying. The judge has the discretion to take evidence out of order. I think it was the judge's appraisal that for their game plan, that's the way the witness load looked. They had doctors available at the time and put them on. The effect, of course, was to preannounce what never was produced in terms of alleged victims, to make the case look larger than it would be eventually. I could have picked these three last children as children that no competent prosecutor could bring to trial. Generally my experience has been that if you have an alleged victim and don't bring him in, the prosecutors drop the counts. But they're not going to do that in this case."

Peggy sat on a bench in the hallway eating her sack lunch, surrounded by her friends and some reporters. One of them asked us, "You said in your book that there are thousands of cases exactly like McMartin going on in every county in the United States. What does that mean?"

"Well," we said, "they're spending billions to build more prisons and courthouses to lock people up for sex and marijuana and consumers of pornography and for touching your children. They're creating a situation very similar to what existed just prior to the French Revolution. They're creating a criminal class so large it takes in almost everybody. That's what happened in France, and the people banded together and butchered the government. The kind of treatment the Buckeys have received used to be reserved for the very poor and disadvantaged, and ethnic minorities. Now, they're going after middle-class, white Republicans by the thousands. And you've got to know there's going to be a day of reckoning. What goes around comes around. Always. Every witch hunt in history follows the same pattern. At first the public cheers and screams for more. Then, once they really understand it they turn on the witch hunters in anger and revulsion. It's also another way [for] the government to get into our bedrooms and snoop."

After several hours of extremely dull direct examination by Gunson, reporters and spectators began leaving the courtroom. Davis repeatedly objected on the ground that the witness's answers were vague, nonresponsive, and irrelevant. Gits stated, during a recess, that the prosecution was trying to minimize MacFarlane's role in the case. He and Davis asserted that they intended to show that she was an integral part of the prosecution in selecting the witnesses and that her career and reputation were at stake in this case. The defense attorneys were also seeking, over the prosecutors' objections, to delve into MacFarlane's alleged romantic relationship with former ABC-TV newsman Wayne Satz, to show that they acted in concert to create the mass hysteria that surrounded the case. One of the lawyers said they had lived together and vacationed together at that time. MacFarlane's new husband was sitting in the courtroom, listening, but showing no emotion.

Prosecutor Lael Rubin stated that the prosecution would rest its case by Labor Day. The defense attorneys said they may take only six months to present the defense portion of the trial. We were nearing the home stretch.

Tuesday afternoon was spent with Gunson showing brief portions of videotaped interviews of the McMartin children by MacFarlane, then asking her why she said certain things to them. This was being done in anticipation of the defense's cross-examination, which would attack the validity of MacFarlane's techniques. MacFarlane gave overly lengthy explanations and defended her techniques.

During the mid-afternoon recess, Peggy told me, "Kee MacFarlane told one little girl that 'all of your friends said it happened.' They hadn't even interviewed her friends yet!"

I don't know whether the lawyers understood it or not, but once you've seen a large number of these videotaped interviews, several things became apparent: (1) they were using a form of Pavlovian conditioning on these children so they would give the desired response to key words and phrases. The reward was praise and the promise of even greater approbation from the parents and the community; in the other direction was anger, loss of love, ostracism, all the things a child fears most; (2) there was also an element of hypnotism. They narrowed the child's focus to one thing and kept it there; and (3) exhaustion—nobody knows exactly how long these interviews lasted or at what point the camera was turned on or off, but in most of the videotapes we saw in this and other cases, at the end the child is clearly and visibly suffering from extreme fatigue and is involuntarily falling asleep on the floor. This, too, is a well-known brainwashing technique. It is not therapy. It is modeled on the classic police interrogation: "All the others talked so you might as well tell us."

Another important element was that interviewers began by making a line drawing of a human body and then establishing what terms the child uses to identify the sexual organs, so that the tapes could be used in court and there would be no confusion as to what specific organ the child was referring to.

On cross-examination, Gits asked Kee MacFarlane about her use of the phrase, "Ray's creepy friends" in the interview with Melinda. "Don't you think that implies that Ray and the teachers are bad?" MacFarlane said she did not.

Referring to the use of naked "anatomical" dolls, Gits asked her, "Aren't you suggesting to the child that naked games were played?"

"I think I'm suggesting that it may come back to her later."

"When Melinda says she doesn't remember any [naked games] you said, 'I know 'em all because other kids told me.' Do you think that puts pressure on Melinda to remember games that she might otherwise not remember?" Gits asks.

"Yes."

MacFarlane was slender, blonde, with a pleasant voice. She looked and spoke like an actress.

"Do you think that having naked dolls with anatomical parts tends to suggest to the child naked games, naked people?"

"No, I don't believe that," MacFarlane responded.

"You made the statement, 'Every kid from the preschool came in and told me.' Do you think that statement puts pressure on a child?"

"No."

"You said, 'That's why we wanted to use puppets. We wanted them to get real brave because more than sixty kids have come in and told yucky secrets, and every day more kids come in and tell us what went on down there.' Do you think that statement might put undue pressure on Melinda to comply with what other kids said?"

"That statement was true," MacFarlane responded.

" 'And we found out all the scary stuff was just a trick to scare the kids to make the kids think that somebody would hurt their moms and dads or hurt them. We found out.' Doesn't that tell the child that you know that something happened?" Gits inquired.

"Yes."

"In this interview, you are the source of contagion, right?"

"Objection."

"Sustained."

" 'All the kids' mommies and dads now know what happened at the school, all the touching, all those sneaky little games.' Do you think by using that statement, and authority figures as sources of knowledge is putting pressure on her?"

"I'm telling her all the parents came to see me and now it's okay," MacFarlane answered.

"Before that did Melinda make any statement about touching?"

"I don't really remember."

" 'Well, I'm glad you're not so dumb, Snake.' Do you think by telling Melinda that, you are telling her she's dumb if she didn't agree?"

"No."

" 'The mommies and daddies are so glad the kids are telling.' When you say 'this stuff happened,' are you telling Melinda touching happened at the preschool?"

"I think I'm trying to tell her I know something happened. I use the word, 'stuff,' on purpose."

"Do you believe these statements tell the children you believe molestation happened at the preschool?" Gits asked.

"No."

". . . with the use of grownups and authority figures."

"No."

" 'Now, Snake, I don't think those teachers should still be teaching children, do you?' Do you think that calls for an opinion?"

"Yes, I think it calls for an opinion."

"Don't you think it tells Melinda the teachers are molesters?"

"No. Not at all."

" 'Well, Mr. Snake, you and any puppets you want to use can help us figure it out so no more kids will have that yucky stuff happen to them. . . .' Do you think this is one of the most fundamental pressure points? 'All the other kids said it happened.' Parents, Kee, authority figures. Isn't that telling Melinda that kids are getting raped and molested? 'Secret police are watching Ray all the time.' Don't you think that statement might influence Melinda to believe that Ray is a bad person?"

"Yes."

" '. . . and we're gonna make sure that no more kids get hurt.' What did you mean, 'we'?" Gits asked.

"I was referring to myself."

" 'If you have a good memory like all the other kids.' Isn't that putting pressure on Melinda?"

"I'm not asking Melinda to comply with my statement," MacFarlane said.

MacFarlane's answers were long and dissembling. Gits read from the transcript of the CII interview: " 'I think we should beat up Mr. Ray. . . . What a bad guy! Don't you think he's a bad guy? He's not gonna do this any more to kids, is he?' Did you encourage Melinda to beat up the Ray doll?"

"In a manner of speaking, yes."

"Is there a clinical reason for doing that? A therapeutic reason?"

"It can be."

There was a series of questions in which Gits attempted to show that she was principally a grant writer rather than a therapist or an "expert." He ended his cross-examination with: "Looking back on Melinda's interview . . . do you think Raymond Buckey ever had a fair chance?"

"The issue of 'fair' may have to be left to the courts to decide," MacFarlane answered.

"No further questions at this time, your honor."

Gits sat down.

Davis's voice angrily echoed across the courtroom. "You probably heard

Mr. Gunson say that that wasn't the purpose of the interview, just now. Did you hear Mr. Gunson say that the purpose of your interview wasn't fairness to Mr. Buckey?"

"No."

After starting with a loud bang, he lightened up his style and just let MacFarlane talk. She was talking too much. Instead of a simple yes or no, she was giving needlessly long answers and seemed to be trying to minimize the apparent bias in her assessments. Davis asked her if she had ever had children of her own. She replied that she had only stepchildren she had acquired in her marriage eight months before. He asked her who had been her teachers in child sexual abuse.

"You indicated you had training from the FBI."

"No," she said. "I was the trainer."

"And who trained you before you trained the FBI?"

MacFarlane was unable to come up with any names. Instead, she simply answered, "I attended numerous workshops." It appeared that it was she who designed and taught the system now being used in similar cases all over the country.

"Did you ever sit down with police officers and did they tell you what law enforcement needs to do in interviewing a child who may have been molested?"

"Yes."

"Who?" Davis asked. Again, MacFarlane could come up with no names. Davis asked her, "Could you please search your records for the names of police officers who trained you in child molestation?" Again, MacFarlane was unable to come up with any names.

Davis asked MacFarlane if the dolls really assisted in determining whether a child had been molested. Her answer was equivocal. "It depends. I don't think you can make an overall statement on these dolls.... They might be able to assist children in conveying things, especially children that have a hard time verbalizing things. They can provide another way to talk about something by saying, 'Can you show me what that looked like.'... I don't associate the dolls with having to do with whether the answer is reliable or not.... They give you another piece of information that doesn't match what the child says.... I think the reliability has many different ways of observing it."

"Do you think that by disrobing a doll and exposing a child to what appears to be an erect penis, that that's suggesting things to the child?"

"Well, we worked very hard on the dolls to have them not appear to be an erect, stimulated penis. In fact we tied them down. If you're asking about whether it can ever affect a child, it's one the research of the last five years has been investigating and ... there's absolutely no evidence in the research that they do that ... providing incorrect or false information just because they've got these dolls."

After the recess, the defense attorneys disclosed that they had subpoenaed Wayne Satz, the former KABC-TV newsman, to inquire about his alleged romantic relationship with Kee MacFarlane at the time he broke the story on Channel 7. Davis asked that the judge order MacFarlane not to discuss this matter with Satz between now and the time he would come to court the next day. Prosecutor Rubin protested that, "There are others in the courtroom who are in contact with Wayne Satz."

"Who?" the judge asked.

Rubin named a husband-and-wife writing team who are working on a script for a television film about the case. The husband was not present but his wife, sitting in the audience section, jumped up and shouted, "That's a lie! That's a lie! That's a lie!" The judge smiled as she asserted that she had never even met Satz.

The next day, the woman's husband approached us in the hallway and said, "Do you think I should go in and talk to the judge?" We told him, "Of course. If you take that lying down, you'll be getting a lot more harassment." The man went into the judge's chambers and spoke with him, and, after lunch, the judge allowed him to stand and speak. He said, "I was very disturbed to hear of the allegation by Miss Rubin that I and my wife talked to and gave testimony to Wayne Satz. I want to go on the record, under oath, that I do not know Mr. Satz. I have never talked to him. I have never seen him. Thank you, your honor."

The cross-examination continued. Davis asked MacFarlane why she had used a black doll to represent Ray Buckey in her interviews. She gave a long, excessively verbose answer asserting the necessity of distinguishing the teachers, one from another.

The next morning there was a hearing on the admissibility of the relationship between MacFarlane and Wayne Satz. Attorneys representing MacFarlane and Satz argued that it violated their right to privacy. Defense attorney Davis then gave a long list of occasions on which MacFarlane allegedly provided Satz with information for his television broadcasts, giving the exact dates and the names of the children involved. Davis also stated that she appeared on Satz's newscasts, soliciting parents to come to CII, and that MacFarlane provided him with exclusive information that other media did not get until after Satz's newscasts.

"In June of 1985," Davis said, "Mr. Satz and Miss MacFarlane took an approximately three-week trip to the South Pacific. It may be appropriate to establish that they lived together." He said that evidence of such a relationship would show that MacFarlane's child interviews were tainted. The judge ruled that this relationship was relevant and should be considered by the jury. He also told Davis, "This is the longest offer of proof I have ever heard." But he added, "It seems clear to me that it is relevant that if Miss MacFarlane imparted to Mr. Satz . . . an exclusive exposé, a great news sotry that would thereby enhance his career and enhance her career . . . [it] seems self-evident, and that's what the offer is."

The cross-examination resumed.

"The reason you used ugly-faced dolls is because you wanted to impress a negative perception of Mr. Buckey . . . and then you go on to use a black doll with funny boobies to represent Peggy Buckey. Right?" Davis asked.

"I couldn't say . . . for the most part children picked the dolls," MacFarlane responded.

"Do you see any harm in telling a child what other children said?"

"Harm? Well I can see it can become a problematical issue in legal cases but it doesn't have any effect one way or the other. You cannot say that it is harmful. In fact I did it because I saw a potential for children sitting and clamming up. I did it to prevent that."

". . . You can't distinguish whether what the child says thereafter is something they actually experienced or something you're telling them other kids said. Isn't that one of the issues?"

"Objection. Speculation."

"Sustained."

"Didn't you tell, in the grand jury, that you did not tell one child what the other children said? . . . Combining your telling [a child] that 'naked games were played at the school because all the other kids told us,' and then to say 'the kids really didn't tell us, the puppets told us,' what was the combined effect of that?"

"What I was trying to do in telling her [that] I already knew was to take from her any burden she might have about the repercussions of telling. . . . I was offering the puppets as a medium to communicate."

"And when you did that, did it occur to you that you might be creating a sort of realm of fantasy in which children might make false accusations in which they believe they're just pretending?"

"No. It's a major issue because there's not any data to show that has ever happened. Any! But because it is consistently raised, all of the studies with the use of anatomical dolls have shown that the use of those dolls does not in any way lead to false reports about abuse, and there are now, because of this case and the many other cases in which these issues have been repeatedly raised in court, we now have research that looks into issues of suggestibility. There are five or six articles which address these exact issues which you are raising. And they are debunking the idea that by suggesting to children even leading and misleading questions suggestive of child sexual abuse they are debunking the idea that children just pick up and just repeat it. It's information that I didn't have when I did these interviews. Now, five years later, the research is out there. Numerous studies . . . and the resistance of children to these questions is in the ninety-three to ninety-nine percentile. . . . There is now research on the subject."

"My gosh! It sounds like there have been a lot of current studies that really back up your techniques. . . . Could you be a little more specific please? The name of the author, the title, the date of publication?" Davis asked.

"I can't recite that off the top of my head," MacFarlane said. She said there were a number of recent articles that concluded that children could not be led to make false statements. She did not note that there were also a number of articles, including that of Dr. William McIver, which concluded that the use of dolls for this purpose was worthless. A 1988 article in *Contemporary Psychology* (volume 33, number 1) states that these techniques

> cast aside professional and scientific standards and substitute reliance on child-care workers' zeal . . . risking the emotional adjustment of incorrectly identified victims and the freedom of wrongly accused perpetrators. In so doing they ignore the limitations such as the unexamined validity of their assessment procedures and the possibility that their highly directive and suggestive questioning tactics unwittingly elicit fictitious abuse scenarios from young children. . . . Some of the statements are hairraising. . . . They advise caseworkers to refrain from videotaping the earlier interviews in which self-reversals are more likely, and to film only later sessions when the accusations are clearer. Interviewers are advised to use candy and trinkets to encourage children to 'talk about molestation,' a procedure that sounds suspiciously like bribery and would be forbidden to researchers and most psychological evaluators.

The article further states that, "There is remarkably little scientific evidence to support many of their assertions," characterizing them as "professional vigilantism."

The article asserted that "The MacFarlane group seems to view such acts as an adult ever touching a child's genitals, and a child or an adult disrobing in front of the other, as heinous sex crimes. These widely disseminated views and recent highly publicized cases have produced a climate of hysteria about possible sexual abuse, and unfounded charges of witchcraft, ritual murders, and other wild accusations against parents, teachers, day care workers, club leaders, coaches."

Davis asked a series of questions to establish that in one of MacFarlane's interviews, the "naked movie star" game was first mentioned by her, not the child. According to the transcript, the child repeatedly denied ever playing naked games.

"Just taking the act of a child beating a doll, do you feel there is a difference in interpreting what is going on when a child beats a doll of their own volition, as opposed to a child beating a doll at the suggestion of an adult?" Davis asked.

"It can be different. It can be the same. It depends on the child. . . . It may be the same, whether they're invited to do it or whether they do it on their own."

"To the extent that you adopted this doll-beating technique, you cannot direct us to the identity of any child in the McMartin case that initiated it in their own right—right?"

"Not off the top of my head."

"And did any of these children, of their own volition, initiate the doll-beating?"

"Not that I recall."

"You suggested it to the children?"

"I don't remember."

"Have you ever been tested for your credentials as an interviewer?"

"Not that I can think of. . . . Over the last several years I have been one of the trainers. . . . Several years ago, California changed its licensing requirements for psychologists and required that they be trained in the area of child abuse and . . . I've trained a number of these and I also teach a course at USC which meets the requirements for psychologists."

Asked about the sources of funding that supported her work, MacFarlane said, "I thought what we needed to do was stop seeing children, write some grants and seek some funding . . . so I just began developing the idea of the multidisciplinary center and writing grants. . . ."

"You accept, don't you, that in some of these interviews you urged these little children to beat up on these dolls?"

"Yes."

"Do you have any meaning in your mind for 'Gestalt therapy'?"

"Yes."

"What is your understanding of Gestalt therapy?"

"Gestalt therapy is a mode of therapy used for adults. . . ."

"And what is your understanding of some of the preliminary aspects of Gestalt therapy?"

MacFarlane was unable to give a definition of Gestalt therapy.

On Wednesday, August 31, 1988, after a lengthy hearing, Judge Pounders ruled that Kee MacFarlane's romance with former television newsman Wayne Satz was not relevant to the trial and would not be told to the jury. MacFarlane admitted that she and Satz had had a personal relationship during the early months of the case, but said the relationship did not begin until after she interviewed the children in the case. Although Davis offered various documents that indicated the two worked together to enhance the high publicity that surrounded the case, Judge Pounders said Davis had failed to show that Satz's relationship with MacFarlane affected the investigation. The judge also said that MacFarlane's credibility was becoming more of an issue because of her apparent evasiveness in answering certain questions which, he felt, she should have been able to answer clearly.

Davis said he strongly believed that the romantic relationship between

Satz and MacFarlane was critical to understanding the case. "The fact that she would broadcast her opinions even before the grand jury convened is in itself evidence."

The jury was brought in and Davis resumed his cross-examination. He played a portion of one of MacFarlane's CII interviews on a television monitor. The child appeared to be enjoying himself and perceiving the interview as a game. He shouted with wild enthusiasm. When the television was turned off, Davis asked, "Miss MacFarlane, from what you observed and recall from that interview, was [the child] scared? Terrorized?"

"I think that has to be judged in the context of more than a little piece like that. But I would say that what I have known of him and the other pieces put together, yes."

"And at the beginning of this piece you're introducing the name of a game and the fact it may or may not be a naked game, correct?"

"Correct," MacFarlane answered.

"Don't you feel that that is overly suggestive to a child to tell the child that it's naked?"

"Absolutely not!"

"I'd like to explore a little of what you said about children naming names of other children . . . looking at the names in this piece on 'horsey game.' . . . Is this the context in which the child names names of people who played the games?"

"We asked the children. That's one way we name names. They pick them out of photographs. That's another way. . . . There are specific places in these interviews where I ask the child, 'Was this child involved?' or 'Did they get touched?' or 'Were they naked?' And if the child confirms those direct questions, I would generally pass that along."

"You would generally pass that along by telling somebody in the police department, wouldn't you?" Davis asked.

"Yes. We're required to do that."

"As a consequence of this conversation with [the child] about this 'horsey game,' did you suggest [that] he might be stupid? Chicken?"

"If you're referring again to my talking to the puppets, I described that every way I know how."

Davis asked MacFarlane to read from the transcript of the interview: "MacFarlane: All right, Mr. Alligator. Are you going to be stupid?"

"And then you introduce in your words, not his, the 'naked movie star' game, correct?" asked Davis.

"Yes."

"And wasn't the essence of what you learned from him that he hadn't seen or heard about this 'naked movie star' game until he heard this song? This chant?"

"Well, that's what he said in this segment."

"And was your response . . . that he was dumb?"

"No. That means you're smart."

"Wouldn't the inevitable impact of this exchange be that any child would figure that you're calling him dumb?" Davis asked.

". . . It was an attempt to reach out [with] the puppets to help the child," MacFarlane responded.

"After he said he didn't see any 'naked movie star' game, you asked him who took pictures for that game, correct?"

"Yeah. I asked him who took pictures of the 'naked movie star' game."

During recess, the husband of the husband-and-wife television-writing team and we were standing near the elevators. Lael Rubin was standing only a few feet away. The television writer walked toward her and said very softly, "Miss Rubin, excuse me." She turned her back and walked toward the elevator door. He followed her and said gently, "Could I ask . . . what was the source of your statement that I provide information for Wayne Satz?"

She turned on him and said furiously, "I do not want to talk to you at any time. I do not want to have any conversation with you under any circumstances. Please go away and leave me alone." Her eyes were wide with anger. She got into the elevator and disappeared.

Back in the courtroom Davis continued his cross-examination of MacFarlane.

"When you talk about 'horsey,' you were the one that added the names of those games and descriptions to that interview, weren't you?"

"No. Some of the children said 'horsey game.' "

"Anyone in this case call it 'horsey game' before you mentioned it?"

"I don't recall."

"How about the 'tickle game'? You're the one who put those words, 'tickle,' in , aren't you?"

"No!"

"Isn't it very easy for you to say there are lots of unnamed children out there in other interviews, without identifying the child?"

". . . I did not make up a single game. These all came by children or by information I had beforehand."

"Did you not introduce every one of the games to [the child] in this interview?"

"No. Of course not."

"You introduced the 'naked movie star,' didn't you?"

"I'm not disputing that I introduced games. You asked me if I introduced every single game and I'm saying I referred to 'lookout.'"

"Your technique . . . Miss MacFarlane, is to take perfectly innocent games and convert them, by the insertion of words like 'naked,' and 'yucky' into accusations of crime, isn't it?"

"No, it is not."

Raymond Buckey: key defendant in the McMartin case; a teacher at the preschool; grandson of Virginia McMartin, founder of the preschool; and son of codefendant Peggy McMartin Buckey. © 1987 Los Angeles Times.

Peggy McMartin Buckey: codefendant, director and teacher at the preschool. © 1987 Los Angeles Times.

William R. Pounders: the Superior Court judge who presided over the case. © 1987 Los Angeles Times.

Lael R. Rubin: coprosecutor. © 1987 Los Angeles Times.

Roger J. Gunson: coprosecutor. © 1987 Los Angeles Times.

Daniel G. Davis: defense attorney who represented Raymond Buckey. © 1987 Los Angeles Times.

Dean R. Gits: defense attorney who represented Peggy McMartin Buckey. © 1987 Los Angeles Times.

The media looks on as jurors review the McMartin Preschool site where much of the alleged sexual abuse occurred. The school was eventually torn down.

One of the classrooms at the McMartin Preschool.

"Then how do you justify, after he tells you 'tug-of-war,' the introduction of the word, 'naked'?"

"I don't think we're talking about the same game. I asked him if any games were played and he says, 'tug of war.'"

Davis read from the transcript of the interview: "MacFarlane: Mr. Pacman, do you remember any naked, tie-up games like other kids remember?" The child answers, "No."

"How can you justify inserting the suggestion that there were naked tie-up games when he just told you about tug-of-war?" Davis asked.

"I can justify it by dozens of other children who told me they were tied up naked, showed me with the dolls, told their parents. . . ."

"After hearing it from the parents, you'd include it in your tapes, right?"

"[The child] says, 'We just wanted to protect each other. . . .'"

"Protect each other from what?" Davis asks.

"'So they wouldn't hurt us.'"

"Contrary to your representations, [the child's best friend] was interviewed three days after [the child], wasn't he?"

"Objection."

"Sustained."

"And did you make an effort to force little Tom to make an accusation of oral copulation on my client in that interview?"

"Absolutely not."

"Your sequence in the technique with Tom was to first talk about sexual acts and then attempt to have him demonstrate them—correct?"

"No. . . . The goal was to take it all and show anything significant to the parents."

"What we saw Tom doing, demonstrating a little doll with its penis in the mouth of another little doll, do you think that had any pornographic effect?"

"Objection."

"Sustained."

Davis reads from the transcript of the CII interview again.

MacFarlane: When Ray comes out, what does Ray do? How does something get in that little hole?
Tom: Well, nothing gets in that little hole.
MacFarlane: Remember when we figured all that out? That's already in the secret machine?
Tom: Oh yeah. Lemme think. . . ."
MacFarlane: Remember that? How did that get in there? Let's just show how that happened. That'll be easy. And that can be in the secret machine, all gone. How did it happen?
Tom: Well, Ray kicked him.

"Does it seem apparent to you at this time," Davis asked, "that . . . he's saying nothing happened to his bottom?" Davis asks.

"No. It doesn't seem apparent. It seems to me that he's having a hard time with those questions. . . ."

"What you were really trying to do was to get him to demonstrate sodomy with the dolls so you could show it to the parents. Wasn't that really what you were doing?"

"Mr. Davis! I never set out to try to prove to three hundred plus parents that I could make them believe by looking at some segment of tape that their children had been molested! I wanted them to see what I saw because they know their kids better than I did . . . so they could know in their own minds whether something happened to their children."

Davis again reads from the transcript of the videotaped interview: "[MacFarlane:] Now remember when we were figuring out what went in that hole? Now let's see how it went in there. That would be easy for us to figure out with these dolls." Tom says he knows. MacFarlane says "Wow!" Tom says, "He pokes him." MacFarlane says, "What did he poke him with?" Tom says, "A chair." MacFarlane says, "How about remember when he poked him with himself?" Tom says, "Oh yeah." MacFarlane says, "Okay . . ." and Tom says, "His foot." MacFarlane says, "Remember when we talked about his penis? You give me the secret for the secret machine so we can see what happens."

"In that section," Davis asked, "is it fair to say that you were telling him to remember that it was a penis and not a chair or a foot that hurt his bottom?"

"I was asking him to ask himself if that's what happened. . . ."

"Doesn't someone in your field have some responsibility for anticipating the effect that their statements have on children?"

"Yes. And that's why a lot of research is being done in the last seven years for exactly that reason. . . ."

"He saw you demonstrate with the dolls, didn't he, after you used the word, 'penis.'"

"Yes."

"Is he demonstrating what happened or is he just going along with the suggestion you're making?"

"Objection."

"Sustained."

Davis read from the transcript again: MacFarlane: "Thanks for helping us figure that out. And how about when he had that yucky stuff in his mouth? How did that get there? What's that look like?" And then Tom: "Well, you taught me about that."

"It was your intent to have him accuse Ray Buckey of oral copulation when you began the next section, wasn't it?" Davis asked.

"No. It was never my intent to interview children for the purpose of accusing. . . ."

"Do you see yourself as a link in the process that led to the children making these accusations?"

"I believe that I enabled children who had not been able to describe things, before they came to me. . . . My job was to uncork the bottle, to see what they had to say, once they had gotten over the fear they had."

MacFarlane was on the stand for five weeks. She repeated her statement that the use of puppets and dolls could not induce a child to make false allegations of child sexual abuse. The defense played the videotape of a 1984 ABC-TV newscast broadcast, during which MacFarlane was briefly interviewed by Wayne Satz. The case was discussed by both MacFarlane and the blonde news anchorwoman as though there was absolutely no question of the defendants' guilt. "Will the victims be able to testify against those who molested them?" the anchorwoman asked. Also, the statement was made that this case is "only the tip of an iceberg."

"What, if any, are the problems of children being exposed to media hype?" Davis asked MacFarlane.

"Objection. Speculation."

"Sustained."

Davis played a portion of another CII-videotaped interview and then asked, "So when Arthur says, 'I never knew that until my mom told me,' did you assume at least that his mother must have been talking to him about what happened to other kids at McMartin Preschool?"

"The fact that a parent talks to a child doesn't necessarily in any way have to affect what they say or what may have happened to them," MacFarlane countered.

"In your presence did Melinda say [that] nothing happened at the car wash?"

"She said no to questions whether anything happened at the car wash." On redirect, MacFarlane said, "One of the things about child sexual abuse that is so predominant is that children can mask their feelings about it and, as I said, the literature has shown that 20 percent or more of children that have been sexually abused show no symptoms that anyone could pick out as fear just from looking at them when they are admitted to hospitals or health clinics. There is nothing that anybody checks on as a fear response."

MacFarlane was no menial social worker. She was one of the leading figures in the child sexual abuse hierarchy created by the child abuse legislation of the 1970s. She was extraordinarily fluent. As Davis had said, she went from nowhere to the very top of this hierarchy in a very short time.

As we shuffled out into the hallway with the rest of the journalists, spectators, lawyers, and their paralegals Shirley saw Peggy sitting on the bench waiting for her ride home. She had enjoyed visiting with Peggy, but the fierce, angry stares of Davis and Gits hovering over us were unpleasant, and they have constant access to the judge. She did not. So by this time Shirley was just greeting Peggy with a friendly hello and continuing to walk.

Paul did not. He enjoyed flaunting his contempt for Gits and Davis and their overly dominating manner. Sometimes, while talking to Peggy, Paul glanced at them with just a vague trace of a smile, affecting the countenance of a big thug looking down at a child. Once when Peggy was complaining that the lawyers were overly bossy and arbitrary in their behavior toward her, Paul told her, "You have got to understand that those lawyers are not your bosses. You are the client. You are the boss. They are your servants. They do not tell you what to do. You tell them what to do." Davis and Gits were sitting only a few feet away, watching, but said nothing.

The prosecution called two teachers from a preschool in San Diego to refute defense evidence that Ray Buckey was attending college in San Diego and working at a preschool there, a hundred miles away, and could not have been at McMartin during the time when some of the child witnesses who said he molested them were there. The teachers said that Buckey had indeed worked at their preschool for several months, that nobody had complained of his behavior there and, in fact, he had been given an award in recognition of his outstanding work there. The teacher testified that this award was given, not as a matter of course to everyone who worked there, but only to those who actually contributed exceptionally valuable and conscientious work. Prosecutors Rubin and Gunson looked jolted. Apparently they had not expected this.

During this period Buckey attended college in San Diego and lived in San Diego. He did occasionally come home to visit his family for a day, according to his mother, Peggy, but this would hardly have given him sufficient time to organize an army of naked nuns to engage in drinking blood, satanic rituals, dismembering animals, and raping infants.

The prosecution called Dr. Carol Berkowitz, a pediatrician who testified, in another case, that there is no finding inconsistent with sexual abuse. There was an anus blazing from the slide projector screen. The photograph was taken several years after its owner last attended McMartin, making the testimony tenuous to say the least. What the prosecution seemed to be doing was simply adding one more doctor to the already excessive array of physicians testifying for the prosecution, knowing that many people worship doctors and naively believe in their infallibility. Berkowitz's testimony was brief and uneventful.

The next presentation by the prosecution was the showing of the videotaped CII interviews of the child witnesses, filmed in 1984 and used as evidence to obtain indictments before the grand jury. The interviews were extremely long and boring, but there were certain techniques used uniformly in every one: The interviewer did almost all of the talking. In a situation where children are alleged to have been abused, it would seem logical that the best way to get them to talk would be simply to assure them that they were absolutely safe and protected, and let them talk, asking, perhaps, if anyone had ever hurt them. But in these evaluations the interviewer did virtually all of the talking. In every videotaped interview offered, the child is told that large numbers of children and parents had already told the "secrets."

"Ray never touched me," one of the children said. He was told, once again, that all of the other children and parents knew: "Johnny told us. You're just as smart as he is, aren't you?" The child was trapped. He was the only one "out of line." He was alone. Finally, after a lengthy interrogation, he reluctantly pointed to the doll's genitals. The interviewer loudly exclaimed, "What a great kid! You're so smart! Your mom and dad will be so happy!"

"It was my mom and dad who told me," one of the children said. But he was in a position where he couldn't back out. All these people were "so happy"; what would they say if he recanted? Looking at the child's face, it was clear that the interview hadn't unearthed any mind-boggling secrets. He was bored, tired, and asked to be allowed to leave.

"No, I wasn't there when that happened," one child said when pressured to make accusations of sexual abuse against the teachers. Then he asked to be allowed to leave. But MacFarlane said, "No! We're not finished yet." Finally after much prodding the boy said, "Well, I heard about it." MacFarlane exclaimed, "Your mom and dad are going to be so proud!" The child was lying on the floor, exhausted, arms outstretched, and tried to crawl away, pleading, "I want my mommy."

"Where did Ray's penis go? In this hole?" MacFarlane persisted. The child gave no audible answer. "Any other place his penis went? Anything else come out of Ray's penis? What color was it?" The child answered tentatively that it was yellow and smelled like "poo," and asked, once again, to be allowed to leave.

"How about in the bottom? Remember what went in the hole?" MacFarlane arranged the dolls in the position of pederasty.

"You told me about that," the child answered. When he finally made the dolls simulate pederasty, MacFarlane cried out, "You were great, Pacman! You are amazing how much you know! I wonder if Peggy did any of those things."

"She didn't hurt anyone," the child answered.

"Did she ever touch you on your private parts?" MacFarlane asked.

"No." Asked again to accuse Ray, the child gave no answer.

"Remember what Ray said he'd do to you if you told what he did?"

"No."

The child asked to be allowed to leave, and tried to throw the Ray doll out of the window, but MacFarlane stopped him.

The videotapes were surprisingly amateurish. The speech on the sound track was almost unintelligible and the jurors complained of this. The interviewer was not asking what happened to the child; she was telling what happened: "Mr. Ray can't hurt you any more. There is a policeman that follows Ray wherever he goes, and if he tries to do anything to the kids, he goes to jail. All the moms and dads know about this."

In one of the interviews MacFarlane selected a doll and the child took one. After a long time and many questions, MacFarlane asked the child, "Did you ever see anything come out of Mr. Ray's penis?" The child made the doll nod. "Wow! You're so smart!" MacFarlane told him to beat up the Ray doll and the child complied. Shirley leaned over and whispered to me, "I'd hate to be convicted by a snake or a cow." How could anyone define this as "evidence"? There was not one spontaneous "disclosure" on any of these tapes. These interviews were shown to the jurors, hour after hour, day after day in the darkened courtroom while the lawyers were off doing something else.

All of the children were told that large numbers of children and parents had already told of sexual abuse at the preschool. Virtually all were told, "We're trying to see who are the smartest kids." When they did make tentative accusation the interviewer exclaimed, "You must not be a dummy after all." On all of the videotapes shown, the children repeatedly denied witnessing any act of sexual abuse of children: "Ray never touched me," and "It never happened to me." The interviewer ignored these exonerating statements and continued to coax and pressure the child for accusations. The child was told that he was stupid if he failed to provide accusations against the teachers.

All of the children on the tapes were told that the teachers should not be allowed to teach children any more. When a child was coaxed or tricked into placing the dolls in a position of pederasty or oral copulation, a sudden torrent of praise was heaped upon him: "Yea! What a great kid! You're so smart! Your mom and dad are going to be so happy!" But the children's faces betrayed no stress fear, shame, pain, none of the emotions one would expert to see on the face of a child telling of being sexually abused. All exonerating statements were ignored and all accusations, no matter how tentative, were met with boisterous praise.

We had lunch with a journalist from London who was writing a piece on McMartin. Visibly distraught, she told us the same kind of witch hunt had been going on in England. "We're going to have a whole generation of children who've been taught to lie!" she said. "And we're going to have social problems like we've never seen before!"

The next witness to be called by the prosecution was a twenty-two-year-old woman who had attended the preschool as a four-year-old and then, at the age of fourteen, was employed there as a teacher's aide. Virginia McMartin had read a newspaper story about her and invited her to come and visit her at the school. The young woman said that her experience at McMartin had inspired her to make the decision to become a teacher of preschoolers. Until then, she had planned to become an interior decorator, like her father.

The prosecutors' stated purpose in calling the woman was to elicit evidence that Ray Buckey did not wear underwear and that his genitals were sometimes visible. They seemed to be grasping at straws.

The witness was very short and had a neurological defect that made it necessary to use crutches. She wore glasses. She appeared to be shy and spoke in a thin, childlike voice. However, the woman impressed nearly everyone as being genuinely sweet and kind and bluntly honest in her answers. She testified that Ray and Peggy were kind to the children and that she never saw any evidence that children were abused or mistreated. She testified that she never saw the defendants engage in any improper conduct, that she never saw anyone take pictures of naked children, mutilate or mistreat animals, or play any "naked games." She said that parents were continually coming and going, that she never heard the "naked movie star" chant, that she never saw children taken away from the school except when Peggy took her own niece and nephew home. She said that none of the children ever appeared to be frightened when Ray or Peggy took them to the bathroom. She said she had been friendly with Ray and that they talked about music but never dated.

As for Buckey's attire, the woman said he sometimes wore shorts but that they were not particularly short and in fact extended almost to his knees. She testified that on occasion, when he was sitting, she could see part of his genitalia, but that it could have been his scrotum rather than his penis. It was her perception, she said that Ray was unaware that his genitals could be seen. She also stated that she had never told anyone that she saw his penis "dangling out."

"How do you feel about Peggy?" Gits asked her on cross-examination.

"Then or now?" she asked.

"Then."

"I liked her very much."

"Don't you like her now?"

"I'm not sure."

"Is that because of what you heard and read in the newspapers?"

"Yes."

"Is that because of Lael Rubin?"

"Objection."

"Sustained."

"Did you ever observe anything that led you to believe that Peggy Buckey was anything but a kind, caring person?"

"No."

The woman also said she had been interviewed by the FBI four times. She was excused and the prosecutors called Virginia Harper, who had been an investigator for the district attorney's office, in order to rebut their own witness. Harper testified that the last witness had told her that Buckey's penis was "always showing . . . always dangling out." On cross-examination the previous witness said that she was never interviewed by Harper and that she had never said she saw Buckey's penis "hanging out."

We had expected the prosecution to finish with a bang—some dramatic, earth-shaking coup that would throw the jurors and everyone in the courtroom into a coma, some shattering blow that would leave the defense in shambles. Instead, Rubin quietly told the court, "We will call no more witnesses."

And so the prosecution rested, leaving some important questions unanswered: (1) what happened to the last four child witnesses, and (2) what happened to the 120 people on the prosecution's witness list who did not testify? When reporters asked the judge to disclose the names of the 120 witnesses who did not come in, Pounders testily refused, stating that their right to privacy would be abridged and that he would not subject them to the embarrassment that had plagued others in the case. And then Judge Pounders said, "This case has poisoned every person who has had contact with it."

The following week Judge Pounders dismissed thirty-five of the counts at the request of the prosecution, leaving only sixty-five. Defense attorney Davis accused the prosecutors of trying to "cut their losses" by eliminating the children who told the most bizarre stories. As for the last four children, Davis said the written information provided by the prosecutors showed that the witnesses' reasons for not wanting to testify were inconsistent with the statements made by Rubin.

Davis also argued that the jurors should view the preschool to receive an accurate impression of the school's size and dimensions. He further stated that people viewing it for the first time are surprised to see how small it is.

The prosecutors sought to block the jurors' viewing of the school, as they had since Davis first moved the court to require it several weeks before.

Monday, October 17, 1988. The defense began. Peggy excitedly told us outside the courtroom, "If you knew who our first witness was you'd fall on the floor! I can't tell you who it is but you'll see in a little while."

Gits and Davis were there waiting for the bailiff to unlock the door. They had a tough job ahead. Children, cops, various "experts," and doctors all said it happened. America worships doctors, cops, and experts, no matter how incompetent and corrupt they may be. The prosecution provided the court with sixty-one witnesses and nearly a thousand exhibits, a tough act to follow. But the doctors contradicted each other, the girls' hymens were intact, almost all of the kids told five different stories, and some of the exhibits were less than enlightening. What were we to infer from the ninety bags of soil stored in the D.A.'s evidence room? And were the graduation gown and the rubber duck sent to us by the devil?

But when the judge entered the courtroom, instead of the defense's first witness, there was Gregory Mooney, the attorney, and Bernard Johnson, father of the child who was the subject of the original police complaint that started the case. Johnson was the ex-husband of Judy Johnson, who reported Ray Buckey's birdlike flight through the air, and his companions, the goat man and the elephant. And the blood-drinking, satanic festivities.

Johnson and Mooney were there to resist the defense subpoena of the child, with the strong support of prosecutors Rubin and Gunson. In support of his motion to quash the subpoena, Mooney had brought Dr. Edith Wolf, a psychologist from the South Bay Counseling Center, of which Mooney's wife, Colleen Mooney, was the director. Wolf testified that forcing the boy to come to court might produce "regressive" behavior such as nightmares and bed wetting. Interestingly, Wolf testified that the child had said that *Mooney* did not want him to testify. Mooney addressed the court and stated that the child "should not be ordered to testify or appear in this proceeding in any fashion. . . . I ask the court to take judicial notice of information that is already in the record, that not only is this child a victim of sexual assault, not only did he undergo the divorce of his parents, the death of his mother, but he also underwent the death of his only sibling. To involve him in these proceedings in any way, shape or form, however mild and gentle, I think the court has sufficient evidence already in the record to take judicial notice of the trauma he has suffered."

"They are going to go to any lengths to keep this kid from coming in and talking," one of the lawyers told us. "If he talked, the whole case would fall apart." The boy was not called by the prosecution to testify. He was never interviewed nor videotaped by CII. He is now seven years old. Davis asserted the boy told two doctors that his father, not Buckey, molested him.

"We are not attacking [the child]. We are refuting George Freeman's testimony," Davis said. "In fact [the child] said, 'It was my father. Ray Buckey didn't do these things.' We don't have a single statement from [the child]. One of the lynchpin assertions in this case . . . against Mr. Buckey. . . . If [the child] has sufficient recollection to come in and say who did it, and when they did it, that person will not have been Raymond Buckey. He can also explain that this was going on at a time when he was in the custody of his parents and Raymond Buckey was incarcerated, so it would have been impossible for him to have done these things."

The judge ordered that the boy be brought into court the following day so that he could speak with him privately to find out whether he would refuse to testify, and if so, for what reason—whether it was his own independent decision or one made under pressure from others.

The following day, Gregory Mooney appeared at court without the child or the father, and said that "irreparable harm" would be done if the boy were forced to appear in court. The judge angrily told him, "You've taken it on your own to cancel a direct order of the court! If he's not here today, I'm going to be very angry. . . . I'm going to issue arrest warrants." About two hours later, the father arrived and spent about forty-five minutes in a private meeting with the judge and attorneys. The judge finally put off the matter for a week but told the father he would be held in contempt if he failed to produce the boy. The defense wanted the boy to testify because the boy had been taken to Harbor-UCLA Hospital, where he told a doctor, "Daddy poked me," according to hospital records. A week later, a physician at Kaiser Hospital made a written report stating that, "Eight days ago, child reported that father poked him in anus with stick." A police officer filed a report stating that the boy said his father "poked him lots of times." The same officer reported that the mother had said that the boy returned from visits with his father with a red anus.

A half day was spent by the judge interviewing each of the jurors separately to inquire whether they had seen a Geraldo Rivera television program on satanism and satanic "ritual abuse" of children. Only four said they had seen any part of the program, and none said they had seen or heard parts pertaining to the McMartin case. The show consisted of a high degree of sensationalism. An off-camera voice had stated that over a thousand children were still suffering "from the horror they experienced at the McMartin Preschool." Later on in the, program, Bob Currie, surrounded by a group of women, declared that Manhattan Beach was the "molestation capital of the world."

Wednesday morning began with more arguments on the defense attorneys' request that the jury be taken to see the preschool. Rubin and Gunson argued vigorously against allowing the jury to see the school, asserting that it was not in exactly the same condition it was in the years 1978 to 1983. Davis had the school cleaned up and painted after it was set afire and abandoned for four years. The prosecutors were also asserting that the shrubbery and foliage had been trimmed, prejudicing their assertion that passersby could not see into the school grounds from the street. Davis said this could easily be corrected, but that the one fact that was immutable was the smallness of the structure, of which, he felt, the jurors were unaware. "There are sixteen different misconceptions that could . . . in a half day, be resolved," he said.

"I've already presumed," Judge Pounders responded, "that there is a strong compulsion to grant the jury viewing. Your position is well taken." The judge said he was startled when he first saw the school and observed that it was about half the size he had imagined it to be "and I assume the jury's going to have the same confusion."

The arguments went on and on but nothing was resolved. The prosecution had rested the previous month, but after days of arguments over various points, we felt like spectators who had just bought a ticket to the World Series and then had to sit for several days, waiting for the game to begin while the referees and officials argued. The jurors' faces reflected the same impatience.

A large portion of the next day was consumed by questioning the jurors, separately, one by one, about a plethora of news stories that had appeared in nearly every California newspaper. This was not a trivial matter; it is one of the great scandals of all time, finally brought to light. The newspaper stories were about a "jailhouse snitch" who, like George Freeman, was used as a witness in criminal cases to report on the "confessions" of defendants.

The man in question, Leslie White, demonstrated to reporters how easy it was to do this, and said that inmates who fabricated testimony for prosecutors were rewarded with leniency, witness relocation money, or the dropping of charges against them. White said he had worked for prosecutors for eleven years, trading perjury for leniency, and had testified as a prosecution witness in more than a dozen felony cases, including murders. "It would shock the public to know the entire truth." White said. His disclosures prompted a massive review of murder convictions in Los Angeles County during the past ten years and massive newspaper coverage. What was indeed strange was that in every one of the newspaper stories, George Freeman and McMartin were scrupulously blanked out. There was no mention of either, in spite of the fact that it was George Freeman's lengthy appearance in the McMartin trial that blew the cover off this "jailhouse snitch" scandal and prompted two enterprising reporters to investigate and go into the county jail to interview Leslie White and other jailhouse informants.

The judge asked each of the jurors if he or she had read any of the stories. Most said they had not. Two said they had read the first few lines and stopped. The judge ordered them not to read any of the stories and not to listen to anyone speaking about them. If they had read the stories, and we strongly suspect some of them did, the only consequence would be to give them greater insight into the case and how the system worked. Apparently the system didn't want that.

Wednesday, October 19, 1988. The defense finally got started. Defense attorney Davis announced, "Your honor, I would like to be sworn as the first witness for Mr. Buckey." Another attorney was brought in to ask the questions as Davis sat at the stand.

Davis testified that when he went to county jail and met with George Freeman in March 1984, Freeman told him that Ray Buckey had denied any involvement in molestation of children and said the case was a setup by a mother who had put her child in the school in order to initiate a lawsuit against McMartin. Davis said he went to talk to Freeman because he had been warned by another attorney that a known snitch (Freeman) had been placed in Buckey's cell, a person "who would concoct a story about my client." Davis denied having threatened Freeman and said that he did not even know at that time that Freeman would be called as a witness. Davis reiterated that Freeman told him that Buckey never confessed to anything.

The next witness to be called by the defense was the director of Northrop University's Institute of Technology. Prosecutor Rubin strenuously objected, saying that the prosecution had not been given time to prepare for this witness. There ensued a long argument in which the judge agreed with Rubin that this was not fair to the prosecution. Several lawyers told us during lunch that California law does not require the defense to give the prosecution advance notice of its next witness. "In any other case, that's true," one of them said, "but in McMartin anything goes. They seem to making up their own rules as they go." The witness's testimony was brief. He read records that showed Ray had had "perfect attendance" at the school, seven hours a day from October 23, 1978, to January 17, 1979, a time period in which he was accused of molesting four of the child witnesses. Since Northrop University is at least ten miles from the preschool, he could hardly have been at McMartin butchering animals and drinking blood with naked nuns.

The next witness was a former teacher at the preschool, an important witness because the prosecution brought no adult eyewitnesses and this woman was present during the time period in which the crimes were alleged to have occurred. Mary Lou Enochson said she saw nothing that raised any suspicion that the children were being abused. "I'm positive it didn't happen," she said. She also testified that she had never seen Ray Buckey at the school, that she had seen no children playing naked games, and that her own two children were happy at the preschool.

There was a meeting that week with the seven-year-old boy whose mother launched the case. His father and his attorney, Gregory Mooney, and both the defense and prosecution lawyers were present. The judge questioned the boy about his willingness to testify.

The next defense witness was Janet Key, a small, slender woman whose two daughters attended the preschool. One was by then fourteen and the other twenty-four. Mrs. Key, the mother, appeared to be hardly more than twenty-four herself. She testified that her youngest daughter attended the school during the time period when the prosecution's child witnesses were there, that she never saw any naked children, nor any children being mistreated at the school. She also said she saw Ray Buckey only once or twice during the two years she brought her children there and that she never saw him teaching or interacting with children. The issue of shrubbery and foliage was raised again. Contrary to the prosecutors' representations, Key stated unequivocally that, "There wasn't shrubbery on the front. There were trees, but you could see all the way to the back. . . . I walked and drove by there several times a day."

"During the time Corey attended, did she ever express any resistance to going to the school?" Davis asked.

"No . . . she loved going," the mother answered. This drew a strident "Objection!" from Lael Rubin and a lengthy argument over the admissibility of the question and answer.

Gits argued against Rubin's motion to strike the answer. "Even though there were eleven complaining witnesses in this case, the reality is that other people would have to have known about it. . . . There were, allegedly, entire groups of children molested in this case . . . and certainly Corey would have been in a position to have known about it and would have suffered anxiety."

"I don't agree with anything you've said, and certainly not that," the judge said. "Whether or not Corey was molested does not prove that the other children were not molested. If you are going to parade in hundreds of children who say they were not molested, we're going to stop you, because that does not prove that children maintained in this case were not molested. . . ."

"The question wasn't 'Was the child molested?' " Davis countered. "But if she expressed something that the jury might consider as evidence that she was very discontented about going to that preschool, one reason might be that every day she went there, the defendants were viciously molesting children. . . . But if other mothers say their children were happy, it becomes circumstantial evidence that maybe what's being claimed by the complaining witnesses is not consistent with the true nature of the activities at the school."

"We're not going to go through this with each child!" Judge Pounders warned. "The idea that there may have been dozens or hundreds of children that didn't express any of these things doesn't prove any issue in this case. If you're trying to show that these children were not molested, then the relation to what you're trying to do is even more remote, and I don't find it relevant."

"I respect your vision," Davis said. "I just don't see why it is [that] I can't ask the parent if her child liked the school."

"What is it relevant to?" the judge demanded. "You're trying to show that the child was not molested but that she would have been unhappy if other children were molested and she knew about it. That's a very remote and speculative inference that you want the jury to hear."

"I don't know a single child," Davis said, "that would have anything but objections if they went every day . . . they were raped and sodomized and animals were slaughtered. It's just not the sort of thing that children would be happy to go back to school about. . . . Life just isn't that way, if it's a good school and nothing happened."

"What you've offered is so speculative that it's not relevant," the judge said.

"Then I move to strike similar behavior observations testified to by (prosecution) parents and children in this case," Davis asserted.

"Your motion is denied."

"I'm saying you almost have to be a defense attorney to see it."

"I don't like that argument!" the judge bristled.

"It's fairly clear to me as a defense attorney," Davis said, "that if you have happy children, then for the likes of Billy saying massive molestations are going on, on a daily basis, it is circumstantially inconsistent in that kind of environment. . . ."

"It is speculation. The objection is sustained."

Rubin cross-examined Key briefly but wasn't able to discredit any of her statements. Her final question, however, was very calculated, "Isn't it true that your daughter has psychological problems?" Both defense attorneys indignantly objected and were sustained. A friend of the family told us, in the hallway, that the only psychological problem Corey had ever had was some distress over the separation and divorce of her parents five years ago.

In the morning the defense called Corey, Key's fourteen-year-old daughter, and the girl was indeed a surprise. She was somewhat taller than her mother, extremely thin, with straight, blonde hair cut to shoulder length. Her classic beauty and poise held everyone's attention, and she spoke with candor, a calm, lucid intelligence, and a subtle wit that twice brought a chorus of laughter from the jurors. They definitely liked her. She testified that she did not remember ever seeing Raymond Buckey at the preschool or anywhere else, that there were no naked teachers or children and no naked games. When she was asked about the "naked movie star" chant, she said it was "just one of lots of rhymes that I've heard all throughout going to school that were stupid like that." She recalled that when the case first surfaced "everybody went berserk."

Corey was not the slightest bit intimidated by Rubin on cross-examination and said, later, that she was amused when Rubin glared at her. Rubin, who had been zealously insistent that her child witnesses have a support person present in the courtroom, argued strenuously against Corey having a support person in the courtroom. Nevertheless, she testified with great poise and told a reporter the defense attorneys had not rehearsed her "because it would have sounded fake. He told me to just tell the truth and not be afraid."

Corey's older sister was called and testified that she had never observed anything that raised any suspicion that children were mistreated at McMartin. No secret rooms, no naked children, no naked games.

A Mrs. Jacobson, who had also been employed at the school, testified that she watched over the children as they slept during naptime in the afternoon, and said that Ray Buckey was not at the preschool during the time she was there. She said he came to the school "maybe two or three times a month" to pick his mother up, and that he stayed only about twenty minutes. She too said she had never seen Peggy naked.

During the examination of these women there were many questions about the foliage in front of the school, and whether the foliage hid the school from passersby. Both Gits and Davis repeatedly pronounced it "foilage."

On Friday, November 4, 1988, Judge Pounders stated that, "There is no way to obtain testimony" from the child whose mother launched the case in 1983. "It is my impression," the judge said, "that [the child] has something that occurred at the preschool that he doesn't want to talk about." Pounders made the statement after a meeting with the boy.

The defense called Charlotte Cravello, another former teacher at the McMartin Preschool. Before the jury was brought in, Rubin protested that Cravello had been unable to remember certain dates when she recently testified at Peggy Ann's hearing across the street, suggesting that she was not competent to give testimony in the trial. When Cravello was brought in, she was lucid and gave clear, succinct answers to the lawyers' questions. She, too, testified that she had seen no naked children at the school except when they put on their bathing suits to go into the wading pool, and that she had never observed anything that raised the slightest suspicion of molestation. She said all the children were kept together during naptime, that she had sat there on a chair and watched them, and that parents were continually coming and going. She stated that one could see into the school from the street, and that the green areas on the prosecution's diagram were deceptive because there were trees, not shrubbery.

"Was there foilage [sic] there?" Davis asked.

"I'm not certain," Cravello answered.

She also said that no child was permitted to go out on the swings alone because it was unsafe, that she had seen no "naked movie star" game, no *Playboy* magazine, no secret photographing of children, no harm done to animals, no secret room.

"Were children taken away secretly in the afternoon?" Davis asked.

"No, because everybody was waiting together."

"Were children snuck back through a side entrance?"

"There was no side entrance."

"How old are you?" Davis asked.

"I'm seventy-seven."

Cravello said that if she had difficulty remembering dates, "it's not my age. I've never cared about dates."

Gits offered into evidence the death certificate of a Mrs. Shelton, who taught at the school but had died since then. The defense wanted to read her testimony from the preliminary hearing. She had testified that she had taught Spanish at the school and that her daughter had attended. She, too, said she had observed no naked children, no secret room, no adults photographing naked children, no children who appeared to be terrified, no child being abused. "They were happy," she said, adding that the teachers were "all very caring and took good care of the kids." Shelton testified that she saw nothing that led her to believe anything improper happened at the school.

The next morning, when the judge entered the courtroom and asked, "Anything to take up before we bring the jurors in?" Davis angrily stated that Leslie White, the notorious "jailhouse snitch," had been placed in close proximity to his client, Ray Buckey, in the county jail. "He is testifying for the prosecution in several cases, and my concern is that he may come in and fabricate a story about my client," Davis said.

Judge Pounders turned toward the prosecution table and asked if the prosecution had anything to say. Rubin and Gunson innocently denied having any knowledge of this, but when the judge asked if Leslie White was on the prosecution's witness list, Rubin hesitatingly admitted that White was indeed on their witness list. It was disclosed later that the prosecutors had on their witness list not only George Freeman and Leslie White, but a total of seven jailhouse informants known to trade perjury for leniency.

A reporter obtained documentary evidence that "jailhouse snitches" were routinely rewarded by the district attorney's office with early release and witness protection money for fabricating the "confessions" of other inmates and testifying against them in trial. He went to the county jail and interviewed a number of these inmates and learned that this was not just an occasional, isolated occurrence but a well-organized system that had been in place for decades. He wrote that "approximately eighty other jailhouse informants are kept in a protective housing unit in Los Angeles County Jail," and that the informants "are planted next to jailed defendants for the purpose of eliciting details . . . that can later be used by the informant to embellish fabricated 'confessions.' " It was also disclosed that there was a law enforcement officer in the county jail whose main function was to act as a liaison between prosecutors and these informants.

Several defense attorneys told the media that the D.A.'s office used these jailhouse informants in almost "every high-publicity case where the evidence is weak." Wilbur Littlefield, head of the public defender's office, stated that prosecutors use jailhouse informants "in well over one hundred cases a year" in the downtown courthouse alone. "The question," he said, "is how many people are in state prisons and on death row as a result of manufactured testimony."

The next witness was Mary Ann Jackson. Before Jackson and the jury were brought in, Rubin asked for a ruling from the court that the attorneys not ask questions pertaining to Jackson's loss of her home and life savings as a result of being charged in this case, "because it might tend to evoke sympathy from the jurors."

Jackson walked to the witness stand and sat down, wearing a white dress, stylish earrings, her hair beautifully coifed. She was remarkably pretty and glamorous for a woman over sixty years old. She stated that she arrived at the school each morninq about eight-thirty and somebody was there to greet the children at the gate. "We took turns. . . . I had music time, rest period, I would be preparing juice and crackers, then I would read a story."

Jackson said she could see into all the classrooms, and never saw anything out of the ordinary in Peggy's classroom or any of the others.

"How did Peggy Buckey get along with the children?"

"She had a gift. She loved children," Jackson said. She said that she had never seen any evidence of molestation or any improper conduct at the preschool. No naked children, no naked games, no secret tunnels or rooms. "It was an especially happy place to be," she said. Jackson also told the court that she had never met Ray Buckey except once, very briefly, when she was introduced to him at an open house, until she appeared in court for her arraignment. Jackson was one of the five defendants whose charges were dismissed in 1986 by District Attorney Ira Reiner, who said the evidence against them was "incredibly weak."

Lael Rubin attempted to show trivial contradictions in Jackson's testimony, but the witness held her own gracefully throughout this sparring match.

"You described a game you played with children called lookout."

"I can't agree to that. I didn't play with them. On rainy days, near the gate, unless it was pouring, the parents came to the room. It wasn't anything organized. It was just something they did." Jackson grinned. Angered, Rubin asked her what was funny.

"Well, it wasn't a game!" Jackson smiled. "They just watched to see which child's parent would come first. We'd take an umbrella to the car. Just something they did."

"You seem to be smiling. Why is that funny?"

"It was not an organized game. You said, 'How was the game played? I don't remember any game called "lookout." ' "

Following the noon recess, at one-thirty, before the jury was brought out, there was a discussion between the judge and the lawyers about one juror. Prosecutors Rubin and Gunson argued strenuously for her removal, asserting that she had laughed, sighed, and manifested other signs of disrespect when prosecutors and their witnesses spoke. Gits seemed to be agreeing with them. She was one of only three blacks on the jury and appeared to be the most sympathetic to the defense. The judge also said he was angry with her but she was not brought out and no action was taken.

When they finished up with Jackson, Davis asked on redirect, "Is there a location at the school where someone might have inserted an object into the private parts of children without anyone knowing it?" Jackson replied that there was none.

"What did I tell you before you came in here to testify?"

"To be myself and tell the truth," Jackson said.

Jackson was then excused. Afterward a lawyer who was in the case during the preliminary hearing spoke with us. "If the Buckeys don't win this trial they have no hope of getting it reversed on appeal. All of the appellate judges in this state are Deukmejian's appointees. And they know Deukmejian wants a conviction."

During the next three days, three witnesses testified briefly in rapid succession: a U.S. Postal Service mail carrier, a fire extinguisher serviceman, and an insurance inspector. The mailman testified that "everything looked normal," that he saw "happy, kids, normal kids."

"What about the foliage? Do you have any recollection of the foliage?" He did not remember the foliage, nor did he remember having seen any child alone in the school yard, nor having seen any children being taken off the school yard.

The insurance inspector testified that he saw no evidence of molestation and that he would "most certainly" have included it in his report if he had. He said that Virginia McMartin was very kind to the children and always took time to answer their questions, even when she was busy.

The fire extinguisher man also said he had never seen any evidence of improper conduct at the preschool. At the end of the day we were told that the next witness would be Peggy Ann Buckey. There was a murmur of excitement. Peggy Ann is an uncommonly charismatic and outspoken person, and it was expected that Rubin's cross-examination of her would be assaultive.

When we arrived in the morning Peggy Ann was sitting on a bench in the hallway near the courtroom door, waiting while the lawyers were inside, arguing. She was slender, with light brown, almost blonde, hair and she was wearing a soft cotton print dress, white and pastel blue, looking very elegant. Hers was not the gaudy look of the typical L.A. blonde, but a softer, more natural beauty. Sitting with her was a paralegal who worked for the defense.

Inside the courtroom Gunson and Rubin were arguing zealously to have Peggy Ann excluded as a witness on the grounds that she was employed by her brother's attorney, Davis, as a paralegal and that she had both "a familial and economic interest" in the case. Pounders looked skeptical and said he did not think ten dollars an hour would "buy perjury" from her. The judge ruled that she was a crucial witness and denied the prosecutors' motion. Rubin asked for a ruling from the judge prohibiting the defense from saying anything about Peggy Ann having been held in jail for two months, lest it evoke sympathy from the jurors. The jurors and Peggy Ann were brought into the courtroom. She raised her hand, swore to tell the truth, and took her seat at the witness stand.

Gits began by covering the main events in her life from childhood. Peggy Ann told the court she had lived in Manhattan Beach all of her life until she went to college. She graduated from the University of California at Irvine, she said, and then went to the University of Southern California for a year to get her M.A. in special education.

Gits brought out a large chart on posterboard showing the dates Peggy Ann taught at the preschool each year from 1978 to 1982. She too denied having observed anything that raised the slightest suspicion of child abuse. Gits brought out the diabolical black robe taken during the search of her home which, she explained once again, was her graduation gown. He brought out the boxes of underwear with the humorous slogans printed on them which, she said, were nothing more than a joke. These were the items that Gunson darkly told reporters were evidence of an interest in oral copulation and pedophilia.

Gits took Peggy Ann through the period when she was employed as a ranger at Wind Cave National Park. She said that she and her brother, Ray, had planned that he would come to Wind Cave and drive back to Los Angeles together, and that these plans had been made in June, long before Judy Johnson told her story and the investigation began, refuting George Freeman's testimony that Ray had gone to South Dakota to hide child pornography. She also said that her brother's suitcase was open most of the time he was there, and that there was no pornography, no film cannisters, just clothing.

Gits asked Peggy Ann about her camera. The prosecutors had asked every witness about cameras in an attempt to create, by insinuation and repetition, the belief that photographs of nude children were taken.

"I worked with aphasic and deaf children," Peggy Ann said, "and one of the techniques that I used is called 'language experience,' where you take a photograph of what they're doing on a field trip and you put it on a posterboard and you write what happened so they visually see what the experience is, and then they get the written words along with it. I bought one of those little, tiny 35mm cameras." Peggy Ann said she bought Ray a ticket to fly to South Dakota so she would not have to drive back alone. She testified that she had seen no naked teachers at the school and the only time she saw naked children was when they went into the wading pool and teachers would help them get into dry clothes afterward. She denied that she or any of the other teachers ever touched the genitals of children at the preschool.

"When did you first learn of the investigation?" Gits asked.

"My mother called me when I was in South Dakota. . . . Ray was supposed to come and meet me. . . . I thought it would be fun to take a couple of extra days and see things along the way and drive back. . . ."

"Did you ever see your brother chop up a horse?"

"No."

When she was asked about the "naked movie star" game Peggy Ann said she first heard of it "on the Wayne Satz TV show."

Hearing this young woman insulted with abusive questions about molesting infants bruised our sensibilities. Davis was even less genteel. He loudly asked if she "lured little children into being photographed in the nude," which she denied. At least he was keeping the jury awake. But this was an indispensable part of the defense process. The prosecutors would throw all of this at her on cross-examination and the more times the jurors heard her denials the more the denials would become impressed upon their minds. One by one, Gits and Davis covered all of the allegations, the naked games, trips to farms, houses, the car wash.

"How was your relationship with your mother and your brother?"

"Excellent."

"Would you lie for them?"

"No."

Rubin began her cross-examination. She asked Peggy Ann why she stated on various radio and television talk shows that she was teaching at the preschool for only five weeks when, according to the chart pinned up in front of the jury, she was there at other times. Peggy Ann explained that these programs were about the allegations made at the preliminary hearing, four years before, "and I referenced my answers to the time frame of the allegations in the preliminary hearing because that was all '60 Minutes' was on."

"Your honor, I move to strike the last sentence," Rubin said.,

"The last portion is stricken," Pounders ruled.

Rubin went on, day after day, pressing Peggy Ann with variations on the same question, and Peggy Ann continued to give the same explanation. The questions seemed rather pointless when there was, right before us in large, black letters, the dates when Peggy Ann was present at the preschool. If it was her intent to deceive the court, why would she have this large piece of posterboard pinned up on a pedestal for all to see?

"You've made various other public statements on radio and television that you were only at the McMartin Preschool for five weeks—correct?" Rubin's face was hard and relentless as she hammered Peggy Ann with her questions.

"Not the way you're saying it," Peggy Ann responded. "Those interviews were about the preliminary hearing, not my whole life. . . ."

"You haven't corrected the misstatement you made in the letter of 1986 —correct?"

"That's not correct."

Rubin continued with her endless variations on the same question and resurrected the defunct charges against Peggy Ann that were dismissed three years before. It wasn't having much impact; the jurors' attention was drifting away and so were the reporters. The audience section was empty and there had been no reporters in the courtroom for days. The trial was interrupted for two days because of the illness of one of the jurors. During this time, Judge Pounders held a bail reduction hearing and reduced Ray's bail to $1.5 million and cut Peggy's bail by $100,000, saying that the original amounts were excessive. "Is it reasonable to hold someone in jail for five years without determining his guilt?" Pounders asked. Prosecutor Lael Rubin argued stridently that, if released on bail, Buckey would pose a risk to society, inferring presumably that he would immediately begin drinking blood, dismembering beasts, and touching children. The judge said he did not believe that either defendant posed a risk to society.

Despite the reduction, Ray was far short of the amount required to obtain his release. In a newspaper story published at the time, it was reported that his family gave up real estate valued at $1.5 million and their life savings to pay his attorney. Various people had offered to pledge real estate to satisfy the bail. A group of friends and supporters of the Buckeys happily speculated that, "Ray just might make it home for Christmas!" Their hopes were diminished when Rubin told the court that the county had the right to assess the true value of any properties before they could be pledged in lieu of cash bail. Peggy told us that the judge had reduced the bail on his own without a motion from the attorneys.

We had lunch with a group of attorneys who were in the preliminary hearing and others who followed the trial because they had lawsuits going on behalf of former defendants. We told them we had heard that Judge Pounders reduced the bail on his own without a motion from the defense attorneys. They were astounded. "Are you sure of that?" one asked.

"That's what Peggy told [us]. We had a long conversation about it."

"I find that astounding!" one of them said. "They should have immediately moved for a bail reduction when the judge dismissed the thirty-five counts, two months ago!"

Rubin continued her cross-examination of Peggy Ann. She had Virginia's personal diaries and was reading from them as she questioned Peggy Ann.

"Isn't it true that in January, 1979, you in fact had lunch with your mother and grandmother in Manhattan Beach?"

"No."

"Your honor, could I approach and show Miss Buckey a portion of exhibit 38.... Does that refresh your memory that you had lunch with your mother and grandmother on January 16, 1979?"

"No, because it doesn't say..."

"If there's an explanation," the judge said, "your attorneys for the defense can ask you about it...."

"But the question misstates what it says," Peggy Ann protested.

"Your honor, I've asked the court for the third time to admonish this witness...." Rubin interrupted.

"Do you have a recollection of having lunch with your mother and grandmother..." Rubin asked.

"No."

"With the court's permission I'd like to show the witness exhibit 36.... Does that refresh your recollection that you had lunch with your mother and your grandmother?"

"Your honor, I can't answer it, because the way she's asking it is not what it says here," Peggy Ann protested. This haggling went on for hours and days. The jurors were drifting off.

"Do you have a recollection of working at the preschool in 1979?"

"I think I was there for the Christmas party...."

"And did you assist with the children?"

"If I was there I probably did if they needed some help."

The jurors were staring off into space. Finally, court was recessed for the weekend.

Monday morning, Rubin continued her cross-examination. She had stacked before her an arsenal of manila folders, bound volumes of transcripts, and yellow notepads. She had, clearly, spent a great deal of time preparing for her assault on Peggy Ann.

"Now, you testified that . . . you were not in Manhattan Beach in '79 and '80 . . . . Isn't it true that . . . there were weekdays when you found yourself in Manhattan Beach at the McMartin School?"

"During that year I was at the John Tracy Clinic and that was from nine to five every single day. . . ."

"Showing you exhibit 38 . . . do you find an entry there that you had lunch with your grandmother?"

"Yes."

"And does that refresh your memory that you had lunch with your mother and grandmother on that date?"

"No."

It went on and on. She was being asked about incidents that, if they occurred at all, occurred nine and ten years before. We wondered how many people remember where they had lunch on January 6, 1979, or with whom. But the questions went on and on, in an attempt to smear and make Peggy Ann appear deceptive or untruthful. At noon, during the recess, we asked Peggy Ann, "What is the big deal about the fact that you told Mike Wallace you were only at the school five weeks and now it says you were there in 1979?"

"Well, if I went to visit my mother and helped set up the tables, I wouldn't call that teaching," Peggy Ann said. The time she spent at the school in 1979 appears to be extremely negligible. Three mornings.

Back in the courtroom, Rubin continued to batter Peggy Ann with questions about her grandmother's diaries. The jurors were slouching and drooping. None of them was looking at the witness or the prosecutor. One was peacefully sleeping. Before court was recessed for the day, Judge Pounders told the jurors that there had been an administrative hearing across the street involving Peggy Ann Buckey, and ordered them to "avoid learning of the outcome of that hearing, and if you do learn of it, draw no inference from it." After the jury had left, we heard Pounders tell the lawyers that he strongly suspected that Judge Gruen, the administrative law judge presiding over Peggy Ann's hearing, would rule against her and recommend that her teaching credentials not be restored because if she began teaching again and anything untoward happened, the judge would share the blame. In other words, Gruen's decision, like most of the others in this case, would be a political one, rather than one based on the evidence. We thought of Peggy Ann, who put a lifetime of hard work and honest hopes into a career teaching deaf and aphasic children, only to be barred from ever teaching on the basis of such ludicrous "evidence."

That evening we were invited to speak at a meeting of an organization of psychologists. When we had finished, one of them picked up a copy of *The Politics of Child Abuse* and asked, "Why did you write about this subject? Were you abused as a child?"

"Battered, neglected, but nothing as dramatic as this," we answered. "No naked nuns drinking blood and dismantling animals."

"Maybe you were molested and don't remember," she diagnosed.

In the morning there were lengthy arguments over the diaries and defense objections on the grounds that they were hearsay. The judge agreed. "You've got no proof that what's in the diaries is accurate."

Resuming the prosecution's marathon cross-examination, Rubin raised, once again, the chilling specter of "pornography."

"Now you are aware that your brother kept pornographic magazines in his residence?"

"I remember seeing *Playboys*, yes," Peggy Ann answered.

"Anything more hardcore than *Playboy*?" Rubin asked eagerly.

"Not that I recall."

Clearly, Rubin was going to hammer away at Ray on this point throughout the trial, to the very end, in an effort to paint a picture in the jurors' minds of Ray Buckey as a man with an unnatural interest in sex. But the "pornography" was the soft-core *Playboy* magazine, and the pictures were of adult women —hardly evidence of an interest in pedophilia. The often-repeated accusation of having *Playboy* in his possession did not really succeed in making Buckey appear to be a man with weird cravings, depraved desires, maniacal longings—just your average heterosexual young man. But Rubin continued to ask question after question in an effort to insinuate that there was something sinister.

There was more nitpicking about Peggy Ann's statements on various radio and television talk shows. Asked again why she said she had worked at the preschool for only five weeks she said, "I referenced it to the preliminary hearing because that was the cause of this . . . and everything I experienced, being in jail and everything else. . . ."

Rubin cut her off. "I move to strike any reference to being in jail."

"Sustained. That portion is stricken."

"Do you believe you might have forgotten some date that you were at the preschool?"

"Yes."

"Do you believe that you might have forgotten whether or not you molested little children at the McMartin Preschool?"

"No."

"Do you believe you might have forgotten that you saw other teachers molest children at the McMartin Preschool?"

"No."

On recross, Rubin ended the day by producing two pay vouchers with the same date on them, one for twelve hours and the other for thirteen hours, making the inference that Peggy Ann had billed the county for twenty-five hours' labor performed in one day, apparently some kind of clerical mixup. But Peggy Ann was paid only $132.50 for that day. The most rudimentary common sense would lead even the simplest juror to conclude that her supervisor would not be so careless as to sign and authorize such a request, nor would the county bureaucracy approve and pay it. Nor would Peggy Ann be foolish enough to sign under oath such a request when she knew it would come under the relentless scrutiny of Lael Rubin.

Davis grinned and asked her, "You were trying to cheat someone out of $132.50, weren't you?"

"No," Peggy Ann smiled.

Court was recessed for the Christmas vacation.

In the evening Peggy Ann sat with us and talked about the case.

"The techniques they use, once those techniques are learned, they can get a kid to say anything. Before this I never knew children could be manipulated so easily. I've heard of some legitimate cases where the kids cried and really did show some emotion because they've been through something terrible. But these kids here, it's like they're reciting from a little script. They show no emotion at all. Dead nuns? Drinking blood at the church? You wouldn't believe how many times those kids were interviewed. If a kid says nothing happened he's told that he's dumb. They use dolls and puppets. The one they used to represent Raymond looked like a vulture. And Kee tells the kids that the teachers at McMartin are sick people and that the police are watching Raymond and following him. And the kids said over and over again that they were not molested. And you see Kee MacFarlane saying, 'I don't want to hear any more "no's."' And she tells the kid that all the other kids said it happened, which wasn't true.

"And they're saying a three-year-old kid can be raped by a grown man, walk out of the school, and no one notices it. That's absurd in the first place. That child would be ripped to shreds. There would be blood. I have a friend who's a doctor and he's seen legitimate cases and he says those kids are not walking in. They're carried in. And they have stitches! And they are ripped! They forget how little a child is. And when they talk about a hymen being a millimeter off I sit there and say, 'Are you kidding?' I can't believe the D.A.s and judges don't apply a little logic. They're saying 'raped' and 'sodomized' day after day. And the kid just skips out of school and goes home," Peggy Ann said.

"If a kid was taken up in an airplane, wouldn't he tell somebody? And there was a child who said he was taken to a Catholic church and the priests and nuns were running around naked. Here's another thing they do at CII. When a child won't say anything the interviewer says, 'I'll point and you say yes or no whether you got touched.' And so it isn't even the children pointing. It's them pointing. And the kid keeps saying no all the way through and they still say he was molested.

"The first kid that testified was a sweet little boy, so he gets up there on the stand. And everything they'd ask him he'd say, 'I don't remember.' And so the prosecutor says, 'He needs a break.' And then the D.A. would bring him back in and he said, 'It was Raymond that did it.' And then our attorney said, 'Did Mr. Stevens tell you to say that?' And he said yes. . . . 'They just want me to tell the story.'

"But that was back when the press was so against us that they just played it down. They could have made a big story out of it. Wayne Satz caused a lot of this because [of] the way he presented it, it made us look like monsters. He said things that made it look like we were guilty and no questions asked. This whole thing of 'innocent until proven guilty,' that's just a bunch of baloney.

"I think if somehow they could get out of this they would. But they've spent eight million dollars and they can't say, 'Oh, sorry. We made a mistake.' No one will admit they were wrong. I think if we'd gone to trial right away it would have been goodbye. But people are starting to realize there's something wrong. They're saying twelve hundred children have been molested! And not one child ever said anything?" Peggy Ann said.

"Every time I see Kee MacFarlane and that group I think about all the pain they've caused. And it wasn't ever needed. And they're getting all this money! All these grants.

"We were getting on the bus and one of the sheriffs talks to all the women that are getting on, and he says, 'These are the child molesters. That's the thing to do now.' And he laughed. Well, there were about a dozen in the back of us and they started screaming and yelling and threatening. And one girl had matches and we were in this locked up little thing with our hands handcuffed and she struck matches and was throwing them, trying to catch our hair on fire!

"And the sheriff just sat there. He'd started the whole thing. And he just sat there. There were two sheriffs on the bus and I yelled to the other guy. He told them all to sit down and quit it. They tried to set our hair on fire! And we were handcuffed. And it was all because of this stupid sheriff. He started the whole thing. And I said, 'Excuse me. Could you tell me your name?' And he says, 'No. What for?' And I said, 'I'd just like to have your name please.' And he said, 'I didn't do anything.' So I went to the other guy and said, 'Could you tell me his name?' And he said, 'No. He can tell you if he wants to.' And the other sheriff looked over and said, 'I didn't do anything. It's all her fault.' But the mentality of the cops! They enjoy cruelty!

"Ray's over in the hospital part where they put informers, police officers, political people, those who can't be put in with the general population. Lael Rubin had him put in the general population and they threw urine and feces on him. She's the one who was responsible for that. The reason why they did that . . . they thought they could break us. She put Babs in with all the people who were crazy. She put me in with all the people who were coming off drugs. They put you in a little cement cell. Just room enough for a mattress. There was no reason for that except Lael Rubin wanted to break us. I sat in this little cell. People screaming, yelling all night long.

"By the way, please don't tell anybody where we live. We've had to move five times. Every time we moved the cops came over and told the neighbors all the juicy details of what we were accused of and we were getting death threats and people calling up and saying, 'You're gonna die!' And people coming by and saying things like that to my parents and my grandmother. I don't know why the cops did that."

Instead of fading away, the disclosures of prosecutors' use of jailhouse informants to fabricate testimony in exchange for leniency and early release has burgeoned into a full-blown scandal with stories and editorials in virtually every newspaper in California. A number of defense attorneys told reporters that the rewards and payoffs are not disclosed at trial because they are made after the informant testifies. Leslie White said he could identify cases in which defendants were sentenced to death row on the testimony of jailhouse informants, and disclosed that police feed details of the testimony to these professional perjurers so they will be more convincing in court. One editorial writer stated that, "Jailhouse informants are no sleazier than the prosecutors who use them to win a case at any cost."

But in all the newspaper stories and editorials, the McMartin connection was entirely blanked out, in spite of the fact that it was the McMartin trial that exposed this practice.

Monday, January 3, 1989. "We are back in *People* v. *Buckey* and all defendants and counsel are present," the judge began. "Anything to take up before we bring in the jury?" There was indeed. The defense had brought a witness but they had apparently discovered that he was once arrested on some kind of trivial misdemeanor charge which was dismissed, but it was a rather embarrassing one, and they were asking for discovery on anything the district attorney's office might have had on this event. Davis asked for a printout from the D.A.'s computer on the man. Lael Rubin stated that it could not be done quickly. The judge said, "I have a number at the state attorney general's office. I can get a printout almost immediately." Rubin then said she could provide the court with a printout. The data arrived and the defense attorneys asked the court that it be suppressed and that the prosecutors be precluded from bringing it up before the jury, knowing they could expect a thoroughgoing smear from Rubin and Gunson if it were not suppressed. Incredibly, Gunson wanted to somehow link it to the underwear Peggy Ann was given as a joke, the jockey shorts with the humorous slogans printed on them. But the offense the man was arrested for had nothing to do with pedophilia. The prosecutors wanted to prove "lewd intent." The judge asserted that, although this case was about "unusual sex," the prosecutors had, so far, failed to show any connection between the act the man was arrested for and the charges pending against the defendants.

"Unusual sex!" the young reporter sitting next to us scoffed. "I wonder if there's anybody in this room who hasn't had unusual sex, or wanted to at some time or other. What a bunch of crap!"

By the middle of the day it was clear that the issue wasn't going to be resolved soon, so the defense attorneys announced that they would not call the witness at this time but would go on to their next witness, who was in the building, waiting.

"May we know who the witness is?" Rubin asked.

"Forrest Latiner," Davis answered. There followed lengthy arguments before Latiner was brought in. He was being called to explain what the judge called "incomprehensible": the fact that a person of Peggy Ann's intelligence could go throught the longest preliminary hearing in history and not know the particulars of the charges against her. Rubin said she feared that this "opens the door" to Latiner volunteering gratuitous statements that not only were the charges against his client false, but that all of the charges in this case were without merit. "I would ask that Mr. Latiner be directed not to volunteer that kind of inference," Rubin said. Davis agreed.

"I do too," the judge said. "I know Mr. Latiner and I know that he's an avid advocate for the defense." When all the discussion was done, Davis went to the telephone on the bailiff's desk and called Forrest Latiner, whose office was on the nineteenth floor in the public defender's office.

"Mr. Latiner, would you join us in Department 130? It's on the fifteenth floor," Davis said. It was a silly remark. Latiner had been there many times.

Latiner walked into the courtroom, stopped and waited. Then he went up to the witness stand and sat down. He had spent nearly thirty years in the courtroom and he sat there with the ease and confidence of a man sitting in his own living room. He was handsomely dressed in a dark suit and a white shirt.

"I know that you are a very avid advocate for the defense position in this case. It is not going to be your opportunity to relate that to the jury," the judge told him. "You are to answer strictly the questions that are asked of you.... Do you have any problem with that?"

"No problem," Latiner answered. He was sworn in.

"Mr. Latiner, what is your profession?" Davis asked.

"I'm an attorney and a member of the public defender's office."

"And did you represent an individual named Peggy Ann Buckey in connection with this case?"

"Yes . . . between April 1984 and January 1986."

"And during the preliminary hearing did you receive a document listing the accusations against your client?"

"I did."

"And what did you receive?"

"A complaint. I also received an indictment."

"In that indictment, did it list a count or counts against Peggy Ann Buckey?"

"It listed one count against her."

"And did it list the name of the child in conection with that count?"

"Yes."

"And what was the name of that child?"

"Your honor, may we approach?" Rubin interrupted. We waited through a long sidebar conference while the lawyers whispered. Gunson looked at the clock, then, three seconds later, looked again. Sometimes he stared at the clock without letup during these sidebars.

"And prior to the arraignment did you receive a copy of the complaint?"

"Yes."

"And do you have a recollection of how many counts?"

"Fifteen, I believe."

"And after you received a copy of that complaint did you show that to Peggy Ann Buckey?"

"No."

"Did you point out allegations involving her?"

"No."

"Why is it that you didn't provide a copy or point out specific counts in that complaint to your client?"

"I have several reasons. One is simple . . . the first is that. . ."

"Your honor, may we approach the bench?" Rubin cut him off. We sat and waited through another lengthy sidebar. The jurors looked annoyed. When it ended, the judge told the jurors, "There is an issue that does not require your presence. I'm going to ask the jurors to step into the jury room." The jurors stoically filed out of the room.

"We need to know what you're going into," the judge said. "The explanation you're going to give as to why you did not give a copy of the complaint or a description of the counts to Peggy Ann Buckey. What was the explanation that you're going to give?"

"Well, three reasons. The first is that I never give a copy of the complaint to a client because the complaint, as you know, is in legal jargon. It doesn't really tell you anything. . . . It's customary to waive the reading of the complaint. Second, and perhaps more importantly, each of the specifics of the case we received on discovery, and the problem there was that we were continually receiving discovery. I was receiving discovery throughout April into May and on into the summer of 1984 and the details were changing. No child told the same accounts as any other child and no child ever told the same account twice. There was no detail that we could sense. Case in point. Billy. He started off with the videotape saying he remembers going to a stage far away and that he remembers a rabbit being slashed. By the time he testified at the preliminary [hearing] the stage became a blue house and he remembered rabbits being mutilated and killed. By the summer of 1984 he remembered going to a farm, and he remembered a horse being killed and slaughtered. Some time later he remembered going to Harry's Market—something he had never remembered earlier. Also, by the time we got to the preliminary hearing he remembered two ponies and some chickens being killed. He also remembered then, for the first time, going to St. Cross Episcopal Church and having to drink a cat's blood on the altar. I remember a young lady, ten days or so before the preliminary hearing, talked about a pig being killed at a farm by Ray Buckey. At the preliminary hearing she was asked about the farm and she said, 'What farm?' And they said, 'the farm you told us about where the pig was killed,' and she said, 'What pig?'

"The details kept changing so it was enough for me to categorize all these details and I made elaborate lists of all these variations, not only between child and child but between one child in each and every occasion when the child was interrogated.

"Then, finally, the third and critical factor was my client, Peggy Ann Buckey, getting her released from jail where she had been held for sixty days, totally unconstitutionally, and on fabrications. Second was the right of confrontation and witnesses. Third was how to temper the media, and change Salem back to Los Angeles. Each and every one of the concerns I had— and I knew they couldn't be dealt with in sequence unless I could get her released from jail, unless I could avoid the denial of the right of confrontation, unless I could somehow make the media take a different perspective. Unless you were there you cannot imagine what was going on in the media, in the press, on the radio and TV. . . . These were things that were of immediate concern. Faced with all this, I didn't see any point in going over with Peggy Ann anything but one question. 'Did you do anything?' And the answer was 'no' and that's all I needed to know. . . . The charges weren't clear. She was charged with witchcraft, judge! It was in the papers every day!"

"But how did you communicate to your client," the judge asked, "When you asked, 'What did you do?' how does she know what you're talking about— from what she read in the papers or from what you gave her?"

"She was already aware that the subject of the case was McMartin Preschool, molestation, child pornography, child prostitution, slaughtering of animals. I asked her if she was involved in any of this. And the answer was a categorical 'No.' "

"Any of you have any questions you want to ask?" the judge looked at the lawyers. There was a sudden, loud shriek of derisive laughter from Rubin that echoed wildly across the room, ridiculing Latiner.

"Obviously what he's related, I can't allow that to go to the jury," the judge said. I was surprised that he did not admonish Rubin for her behavior, and that the defense attorneys did not protest this insult to their witness.

During the short three o'clock recess, we spoke with Latiner outside the courtroom. "The judge said the jurors cannot be allowed to hear what you said. Why not?" we asked. "Isn't that the heart of the case?"

"I think they should hear all of it," Latiner said. "It's not some gratuitous opinion. It's simply the facts of the case. I see absolutely no reason why they shouldn't hear it. Without that, they're not getting full and complete information."

"Gits and Davis seem to go along with the judge and Rubin. What does that mean?" someone asked.

"I don't interfere in this case," Latiner shrugged. "Davis gets mad if you ask any questions or offer any advice. You know, I've been a public defender for twenty-five years. I've defended some bad people and some good people who did bad things. But this case is unlike any I've ever seen. I am absolutely 100 percent certain that these people are innocent. They didn't molest anybody. This case reminds me of what happened to the Japanese Americans during World War Two. They just got caught up in something that wasn't of their making and they got locked up. Innocent people do go to prison.

"Of the kid witnesses that testified not one said he was molested before he was interviewed at CII. They all denied they were molested before they were interviewed at CII. And the interviewer said, 'We don't want any dummies here. We only want to talk to the smart ones. You're smart, aren't you? Your friends all told us. I don't want to hear you say no! If you say no you're a dummy.' Gross! Even if you accept Kee MacFarlane's explanation that she had a social worker's purpose in mind and you've got to use all kinds of pressure tactics to get the kid to own up—that's Roland Summit's theory—even if you accept that at face value it taints the stories you're receiving. . . . It's debatable whether that's a viable approach even for a social worker. But I don't think there's any question that for prosecutorial purposes that information you've got in that manner with those methods is totally worthless. Those videotapes are the defense's best weapons in this case.

"But when you look at the so-called medical evidence, it doesn't exist. There is no corroborating evidence. There is no case. As an attorney there are some things I can do and some things I can't do. I work within a system that has its limitations. That doesn't mean I have to like it but I have to recognize it. The no-bail holds were bogus and sham. And I criticize the presiding judge [Judge Ronald George] in the master calendar for allowing it to happen. I have known him for years and I have a high regard for that man. But I know he is extremely ambitious. I know he is seeking appellate appointment [which he later received] and I have a deep, nagging suspicion that somewhere in the back of his mind he believed that being of some help to Philibosian would stand him in good stead with the governor. But there was never a reason to lock these people up without bail."

We asked Latiner, "These allegations of drinking blood and satanic rituals and animal sacrifices and naked nuns and chopping up babies and worshipping the devil in ritual molestations . . . do you think the prosecutors really believe that stuff?"

"No. I think they're amoral," Latiner said.

The next witness was Jack, the father of a young man who was a close friend of Peggy Ann. He was brought into the courtroom by Gits. He was in his mid-sixties with thinning gray hair. Dressed in rather drab, brown clothes, he contrasted with the overdressed young lawyers in their showy, three-piece litigation suits and fastidiously blow-dried hair. He was tall. His face was wrinkled but friendly. He waited by the railing until he was motioned to go to the witness stand, where he sat down and was sworn in. We now had a witness to corroborate Peggy Ann's statement that the underwear with the humorous decals were given to her as a friendly joke and not as part of some satanic conspiracy. Gunson stated that they were introduced "to show a lewd and lascivious interest," and a morbid preoccupation with oral sex and children. We had gone far afield. The attack of the killer underwear!

Davis took out the jockey shorts and showed them to Jack, who stated he had bought them at a swap meet and given them to Peggy Ann as a Christmas gift, in gift wrapping. One of them had a decal that read: "HOT STUFF." The shorts were contained in flat, cardboard boxes. Jack took out one that read, "Be my baby." Davis asked that it be marked exhibit 986. On the box was also printed the words: "Underwear that's funtawear." The witness testified that his son had been a boyfriend of Peggy Ann and that he had asked his father not to give any more of these items to her.

Gunson rose to cross-examine the witness. When Davis asked the question his voice echoed, loud and clear across the room, but when Gits and Gunson spoke, it was necessary to move to the front row in order to hear. Even then, from behind, they were almost inaudible.

"You gave this to Peggy Ann Buckey?" Gunson began.

"Yes."

"Was there something about Peggy Ann Buckey that suggested that this would be a good Christmas gift to give her?"

"No. Not a thing."

"What was it that indicated this would be a good choice?"

"It's just a humorous joke that I thought was harmless."

"Now you said 'a joke.' What do you mean by a joke?"

"The usual definition of a joke, I guess . . .something that somebody might have found amusing."

"And what did you intend to do with them?"

"I intended to sell some of them. I had a garage sale . . ."

"And where was it that you saw these items?"

"It was either in Las Vegas or Reno at a trade show. . . . I just thought they would be a cute item to sell. They weren't very salable."

". . . because of the subject matter printed on them?"

"No. On the contrary, even those who didn't buy them enjoyed them. They'd look at them and laugh."

"When you say, 'enjoyed them,' what do you mean by that?" Gunson's harsh countenance, his dark look of loathing and moral condemnation, sent the message that they were not funny, or trivial, or forgivable, but that they were vile evidence of odious crimes, depraved desires, maniacal longings.

"Oh, they'd laugh and call their friends over," Jack answered cheerfully.

"You indicated that they were durable. . . . What did you mean?"

"They last."

"Is that because you were wearing them?"

"Yes."

"Did you sign over an interest in your residence for the purpose of giving it to Mrs. Buckey?"

"I put up my property as bail for her with the county . . . so she could make bail and be out on bail."

"How did she benefit by that?"

"She benefitted with her freedom."

"The idea of that underwear being a joke. How did you view that as being a joke?" Gunson asked.

"I viewed it as a humorous, harmless item."

"Do you know what they did with these things?"

"They refused to put them out for sale."

"And was the reason you gave them to her that it had a little bit of shock value?"

"A harmless joke. Like it says on the box. Underwear that's funtawear."

"And you found them fun to wear."

"I found them useful to wear."

"What do you mean by useful?"

"They wear well. They last. I washed them a dozen times."

"Well, there's something different about these underwear, isn't there?" Gunson asked severely.

"No . . . except they have a decal on them. That's all."

"Is that part of the fun of wearing them? The shocking part of showing the decal?" Gunson was trying to insinuate that the man exposed himself.

"No."

up something that could be used to color him as a sexual deviate of some sort and, by association, implicate Ray and Peggy. Each time the judge denied his request, Gunson tried another approach, insisting that this case was about unusual sex and asserting his right to go into the possibility of unusual sexual behavior of this man, in the presence of the jury. Finally, the judge told Gunson that unless he could establish some connection between the man's past and the charges against the Buckeys, it was inadmissible. "It would taint and degrade the defendants. . . . The prejudice would outweigh the probative value and therefore it is inadmissible under 352. I can't allow that. You haven't shown any connection." Judge Pounders was a man of intelligence and perspicacity. But his statements throughout the trial, to us at least, indicated that he believed there was some substance to the charges.

The jury was brought in and Gunson resumed his cross-examination. He wanted to talk about the underwear some more. There were stacks of boxes of the underwear on the witness stand. There followed hours of questions suggesting that the underwear was evidence of some unspeakable depravity. One of the garments had a drawing of a champagne bottle with the words, "Happy Birthday."

"And you don't see any phallic symbolism in that?" Gunson demanded.

"I wouldn't think of it that way." Jack responded. "*Your* mind is looking for that. You could find sexual symbolism in that."

"Do you see any sexual symbolism in the champagne bottle popping?" Gunson asks. His face was mean and ascerbic.

"I guess *you* could make that. . . . I hadn't thought of it. It's possible. . . . Until *you* mentioned it I hadn't thought of it."

"And when you were in that trade show and you were walking by and you saw, and you had this desperate urge that caused you to purchase these items, what was that urge?"

"I decided I would purchase some for gifts and possibly sell some."

"When you saw these exposed phallic symbols and you were desperate and you went and purchased these items, isn't that so?"

"I didn't look at them the way you do. I looked at them as a humorless, harmless joke."

As we listened to the prosecutor go on, hour after hour, with this absurd cross-examination, we wondered why anyone would choose to go into such a profession. But it's not the profession itself that's necessarily loathsome; it's the way it's practiced: the purchase of false testimony from murderers; the use of smear, blackmail, deception, distortion; the casual, remorseless ruin of innocent people.

Gunson brought out another box of the humorous undergarments. On the front there was a picture of a teapot. Gunson sprinkled his questions with words like: "desperate urge," and "lust," and "harmful," and "sexually stimulating."

"When you look at the board there, the one on the left, does that indicate a genital?"

"I never thought of it that way. It might if *you* think so," Jack said.

"Is there anything on that decal that relates to a male genital?"

"I hadn't thought of it until *you* mentioned it."

Not bad!

"Looking at the one on the end there, do you see it as relating to a male genital?"

"Unless *you* interpret it as a male genital or something."

"What was it you interpreted in this underwear as a joke?"

"Well . . . the fact that there were decals . . . I thought it was a harmless joke. And everyone that's looked at them seemed to see something that made them laugh."

"And if you saw that pair of underwear, would you say that it relates to just a hot dog and nothing else?"

"No, it could relate to the genitals."

"And that's why you thought it's humorous! Isn't it?"

"That's a way *you* could take it, yes."

"No. I'm asking you if that was the reason you thought it was humorous. Because it relates to the genitals. The male penis."

"I didn't sit down to analyze. . . . You just get caught up in shopping at those shop meets."

This absurd cross-examination went on, hour after hour as Gunson tried, relentlessly, to transform the underwear into something dark and sinister. For eighteen months they had been pounding Ray with the allegation that he did not wear underwear, as an insinuation of depravity. Now, they are trying to smear him with the allegation that he did wear underwear, as an insinuation of depravity. Is he depraved because he did not wear underwear, or because he did? Or both? For the answers to these and other questions we continued to listen and it seemed as though it would never end. Finally, the judge looked at the clock and said, "We will be in recess until 10:30 tomorrow morning." As we left the courtroom we saw the witness sitting sadly on a bench in the hallway and smiled. We introduced ourselves. "I guess you think I'm a dirty old man," he said.

"Certainly not!" we answered. "You should tell that prosecutor he has a dirty mind."

"Well," he grinned broadly, "I sort of did when I said I didn't see a male penis until *he* thought of it." We all laughed.

In the morning when we entered the courtroom we saw the witness sitting in the back row. We smiled and exchanged greetings. Then we looked and saw the prosecutors, Rubin and Gunson, squinting at us fiercely. Before the jury was brought in, Gunson argued furiously that he should be allowed to go into the witness's private, personal history for the purpose of bringing

On recross, Gunson asked Jack, "Before you came up here today and testified, did you talk with someone in the audience?" Gunson's tone and facial expression indicated that a heinous crime had just been detected.

"Yes," Jack answered.

"Was it Paul Eberle?"

"I believe so," he answered.

The judge laughed. During the recess, in the cafeteria, one of the lawyers said to us, "I notice the prosecution took another dig at you. It's about the fifth time they've done that. They don't want any books written about this."

"Yeah," Paul agreed.

"And they see you laughing at them with that look of ridicule and contempt and loathing. You should cool it with that."

"Yeah, I think that's good advice."

The next witness was a Mexican man, employed at the Red Carpet Car Wash, called to show the impossibility of child molestation occurring there. The prosecution made objections to all of the photographs and diagrams brought in by the defense. They routinely tried to block everything the defense did, but the objections were overruled.

"Customers could see the car all the way through," the witness said. "You can see very clearly." He testified that customers were never allowed to remain in their vehicles while they were going through the wash, and that they checked all cars carefully "because we are responsible if anything happens."

In the morning, Thursday, January 5, 1989, we received the astonishing news that Judge Ronald M. Gruen, the administrative law judge in Peggy Ann's hearing, had ruled in favor of Peggy Ann and recommended that her request for a new teaching credential be granted. Gruen literally blasted the state's case from beginning to end and said he did not have to consider whether a "preponderance of the evidence" existed because there was no case on the face of it! We got a copy of the judge's eleven-page ruling, in which he stated there was "no credible evidence" and "no corroboration," and that the interviewing agency (CII) had done "incalculable damage" with a "pervasive use of leading and suggestive questions." He further stated that the videotaped evidence "reveals a pronounced absence of any evidence implicating the respondent [Peggy Ann] in any wrongdoing and . . . raises additional doubts of credibility with respect to the children interviewed or with respect to the value of CII interviewing techniques themselves."

Gruen concluded that there had been a "serious violation" of Peggy Ann's due process rights, and that "cause does not exist for the denial of the credential applications of the respondent under the Education Code Section 44345 for the commission of acts involving moral turpitude or for failing to furnish evidence of good moral character."

The next day, the state Commission on Teacher Credentialing met in

Sacramento and voted, seven to six with one member abstaining, to endorse Gruen's ruling and restore Peggy Ann's right to teach. It was a stunning victory for the defendants, and a stunning blow to the prosecution, even though the commission voted in Peggy Ann's favor by a margin of only one vote.

Monday, Judge Pounders spent almost the entire day interviewing each of the jurors individually to ask whether they had learned of Judge Gruen's ruling in Peggy Ann's favor, or of the state Commission on Teacher Credentialing's vote in her favor. Two said they had caught a fleeting glimpse of headlines but read nothing else. The others said they had neither read nor heard anything of these events. We found that difficult to believe because it was on the front page of every newspaper in Los Angeles and on every television station. But the electronic media made no mention of the judge's damning statements about the state's "evidence" and only reported briefly that Peggy Ann's teaching credentials had been restored and showed parents protesting with picket signs. During the same day, we received the shocking news that the trial, which we had been told would end in April, would go far beyond that date, possibly into October or November. At one point, the judge said, "When we tell the jurors, I'm afraid they'll rise up and hack us to pieces. I am farther away from them than you are."

Tuesday morning when we arrived at the fifteenth floor, a large group of people surrounding Peggy were talking excitedly. Peggy called us over and told us, "Yesterday the jurors, while they were in the jury room, they wrote a bunch of things on the blackboard, like, 'TWO AND A HALF YEARS WASTED' and 'MISTRIAL,' and 'HANGMAN.' The judge is in a state of shock."

"It looks like the jurors have risen up in rebellion," we said. More reporters came running out of the elevator. It was a good newspaper story. And so another day was spent questioning the jurors, individually, about this. The jurors explained that one of them was buying a new car and wanted to get personalized license plates and asked for suggestions from the others. The jurors' answers were polite and guarded and they did not inform on each other. None would say who gave the phrases, "TWO AND A HALF YEARS WASTED," and "MISTRIAL." The judge expressed concern about the danger of a mistrial and said, "I don't think we could try this case again."

At the end of the day, the judge sternly told the lawyers that he wanted to get it over with. "I will allow you some latitude with the defendants and expert witnesses but if you present testimony that is redundant I will cut you off."

We walked out of the parking lot with Peggy. She was ill and looked pale and tired. "I think it's terribly unfair," she said. "The judge let the prosecution go on for sixteen months! And now he's only going to let us have five or six. They get sixty-one witnesses and we get thirty-seven. He's trying to cripple the defense!"

Thursday, January 12, 1989. The Mexican man from the car wash is still on direct, with Gits asking the questions. He said it took only about one minute for a car to make its journey through the "tunnel." He said that anyone could see into the car at all times, that there were as many as fifteen to twenty-five workers and there were men waiting at the end to dry the cars. He was asked if it would be possible for a person going through the car wash to take off his clothes, take off the clothes of seven or more pre-schoolers, put his clothes on, and put on the clothes of all seven children. He said no. His answer was drowned out by objections (on the grounds the answer was only speculation), but I think the jury got the message. He also testified that there were always large numbers of customers present in the car wash. He said that anyone attempting to molest children in the car wash would have been detected at the earliest stage of the process.

"Did you ever see some kind of sexual activity inside a car?"

"No. Never."

The man said the length of the "tunnel" was only about forty feet.

Gunson rose to cross-examine. At the lectern he marshalled his stacks of notes and documents for his assault on the witness, but was put to rout. The witnesses' answers strongly showed the impossibility of the allegations of the car wash kids. "They are not going to let you go inside the car!" he told Gunson. He described in great detail why it would be impossible to molest children at the car wash. "The workers always look inside the cars," he said.

"What if a van had a curtain behind the seat? And curtains on all the windows?" Gunson asked.

"They would look to see what it looked like inside."

When court was recessed at the end of the day, we saw Peggy sitting on a bench, waiting for her driver. She had been ill and was not looking well.

The Mexican man concluded his testimony, saying that all of the workers at the car wash checked everything well. The defense also called the manager and the owner of the car wash. Both testified that there were as many as twenty-five workers at the car wash at any given time, that people in the lavatories could be heard speaking to each other.

"Would it be possible, if a customer made a deal and bribed the drive-on men . . . the assistant manager, the window man, and you, to let him go through the car wash?"

"Wait a minute!" the manager interrupted impatiently. "You've bought me. You've bought the drive-on men, the window men; you've bought the drive-off men, and the assistant manager. You will still have to buy several other workers."

"What if a van had curtains behind the seats? Would you see into the van?"

"The window man would."

Davis asked the owner, "Could anyone molest a child in the car wash?"

"He would be detected," the owner said.

The defense did a thorough job of showing the impossibility of the car wash stories. Why, we wondered, would anyone take a child to a car wash to molest him, and why would the court even entertain such a ludicrous tale?

The defense called a woman who was a secretary at the St. Cross Episcopal Church, and had been so employed for the past twenty years. She, too, said she had not seen anything that raised the slightest suspicion of child molestation. She was asked if someone could enter the church without being seen. "There were three other secretaries there," she said.

In the morning, before the jury was brought in, the lawyers and the judge spent most of the morning arguing. Prosecutors Gunson and Rubin wanted to be allowed to ask questions, in front of the jury, about a man who was a janitor at the church who allegedly touched a child in some improper manner and was quietly dismissed. Gunson added that there was also an organist who touched a child on the leg, and another man who, although he was not accused of any improper conduct at the church, "has a record of pedophilia."

"We have no discovery on this," Gits protested.

"The rest of my cross-examination relates to this!" Rubin protested. "She's sitting up there and saying that nothing could have happened at the church."

The defense attorneys were handed eighty-one pages of material on the alleged molesters at the church. Gits told the judge, "We cannot absorb this much material in the few minutes before the witness is called." The judge gave them an hour to read the material.

We asked one of the attorneys, a woman who is a law partner or associate of Buckeys' attorney, "Shouldn't this have been received on discovery long ago?"

"Yes," she said, "but they seem to be making their own rules in this case."

"We don't understand why Gits and Davis didn't object more forcefully," we said. "They tried to ambush you."

"This has happened so many times that all we can do is object and make a record," she said. This record could then be used as the basis for an appeal if need be.

Another attorney sitting with us said, "Lael Rubin testified at a congressional committee hearing and lobbied for the abrogation of the Sixth Amendment right of confrontation, the right of public proceedings, the rule against hearsay evidence, the rule against leading questions. She wanted the preliminary hearings closed to the public."

After reading the eighty-one pages of discovery, Gits told the judge, "There are no dates!" He also protested that, according to the documents, the alleged molestations occurred in a different place, not in the building where,

Billy had testified, he had been forced to drink blood by figures in black robes. Mutants.

"It shows she has knowledge of these events," Rubin asserted.

"It's too remote," the judge said. "I will preclude any inquiry into [one of the alleged church molesters]. Mr. Buckey would be soiled by this. . . . He would be tainted by guilt of association. You have got to show some relationship to the defendants. . . . I will sustain the objection."

The prosecutors continued to argue. Gunson suddenly began to shout. Even when he shouted, his voice was flat, dry, unclear, and difficult to understand. This was the first time he had ever raised his voice to this level. Finally the judge cut off the quarrel and said he would preclude the line of questioning.

Another juror was dismissed. She had already suffered the loss of a $6,000-a-year pay raise and was now faced with the loss of her job if she did not return to work. There were only two alternates left.

After the young woman departed, prosecutor Gunson asserted that he was concerned about persons other than the judge viewing the notebooks of the jurors. He stated that the court reporter, the young woman who typed up the transcript of the proceedings, had read jurors' notebooks and relayed information "to Mr. Buckey's attorneys."

"Oh my God!" the judge threw back his head and slapped his forehead in the manner of one who has just witnessed an act of insanity. A burst of laughter erupted from the audience section, mostly from lawyers who knew both the court reporter and Davis. Gunson said that "a relationship" existed between the court reporter and Buckey's attorney. For the first time in memory, Davis was speechless. The lawyers continued to laugh.

"This is a rather shocking allegation," the judge told Gunson and inquired as to the nature of the "relationship." Gunson said he had observed the young woman engaging in conversation with the attorney, and that it was not Daniel Davis but another lawyer representing Buckey in a civil matter pertaining to insurance, a Mr. Scott Bernstein. The judge asked Gunson to be more specific about the nature of the "relationship." Gunson continued to speak but seemed to be just spewing out words without saying anything. The judge shrugged.

The jurors had been sitting in the jury room all day and the witness, the church secretary, had been sitting in the hallway since 10 A.M. With only ten minutes left in the day, the jurors were brought in and dismissed until morning. They looked angry.

In the morning, the judge did an about-face and allowed Rubin, on cross-examination, to ask the church secretary if she was aware that a janitor had confessed to touching a child at St. Cross Episcopal Church. She showed the woman newspaper clippings about the incident. The secretary denied ever having heard of this and her face showed extreme anger at this vilification of her church.

In the cafeteria, Irene asked, "How's McMartin going?"

"Tiresome," we said. "They follow us when we go to lunch. They follow us when we go shopping. They follow us into the restrooms."

"I wish they'd try that with me just once!" she laughed. Irene had a great flair for raunchy humor. Our friend, Frank, a former state senator, told us, "I hope you understand that you're not going to learn anything about molestation here. But you're going to learn a lot about the quality of our leaders."

Several more newspaper articles about the D.A.'s snitch system appeared during this week. Inmates who tried to expose this practice were brutally beaten by law enforcement officers in the county jail, according to the newspaper stories. One inmate, according to his mother, was attacked by six sheriff's deputies who beat him into unconsciousness and squeezed his testicles, then dragged his comatose body while she watched helplessly from the visiting room. According to the article, George Freeman had told other inmates that the testimony he gave against Ray Buckey was fabricated.

We saw Scott Bernstein and we all laughed about Gunson's statement that he had a "relationship" with the court reporter. "Why would they accuse you of a thing like that?" we asked.

"They're desperate," he said. "They don't have anything."

The defense called a priest from St. Cross Episcopal Church to impeach the testimony of Billy, who said he was molested by atomic mutants in black, hooded robes and forced to drink blood at the church. Rubin objected, trying to block another defense witness, because, she said, his priestly robes and collar gave him greater credibility and would put the prosecution at a disadvantage. Nevertheless, the priest was called. He was seventy-nine but still extremely lucid and articulate. He said that he had seen no visitors in black, hooded robes and that since he spent almost all of his time at the church it would be unlikely that anyone could enter the church without being observed because the doors were always locked. When asked about the janitor, he said the man was not an employee of the church, but was the husband of a woman who worked there and that he did volunteer work without pay and built toys for the children.

Another woman who was employed as a bookkeeper at the church testified that she had never seen any hooded figures in black robes or any blood on the altar. She was shown photographs of Billy and Ray Buckey and said she had never seen either. Another woman employed at the church said, "We kept a lookout as to who went in and out of the church. It had things that can be stolen, and there were three women working there."

The defense called a woman who had been employed at Harry's Market for twenty-one years. She said she was there all day and did not leave the building during her breaks. "There were meat men there. The produce men were there. The bookkeeper was there every day. The owner was there every day." She said she could see into the storage area where Billy claimed to have been molested, because the lower edge of the swinging doors was more than two feet above the floor. She said children were not allowed in that area because it would have been unsafe for them.

On cross-examination Gunson asked the woman if it would be possible for children to be concealed from public view if they were to the side of the doorway. She answered that that would be impossible because there were always boxes stacked up on both sides of the doorway.

It was the day of Buckey's bail hearing. It was nearly three o'clock, and the jurors were dismissed for the rest of the day. Twenty-two property owners had put up equity in their homes. Each was shown the documents they signed in order to post their homes as bail for Raymond Buckey and asked if they understood the consequences of what they were doing. All of them emphatically said they did. It was a very moving event. Predictably, Rubin raised every possible obstacle to Buckey's release, but Judge Pounders said he was concerned over the fact that Buckey had already served more time in custody without having been convicted of any crime than most people convicted of felonies. Judge Pounders ordered Buckey released, but he would not be free for a few days, until after the paperwork was processed.

After the hearing, television camera crews converged on Rubin, and the young reporters with their trendy clothes and epoxy hairdos barraged her with questions. "Raymond Buckey continues to be a danger to society," she said.

Buckey said he had not been in the company of so many friends in five years, that it had restored his faith in people, and that he was only disappointed that he couldn't say something to the people who put up their houses. Asked what he wanted to do when he was free, he said he would like to go to the beach and look at the water. Unlike Rubin's, his statements were not broadcast on the media.

Gregory Mooney, the attorney close to the prosecution who repeatedly tried to prevent exonerated witnesses from testifying, argued against Ray Buckey's release by stating his concern about the safety of children and of the community at large. Would Ray Buckey begin drinking blood and single-handedly demolish the community?

The elderly woman from Harry's Market was back on the stand. The defense was almost finished examining her. Davis asked, "Did you ever see children without clothing?" She said she had not.

"Would you have noticed five or ten preschoolers?"
"Yes."
"Is that something that could happen without your seeing it?"
"That is impossible."

"No further questions."

The next witness was the meat man from Harry's Market. He stated that all of the storage areas could be seen by all customers, and that he was there all day and frequently went to the meat cooler.

"Did you ever see naked children there?" Davis asked.

"In the meat cooler?" he exclaimed incredulously. He said it would have been virtually impossible for anyone to bring children into the market, undress them, and molest them without being seen.

After the jury and the witness were excused and had departed, the judge asked, "Anything else before recess?" Davis told the judge that there had been a flirtatious relationship between Billy's mother and Ray Fadel, the owner of Harry's Market, "and it may be that because he didn't respond to her overtures, he found himself the target of accusations." The next day, Davis stated that, "Our next witness, Ray Fadel, caught young Billy stealing some items from the store and the real reason he didn't return to the market didn't have anything to do with molestation."

"It's a collateral matter and isn't probative," Gunson argued. The judge agreed, and would not allow it.

The defense called Fadel. He was sworn in and asked to give and spell his name, which he did: Rachid Abou Fadel. Fadel testified that he had never seen any of the defendants come into the market with children, that he was there seven days a week from seven in the morning until seven at night. There were fifteen employees at the market. Fadel said that he had never witnessed mistreatment of children by anyone at the market. At the end of the day, after the jurors were excused, Davis asked Fadel, "Did you have an encounter with Billy at one time when he stole something from the store?"

"Yes. . . . I told the employees to watch Billy because he was stealing. . . . I saw Billy putting stuff in his shoes and pockets. I went out and told him, 'Put them back, or you can never come in here again.' "

"Did you hear that Billy accused you?"

"Yes. Police cars came and searched."

Fadel testified that Billy's mother came and told Fadel to forbid Peggy from coming to the store and to refuse to sell merchandise to her.

"I told her, 'It's a neighborhood store,' " he said.

He refused to ban Peggy from his market.

During recess, we spoke with one of the attorneys from the preliminary hearing. He asked us what was going on in the trial.

"It's a little unnerving," we said. "Rubin and Gunson stare at us and then whisper and then stare some more."

"I've noticed that," he said. "Better watch yourself. Prosecutors play a very dirty game. All they have to do is put something in your stuff and you're gone. They do that all the time, to defense witnesses and anybody who becomes a pain in the ass to them. They might even try something right in the courtroom. And there isn't one person in there who would lift a finger to help you."

In the morning, we entered the elevator breathing hard, red-faced and perspiring after the long, uphill run from the parking lot. An elderly lawyer whom we knew said, "Us older guys have to take it easy in this warm weather."

"We take exception to the 'old,' " we answered.

"Your exception is noted," he said solemnly. "How old are you?"

"Objection. Assumes facts not in evidence, calls for hearsay and speculation, irrelevant, prejudicial under 352, no foundation as to personal knowledge," we recited.

The man stared at us and said, "You need a vacation."

One of the unescapable facts of living in L.A. is the extraordinary heat that blows in off the desert. It's like an oven. From July to early October it is usually in the high nineties and in the suburbs, a few miles of freeway to the north, it rises above one hundred degrees almost daily. But we never saw the lawyers perspiring. They arrived in their air-conditioned Mercedes Benzes, cool and dry.

When we reached the fifteenth floor there were reporters everywhere. Ray had been released from custody. At the far end of the hallway was a large confluence of young lawyers with their plastic suits and aluminum hair. There were television camera crews and reporters following Ray; he was blinded by the strobes flashing in his face. He looked dazed.

Peggy, his mother, brought us over to where Ray was sitting on a bench and introduced us to him. He smiled and said, "I read your book! You were the first to tell what was really happening."

"Yes, and we've taken a lot of heat for it."

"I'm not surprised," he answered.

"We've been watching you, sitting there for five years, wondering what's going through your head."

"You get adjusted to it," he shrugged.

As we sat and talked, Gits and Davis stood over us and listened, looking extremely angry. Ray was taller than we had realized, and thin. He was handsome and had a deep, crisp voice. We thought he would be a good witness.

The jurors were asked for a show of hands to find out whether any had seen or read of Buckey's release. Not one hand was raised. I found that hard to believe because it was on all the media. The judge ordered twenty-four-hour security for Buckey and forbade him from visiting Manhattan Beach, where he had spent most of his life. Ray was also forbidden from associating with persons under the age of fourteen.

The next witness to be called by the defense was the daughter of Maxine Cobb, now deceased. Rubin objected, but Gits explained that one of the children identified Maxine Cobb as being at a farm where horses were killed and children were allegedly molested. "We have to eliminate her as a co-conspirator," Gits said, "and we have to exclude the ranch where Mrs. Cobb lived." Gits asked to introduce into evidence a diagram of the farm. Rubin objected. The judge said that if there were inaccuracies in the diagram they could be corrected during the taking of testimony.

The woman stated that she had lived with her mother on Desire Avenue since 1975. "It was horse property," she said. "About two acres." There were stables and barns, she said, and she lived there with her husband and son. Peggy Buckey was her cousin. She said that both her house and barn were white.

"Did Ray Buckey ever come to the residence?" Gits asked.

"No."

"What kind of horses did you raise?"

"Arabian horses."

"How big are they?"

"Fifteen hands high." (Five or six feet.)

"Are these horses valuable?" Gits asked.

"Yes."

"For what are they valuable?"

"For their breeding, their disposition, for their blood lines, for the way they look in a show."

"Are they valuable if they are dead?"

"Dead?" the astonished woman asked. "No."

"Did you ever come home and see a dead horse?"

"No."

"Between 1979 and 1982 did any horse die?"

"No."

"If one had, would you have noticed?"

"Yes."

The woman said that no preschool children ever visited the farm.

"Would a horse stand and do nothing while somebody hacked it or beat it to death?" Davis asked.

"Oh no!" she exclaimed. "It would run away. It would bolt."

The farm was searched in 1984 and no knives, bats, or machetes were found. The witness said she had never seen any evidence of harm done to animals on her farm, nor had she ever been visited by anyone driving a beige station wagon.

A city official testified that about 17,000 cars passed by the school every day at a speed of about 29 miles per hour.

A woman employed in a building directly across from the preschool testified that she had a direct view of the school, and that other people in the building had a direct view of the school and that she had never seen a child alone on a swing or a slide, that she could hear the children from where she sat, and that she had never heard screams of pain coming from children or animals. She said the shrubbery and weeds at the front of the school were cleared away. She also testified that if she had seen or heard a child being mistreated, "it would have stuck in my head." Other neighbors gave similar testimony.

During recess we spoke with a lawyer friend we've known for years and told him, "What we don't understand is why this should take three years. Some murder trials only take three weeks."

"The system is designed for those who are guilty," he said. "They don't know what to do with those who are not guilty."

All of the Los Angeles media carried brief stories giving the news that Peggy Ann had returned to her teaching job in Anaheim. Most of the stories were neutral, but the *Los Angeles Times* printed a photograph of a woman holding a poster showing a small child weeping, with the word, "VICTIM" on his shirt and a caption that read, "CITIZENS AGAINST CHILD ABUSE." With her were a group of protestors. There was a photograph of Peggy Ann that made her look like a demonic witch. Peggy Ann is an uncommonly good-looking woman, and it is almost certain that they picked through dozens of photographs until they found the ugliest one they could find. Lawyers, friends, and supporters of the Buckeys believed that the prosecutors tipped off the *Times*, and may have actually staged the protest demonstration and picketing.

"For the record we are back in *People* v. *Buckey* and all defendants and counsel are present," the judge began, as court reconvened. "Anything to take up before we bring in the jurors?" He looked at all four lawyers and waited.

"We call Dr. Michael Maloney," Gits said. Maloney is a clinical psychologist and a professor of psychiatry at USC School of Medicine. He was to be the defense's first expert witness. At last they were bringing up their heavy artillery. Going over his credentials consumed a large part of the morning. He had evaluated hundreds of children alleged to be victims of child abuse. He had testified not only for the defense but also for the prosecution. Gunson objected to allowing him to testify. Before the jury was brought into the courtroom, Maloney told the judge that after reviewing the CII videotaped interviews, he had concluded that the interviews were "definitely invalid," that the children were "so contaminated by the process itself that, no matter what they said . . . you'd have a hard time saying where it came from."

He did not testify until late in the afternoon, and was quickly cut off by objections from the prosecution to nearly every question and answer. The judge recessed the proceeding until morning.

"Anything to take up before the jury is brought in?" the judge asked when court began the following day. There was indeed. The prosecution objected to a large bar graph the defense had prepared, showing the number of words spoken by the interviewer and those of the child, which showed that in these CII interviews, the adults did almost all of the talking. The prosecutors objected also to seventeen videotaped presentations the defense had prepared on the grounds that they were irrelevant, argumentative, and repetitive. The judge stated that he wanted to speed up the trial and that showing the videotape would waste an hour of court time. (And so, instead, they wasted an hour with arguments.) Gits pleaded with the judge, saying, "Whatever you cut, please don't cut these!" Gits said that the interviews were the heart of the case, a statement the judge, himself, had made. But Pounders finally said, "I will sustain the People's objections on all three of these grounds. . . . You can show them in closing arguments." Anyway, the jury was going to have the tapes in the jury room during deliberations. Before the jury was brought in, Davis complained to the judge that, having disallowed the chart and the videotapes, "You've cut us down to nothing."

Finally, Dr. Maloney was brought in. He was short, bearded, and wore thick eyeglasses and a patch over one eye. He sat down at the stand. Judge Pounders remarked to Maloney that he was greatly impressed with the doctor's credentials and reputation.

Gits began. "Doctor . . . do you recall that your first function when you were appointed to assist the defense was to start looking at the tapes—is that correct?"

"Yes."

"When you started looking at the tapes, initially, did you come to any initial conclusion with respect to the interview techniques utilized by CII?"

"Yes, I came to several after watching perhaps five or six tapes in their entirety. . . . One conclusion was that the interviews were clearly led by the interviewer rather than focused on the child, or the interviewee. And the other was that the vast amount of verbiage, or words said, were said by the interviewer, not by the children. Another observation was that these children indeed could talk and did seem quite willing to talk at the outset of the interview, and there did not appear to be a need for that kind of approach. In fact, that kind of an approach would be counterproductive in the sense that the interviewers were saying too much, and providing too much information, what I would refer to as a 'stage setting.'"

"Were those your only conclusions?"

"There were many more. Those were the primary, first ideas that I had, the first conclusions that I did come to, yes."

"Was it your conclusion that the number of words used by the interviewer were too many?"

"Yes, definitely. . . . I'm really talking about the ratio of words between the interviewer and the interviewee, the child. Given the premise that the goal of this kind of interview is to get information from a child, to learn about their experiences, their memories, what has been done with them, then we want to hear the child talk. And if the child is able to talk and is willing to talk, the interviewer's job is to facilitate that and get them to talk."

"Doctor, would it be fair to say that you are going to find children who are too scared to talk, so the interviewer has to talk more?" asked Gits.

"They were verbal kids. They seemed relaxed. They were talking. So there did not appear to be any basis for taking over the interview," said Maloney.

"So the interviewer spoke more. What's wrong with that?"

"There are many things. One is that you are presenting a template, or a design for what's going to happen. You're communicating to the child: 'I'm gonna talk. I'm gonna ask questions. Your job is to sit back and follow my lead. . . .'"

"Why is that wrong?"

"Because you avoid being able to learn from the child, in the child's own language, what their experience is, how they organize their own history, their own memories."

"Why is that bad?"

"Because your task really is to find out that information. What is this child saying? What does the child remember. The more you use an interviewer to effect that, or provide them with information, that could contaminate them, the less you can rely on anything you get out of them. . . . These interviews did not flow in the direction of the child. In other words, typical child evaluation interview, you let the child talk, and you follow their lead. You keep them speaking. In these interviews the kids all were machined through the exact same process. Toward the end of that process they were being asked very direct and almost coercive questions about sexual behavior. At those times some of the children became fairly nonverbal and were simply pointing and did so in a somewhat passive way and sometimes even in a questioning way."

"Did you form any opinion as to whether these children were such that numerous questions by the interviewer were inappropriate?"

"In all cases, yes. . . . As I was saying previously, one of the first observations I made was that the interviewers were doing the vast majority of verbal output. And there are reasons why that could be very problematical in an evaluation interview."

"Without knowing anything about the children . . . would you be able to come to any conclusion, based on the numbers alone, as to whether or not the interview techniques were proper?"

"I would have to integrate one premise which I've already measured—that the children were willing to talk. They did talk. . . . If you gave me a random sample of children, nine children roughly aged four and a half to nine, and I knew they were picked out of some kind of normal population, I would say that it was backwards, and it would be wrong."

"Can you tell us what else you did with respect to your analysis of the interview techniques of the CII tape?" asked Gits.

"The next step I took was to categorize various aspects of these interviews and classify the type of behavior that was occurring, the type of interchange between the interviewer and the child," Maloney answered.

"Can you tell us how you went about that?"

"Several different ways. My first impression when I watched the very first tapes, was that these were done in some systematic way. These were not interviews that followed the lead of the child. I watched probably forty or fifty tapes of different children and developed what I have referred to as a script. And what I was trying to do in reviewing those tapes was to isolate out certain kinds of activities, behaviors, statements made by the examiners to all or most of the children."

"Why do you call it a script?"

"The reason I called it a script is that in interviewing children the focus is on the child. The opposite of following the child is following some kind of predetermined program. I used the word, 'script,' for that—to refer to that program, but I also use the word, 'script' because even word usage by the various examiners with the various children was very close. It was if they were reading a script. . . ."

"Can you tell us, doctor, what's wrong with the script?"

"The very concept of using a program or a script in an interview of a child is wrong in the sense that it is putting in the interview situation material from the interviewer rather than obtaining spontaneous information from the child. The more that's done the less you will be able to conclude about the child's behavior and statements."

"But doesn't that depend, doctor, on the particular child at hand?"

"It certainly depends on the particular child. . . . Generally the same script was used for all the children. That simply underscores that it was programmed that way. It was planned that way."

"Is there something wrong with using the same methodology or script with children throughout that age range?"

"There's something basically and inherently wrong with using a script in any type of evaluation interview."

"What's wrong with it? Why is it wrong?"

"Several things. First is that there does not appear to have been any consideration from the cognitive development of the children. Second, there is no consideration of the relative brightness of the children and the relative fluency of the children, the sex of the children. They are all considered, at least by implication, as a homogenous mass that you must treat the same way. . . ."

"Doctor, do you believe you have the ability, from looking at the CII tapes . . . to come to a conclusion of the cognitive development level of any given child?"

"Other than in a very general sense, without a complete evaluation of the child, it is very difficult to say. We don't have enough data in terms of their own responses on those tapes, to make that kind of a conclusion."

"Would it be improper in your opinion to conduct an interview of a child for child sexual abuse without doing some kind of analysis as to the cognitive development of the child?"

"I believe it generally would because the cognitive evaluation provides you the additional data to assess what a child is saying. The bottom line of all this is: the child is saying something. How would we know why they're saying it? Is it their own experience or did it occur some other way?"

"In your viewing of the videotapes in this case, did you observe any testing of a child to ascertain cognitive developmental level?"

"Not to determine cognitive level. There was some testing to see if they knew the names of certain body parts, but it wasn't cognitive."

"Can you tell us what particular things you observed that were repeated from child to child that led you to believe that there was a script being utilized?"

"In almost all cases the interviews started with drawing a picture that was typically outlined by the interviewer. After that there was a procedure where they went into naming body parts, the specific focus being on the sexual body parts. There was then an introduction of so-called anatomically correct dolls, with the focus again on sexual body parts of the dolls. There was an introduction of pictures of students and teachers from the school, where persons were identified by the examiner and by the child with specific focus on certain teachers in the school, and sometimes the child himself. There was an introduction of puppets as a method of presenting information. There was an introduction of the nature of these dolls, that they were dolls that you could not find in a store. There was an introduction of variously referred to 'yucky,' 'sneaky,' 'tricky' games. There was an introduction of Ray Buckey being a bad person, surveilled by police. There was an introduction of ejaculation in terms of Ray Buckey, and what that might look like, taste like, and so forth. Those items were in almost every case here and in many others as well. . . .

"I would like to add, however, in a number of these tapes, there is something going on. You don't see a picture of a child walking in, and an examiner walking in and sitting down. They are already in process, so something could have happened before. I don't know what. But when they are sitting down in this phase, they are drawing a picture of the person, frequently outlined by the examiner."

"Is there something wrong with what occurred in that type of interaction?"

"The first thing that I would suggest that is wrong about that is that there is a subtle communication—and sometimes not so subtle—that what is going to happen between these two people is going to be controlled by the interviewer. And what you want is information that is controlled and generated by the interviewee, the child."

"How is that communicated by this drawing?" asked Gits.

"It's pretty straightforward, in the sense that if I want you to draw something and I want you to look at it and help me with it, the examiner is taking over the behavior," answered Maloney.

"Anything else that appeared improper about that kind of activity?"

"Drawing that picture is a stage-setting behavior for identifying sexual parts."

"You said a 'stage-setting' behavior. What does that mean?"

"It simply means that it provides a certain kind of information, a certain kind of activity from which more information will be based or evolved from."

"What information does that drawing of a picture provide to the child?"

"It goes into the next part of it where they say, 'What are these?' and if you recall that, they will often say, 'What's this?' and they will have a mark in the middle of the torso, usually identified as the belly button. Then, they will have two marks up above, usually identified as breasts. Then they will identify private parts. They also do identify hair, fingers, and so forth, but very soon on—in one case, for example, it was four minutes into the interview—the child was saying 'private parts,' and 'What's another name for that?' 'Vagina,' and 'weenie,' or whatever. That was introduced that soon into the interview."

"You talked about naming body parts as something that gradually evolves from this situation. Can you tell us what's wrong with naming body parts?"

"In isolation, nothing. The primary problem with that is that the end result of this identifying body parts is to identify the sexual body parts. In almost all cases, that's where it ends. At that point in the interview the child[ren have], typically, said zero about their own sexual experiences. But they have been directed to talk about genitalia and other so-called private parts. Again, in doing that, you run the risk of stage-setting. . . . It also presents data that the children may not know. There are a lot of the children, four, five, six, that have not been able to say what even the difference between a boy and a girl is."

"Wouldn't naming body parts be an appropriate activity if you were simply trying to determine the terminology used by the children? . . . Would it be appropriate at that point?" Gits asked.

"No . . . because it's setting the stage that we are talking about sexual matters. . . . Once you do that you never know what they know before you got to that point," Maloney answered.

"Couldn't that kind of activity be justified by virtue of the interviewer wanting to use the same terms that the child used?"

"You could argue that. But what I'm saying is that you are presenting that as a topic when the child never spontaneously brought it up."

"What else was there that you observed about the scripting that occurred in this particular case?"

"The next one is the introduction of the dolls. . . . We are talking about dolls that are usually referred to as 'sexually anatomically correct dolls,' or so-called S.A.C. dolls."

"Is it your opinion that there was something improper about the introduction of those anatomically correct dolls?"

"Yes."

"Was it your opinion that the use of the dolls in these nine cases was improper?"

"Yes . . . they were very systematically introduced in a fashion suggesting that they were silly, that it was funny. They referred to the breasts as 'cupcakes.' In some of the later interviews, after the dolls had been used a lot, they got parts all over. The kids wrote on them, beat them up, and they had to repair them. There was definite levity in that, matched—or mismatched—with very serious content material for children this age. Obvious sex characteristics . . . sexual education for children is very serious. They're concerned about it. It's not funny to them. In many cases the way it was presented to them was in a derogatory way, a negative way. I can't imagine a rationale for doing that. You might say it makes them more at ease, but it might not make them see it as a serious issue.

"Secondly, the dolls are almost always presented clothed, and the children are allowed to experiment with them, at their own rate, at their own speed. In this case, they are dumped out of bags and said, 'These are funny dolls. You can't find them in a store. They're really silly.' And they strip them, and they show them. You asked, initially, what's wrong. We're really forcing the focus on sex in these interviews. You might say, ahead of time, 'I don't know whether these kids were ever abused or not abused.' "

"You talked about reinforcement, doctor. When you say 'reinforcement,' what do you mean?"

"I could give it to you in example form. If a child were to have identified a private part of the drawing, the dolls were then introduced, and they say, 'What was this part again?' and the child says, 'vagina,' and they say, 'Great! You're smart! You're really a smart kid!' That's the reinforcement."

"Is there anything wrong with reidentifying the body parts on the anatomicaly correct dolls?"

"What it does is it gets these children farther away from their own spontaneous remarks about sex. You are presenting it to them in a drawing form. You're presenting it to them in a doll form. It's almost as if you wanted to make sure that they're going to focus on those areas. If you're interested in getting spontaneous information, it's obvious to me that that would be wrong."

"Couldn't the use of dolls be justified in terms of trying to desensitize the child?" Gits asked.

"You can say that, sure, but you are presenting them with sexual material and saying this is a big deal," Maloney responded.

"Is there a danger that using these dolls might result in leading the child to react in terms of fantasy rather than actual events?"

"There is a danger, yes."

"You mentioned that the focusing in on the body parts was done a second time when the anatomically correct dolls were introduced. In your opinion is there any justification for doing that a second time, that is, naming the same body part that the child picked on the picture and hooking it into the body part?"

"To me there is no justification. . . ."

"Can you tell us what other aspects of these interviews constituted a script?"

"Yes. Another one related to the dolls is a scenario wherein there is a presentation that these dolls 'help us figure it out.' Now that word, 'it,' has several different references but it is usually vague. But that kind of specific statement was used with most of the children."

"What's wrong with that?"

"Many things. The first one is the way that it is presented. There is an implication, if not a statement, that there is something wrong. At this point, from the children, we don't know if there's anything wrong or not. But saying, 'These dolls help us figure out some of these things,' presents the idea that there is something there that needs to be figured out. So that's a stage-setting behavior as well. There's ground laid that we're going to have to work on something here. In some cases there's something much more specific about that, saying that negative things happened. There are words like 'yucky' used very frequently in these statements. . . .

"Secondly, there is a game-playing quality to this. Before the dolls were being used to identify body parts to look at, this time, we're using the dolls as an intermediary. 'The dolls will help us figure it out.' This is where you could really get into the risk of a fantasy problem. You are removing responsibility from the child. You're not saying to that child, 'I want you to only tell me what you know.' You're saying, 'We can use the dolls. They'll help us.' "

"Generally speaking, when the interviewer is using these dolls, to help us figure it out, is the doll clothed or unclothed?" Gits asked.

"I believe they're usually unclothed at that point. This comes after the other parts of the script, which brings up a focus again, or contamination about sex," Maloney answered.

"Is it your opinion that at that point in time, having pulled the clothes off the anatomical doll and making references to 'dolls helping us figure it out,' were you able to render an opinion as to whether or not the child would understand that that's what it was about?"

"There's no way to know exactly, but I think there's a very high probability that sex has been emphasized so much, prior to that, that now we're presented with a problem that needs to be figured, that would be one of the high-probability associations: 'Figuring means sex.' "

Summing it all up, Maloney said the CII interview techniques were "about as backwards as you can get," and that "many of the kids' statements in the interviews were generated by the examiner."

Having covered the dolls and puppets, Gits asked, "Are there other areas and portions of the script that you have identified?"

"Yes. Another portion of the script would be the presentation of photos of either classes or teachers or students at McMartin."

"What is there about that that is improper?"

"The risk that this technique runs, and the potential harm it causes, is that it could be looked at as a teaching and rehearsal strategy, rather than a strategy wherein an interviewer independently determines what a child remembers."

"You say, 'a teaching and rehearsal strategy.' Could you tell us what you mean by that phrase?"

"What usually is involved when this is done is, photos are pulled out, regarding the child, usually, and the class that the child was in . . . photos of the school, and the technique is to say, 'Well, let's look at this. Do you remember some of these people?' Now if the child spontaneously says, 'Yes. This is so-and-so . . .' and they recall them, I don't see much harm in doing that. There are some cases, however, where children said they didn't remember who they were. Sometimes they would misidentify people. And then they were corrected in that regard. The risk that you're running here is that you're not getting a spontaneous recall from the child. . . . The role in this kind of interview is to try to obtain spontaneous information from children. . . . Once a child identifies someone, verbally, in a spontaneous way, I think it might be a good procedure to go back and say, 'Is this who we're talking about?' If you do it the other way around there is a contamination or a potential for a contamination that you can't rectify."

"How is it a contamination?"

". . . Some of the other parts of the script say 'things happened at the school,' or 'yucky things happened at the school.' There's an implication that some people might have done these things. The child might not even remember a given person. . . ."

"Anything else about using class photos that appears to be inappropriate to you?" Gits asked.

"In some cases the key figures are simply pointed out to the child. Some of the children didn't recall who they were," Maloney responded.

"Are there other areas that you've identified as 'script'?"

"Yes . . . which I have titled, 'Mention of Children Who Have Attended CII.' Children who had been evaluated there before. And I could give some of these examples . . . what we're talking about here is statements wherein the interviewers say, 'All these kids have been here before.' "

"What's wrong with that?"

"That, in isolation, I wouldn't say there's something specifically wrong, other than that there starts to be a cumulative effect that something of a major nature went on. . . . There is also a social pressure and coercion in that they don't just say that all these kids have been here. They tend to say that all these kids have been here and they've told us all these yucky things. There's another part of the script and it's integrated with this part of the script."

"You say it's social pressure. What do you mean by that?"

"Social pressure in the sense that these children are told that . . . 'hundreds,' 'every child in this picture.' So they're presenting this child in contrast to all the other children."

"You talked about an element of coercion in this kind of technique. How is that coercive?"

"They are saying, 'All of your mates have told us these secrets.' There becomes an expectation that the child should do the same."

"What danger could that have on the propriety of the interview?"

"It does present that expectation and there are data available to indicate that adults and kids do respond to social pressure."

"Couldn't that be justified on the theory of an attempt to put the child at ease?" Gits asked.

"It could be . . . [if] the child manifested anxiety. . . . But if you do it before that . . . there's no way to get back to spontaneity. You've already laid out that part," Maloney answered.

"In viewing the nine videotapes in question here, did you observe any kind of anxiety reaction that preceded these kinds of words, 'All the kids have told us about the yucky secrets'?"

". . . I did not see what I would operationally define as anxiety."

"Anything else about mentioning that other children had already been to CII that appeared improper?"

"In some of the cases there is a specific reference—it isn't just that 'children have already been here.' There is an indication 'we already know what happened.' . . . It's presenting that as a fact, as an authority, and the authority is based not only on the interviewer but on all the other children."

"What effect could that have on the child?"

"I would see it as another form of pressure, another attempt at forcing conformity. . . . It decreases spontaneity."

"Any other aspects to the script you've isolated or identified?"

"Yes. There is a part that presents the puppets as a vehicle for telling secrets. . . . You know what we have here are puppets, and they really help us. The kids don't even have to do it.' "

"What's wrong with that?"

"Well, from a purely clinical point of view . . . it's an inappropriate start-off technique. . . . It tends to decrease personal responsibility. 'The puppets tell us. The kids don't have to say anything.' "

"Do you have a recollection of the interview between Kee MacFarlane and Veronica?"

"Yes, I do."

"Can you tell us, in general, how you would characterize that interview?"

"It was a very long interview. A great deal of discussion by the examiner.... Veronica says very little. Maybe two or three words."

"Any other areas of the script you've noted?" Gits asked.

"Yes. The next one I have is titled, 'Kids Have Been Scared.' It's a statement that ties in with mention of the kids to CII, but it adds information that either kids have been scared to talk or that kids simply have been scared," Maloney said.

"The interviewer provides the information. What's wrong with that?"

"It is what I would describe as 'stage-setting.' If you're trying to obtain information from a child, once you say that, it's difficult to determine whether that child himself has been scared or is simply responding to that kind of a statement."

"If a child had not been threatened, what would or could be the potential effect on the child?"

"It presents information that something might have occurred that people were scared about.... 'Listen, we've seen about a hundred kids and they've all been scared.' "

"Did you, in your view of the videotapes, ... note any behavior that would indicate anxiousness on the part of the children?"

"I don't recall any."

"What about the response of an interviewer when Mary points to a particular picture?"

"The response is reinforcing, since the interviewer says, 'Yeah!' and 'That's what a whole lot of kids told us.' "

"So what if it reinforces the answers? What's wrong with that?"

"The next time you get into another area and say, 'Can you point?' there would be a higher probability they would point to Kay."

"What about the next area?" Gits asked.

"The next area is titled, 'The Secret Machine,' " Maloney said.

"Could you tell us what that area involves?"

"It's an instruction to the children that if they have a secret they can say it into the microphone ... and they tell them that the secret will go down the wire and into a box and will be gone forever, or they won't have to worry.... First, it can be confusing.... I don't know if there's any clarity as to what that word really means to children.... If these children were molested, if they were traumatized, it's simply a misrepresentation. It wouldn't go away."

"And would you go into the next area of the script?"

"There is a part that I have titled, 'Older Kids/Younger Kids.' "

"Would you tell us what that involves, please?"

"There's a fairly systematic statement given to the children that the older kids are very helpful because they are able to give a report the younger children can't give. They are better detectives. They are smarter. They need to help out the younger kids."

"And what is wrong with that approach?"

"It is an inducement to the children to talk. It presents some external pressure, and in some cases the pressure is relatively severe. . . . You run the risk of telling the children that if they don't say something they are not smart, they are not like the other, older kids, and they are not helping out the younger children. All of that could be subsumed under the implication of stage-setting: 'This is what everybody else did. Who is not bright? Who is older? Who is helping?' "

"Could this kind of pressure change the behavior of children in terms of responding correctly?"

"Yes it could."

Maloney cited several studies showing that this pressure could induce most children to give false answers.

"What is the next area of the script that you've isolated?" Gits asked.

"It's an area called 'Secret Policeman,' " Maloney said.

"Generally, what does that area involve?"

"It involves a fairly specific description that Ray Buckey is being surveilled. . . . It identifies him as a bad person."

"How does it do that?"

"Some of the things were quite direct in that area: 'He needs to be watched.' 'He needs to be put in jail.' . . . It identifies him as a bad person who needs watching. There's no other explanation."

"But the mere fact that that kind of communication is communicated to the child, can you say thereby that it might have an effect on the child's behavior or responses?"

"Certainly. . . . If the child believes that something happened at the school, that hundreds of kids have said it. A 'yucky' thing, they've been presented with issues of sex . . . and now Ray is introduced as a person who needs police surveillance. I don't think it takes a great leap to identify him as a person who is involved in all those things and he has already been placed on the stage."

"The next area, please," Gits said.

" 'Naming of Dolls.' It deals with an interaction between the interviewer and the child where they are looking at these dolls. I believe in almost all cases the dolls were unclothed. And they are saying who played the game and they want to identify these dolls as various players. The players have been identified by the pictures. That's generally this part of the script."

"What's wrong with that?"

"They now take these dolls and use them as a personification of these people. In almost all the cases that we have here, Peggy is identified as the fattest one. They use that kind of terminology and the kids call her 'Miss Piggy.' So the dolls are derogatory. Then they use the introduction of these people as derogatory as well."

"And your next area, doctor?"

"This is 'Names Introduced.' This is a general category that involves the examiner presenting to the child some idea that certain games were played at the school. The games are typically referred to as 'sneaky' or 'tricky' or 'naked.' It presents the child with that information. They're essentially telling them that this is what happened. If you have a child [who] did not have that experience, the impact may be that within the context of the interview the child may say yes, that something happened.... It's an information-giving technique."

"And the final category?"

"The final category I have titled 'Stuff Out Of Ray's Penis.' It involves a series of quite direct questions about Ray ejaculating and certainly the implication is made to the kids of oral copulation. I don't recall any child saying that Ray ejaculated before this was brought up.... The children simply didn't say anything about it. The second thing about it was to me the most ridiculous set of questions in the whole interview because they start off and they use, with the majority of the children, the same terms. 'Did it taste like candy?' 'Did it taste like strawberry?' 'Did it taste like pizza?' 'Did it taste like chocolate?' This has already been identified with the penis area of the Ray doll. Children of that age ... think of that as an area of excretion."

"If you would take these scripts that you have isolated or identified here, how would you characterize them in terms of the propriety of the interview?" Gits asked.

"... With that many things wrong, with that significant amount of negative influence, I would say that these were very inappropriate interviews for this purpose," Maloney answered.

"If we were to take the various aspects of this script that you have isolated, and put those together, is there a joint conclusion that you can reach in terms of the propriety of the interviews?"

"I think the risk that you run, very strongly in this case, is getting kids to acquiesce in saying things, or point to things that we are not sure of at all. There's a great deal of pressure on them to do that.... In evaluation for sexual abuse, this would be an inappropriate way to proceed for all the reasons I have given ... in summary, it presents information to the children that we don't know if they had or did not have before. It tells them that things happened at the school. It gives the general nature of the things. It presents the players in the situation and, essentially, presents all the pieces to a puzzle. And there was very strong motivation for the children to solve the puzzle. The motivation comes out of things like, 'Are you smart or dumb?' 'Are you a good detective?' 'Are you going to please your mother and father?' And then, finally, it gives a vehicle for solution, which are these puppets, these dolls. So what you're doing is presenting a situation that you could take with any children, and not know why you got the results you got out of it, no matter what their experience was before that."

"And is it your view that these nine CII interviews are worse than just plain useless?" Gits asked.

"Objection."

"Sustained."

"Would it be fair to say, doctor, that the only end result of these interviews is that they can't be relied upon because of the techniques that were utilized?"

"Objection."

There was a very long sidebar. We never did get the answer.

"Are there, or could there be, factors occurring to a child before a CII interview, that might affect the child's response, both in the CII interview and later?" Gits asked.

"Sure."

"Hypothetically, what factors might affect a child's report at a CII interview?"

"Any interaction with other persons that dealt with the same type of material. Multiple interviews, or any interviews. Now, it's presented to them by other persons. Siblings, family members, police officers, any information. . . ."

"If you could . . . hypothetically again, assume that the child loves and respects his or her parents. And assume that the parent believes that the interviewer is qualified to do a child sexual abuse evaluation. Then assume, if you would, that after the CII interview, the interviewer goes in and tells the parents that his or her child was molested. Could that have an impact on the child's later behavior?"

"Objection. Speculative."

"Sustained."

"Doctor Maloney, are there psychological factors that might affect a child's behavior after the CII interview?"

"There's many possibilities."

"Can you tell us how it is that you came to that conclusion?"

There is another objection from Gunson, followed by a long sidebar. The objection is sustained and we don't get the answer to the question.

"Doctor, are you aware of any recognized body of experts in the field of interview methodology who espouse the interview techniques that you've isolated in this particular case?"

"No."

"Thank you. No further questions."

Davis rose to examine the witness. He walked to the lectern and asked, "In these nine interviews, did you find that the techniques employed were so inappropriate that you, in your opinion, cannot determine whether or not these children were molested?"

"Objection."

"Sustained."

"Did you, in looking at these interviews reach an opinion whether or not the process employed was valid for purposes of determining the truth of whether these children were or were not molested?"

"In my analysis I would conclude that the interviewing techniques contaminated a great deal . . . it's not a valid method."

"And in what you saw . . . did it appear to you that the information provided to the children assumed that Raymond Buckey molested children at the McMartin Preschool?"

"The comments of the interviewer said that, yes."

"Was there information related by the children that they received information from the news media before they were interviewed?"

"Objection."

"Sustained."

"Was there information contained within the interview that they had received information about the inquiry from their parents?"

"Objection."

"Sustained."

"Was there information on the interviews that directly or indirectly indicated [that] the child[ren] had learned information relating to the subject of the questions being asked, from other children?"

"Objection."

"Sustained."

"Did the videotapes contain information indicating the children were given prior information about the subject matter?"

"Objection."

"Sustained."

"Before they were interviewed at CII, if any of these children were given information through news media, parents, siblings, classmates, would that, in your experience, regarding the contamination, affect what they said in those interviews?"

"Objection."

"Sustained."

Davis eventually successfully rephrased the question—or so it seemed. The doctor answered, "When we're attempting to find out the truth of their experience in this type of evaluative interview, some of the experience could be vicarious, meaning that they did not personally experience it but heard of it through some other mode. That would have to be clarified through the course of the interview itself—what they were saying from their own experience, and what they were saying of what they know or had heard."

"Objection."

"Sustained. The question and answer are stricken."

In one interview, the doctor said, the child did not even know who Raymond Buckey was at the beginning, but after a lengthy evaluation, was making many statements about him. In another videotaped interview, Kee MacFarlane repeatedly tried to get a boy to "remember" the "naked movie star" game, telling him that numerous other children had already told about it. When the boy insisted he never saw anyone play the game, MacFarlane said, "Well, what good are you? You must be dumb."

At the end of the day, friends of the defendants were pleased with Maloney's testimony and said they felt he had effectively dismantled the credibility of the CII evaluations. Judge Pounders did not like Maloney's testimony. In fact, he was so displeased with it that he said he had done research to explore the possibility of striking it. That, of course, would have crippled the defense, since the CII evaluations were the "evidence" on which the original charges were filed, and the defense strategy depended upon discrediting them.

Deputy District Attorney Gunson began his cross-examination. He asked a series of questions about establishing rapport with a child. Gunson also attempted to establish that the CII techniques were indispensable to getting children to talk about their alleged molestations, and attacked Maloney's statements that children are suggestible and can be led to make false allegations. Even when he affected a look of fierce indignation while asking his questions, Gunson did not have a powerful presence. What we saw was a small man with a voice so weak that it was barely audible. The jurors were staring off into space and did not appear to be listening. They looked tired and bored. Gunson asked Maloney if it wasn't appropriate to present a child with information if he failed to recall. Maloney answered that, "It's not necessarily wrong to present information to a child, but I must realize that I may have given them the answer."

This testimony was limited to the nine children called as witnesses in the trial. We know very little about the other children—several hundred—who also were interviewed at CII. We do know from the testimony of several witnesses that there were some who wanted nothing to do with the "evaluations" and refused to participate. And there was at least one child who swore at Kee MacFarlane and walked out. Initially, according to testimony in the preliminary hearing and the trial, all of the children denied any knowledge of molestation at the preschool, except for one whose stories were so bizarre that even the prosecution chose not to call her as a witness.

If CII's evaluations were unsound, the writing of their grant proposals was not. We received a large pile of documents from the state government in Sacramento listing the grants and funding received by CII since the beginning of the McMartin case. It added up to millions—grants from county, state, and federal agencies, not to mention the many private donations. Non-profit corporations are required to disclose all of their funding to the state and these disclosures are public records accessible to all. In the 250 pages we received, which tell what was done with the money, there is not one item that indicates any concern for the falsely accused.

In 1985, at least one million people were falsely accused of child abuse, according to Mary Pride's 1986 book *The Child Abuse Industry*. Since then, the government has been less forthcoming with this kind of information, but the number of reports and sexual abuse cases has grown exponentially. They seem to have cast all discretion to the wind. Recently in Oregon, a preschool teacher, an elderly woman, was given a long prison sentence for touching a four-year-old child on the chest! There are enough equally ludicrous cases to fill several volumes.

There is a missing piece in this puzzle. Not very much is known about pedophilia. Most of the scientific studies on this subject have been done outside the United States. Most of the few done in America are so tainted by hysteria and greed that they are worthless. Studies done in Europe suggest that most pedophiles are either consistently heterosexual or consistently homosexual, and that only about 2 percent have a desire for sexual contact with children of both sexes. It is also apparent that almost all pedophiles prefer children between the ages of nine and seventeen, not infants. The probability of thousands of preschool teachers randomly raping two-year-old infants of both sexes is so remote as to be almost nonexistent. Yet thousands of people all over America were accused of doing exactly that. The prosecutors did not do their homework. Neither did the defense attorneys.

It can hardly be denied that Maloney's testimony was a clear, accurate, common-sense analysis but, not surprisingly, the *Los Angeles Times* published a story the day after Maloney was excused stating that he had failed to discredit the CII evaluations.

After Maloney was excused, the defense attempted, in a hearing, to bring in a presentation by a psychologist to further demonstrate the invalidity of the CII evaluations, but Judge Pounders ruled that the presentation was inadmissible on the grounds that it was misleading and time-consuming. And so there were lengthy arguments that were also time-consuming. The psychologist's presentation could hardly have been as misleading or as time-consuming as the prosecution's overkill of doctors and other "experts." Nevertheless, the presentation—one that the defense considered crucial—did not get in. There was an angry exchange between the judge and Davis in which Judge Pounders said, "We have got to conclude this trial. We are going to do that, even if it's over your dead body!"

"Excuse me," Davis responded. "I don't think you meant 'over my dead body.'"

"I mean exactly that!" the judge shouted. He repeatedly chastised the defense loudly and angrily for taking too much time.

It was reported in several newspapers that day that Mary Ann Jackson's lawsuit against Los Angeles County had been dismissed on the grounds that both state and federal statutes provide total immunity to any person who reports or prosecutes a person for alleged child abuse, even if the accusations are made with malice and with the knowledge that they are false. Several similar lawsuits have been dismissed on the same grounds. They have all been appealed.

We asked our attorney friend Irene, "What does it mean when people in government can falsely imprison you, ruin you, brand you for life as a monster, and there's no way you can get restitution?"

"I believe it's called fascism," she said. "Theoretically, in a civilized world, the government is a bunch of people who work to enhance the quality of life. We don't have that."

The defense called, as their next witness, Sandra Krebs, one of the women who, along with Kee MacFarlane, interviewed the children.

". . . What training did you have to evaluate children on sexual abuse?" Davis asked.

"Just the classes I had in college, talking to children and talking to adolescents. . . . In college I did some counseling, different things. Sometimes drug abuse."

"What courses did you have in college on child abuse to connect with evaluating children?"

"Just any psychology class and just a sense I can establish rapport with other people and facilitate their talking about different subjects . . . even though they might not want to. . . ."

"You agree, don't you, that when it comes to evaluating children who may or may not have been molested, there is a certain minimal amount of professional training necessary for someone to do that. . . . Don't you need training for that sort of thing?"

"Objection."

"Sustained."

"Did anyone assist you in evaluating those children?"

"I was assisted and supervised in certain instances that maybe had something to do with disorders. . . ."

"Would it be fair to say that whatever training you did before CII, you were essentially self-taught?"

"With the exception of conferences I attended in 1980 and 1982."

Asked whether she told parents that their children had been molested Krebs replied, "I told them what was on the tape." To most of the questions, she answered, "I don't remember," so many times we lost count. Asked why she concluded that certain children had been sexually abused, she gave answers like, "What struck me on this tape was long pauses that I thought were a sign of fear," and "one of the things she [one of the children] did was answer the questions before I finished them," and "He [another child] said he didn't remember, but the way he said it, he said it quickly . . . and that, in my mind, was possible repression."

"Isn't there an alternative?" Davis asked.

"That he was nervous. . . ."

All of Krebs's answers were speculative. She denied that she had, after the conclusion of the videotaped interviews, urged the parents to make criminal complaints to the police so that they could get money from the state under the California crime victims' statute. But Davis read from the transcript of her testimony in the preliminary hearing when her answer to the same question was the opposite. Asked why she changed her answer, Krebs replied with a long, rambling recitation that did not provide any enlightenment.

"Did you or did you not tell the parents [that] their kids were molested after these interviews?"

"I did not say they were molested. I told them what happened in the interview."

Davis read, again, from the transcript of the preliminary hearing when she was asked the same question, and her answer then was, "Yes, I did."

Krebs also acknowledged that she had been a guest at the home of Billy, the boy who said he was forced to drink blood by "atomic mutants" in a church, and molested in a supermarket. She said she had visited this family about fifteen times, and that she had also attended the meetings in Manhattan Beach.

When Davis had finished, Gits asked her why she found it necessary to ask a child, six times, if the teachers had done any "yucky touching." She said, "I thought that maybe I could find another way to make it more comfortable."

Gits asked her why she always picked the black, naked doll to represent Peggy. Krebs denied having done this and said it was the children who picked the doll. During recess, outside the courtroom, Peggy told us, "That was a lie. They always picked the black doll to represent me, not the kids."

The next defense witness was Evelyn Pencheff, who taught at the preschool during the summers of 1981 and 1982. She was the sister of Charles Buckey, Peggy's husband. She had white hair, neatly trimmed, and stood tall and gracefully as she raised her right hand for the ritual of being sworn in. She had a cheerful, friendly face and she spoke clearly, having spent many years working as a teacher.

Pencheff testified that she had seen no naked children at the school, no child alone on the swing or the slide, no child tied up, and that the children showed no fear of Ray Buckey. She said she thought Buckey did "an excellent job conducting his classes. He seemed to be very friendly and enjoyed working in the classroom." Pencheff also testified that she never saw children or animals mistreated at the school. She said she frequently gave Ray advice on how to conduct his classes, and that she never saw anything that raised the slightest suspicion that children were being molested.

Panic struck again. One of the jurors informed the judge that the computer firm he worked for was likely to go out of business within the next six months and had just laid off a third of its work force. If he became unemployed he would have no income except the ten dollars a day he received for jury service, and he would have to be excused. This would leave only one alternate. The trial started with six alternates, but four jurors were excused for various reasons and now several were complaining that they were in serious danger of losing their jobs because the trial had gone on far longer than they were originally led to believe. If the number of jurors fell below twelve, it could cause a mistrial. Judge Pounders eliminated eight witnesses the defense had planned to call and said, "I have an obligation to see that it's a fair trial and that it gets to a jury that still exists." The cost of the case was now moving close to fifteen million dollars, and the defense had yet to call its most important witnesses: two former teachers from the school, and at least one medical expert witness to refute the testimony of the three prosecution doctors, and Ray and Peggy Buckey. Then there would have to be at least three months of rebuttal, surrebuttal, jury instructions, and deliberations.

Wednesday, April 19, 1989. The jury finally got a look at the McMartin Preschool after the prosecutors had tried for months to block it. The jurors spent an hour going through the tiny structure while reporters were ordered to stay on the other side of the street. It was a bright, balmy day. Summer comes early in Los Angeles.

The jury was brought to Manhattan Beach, along with the judge, in a sheriff's department van. After going through the classrooms and the playground, the jurors went across the street, where they were able to see directly into Buckey's classroom. They were definitely interested and were scribbling notes and measuring distances between the slide and the front gate, and other parts of the school.

After the jurors were gone, we were allowed to go into the preschool. It was all there, the wooden animals Chuck Buckey had made, the rooms with tables and little chairs, toys, children's books, puppets, blackboards. We were surprised to find that we could easily hear people in the next room, talking, and could understand every word and this was true of every classroom, because each room had a hole cut in the wall, where a heater was installed. If you raised the grille, there was nothing but empty space between the rooms. It seemed strange that the prosecution was asking us to believe that "mass molestations" and mutilation of animals could have occurred in such a tiny place.

The media confronted Lael Rubin with their microphones and asked her questions about the jury's viewing of the school. She said it was "a good thing" that the jurors were able to see the school. She made no mention of the fact that she had tried to prevent it.

The next witness was Babette Spitler. She was an especially good witness because she looked angelic; at forty-one she was still a beautiful woman and her soft voice and gentle smile charmed nearly everyone—except, of course, the prosecutors, who objected to question after question and repeatedly moved to have her answers stricken. Spitler taught at the school beginning in 1973 and was there full-time from July 1980 until the school was closed in 1984. She said she never saw Ray Buckey there before 1981, contradicting the testimony of several of the child witnesses. She also testified that the two-year-old boy whose mother launched the case was never taught by Ray Buckey.

Spitler said she brought her own two children to the preschool. She said she never saw any child molested and that she would have reported it if she had. She denied seeing any naked games or naked children and said she never saw Buckey leave the school with children. She spent two-and-a-half months in jail after the prosecutor persuaded Judge Ronald George that she was a danger to society. Spitler said her children had been taken from her and that it had taken two years to get them back. She said that Peggy Buckey was "supportive, loving . . . she helped the children develop social skills, which was one of the biggest focuses we had at McMartin."

After a long and unproductive cross-examination in which Rubin insinuated that Spitler had been told what to say on the stand, Rubin faced the television cameras and said, "I think it was very clear from her testimony that she's simply not a credible witness, someone who has to lie and give false testimony about very simple matters, really suggests and implies that there's something more serious that she's not being truthful about."

Spitler told the television newspeople, "There's really no way to describe what happened. Our lives were destroyed. We're putting everything back together, but it takes a long time. We lost everything." Spitler's statement was not broadcast on television. Rubin's was.

All seven of the original defendants lost their homes and all of their assets in the process of developing a defense against these accusations. It was an unequal struggle. The prosecutors did not have to divest themselves of their homes and their savings; they had massive amounts of public money behind them. They just collected their salaries and basked in the credibility of the state and the full support of the media.

* * *

Thursday, April 20, 1989. It was the second anniversary of the beginning of the trial. The judge said it was now the longest trial in world history. The mood had changed. Everyone seemed weary of the seemingly endless proceeding and hoped to get it over with. But the most interesting witnesses were yet to come. The outcome of the trial rested largely on their testimony.

The public still had little or no understanding of what the trial was about. A California man wrote a letter to the editor of a newspaper in which he angrily stated that he did not think any of the defendants in all these thousands of molestation cases were falsely accused, and that they should all be executed. A few days later, he himself was accused of child sexual abuse by his former wife, with whom he was engaged in a bitter divorce and custody dispute. After a terrifying ordeal, he was exonerated, and the charges were dropped. His lawyers then asked him to read aloud the letter he had written to the newspaper. He was too embarrassed to do it.

The defense called Charles Buckey, the husband of Peggy and the father of Ray, as its next witness. Buckey had white hair; a square face; and a deep, crisp voice like that of a television anchorman. He presented a very manly image. His answers were quick, short, and straightforward. On direct questioning, Davis's questions focused on the fact that the senior Buckey performed all of the maintenance on the school and trimmed the trees and foliage. Buckey said the school could easily be seen from the outside. Davis surveyed the entire school, piece by piece, with his questions.

Gunson began his cross-examination with questions about the fence, the trees, boards, measurements, leaves, branches, in his barely audible voice. But after the noon break, it got dirty! We were once again given a recital of the accusation of Ray Buckey's atrocious crime: going without underwear. But instead of asking when questioning the father, whether Mr. Buckey was aware of the allegations that Ray's genitals were seen when he was wearing shorts, Gunson, instead, repeatedly used the phrase "exposed himself to children," making the insinuation that Ray Buckey intentionally exposed himself to children, although there was no evidence to support such a belief. The diabolical *Playboy* magazine was brought into the colloquy once again. Gunson did not say, "*Playboy*," but asked the father if he was aware that his son had "pornography" in his possession.

Then it got really dirty. After the afternoon break, before the jury was brought in, Gunson asked the court's permission to read a police report alleging that neighbors saw Ray through his window masturbating with sexually oriented magazines. Gunson stated that the police report contained a complaint by neighbors who had witnessed this spectacle. The message, of course, was that Ray had been masturbating in a place where he could be seen by passersby, as an exhibitionist might do. Gunson said that neighbors would testify for the prosecution that they had seen this through Buckey's window.

A heated argument ensued. The defense attorneys asserted that this was too remote to be admissible, since it "does not connect with the charges." They also contended that it was more prejudicial than probative and therefore inadmissible under section 352 in the evidence code. The judge said, however, that it pertained to "unusual sex" and that this was what the trial was about. But it appeared to be not so much about "unusual sex" as about sexual hysteria. All the prosecution seemed to have going for it was the allegation that Ray looked at *Playboy* and didn't wear underwear, high crimes indeed, although hardly worth fifteen million dollars and a six-year ordeal. But what, exactly, was "unusual sex," and could any two people agree on where the line was drawn? And if the "unusual sex" was nonassaultive and nonabusive, what connection did it have to the charges against the defendants?

The next day, April 21, the couple who the prosecutors said had made the police report and were willing to testify for the prosecution told reporters they had never made any complaint against Buckey to the police, that they had not agreed to testify for the prosecution, and had not even been asked to.

"I am amazed," said the neighbor, John Doeppel. "I never said that Buckey posted pictures on his windows! I don't even know where they got that." He also stated that, during the three years they were neighbors, he had never had any problems with the Buckeys.

Gunson had said, the day before, that the prosecution would call the Doeppels to rebut the testimony given by Charles Buckey, namely, that his son's interest in *Playboy* and *Penthouse* was perfectly normal. But Doeppel said the prosecutors knew he could not be their witness.

Davis stated that the Doeppels had been denying the allegations for years, that it was a false promise of false evidence, made with the intent to poison the jurors' minds. He went on to say that the prosecution had repeatedly introduced unsubstantiated allegations against Buckey, with the promise of later bringing in corroborating witnesses who, somehow, never appeared. He recalled the prosecution's lengthy medical testimony pertaining to three children who never appeared as witnesses, resulting in dropping of the charges related to those children. He also spoke of Lael Rubin's assertion, during her cross-examination of Virginia McMartin, that Ray Buckey had gone to a clergyman for counseling for pedophilia, and the clergyman had told reporters he had counseled Buckey for alcohol abuse, and that pedophilia had never even been mentioned during the counseling.

Peggy shook her head in disbelief. Outside the courtroom, she told us, "They're just trying to make Ray look bad because they don't have anything. The whole thing was a hoax!"

On redirect, Ray's father, Charles Buckey, said that he had had a conversation with his wife about the fact that Ray did not wear underwear, and that, although he did not approve, his wife had said, "In an age when women go around not wearing bras, it's certainly no big deal."

"How long before he taught at the school was it that you knew he didn't wear underwear?" Gits asked.

"About the time he got out of high school, so probably two or three years."

On recross, Gunson asked Charles Buckey, "Before Raymond Buckey started working at the preschool, did Mrs. Buckey talk to you about whether it would be appropriate for Raymond Buckey to work at the preschool?"

"Yes."

"And in that conversation did you talk about Mr. [Raymond] Buckey's viewing these *Playboy* and *Penthouse* magazines?"

"That was never discussed," the father answered.

"Did you talk with Mrs. Buckey about Raymond Buckey looking at this more explicit material and also working at the preschool?"

"No."

"Did you discuss with Mrs. Peggy Buckey the appropriateness of Mr. Raymond Buckey working at the preschool without wearing underpants?"

"It was discussed."

"And did that conversation take place before Raymond Buckey was arrested?"

"Yes."

"And did you decide that it was okay for Mr. Raymond Buckey to not wear underwear?"

"Considering the times, I did not approve but I did not disapprove."

"And did you discuss your not approving to Mrs. Peggy Buckey?"

"Yes."

"Did Mrs. Peggy Buckey tell you about Raymond Buckey exposing himself at the preschool?"

"She never told me that."

"Did Mrs. Peggy Buckey tell you about Raymond Buckey exposing himself at the soccer team practice?"

"When you say 'exposing himself' I think you have the wrong connotation. The answer to that would be 'no.'"

"Is there some understanding that you had with Raymond Buckey that his genitals were viewed by girls on the soccer team?"

"Never."

"Did you hear any other complaints by other persons that Mr. Raymond Buckey's genitals were observed?"

"No."

"Was there a complaint about someone seeing Mr. Raymond Buckey's genitals in a private setting?"

"I never heard it, no."

Gunson showed Charles Buckey the police report, the contents of which were not disclosed, and asked, "Does that refresh your memory?"

"No, it does not! I don't know when that was published, and I don't know who published it."

"Did anyone complain to you about anything related to that?"

"No."

"Did you have a feeling that he should not be at the school without underwear?"

"No, I did not have that feeling."

"Did you disapprove of him being at the school without underwear?"

"No."

"I have no further questions."

Davis asked on redirect, "Mr. Buckey, did you ever talk to Raymond Buckey about why it is that he wasn't wearing underwear?"

"Yes."

"And after you talked to Ray about why he wasn't wearing underwear, did you instruct him that he probably should wear underwear?"

"No, I did not."

"How was it that you came to determine that your son wasn't wearing underwear?"

"I think it became a topic of conversation that he and many of his friends did not, and he sided with his friends."

Gunson again: "Mr. Buckey, did you have any concern about Raymond Buckey being in the preschool not wearing underwear?"

"No."

"Did you have a concern that the children may see his genitals?"

"No."

"Did you have a concern that children were sitting on Raymond Buckey's lap while he did not have underwear on?"

"Not my concern."

"Did you tell Mrs. Buckey that you disapproved of Mr. Buckey's not wearing underwear while children were sitting on his lap?"

"I never made that comment."

"Did you have a concern that preschoolers at McMartin Preschool would see Mr. Raymond Buckey's genitals because his shorts were shorter than his legs?"

"Never entered my mind."

"Did you have a concern that children would be moving in front of Raymond Buckey and they would see his genitals?"

"It never entered my mind."

"In conversation did you explore the possible effect upon the children if they were to see the genitals of Mr. Raymond Buckey?"

"No."

"In conversation did Raymond Buckey tell you the reasons for his not wearing underwear?" Gunson asked.

"Objection. Vague."

"Sustained."

"Did Raymond Buckey tell you the reasons why he didn't wear underwear?"

"Yes."

"And was one of those reasons comfort?"

"The word was 'constricting,' so comfort would be the answer, yes."

"So Raymond Buckey told you that he wanted to be able to wear loose-fitting clothing?"

"Yes."

"Did you at any time go into the bedroom and see him lying without his clothing on?"

"Never."

"Did you ever see him lying on the bed with pornographic pictures surrounding him?"

"No."

"And when Raymond Buckey started teaching at the preschool you had no concern about him wearing loose-fitting clothing at the preschool?"

"Objection. Asked and answered."

"Sustained."

"I have no further questions."

Davis again: "Did you have a concern then that other people might see his testicles?"

"I was not concerned with other people. No."

"You mentioned once or twice that you saw part of your son's testicles. . . . From what you observed in those situations, did it look like he was intentionally trying to expose his genitals?"

"No."

"Did you ever see gestures, circumstances, statements being made that he intentionally exposed himself to children?"

"No."

"During the time you and your wife operated the preschool, did you receive large sums of money from the worldwide sale of child pornography?"

"No."

"From 1979 to 1983 did you and your wife come into huge amounts of money from unknown sources?"

"No."

Finally, Charles Buckey was excused. A reporter sitting next to us whispered, "I've never seen anything as dirty as this!"

"Stick around for a while," we said. "You will."

* * *

"We call Chad Spitler," Gits said softly. A thirteen-year-old boy came forward and was directed toward the witness stand. He said that Ray Buckey came to the school after graduating from college.

"During the times you saw Ray Buckey at the preschool, did you ever see him touch children in their private parts?" Davis asked.

"No," the boy answered.

"Did anyone ever touch you on your bottom?"

"No."

". . . on your penis?"

"No."

The boy denied all the prosecution's allegations and said that the "naked movie star" rhyme was just a taunt, or an insult, that children frequently said to each other, nothing more than that.

He said that he and his sister were taken out of their school classrooms, driven to CII, and informed that their mother was in jail. Both he and his sister were crying, he said. Then, he said, he was told that his sister had been molested, that all his friends had been molested, and that all of them had said that he, Chad, had been molested at the preschool.

Davis asked him about all the acts that were alleged to have been perpetrated upon him in the videotaped interview, one by one, and said, "Did that ever happen to you?" The answer to all of the questions was "no."

Lael Rubin, on cross-examination, asked the boy a long series of questions suggesting that he had been coached, or told what to say, by the defense attorneys. Again, the boy answered all of these questions in the negative.

The juror who had said the week before that his employer was likely to go out of business told the judge that the company was definitely going out of business within a few weeks. The judge said that he was going to try to get the county to pay the man a salary during the remaining months of the trial, to avert a mistrial.

The judge also told the attorneys, "I am going to be in a situation, out of necessary time limitation, to preclude all but the defendants' testimony, Virginia McMartin's testimony, and Dr. Robert tenBensel's testimony. I'm not doing that with the suggestion that I'm going to argue with you at this point, but to tell you that with even limiting it to those witnesses, we cannot, in my view, end by break time and with the limitations that follow. It is because I believe we will not have a jury that I'm going to make those limitations. The warning is simply this: if you have witnesses other than the four people I've named, prepare to have them rejected and have others standing by. If you fail to do that, I'll require that the defendants testify, and if you decline to put them on the stand, I will rest the defense's case. I plan to move it as rapidly as I can. I recognize that I don't save any time by sustaining objections, but I do save time by cutting witnesses, so that's what I'm going to do."

The prosecution had been allowed to call sixty-one witnesses, and the defense had called only thirty-seven. The prosecution brought in seven physicians. Apparently, the defense would get only one.

"We call Betty Raidor," Dean Gits announced, almost inaudibly. Betty was directed to the witness stand and sworn in. She was now sixty-nine years old and, since the preliminary hearing, had lost the sight in one eye and had had two corneal transplants in the other. She was somewhat overweight, wore thick eyeglasses, and had the kindly face of the quintessential loving grandmother. We had expected that her testimony would be less than exciting, but we were wrong. She turned out to be one of the most interesting and memorable witnesses in the trial.

Raidor held her head high. She sat comfortably in the witness chair, her face tilted slightly upward in an attitude of extreme attentiveness, which is important because the jury saw this and got the message: as with Chuck Buckey, they saw a person with a very solid sense of her own worth.

When asked, on direct examination, if she had witnessed or engaged in any of the alleged acts of molestation, Raidor replied emphatically, "Most certainly not!" She told that when she was arrested and interrogated in jail, in 1984, "Jane Hoag accused me of things I'd never even heard of before, things I never knew people did. Things I never even imagined."

Raidor was a crucial witness, because she testified that Ray Buckey did not teach at the preschool during the time when most of the child witnesses said they were sexually abused. Because Raidor was employed at the time of the alleged molestations, Davis said she was "an exact stencil of the time period."

Raidor testified that the only trip to a farm was an imaginary one in which the children pantomimed, with music playing on a phonograph, pretending to be horses and other animals, hopping, crawling, and flying. She said the trip to a supermarket was also a make-believe game played in her classroom. After other witnesses testified that the alleged molestations could not have happened in the morning, Raidor told the court that she was there with Ray in the afternoon when he was in charge of the "stay-up" group who did not take naps. Raidor's only negative statement about Ray was that she felt his classroom was too noisy and undisciplined. She said the children were having a wonderful time, and were always hanging and climbing on Ray. She said the children adored him.

She had known Peggy Buckey for over thirty-five years. When Gits asked her, "How long have you known Ray Buckey?" she replied, "Ever since Peggy brought him home from the hospital."

"Was there a reason why he was in the hospital?" Gits asked.

"He was born," she answered.

For hours, Gits went over the attendance records and time sheets and other records to show that she was there with Ray in the afternoon, and that Ray was not there from 1978 to 1980.

At one point, Raidor interrupted the proceeding to explain why she had been uncertain of the answer to one of the questions put to her: "I didn't have a clear picture in my memory of the events, and when I got home, the first thing I saw was my daughter's portrait, and I remembered that the events just after the summer session started, my daughter had returned home because she was ill. She was hospitalized and after some examinations they determined she had cancer. She was released from that hospital the weekend after the Fourth of July and was returned to the hospital for some new kind of intensive intravenous chemotherapy. And, five days later, she passed on." Although Raidor maintained her composure, we saw the pain and sadness on her face. For a moment her voice quavered.

Raidor testified that the "lookout game" was simply an occasion when children were told to watch for their parents because parking was prohibited on the street in front of the school and parents had to pick up their children quickly and leave to avoid getting a parking citation from the police.

"Did you ever see dead animals at the preschool?" Raidor was asked.

"If you call a bird an animal, yes."

"Did you see the bird die?"

Raidor explained that, on one occasion there was a bird perched on the top of a door, and Peggy had closed the door, crushing the bird and killing it.

"And what was done with the bird after it died?"

"Peggy went out and buried it."

"Objection."

"Sustained."

"She told me she was going to bury it."

"Objection. Hearsay."

"Sustained. The answer is stricken."

"She went into her office in tears," Raidor said later on.

"What was done with the bird?"

"She was holding the bird."

Raidor testified that no child was ever allowed to be alone in the yard without a teacher being present.

"Did you ever see Peggy Buckey naked?"

"Never!"

"Did you ever see naked children?"

"No."

"Did you ever see Ray Buckey naked?"

"No."

During recess, Ray greeted us in the snack bar and said, "I see you hiding back in the third row."

"Well, every time we make the slightest sound or even move, Rubin tells the judge and tries to get him to bust us."

"I know," he said. "I heard her."

"Well, we see you're not drinking blood today," we remarked. Ray laughed: "They don't have any in the snack bar."

Raidor was warned by her doctor, after the corneal transplant, not to expose herself to stress. Nevertheless, she elected to come into court and testify for the defendants. But when Rubin began her cross-examination, she raised the stress level to maximum: "All right, Mrs. Raidor, let's try it one more time. . . ." It did not appear to play well with the jurors. They did not look pleased with the spectacle of this harsh-voiced, younger woman bullying and scolding the benign, gentle grandmother.

"On several occasions, you told [a mother] that you didn't like to leave Raymond Buckey alone with kids, correct?"

"That is not correct."

"Did you say that you told Mrs. B——— that Raymond Buckey was not a qualified teacher?"

"That is different from behaving improperly."

"Mrs. Raidor, please answer my question! The question was 'Did you tell Mrs. B——— that Raymond Buckey was not a qualified teacher?'"

"Yes."

"My question was, Mrs. Raidor, what caused you to say Raymond Buckey was not a qualified teacher?"

"His lack of experience and not having a very definite program, but then that was my opinion."

Rubin made reference, in a number of questions, to the earlier testimony that, because he did not wear underwear, parts of Ray's genitalia were sometimes visible, but instead of stating it that way she used the phrase, "Ray Buckey exposed himself to children." There was nothing in the record to support this, but Rubin did it over and over again, and the defense attorneys did not protest.

There were a number of questions about allegations that Ray once had a "body builder" magazine in his classroom, a magazine about physical fitness. There was strong insinuation that there was something perverse in this, but it was never made clear what kind of depravity was being inferred.

Toward the end of her cross-examination of Raidor, Rubin eagerly brought out some small inconsistencies in the witness's time records, but they were minor at best—certainly not enough time for mass molestations, butchery of animals, drinking blood, worshipping the devil with naked nuns, or any of the other alleged events described by the children.

Raidor was on the witness stand for eight days. When it was finally over, Rubin told reporters that Raidor's testimony was "a bunch of garbage." Rubin said, "She is lying."

There was no court the following Monday because one of the jurors required medical attention. Tuesday morning we arrived in a state of great curiosity because the judge had said he would allow only three more defense witnesses: Ray, Peggy, and Dr. tenBensel, the medical expert.

We were told that the judge and the lawyers were in chambers arguing over a number of issues, and we sat and waited. An hour passed. The press box was filled. Eventually they became impatient and moved out into the hallway and sat in a group. Reporters are a dull lot. They do not converse. They just sit there, expressionless. Finally, we were told by the bailiff that nothing more would be happening until one-thirty and that the jury was being released until then. Everybody trudged out of the courtroom and went to lunch.

At one-thirty we were told, again, that the judge and the lawyers were still in chambers arguing about stipulations and other matters. We waited another hour. Out in the hallway we saw Ray, standing alone against the wall. Paul told him, "When Rubin and Gunson come out, ask them if they are wearing underwear." He laughed and said, "Yeah. And what's written on it."

A reporter turned to Paul and complained, "Jesus! We've been here for five hours and nothing's happened."

"What will you do when your editor asks to see your notes and your worksheet?" Paul asked.

"I don't know. I guess I'll have to make something up."

Finally, at three-thirty, the lawyers came back into the courtroom, then the judge. "Remain seated and come to order. Division one hundred thirty is now in session," the bailiff chanted perfunctorily.

"All of the jurors are present," said Judge Pounders. "And all of the defendants and counsel are present. Do you have a witness, Mr. Gits?"

"We call my client, Peggy Buckey," he said. You could hardly hear him in the crowded courtroom. Peggy walked to the witness stand and was sworn in and asked to give and spell her name. She spoke well, had a pleasant voice, and you could see that, although she was now sixty-two, gray-haired, and overweight, she was once a beautiful woman.

Gits briefly went over the history of the school and Peggy and Ray's duties there, discrediting, again, the prosecution witnesses' testimony. Peggy testified that during much of the time Ray taught at the school there was another, more experienced teacher there to assist him. Then, Gits quickly got to the point. He showed Peggy photographs of the child witnesses and asked, "Did you ever molest any of those children?"

"Never."

"Did you ever touch them on any part of their bodies for the purpose of sexual gratification either of yourself or of anybody else?"
"No."
"Were you ever naked in front of any of these children?"
"Was I ever what?"
"Were you ever naked in front of these children?"
"No."
"Did you ever make any of these children get naked?"
"No."
"Did you ever make any of these children get partially naked?"
"No."
"Did you ever transport any of these children off the school grounds for the purpose of molesting them?"
"Never."
"Did you ever transport any of these children off the school grounds for the purpose of permitting other adults to touch them?"
"No."
"Did you ever transport any of these children off the school grounds for the purpose of engaging in satanic acts at a church?"
"Never."
"Did you ever threaten these children in any manner?"
"No."
"Did you ever see any person molest these children while you were at the preschool?"
"Never."
"Did you see any other person any place in the world molest these children?"
"No."
"Did you ever see these children naked with any other teacher at the preschool?"
"No."
"With any other adult at the preschool?"
"No."
"Did you ever see anything at the preschool that ever once gave you the slightest suspicion that any of those children were being molested in any manner whatsoever?" Gits asked.
"Never."
"Are you aware of the other complaining witnesses in this case?"
"Yes."
"Did you ever see any person molest those children?"
"Never."
"Did you ever see those children naked with any other adult?"
"Never."

"Did you ever see anything at the school that gave you the slightest suspicion that those children were being molested or mistreated in any manner?"

"Never."

"Did you ever conspire or agree with anyone to molest any children at the preschool?"

"No."

"Did you ever conspire or agree to permit others to molest any of those children?"

"No."

"Any other children at the preschool?"

"No."

There was a long series of questions about naptime, who was in charge, and about the request that parents not come during naptime and wake up the children. Peggy answered the questions in an open, smooth-flowing, candid manner: "The parents would come in and wake other children up when they woke their children up to take them home, and this was not fair to the other children because their parents wanted them napping. That's why we made the rule."

Asked about the games that were played at the preschool, Peggy told of "hokey-pokey," "duck duck goose," and "ring around the rosey," and songs about animals and trains. When she was unable to remember the name of one of the songs, Peggy asked the attorney, "Want me to sing it?" The jurors broke into laughter.

The jurors liked her. She was wholesome. The Buckey family was very much like the family in the Andy Hardy movies of the forties, which portrayed the idyllic American dream, the ideal American family. The Buckeys not only resembled those people, they *are* those people. The jurors' eyes were riveted on Peggy and, once again, they were taking notes, no longer bored. The prosecutors, Rubin and Gunson, were not pleased. Their faces were stiff and angry. Their early advantage was slipping away.

At four-thirty Gits glanced at the clock and the judge said, "We will be in recess until tomorrow morning at ten-thirty." Friends, family, and supporters of the Buckeys gathered around Peggy in the hallway. Their faces were like those of a group of people who had just seen their favorite team win the World Series.

"Were you scared?" a reporter asked.

"I was scared at first, but it went away."

A television reporter held a microphone in front of Peggy and asked her if she was angered by the accusations.

"I don't like the accusations," she answered, in a clear, pleasant voice, "because it never happened. I didn't do anything. My son didn't do anything. Or my mother and my daughter, or any of the teachers. I just can't imagine anyone molesting a child, or ever being naked or making children be naked. I just can't imagine . . . I've never in my life . . . I just can't imagine any such things going on. So, yes, it bothers me. And it's bothered me ever since these accusations were made towards all of us. There isn't one of us that would ever harm a child. I just can't imagine harming a child! Or molesting him in any way."

Gits spoke into the microphone and said, "When the truth speaks, it speaks loud and clear. And that's what I heard."

Davis told the television newsman, "It's the beginning of the end . . . for the prosecution."

Wednesday morning, before the taking of testimony began, Davis asked the court to subpoena Dr. John J. McCann, a San Francisco pediatrician, who had just completed a study that showed that "signs" and marks the prosecution's doctors described as evidence of sexual abuse were also found on normal children, that the anuses and genitalia of molested children were often indistinguishable from those of nonmolested children. Davis said that the defense's efforts to find medical experts had been "dismal" because doctors generally didn't want to be attacked and stigmatized in this kind of case.

The judge denied Davis's request. McCann's study of 320 children, both male and female, produced findings that discredited the medical evidence in the McMartin case and many other cases in the recent epidemic of child abuse accusations. The first half of the study was to be published in June 1990.

Gits continued his direct examination.

"Mrs. Buckey, why was it that you hired your son, Raymond, as an aide at the preschool?"

"He was my son, and he was interested in working with children. And I felt he had the potential of being a good teacher."

"Was there a particular teacher that was assigned to be present with Raymond in the afternoon hours?"

"Yes, it would have been Betty [Raidor]."

There were hours of tedious but necessary questions about Peggy's comings and goings and about the day-to-day operation of the school to refute, one by one, the allegations of the prosecution witnesses. Peggy told of her shock and disbelief when parents began calling her in August 1983 telling her of the letter the police had sent out saying that Ray had been arrested on a charge of child molestation and asking parents to question their children about sexual abuse at the preschool.

Before the letter went out, there had been a six-month waiting list for parents who wanted to put their children in the preschool. After that, "the enrollment dropped way down, and we only needed three teachers," Peggy said. "I tried to defend my son because he had done nothing."

"Objection. Move to strike the answer."

"Sustained."

"When did you first become aware that you were a suspect?"

"I never did find out until I was arrested."
"When were you arrested?"
"March 22, 1984."

Gits showed Peggy a photograph of a woman's face and placed it on the blackboard. "Do you recognize the person in that photograph?"
"Yes."
"Who is that?"
"Me. Peggy Buckey."

In the photograph Peggy looked much younger.
"Do you know when that photograph was taken?"
"Yes."
"When?"
"When I was arrested. In jail."
"Do you know who it was that took that photograph?"
"Yes. One of the deputies."
"And where was that photograph taken?"
"Sybil Brand."
"And what is Sybil Brand?"
"Well, it's a jail."

Gits concluded, and the judge turned and asked, "Mr. Davis?"
"I have no questions at this time, your honor."

Lael Rubin rose, walked to the podium and began arranging her notes. On the prosecution table she had stacks of Virginia's personal diaries.

"You told the court that, as director of the preschool, you were interested in having your son work at the preschool because he had some interest in working with children and that he had the potential to be a good teacher, correct?"
"Yes."
"What was it at the time that caused you to believe that he had an interest in working with children?"
"He had a very gentle, loving way with children, which you need when you work with children."
"Your honor, I move to strike the answer as nonresponsive."
"Overruled. The answer will stand."
"What was it that was communicated to you by your son that explained his having an interest in working with children, and I guess my question is, did he tell you that he had an interest in working with children?"
"Yes. He did some volunteer work in San Diego."
"Objection, the answer is nonresponsive. Move that it be stricken."
"Sustained."
"Did your son specifically tell you that he had an interest in working with children?"
"He enjoyed working with children."

"And how was it that the subject came up, that your son told you he was interested in working with children?"

"As I just mentioned, he did volunteer work in San Diego and . . ."

"Your honor that is not responsive. Move to strike."

"Sustained."

"How is it that the subject came up, that your son wanted to work with children?"

"He was at the school one morning and . . . we were out to lunch, and he just told me how he enjoyed working with children, and he would like to come and work at our school."

"And were you surprised when your son . . . offered to work at the McMartin Preschool?"

"Yes."

"And why were you surprised?"

"Because he had never been interested before."

"Did you ask him how it came to be that he was interested in working with children?"

"Yes."

"And what did he say?"

"That he had volunteered in San Diego . . . and he got a certificate . . ."

"Objection. Move to strike . . ."

"Mrs. Buckey, did your son tell you that part of his duties were cleaning up?"

"Yes. He worked out in the yard, supervising the children."

"And was the award specifically for this?"

"I don't remember."

"And what is it he said?"

"He said he would like to come home and work at the school."

"Did you ask him about his qualifications?"

"No."

"Is there a reason you didn't ask him about his qualifications to work with children?"

"Yes."

"And what was that?"

"If you employ someone and you feel they have the potential to be a good teacher, they take certain courses, and that is what I told him he would have to do."

"And from the time your son became employed at the preschool, was he taking courses?"

"Yes."

"Do you know where it was he was taking courses?" Rubin asked.

"El Camino College . . . some of my parents were in the same classes," Peggy answered.

"Now, you told us there are requirements essential for working with children . . . how would you define that?"

"First, you have to care for children. You have to love children. Ray was very gentle. He had a wonderful rapport with children."

"Now, you told us that you never saw anything that gave you the slightest suspicion that children were being molested at the preschool. Were you aware that your son didn't wear underwear? Isn't that right?"

Two of the jurors rolled their eyes in exasperation and put their hands to their faces. We were going to have to listen to the endless litany of the underwear once more.

"And you were aware that his penis was seen, correct?"

"No."

"And you had the belief that it was okay for Raymond Buckey to be in the preschool and not wear underwear?"

"I do not remember that."

"You heard your husband testify that you said that women don't wear bras, so it's no big deal. Do you remember that?"

"Yes."

"And what did you say?"

"I see nothing wrong with not wearing underwear."

"Why not?"

"Many of the young men who came to our house did not wear underwear. Kids at the beach did not wear underwear. Lots of them."

"And did you . . . see their genitals?"

"I never saw anybody's genitals."

"Your honor I move to have the answer stricken."

"Overruled."

"Now, Mrs. Buckey . . . did you recognize that there may be a difference between not wearing underwear at the beach and not wearing underwear at the preschool?"

"Never gave it a thought."

"Now, did you make statements in the past that some women don't wear bras so it's no big deal?"

"I don't remember that."

"Now, with a child sitting on his lap and his not wearing underwear, might that make it easier for a child to touch his genitals?"

"No."

"Now, with a child sitting on his lap and not wearing underwear, wouldn't that make it easier for him to get aroused with a child sitting on his lap, correct?"

"No."

The underwear interrogation went on and on, endlessly. It would seem that this entire line of questioning was irrelevant and speculative, but the defense lawyers did not object nor did the judge. When asked about this, another lawyer, no longer on the case, said, "I think they may be setting them up for reversal," he said. "You only have to object once." In other words, if the defendants were found guilty on any or all of the charges, their attorneys could use this part of the court record as the basis for obtaining an appeal as a result of the claim that the judge erred in allowing these irrelevant and prejudicial questions.

Tuesday morning we were told that we had just lost another juror. His father had just died, and the court would be in recess for the rest of the week. That meant seven days, since Monday was Memorial Day. The saga of the underwear would resume Tuesday.

"We are back in *People* v. *Buckey* . . . " the judge began. Rubin rose to resume her cross-examination.

"Now one of the differences might be that having a child sitting on your son's lap and his not wearing underwear might make it easier for him to get aroused, correct?"

"No."

"Are you aware that A——— grabbed your son in his penis or had you heard that she grabbed your son in his penis?"

"I certainly did."

"Was that something that you observed?"

"No."

"How was it that you heard that?"

"My son told me."

"And how was it that your son told you that?"

"I asked my son if anything happened at the school . . . so I could tell the parents."

"And after asking if anything happened, what were you told?"

"That A——— grabbed him in the genitals through his clothes."

"And what did your son say?"

"He told me that he told her she shouldn't do that."

When the proceedings began again the next day it was announced that the prosecution had asked for a three-day recess the following week—this in spite of the fact that the three-week summer vacation was less than a month away. Reporters, lawyers, and other courtroom "insiders" were speculating that the D.A.'s office was stalling in the hope of a mistrial to spare themselves the humiliation of a not guilty verdict. If the number of jurors fell below twelve, it would achieve that result. We had already lost four jurors. Several others had complained that they were in danger of losing their jobs because of the extraordinary length of the trial. The jurors had been told by the lawyers that the trial would end in 1988, or, at the very latest, in the beginning of 1989. It now seemed clear that the trial would not go to the jury until close to the end of 1989.

The questions continued. Rubin asked, "Now at the time your son told you about A——— grabbing his genitals, did he tell you that A——— was sitting on his lap?"

"All I remember is that he just told her not to do that again. He did not make a big thing of it to the child."

"Did you ask your son where it happened?"

"All I know is he was sitting."

"Did you ask your son how long she had her hand on his genitals?"

"She just grabbed him and let go."

After a long series of questions and answers, Peggy's answer was a simple one. She told us, during recess, that the child's mother had told Peggy that her daughter frequently took showers with her father and was in the habit of pulling his penis. The mother had apologized to Peggy and promised to tell her daughter not to do it again. But the jury was never allowed to hear this simple explanation.

Peggy testified that she had never been interviewed by any law enforcement officer, further confirming the fact that the police were looking only for incriminating evidence and scrupulously avoiding any exonerating evidence. This definitely raised some eyebrows. Peggy also said she had never been given her *Miranda* rights. She was unaware that she was even a suspect until her arrest, she said. "They never questioned my son, daughter, or any of the other teachers."

Throughout the marathon cross-examination Peggy Buckey stood her ground extremely well. The Buckeys are a family of uncommonly wholesome people and they faced the vilification with dignity and candor. Paul was sure that the jurors perceived this.

When she was asked what she would have done if she had believed her son was molesting children at the preschool, Peggy said "I had a twenty-eight-year reputation and so did my mother. I would not have spoiled my reputation or my mother's, who is my dearest friend, for my son, my daughter, or anybody. I would have taken my son in my office. I would have told him to get help and I would have fired him."

Throughout the day, the dialogue between Peggy and prosecutor Rubin was extremely antagonistic. Rubin asked Peggy about a father distressed by the fact that a male was teaching preschoolers and who had asked Peggy if she had checked to see if he had an erection after children sat on his lap. Rubin used the words "hard on" repeatedly throughout the day. Peggy explained that, "As director of the school I had to think as other people think." She said she looked at Ray to see if he had an erection "only one time."

"When you checked, that one time, you saw he did have a hard on, correct?" Rubin charged.

"He certainly did not!" Peggy answered angrily.

"Would you agree it is an unusual event when the director of a preschool checks her son for an erection?" Rubin asked.

"I told you I did it one time and one time only," Peggy said, looking at Rubin with loathing. "It's such a dumb question!"

Peggy also stated that the parent's concern had nothing to do with Ray. "It had to do with his being male."

"Have you ever seen your son with an erection on any other occasion?" Rubin asked.

"Objection. Assumes facts not in evidence," Davis interrupted. The jurors burst into laughter. Even the judge smiled as he sustained the objection.

Asked about the muscle magazines allegedly seen in Ray's room, Peggy said she had told Ray to keep a body-building magazine out of his classroom. "I think they're gross," she said. "I don't like muscle magazines at all." Again, she got a laugh out of the jurors.

Several times during the day, Judge Pounders warned Rubin not to ask deliberately argumentative questions. Toward the end of the day, Rubin asked Peggy if she had told parents that she, herself, had been molested as a child. She acknowledged that this was true. According to parents, she said that a neighbor had put his hand up her dress. She stated that both she and her parents felt it was preferable to deal with this type of event face to face, with the perpetrator, than to call the police, but that it "would depend on what had happened."

Asking about accusations made by a mother of one of the children who attended the preschool, Rubin said, "Was she lying?"

"Yes, she was lying," Peggy answered.

"Why would she lie?" Rubin asked.

"Why did everybody lie in this case?" Peggy answered angrily.

"Do you have a reason to lie in this courtroom?" Rubin asked.

"I don't lie. . . . I'm telling the truth."

Peggy added that she did not use the word "lie" before the case began, but "I've heard the word, 'lie,' so much in this case I've learned to say 'lie' like the rest of you. . . ."

"Are you accusing me of lying?" Rubin shot back hotly.

"No, I'm not."

There were hours of irrelevant questions that did not connect with any of the issues before the court, questions as to whether Ray had tried marijuana, alcohol, or other psychoactive substances, and whether he had quarrelled with his parents.

Rubin had a stack of Virginia's personal diaries before her on the lectern, the ones seized during the police search of her home in 1984. Members of the Buckey family were deeply offended by this violation of Virginia's privacy, and the diaries disclosed nothing supportive of the charges. However, they were used to distort the facts of the Buckeys' lives.

The prosecution subpoenaed Dr. Frank Richelieu once again to delve into the content of Ray's counseling sessions with him. The minister was sworn in and asked about Rubin's assertion that the counseling had to do with "Ray's problem with touching children."

"I never discussed with Raymond Buckey sexual problems with children," Dr. Richelieu said. "It was mostly Raymond wanting to discuss himself, his life, his attitudes, his direction. It was more or less self-improvement."

Davis asked if Rubin had lied about the counseling sessions.

"Yes," the clergyman answered unhesitatingly.

Questioned about this outside the courtroom, Rubin did not directly accuse Dr. Richelieu of perjury but cryptically told reporters, "What I'm suggesting is that he may have other motivations."

Davis was less restrained: "I agree with Dr. Richelieu. She is a liar."

Rubin said she still stuck to her statement that Buckey was counseled "for his sexual problem with children." Gunson asked Richelieu if he was aware that he was required to report to police any confession of child sexual abuse. Richelieu said it was not an issue with Buckey.

All of this occurred with the jury absent from the courtroom. The judge had yet to rule whether the therapy sessions were privileged communication under sections 1032 and 1033 in the evidence code. At one point during Gunson's questioning of Dr. Richelieu, Davis interrupted, "Objection. Counsel is harassing the witness and I ask that he be admonished."

"The objection is overruled. I ask that both of you calm down somewhat," Judge Pounders said, looking at Dr. Richelieu. "I've noticed some animosity on your part in the last few questions, and Mr. Gunson's responding to it. I want you to calm down."

"For the record, I've noticed animosity on Mr. Gunson's part," Davis contradicted the judge.

"I don't care what you noticed!" the judge snapped hotly. Antagonism between Davis and Judge Pounders had erupted frequently during the previous two weeks.

There were lengthy arguments over the judge's statement that the child who was the subject of the complaint could not be compelled to come in and testify. Davis asserted that the child was "a critical witness in this case, and ruling not to compel him to testify for Ray Buckey is critical to the defense for Mr. Buckey. For example, Peter . . . told many people that it was his father who had done damage to his anal area. That was at the time when Ray Buckey was in jail. . . . I believe that Peter's father should be a witness for the defense. He is a man whom Peter accused of molesting him at a time when it would have been impossible for Ray Buckey . . . but it was in fact [the father who] was doing it. He will deny it, predictably, but his son will impeach him. . . . If you eliminate Peter then you eliminate an important circumstance to the defense."

"That was my ruling then, and it is now," the judge said. "He is not available to either side. . . . There is obviously a conclusion that I drew that he could not be a witness for anybody. This is ridiculous! . . . We have more than enough to do to try to finish the longest case the world has ever seen. . . . This case has got to conclude, and I'm not convinced that a jury will be here!"

"It is an aggravation I didn't see when we were wasting time with the People's case," Davis commented.

There was another matter Rubin wanted to bring up before the jury. She had a report from a law enforcement agency based on an interview of Peggy's niece, a report of questionable authenticity, and she wanted to read a paragraph in which the tenuous implication is made that Ray Buckey went to Dr. Richelieu at approximately the time of his arrest and therefore, by insinuation, went there for counseling about pedophilia, even though Dr. Richelieu had already testified that the subject was never mentioned.

"The insinuation," Davis responded, "from the FBI agent's report could dangerously be invoked in front of the jury, the suggestion that Ray was sent to Dr. Richelieu for sex problems in connection with getting in trouble. Child molestation. None of this is true. Another person, talking to an FBI agent whose report here I'm seeing as being used by the district attorney to bootstrap false facts, facts that they have never proved except by insinuation and selective reading of these words."

"I agree with that," the judge said. ". . . it certainly is critical evidence . . . I have no idea what kind of credibility we're dealing with. Is this individual available to testify?"

"Your honor, she is the niece of Peggy Buckey," Rubin replied. "I believe testimony came up during the examination of Virginia McMartin. There was an entry in Virginia McMartin's diary that referred to her as a traitor. . . . I believe in November or December of 1983 she took her children to Children's Institute. They had been at the McMartin Preschool and thereafter [she] believed that her children had been molested at the preschool. . . ."

"I do need to have some assurance, though," Pounders said, "that what may have existed in 1984 is still true today, five years later. The suggestion itself is going to have tremendous impact, and if it isn't backed up by specific testimony, I would tend to preclude it. . . . Do we know now that this lady is available to testify?"

"She no longer lives in this jurisdiction," Rubin answered.

"But the International Compact would reach her, unless she is in one state. One state didn't sign the compact. Utah? It doesn't do any good to drag her in unless she is going to confirm this statement. What is your most recent contact with her?"

"On May 23 of this year," Rubin said.

That was two weeks previous.

"Although I don't believe that specific question was asked of her . . . We certainly know where to locate her," Rubin said.

"I need some assurance that this lady is available to testify and to know what her testimony is going to be. I don't think it's appropriate if she's going to deny a statement made by impeachment, but it is extremely condemning testimony, and it should come from the witness herself. . . . I don't want the suggestion without proof, for this subject to be brought up until we know what kind of evidence the prosecution can offer on that subject," the judge concluded.

"It's such damning evidence that, in my view, if it comes in, it tilts the balance heavily in favor of the prosecution. . . . This is the kind of thing where the mere suggestion of it, even if denied, by defense witnesses, is going to have a tremendous impact on the case. . . . I agree that it's ambiguous and subject to different interpretations. . . . It's a subtle suggestion that would destroy the defense in this case, and that's not appropriate. It is far too prejudicial to be brought in in this manner. At this time it is precluded without some showing as to what the evidence will be."

Rubin's statements implied that the niece moved away from California because of pressure from Ray, which was unlikely since he had been in jail since 1984.

One other matter was raised before the jury was brought in. Davis accused the prosecution of destroying evidence. He claimed that a videotaped interview of Peter had mysteriously disappeared, and that the interview discredited the prosecution's case so badly that it had been "intentionally destroyed." He stated that the tape may have shown that the child identified his father as the abuser, and could exculpate Buckey. The defense position had been that the child accused his father in several interviews but was pressured to accuse Ray instead. The judge had ruled that the child would not testify.

Outside the courtroom, Rubin said, "We've never destroyed evidence and I think this harangue is because they've finally become worried about how their defense is going down the toilet."

Davis subpoenaed Dr. Gloria Johnson-Powell, director of the Family Support Programs for Abused Children at the University of California at Los Angeles. The organization had interviewed the boy, but Judge Pounders did not allow her to testify.

Finally, at four o'clock, only half an hour before recess, Peggy took the stand and the jurors were brought in. They looked like somnambulists. Several of their faces betrayed the fact that they had been sleeping.

"It's true, Mrs. Buckey, that as time went on, there were more and more complaints about your son, Raymond Buckey, correct?" asked Rubin.

"No."

"Mrs. Buckey, when Mrs. D—— first informed you that she had been notified by the police, did she tell you during the conversation that she was informed as to when the molestation was supposed to have taken place?"

"Objection. Calls for hearsay."

"Not offered for the truth," Rubin countered.

"Overruled. You may answer."

"No. All I remember is . . ." Peggy said.

"Objection. Motion to strike after 'no.' " Rubin interrupted.

Rubin went on and on with her questions, eliciting nothing of any significance, except that Peggy called a number of parents and police officers in the mistaken belief that they were her friends and would provide her with some explanation of what was going on, and help her. Most of these people, instead, became part of the band of accusers, screaming for her conviction and imprisonment, after the police department's letter went out and the CII "evaluations" took place.

"Now, when you talked to Det. Hoag, whether it be the thirtieth or the thirty-first of August 1983, you in fact told Det. Hoag that the parent should have come to you first before going to the police, correct?"

"I don't remember saying that."

"That's something you believe, isn't it?"

"No, I think that's up to the parents to make their decision. I've said that I think it would be nice if they would come to me, but that was up to the parents to do what they thought was the right thing, not for me to tell them what to do."

"Now, from the thirtieth or thirty-first of August, within the next few days after that, on the second of September, that was when your residence was searched, correct?"

"Yes."

"And before the search actually began, you told one of the police officers that 'You can't believe little kids. They'll lie.' Correct?"

"I do not recall saying that."

"Mrs. Buckey, showing you this document, I would ask you to read the end of the first paragraph. . . . And doesn't that refresh your recollection that, shortly after Det. Hoag arrived at your residence, you remarked that 'You can't believe little kids. They all lie.'?"

"I do not remember saying that."

"Mrs. Buckey, if Det. Hoag put that in her police report, would that be untrue?"

"It certainly would be. She lied about a lot of things."

"Would this be an appropriate time?" Rubin asked the judge.

"Yes. We will be in recess until Monday morning at ten-thirty. . . ."

Peggy told us privately, in a long conversation that evening, that the lawyers believed the prosecution had revised its strategy. "We think they have given up hope of convicting me and they are now going to put all their efforts into trying to convict Ray. I'll only be on the stand a couple more days. Then, when Ray testifies, we are going to drop something on them so stunning that Pounders is going to have a heart attack. I can't tell you what it is, but you'll see in a few days."

That evening, we attended a large dinner party and a young woman who is well-known in the pop music recording industry said, "Shirley, I heard you were writing a book about McMartin."

"Yes." Shirley nodded wearily.

"Wow! Are they guilty?"

"Absolutely not."

"But all those kids said it happened, and the doctors!"

"Those kids were brainwashed," Shirley said.

"But why would they want to brainwash them?" she asked.

"Big bucks."

"What about the doctors?"

"They get $2,500 a day for sitting in court and saying the kids were molested. Some of them testify for weeks. If they say the kids were not molested, all that's gone."

The woman panicked, quickly turned her back and left. Another young woman sitting at our table said, "I think Buckey's probably guilty."

"How much of the evidence have you seen?" we asked.

The woman looked at us blankly.

"Which witnesses did you think were the most convincing? Which of the counts do you think were the most believable? Do you know who the witnesses were?"

The second woman also turned her back and started a conversation with another woman at the table.

"I read an article about child abuse," another woman at the table said. "It says that children never lie. It says we should always believe the children."

"Well," Shirley said, "an awful lot of the kids said it never happened at McMartin. In fact, all of them said it before they got worked over. Which ones should we believe?"

"You know," the woman said, "I can't believe I'm hearing this!"

Monday morning, as we got out of our car, a loud boom echoed across the city and the sidewalk buckled and bounced under our feet. Earthquake! It wasn't a big one, but it was sufficient to jam the elevators in the state office building next door. Thousands of people were evacuated from all the downtown buildings and crowded together on the sidewalks. We saw the jurors and all the "regulars" coming out of the courthouse. One of the jurors said, "You can go home. The judge is sending everybody home." The up side was that we got a day of rest. The down side was that the trial would last a day longer. But after two years and three months it really didn't seem to make much difference. It seemed as though time had stopped.

Most of the following morning was spent arguing about the FBI report on Peggy's niece, Glendee Lauerman. Rubin had maintained throughout the trial that she had evidence that Ray went to Dr. Frank Richelieu for counseling about an alleged penchant for child molestation. However, when she handed over to the defense notes of a telephone conversation between her own investigators and Lauerman, the notes disclosed that Lauerman said she believed the counseling sessions were for the purpose of coping with the stress of being accused of child sexual abuse, which refuted Rubin's allegations about Glendee Lauerman's beliefs. Rubin, nevertheless wanted the court's permission to question Peggy Buckey about the matter. Judge Pounders precluded her from going into that subject before the jury on the grounds that it was too prejudicial and would carry with it the insinuation that Buckey had confessed to molesting children.

However, in the afternoon Rubin continued to harp on the sessions with Richelieu, insinuating that there was something more sinister than what had already been disclosed. It was an extremely poor strategy because it told the jurors that Peggy was a person who, in time of trouble, went to her pastor, not to Satan, as the prosecutors wanted them to believe.

Peggy said she had also sought counseling with "Dr. Frank" because eight people who were close to her, including her brother, had died or were terminally ill. She said she had never discussed child molestation with him.

At times the antagonism between Peggy McMartin Buckey and Lael Rubin erupted. "You're trying to mix me up and you can't do it because I know what I did," Peggy said in response to one of Rubin's questions. When she was asked if she was ever naked in front of children she answered, "Are you kidding?"

Toward the end of her cross-examination, Rubin recalled Peggy's statements to parents—in 1948, that she had been molested as a child—and then asked her if she thought it was a serious offense, or did she think it was "no big deal." It was a trap. Rubin was trying to get Peggy to say that she did not see it as a serious matter, which would have sent a message to the jurors that Peggy was a person who condoned sexual molestation of children, or at least did not see it as a serious offense. Soft on molestation, as Joe McCarthy might have said if he were still living.

But Peggy wasn't having any of it. "Yes, I thought it was serious." It was an acrimonious exchange between the two women, Rubin, who'd put Peggy in jail with no bail for two years, her son for five years; and Peggy Buckey, who was equally committed to vindicating herself and her son. But Rubin never directly asked Peggy whether she'd committed any of the crimes of which she was charged.

"They had nothing, in all the thousands of pages of documents they have collected over the years," one of the attorneys said.

A former police officer who had been assigned to a child abuse unit told us during recess, "This case has set child protection back twenty years."

Outside the courtroom, Peggy told reporters, "I looked at her [Rubin] and realized this woman has tried to destroy my son and me for five years and I realized there was nothing to be afraid of because I hadn't done anything wrong and neither had my son." If Rubin got a conviction both mother and son would probably spend the rest of their lives in prison. The media did not broadcast Peggy's statement, only Rubin's. Rubin told the reporters that Peggy "has a lot that she is hiding," a comment she made about virtually every defense witness.

Peggy was excused and, for the rest of the afternoon, there were lengthy arguments over the defense attorneys' request that the court allow them to call Astrid Heger, Kee MacFarlane, and two district attorney's investigators, Augusta ("Gusty") Bell and Anthony Brunetti. The judge became testy. Gits said, "Mr. Brunetti's testimony is absolutely critical to Mrs. Buckey." The judge was not impressed. "Everything you offer is absolutely critical!"

"There are some that are more absolutely critical than others," Gits said. "Mr. Brunetti is another. This is a different and unique thing. We are not talking about impeaching the children with prior, inconsistent statements. We are talking about looking under rocks and not finding anything. This is absolutely critical to our case. . . . The jury doesn't know, for instance, that Mrs. Buckey and Raymond Buckey were electronically surveilled for months, hoping to overhear some incriminating statements. . . ."

"What does that prove?" the judge asked.

"I've seen Mr. Brunetti testify on two occasions," Davis said. "No pornography after a big search. No identification of Raymond Buckey by [the first child], and he was shown pictures of Ray Buckey. We haven't heard from the boy. The fact that he looks at a photograph of my client and doesn't name him as a suspect, and names three or four other existing human beings . . . is something that is very crucial to Mr. Buckey." The judge countered that the boy was not going to be a witness "and therefore you cannot impeach him."

"Brunetti can come in here and say," Davis asserted, "that he searched the world . . . and if Ray Buckey had something to do with distribution of pornography, they would have to come up with some photographs, some magazines. . . . This child was given an opportunity, with law enforcement supervising—not CII—did not name my client as having molested him! How am I going to do this at this late date? If the child's not coming on, we have to look at the impact . . . of the doctor and George Freeman [the jailhouse snitch]. This, I'm saying, is unfair. . . . If the judge is not going to put [the boy] on the stand . . . then I think something has to be done about a person charged with molestation where two things have happened in this case, and this is Ray Buckey's crucial issue in this offer. If the child says, 'I don't want to come to court. I don't want to talk about it,' there has to be something fashioned . . . to pull out these very clear events that happened that demonstrate that the child was accusing someone else.

"And this is a case where it's not Ray Buckey! He's looking at a picture of Ray Buckey under the supervision of law enforcement and he does not name Ray Buckey as a suspect. Can't we fashion something that recognizes that that's so inherently unfair? You can charge somebody with ten counts by ten children, and never bring the child in. And everything that might have shown that that child accused his father, or a man down the street, would never come in! And the defendant is sitting there with a doctor, and an informant. And nobody's going to come in and testify that this boy did not name Ray Buckey as a suspect. We don't have any testimony from [the boy] in this case! He never accused Ray Buckey. He accused his father, in front of objective, professional people, and he accused other people. It seems fair enough to require that that be brought in front of a jury. It's not enough to say, 'I'm not going to bring him into court because he doesn't want to.' Unless you're willing to look at what can be done in his absence, unless you can make some accommodation . . . to a crucial, fundamental constitutional right with the seminal child in this case. . . .

"Isn't this unfair? We have information out there that he accused his father to two different physicians who diagnosed him . . . at a time when my client was continuously in prison. . . . What we have is that the father did have the child on the evenings of August the tenth and eleventh, before he was brought to the doctor . . . and shortly after, when Brunetti and Hoag said, 'Name the suspect,' showing him a picture of Raymond Buckey, he does not name Ray Buckey. . . . When a doctor totally unconnected to this case diagnoses him as acutely sodomized, and Ray Buckey is in jail! Someone else had to do that to that boy. And that someone else is not a figment of my imagination or an argument.

"We are talking about someone who did harm to the boy, after my client was put in jail, and we're talking about him not naming Ray Buckey when he was given the chance to tell who did it to him. I can't imagine how this count can go forward without that evidence coming in by an exception devised by this court, acknowledging that when you do not compel a child . . . and that child would help Ray Buckey, then you cannot keep Ray Buckey from bringing in alternate reasonable inferences of the same type of evidence in which the child would give if he testified."

At the end of the day, after recess, one of the paralegals told us in the hallway, "That judge is under a lot of pressure. The governor and all of the most powerful political figures in the state want the Buckeys convicted. This case has put the credibility and the integrity of the whole system on trial and they think a conviction would take the heat off them."

Monday morning there appeared in the *Los Angeles Times* a story about the previous week's examination of Peggy Buckey in which the Buckeys were described as "a very dark American family which tried for a long time to keep its problems hidden." This statement was attributed to Lael Rubin, who called Peggy's statements "prepared, canned answers." There were also references to Ray's "serious problems with drinking and marijuana," which, if the record is correct, were minimal. The reporter described Ray Buckey as "a shy young man who was uncomfortable with his peers and adults, preferred the company of children." It was astoundingly inaccurate. The headline read:

BUCKEY FAMILY PROBLEMS REVEALED IN TRIAL
CHILDHOOD SEXUAL ABUSE, EMOTIONAL UPSETS
TOLD IN 11 DAYS ON STAND

When we arrived on the fifteenth floor, just before the courtroom was unlocked, friends of the Buckey family were reading the story. They were aghast. "A dark American family? Kept its problems hidden? If anything Peggy talks too much!" One of them said. "That's really dirty! And everything in it was false!"

The arguments about the proposed additional witnesses continued. The defense wanted to show, through Heger, MacFarlane, and Bell, that the children recanted and/or could not remember their prior statements. If they had really been sexually abused, they would not have forgotten, Gits said. The judge said he did not think it was important that each child told five different stories. The lawyers' voices droned on and on. We saw Ray Buckey laugh silently as the judge spoke of "satanic rituals." The defense was trying to show that Ray Buckey did not take child pornography to South Dakota in his luggage. The judge responded: "He might have taken the pornography in carry-on luggage and stored it under his seat." Buckey looked astonished. "His luggage arrived two days before he arrived," Davis said. "A man disposing of pornography, nationwide, would be unlikely to send it, and have it sit there for two days before he arrived. . . ."

Eventually, Judge Pounders ruled that he would allow the defense to call Brunetti, the D.A.'s investigator, to testify in limited, circumscribed areas, including the unsuccessful search for pornography. The prosecutors told the media, and the public, that the Buckeys were part of an international child pornography distribution organization, and used the admitted perjurer, George Freeman, to deliver that message to the jury. A worldwide search, engaging the FBI, Interpol, and other police organizations, came up empty. The judge also ruled that he would *not* allow the defense to ask Brunetti about the months of electronic surveillance of Ray and Peggy, and the million-dollar, year-long investigation, both of which came up empty.

At one point in the tense debate, Davis said, "As I listen to your arguments, I am hearing the arguments of a prosecutor."

"No! They're the arguments of a judge trying to get this case to the jury and cut out the crap!" Pounders exploded. Later, outside the courtroom during a recess, Davis said, "I am seriously alarmed. . . . I have heard witnesses critical to the defense described as 'crap' and deeply fear the jury will not hear Ray Buckey's defense."

The judge did allow the testimony of Janie Friedkin, a former teacher at the preschool who was also a travel agent. She testified that Buckey had planned his trip to South Dakota before the investigation began, to refute George Freeman's statement that Buckey had hastily, in panic, flown there to bury child pornography. It all seemed rather superfluous. If the child pornography existed, why would Ray not simply burn it or destroy it in some easier way, rather than fly all the way to Wind Caves National Park?

The defense called Janie Friedkin to the stand. She was an excellent witness. She was somewhat plump, had blonde hair, and sat on the stand with a radiant smile as she answered the questions. Friedkin said that Ray was "very much loved" by the children, that he was their favorite teacher, that she never saw anything in his interaction with the children that was not positive.

"Did you ever see Ray Buckey with a child on his lap?"

"Yes, that's very normal."

"Objection! Move that the answer be stricken," Rubin cut in.

"Sustained."

"Did you ever see Ray Buckey grope, or touch a child improperly?"

"No!" Friedkin laughed exuberantly.

Friedkin was put through the entire repertoire of questions about the "naked movie star" game, naked children, mistreatment of animals, naked teachers, assisting children in the bathroom. She said she had never seen the slightest evidence of anything improper at the school. When one of the attorneys asked, "Your honor, may we approach?" Friedkin laughed as the pompous lawyers whispered, arguing over some trivial point of law. She was definitely a breath of fresh air in this grim drama. She told of making a reservation for Buckey's trip to South Dakota, before the accusations surfaced. She was asked many questions about the process of making the reservation, about her hours at the preschool and other details of her life in the 1981-1983 period.

When it was Rubin's turn to cross-examine, her attempts to bully Friedkin fizzled and not once was she able to shake the witness's buoyant good humor. Occasionally, Friedkin turned things around and began questioning Rubin, who then tersely asked the judge to admonish the witness. Friedkin had a pleasant, musical voice and was surprisingly articulate. She said she spent most of her time at the preschool working with Ray.

Rubin again did not address any of the specific charges pending against the Buckeys. Instead, she asked about Ray's alleged use of drugs and alcohol, and Peggy's denial that she had ever seen Ray with an erection. Friedkin answered all of the questions with clear, forthright answers. During a recess we told Friedkin that we thought she had done marvelously. She told us that Gits and Davis had told her that she talked too much.

At the end of the day, after Friedkin was excused, the judge told the jurors that there was going to be a piece on McMartin the following morning, on NBC television's "Today Show," and admonished them to avoid seeing it. In the morning we turned on the television and watched. Predictably, we saw and heard the zealots cursing Ray and Peggy and saying they wanted to jump over the railing and tear them apart. Lael Rubin's face appeared on the screen, saying, "It is obviously my hope and my belief that the jury is going to come back and convict these defendants, and that the world will say, 'This is a jury and this is a courtroom in which children were believed.'" There were also murky statements by the attorneys, and one by the judge, expressing his concern that juror attrition would force a mistrial. NBC newsperson Heidi Schulman spoke the truth when she said: "What's really on trial here is the legal system."

Davis argued at length that two physicians should be permitted to testify for the defense because, he asserted, Peter, the first child, told two physicians, in the presence of other witnesses, that it was his father who had "poked" him. The judge countered that "even if his father molested him, that doesn't prove that Mr. Buckey is not a molester." The judge also ruled that the defense could not call the boy or his father to testify.

Davis again brought up the fact that two other doctors testified that the boy's mother was definitely protecting the perpetrator and would not allow any question or examination that would identify him.

"That's very important evidence," the judge acknowledged. "[The boy] never accused anyone else. . . . But even though that is very strong, that does not exclude evidence in the case that refers to a confession."

The confession referred to by the judge was the confession alleged by George Freeman.

Judge Pounders stated, "I must preclude this evidence." He had, to date, eliminated twenty-eight witnesses the defense wanted to call, saying they were "too time-consuming."

The next witness was Anthony Brunetti, an investigator for the D.A.'s office assigned as lead investigator for the McMartin case from January 4, 1984, on a full-time basis, until October 1987. He was a handsome man, wore a moustache and looked like a television cop. He testified that a search of Ray Abou Fadel's market for evidence of child pornography and molestation came up empty, as did a search of Mr. Fadel's home. He also testified that repeated searches of the preschool revealed no secret rooms, and that a worldwide search for child pornography, engaging the Los Angeles police, the FBI, postal inspectors, and almost every major law enforcement agency in the world, including the viewing of numerous caches of "pornography," both foreign and domestic, turned up nothing that could in any way be connected with the Buckeys.

On cross-examination, Gunson launched into a long series of questions about conversations with law enforcement about child pornography in other, unrelated cases. The defense attorneys objected indignantly on the grounds that the questions were hearsay and did not connect in any way with the Buckeys. It was a massive negative campaign of the most vile sort, very deliberately done to insinuate that the child pornography did connect in some way with the Buckeys, which the jurors might well have inferred if they were not paying close attention, and if they were not familiar with the way some lawyers operate. Gunson was allowed to go on with this line of questioning for nearly an hour, eliciting hearsay statements about the practices of child pornographers and pedophiles.

At one point, Davis asked, "What does this have to do with the charges?" The defense continued to object, but Pounders told them, "The defense objections are overruled." That was the breaking point.

"Excuse me," Davis said. "Does that mean that the prosecution can now elicit, from this witness, hearsay?"

"Yes. From the information that was just cited. We're not going into anything and everything . . ."

"Your honor, if I understand what you just said," Davis responded, "that was the subject of the stipulation!"

"I'm not sure it limits it to everything you wanted it to."

"May I have appropriate time, if the court please, to prepare an affidavit of prejudice against this court? I believe your ruling in this instance and earlier on Peter is sufficient evidence to prove just that, and I would ask that I have at least a day to prepare such a document." An affidavit of prejudice is an action to remove the judge from the case.

"Certainly you may always file a petition under section 170.1 but we will not halt the proceedings," the judge answered.

"May I have until tomorrow, your honor? It's going to take time and I feel you should not have jurisdiction until I'm given reasonable opportunity to complete such a document."

"Your request is denied."

Gunson continued with his cross-examination. He used the words, "pornography," and "child pornography" in virtually every question. The questions were about cases that had not the slightest connection with the Buckeys, but, over the repeated objections of the defense, the judge allowed it to go on and on. All of the defense objections were overruled.

At recess, Davis faced reporters and accused the judge of prejudice against himself and his client, Ray, and of making "rulings that I believe change the rules of evidence to prejudicially shift the evidence the jury may be hearing. What I heard today was that traditional rules of evidence would be set aside. . . . The record doesn't reflect the understanding we reached when the judge said that opinion evidence could come through Brunetti."

Asked about the affidavit of prejudice, Davis said, "I file it here in court. It's a public document. The court has a period of time to respond, as I do.

Then, it's reviewed by a judicial committee, to decide whether he should continue as judge in this trial. It's a group of judges appointed by the Supreme Court who serve in that function from time to time when issues like this arrive. The judge has to respond under oath."

"Are there other issues of prejudice besides this Brunetti thing?" a reporter asked.

"I will talk about the entire history of his prejudice in this case," Davis said. He also criticized specific rulings by the judge, such as excluding witnesses Davis said were crucial to Ray Buckey's defense, particularly the ruling of that day barring testimony of the doctors to whom Peter had allegedly said that his father had molested him.

"George Freeman was permitted to testify," Davis said, "because the prosecution alleged a count involving [the boy]. We presented square evidence that two doctors heard [the boy] accuse his father. This is a reasonable alternative . . . the only one, that on August 11, 1983, the boy was sodomized, the inference being my client. We haven't heard from the boy. We will not hear from the two doctors. We will not hear from the father. . . . We will not hear from the doctors on his being sodomized on at least two occasions . . . when my client was in custody. And the court won't let it come to the jury! We're talking about a time when my client could not have been the perpetrator because he was in jail. If you were accused in this kind of a case and you knew the confession of George Freeman was bootstrapped on this type of a count, only to find out that the boy will not testify and the doctors who knew his true medical state, and the father, will not be coming in, that's about it."

"Do you think the judge is so obsessed with the jury falling apart that he's throwing away due process?" a reporter asked.

"My concern is a personal prejudice against my client and against myself. It has now escalated into a manipulation of the evidence. So his personal prejudice may well affect the course of this trial. So I'm going to detail the history of personal prejudice against my client, against myself, and then try to present to this court, and the reviewing court, how it is that he manipulated the evidence into a one-sided, prejudicial event. This trial, as far as I am concerned, is no longer a fair trial," Davis said.

"Tomorrow I'm going to file an affidavit of prejudice against the judge," Davis told reporters, "saying as competently as I can the history of prejudice and how it reaches into manipulation of the evidence and the rules of evidence in this case . . . whacking off scores of witnesses for the defense with the stated argument that it is a matter of time. Statements to the press that put him outside the neutrality of a constitutional proceeding. . . . I don't join in his assertion that the jury is being held together with spit and bailing wire. I do say that an evil has infected the rulings and the destiny of this case and I intend to bring it to the attention of the judiciary in terms of this judge."

"Don't you agree that there's a chance of losing the jury?" a television reporter asked.

"They look healthy to me and the attrition rate over a long haul indicates that we'll have plenty of jurors and extras when it's over. I don't join in this kind of karmic doom that emanates from the judge. We have two extra jurors. It would take three lost to mistrial this case. My concern now is the fairness of the proceeding. The jury looks healthy. No. We'll reach a verdict. I'm confident of that. Whether we reach it fairly or not is in serious question. . . . The prosecution had plenty of time to put their [witnesses] on. Now, with the most critical witnesses we're out of time. . . . And I'm concerned that the evil is one that's created an attitude. If we continue it that way we're going to end up with a decision in a case that is going to end in disaster. There's a difference between a mistrial based on juror attrition and rulings that in effect cut one side down to its knees, in the last stages of its own presentation, in favor of another. That to me is an evil. Who's the source of it? I think it's a conjoint effect of what is the McMartin problem," Davis said.

"I would think that when we saw an informant admit his perjury and he got immunity from the same court—to me, in terms of the credibility of our system, the low point in this trial—that we should have suffered a mistrial then. We didn't then so I don't expect it now," Davis said.

"What will be the effect of this affidavit of prejudice in real terms?" the television announcer asked.

"He will respond. Judicial counsel will review it, and I don't make predictions. The case goes on."

"What is your goal in filing this affidavit?" a reporter asked.

"That he remove himself and we have a new trial. That we look for a judge who is neutral."

"And that you start a new trial all over again? After two years?"

"Absolutely. I don't want to continue the way we're going. Would you want to go to a verdict when the defendant isn't putting on his case? It's predictable what happens in trials like that."

"Now you'll file this thing and then what happens?" the announcer asked.

"He has time to respond. If he responds, he can still remove himself. What will happen in all probability is he'll respond and won't remove himself, and it goes up for review."

"Is this brought on by the fact that he has disallowed forty or fifty witnesses?"

"We have a history in this case. This is just the latest batch that have been denied. The judge made a ruling today that what was supposed to be a hearsay review of searches became a hearsay presentation of experts that we aren't even going to hear from. Two physicians in June 1984, examined Peter and saw that he was acutely sodomized. Both of them were told in the presence of many other witnesses that his father was the perpetrator. My client at that time had been in jail since March."

* * *

Gunson's cross-examination of Brunetti continued with more questions about child pornography. He asked the witness if he had viewed a collection of pornography that had been seized from a Mr. Salmi. He said he had.

"Did you engage in a search for animal hair?"

"Yes."

Brunetti testified that of all the massive quantities of pornography he viewed, only a very small amount contained photographs of small children, less than twenty.

Davis, on redirect, asked Brunetti a series of questions about Mr. Salmi in which he repeatedly pronounced his name "Mr. Salami," until he had been corrected several times.

Brunetti stated that Mr. Salmi's collection was the best pornography he had ever seen. He was asked to explain what he meant by "best." A roar of laughter burst forth from the jurors and spectators. Even the judge shook with laughter, although he appeared to be making a futile attempt to control it.

"Naked, good-looking women?" Davis asked.

"Yes."

Davis continued to refer to the collector as "Mr. Salami," and was again corrected.

"Did you find any kiddie porn that you could associate with the McMartin Preschool?" Davis asked.

"No."

"Did you find any network associated with Mr. Buckey?"

"No."

Davis elicited from Brunetti the fact that the foray to Wind Caves National Park in South Dakota was prompted by "information" provided by the informant, George Freeman. It would seem that any reasonable person would wonder why Ray Buckey, or anybody, would take a cache of child pornography to South Dakota when it could so easily have been disposed of in California. Freeman certainly led them on a wild goose chase.

"You also, in an effort to find pornography, went to a psychic, didn't you?" Davis asked.

"I listened to what she had to say," Brunetti said.

"Did you put her out in the field?"

"No."

"For all that you reviewed, did you find anything that connected with Ray Buckey?"

"No, I didn't."

The antagonism between the judge and Davis continued to escalate. During a sidebar conference the judge called Davis an "ass."

When they were finished with Brunetti and he was excused, Dr. Frank

Richelieu came in with his attorney to offer a motion to have his subpoena quashed. The defense wanted his testimony, which the jury never heard, to dispel the prosecution's insinuation that Buckey went to him for counseling about pedophilia. The judge quashed the subpoena, which in effect, meant that Richelieu would not be testifying. During the arguments, Pounders said, "I have the greatest respect for religion. I have two ministers in my family and I have taught religion in my own church."

The next witness, David Sugiyama, testified briefly that he was employed as a serologist at the sheriff's crime lab in 1984 and participated in the examination of numerous items seized from the preschool: blankets, clothing, undergarments, and the like, for the purpose of finding blood and semen. Small residues of blood were found on a mop, he said, but no semen was found anywhere in the school.

On Monday, July 24, another juror was excused because she had been told by her doctors that she had to have surgery for a gall bladder infection. We were now down to one alternate. If we lost two more jurors, it would be over, and a mistrial declared. Lawyers tangentially involved in the case and other insiders told us that all of the most powerful political figures in the state were hoping for a conviction because the stunning disclosures of prosecutorial misconduct, fraud, and perjury arising from the case had put the entire system on trial, and they felt that a conviction would "take the heat off" them.

But now, one of the lawyers told us, "the probability of a conviction has greatly diminished and everybody would be satisfied with a mistrial. That way, they could just keep moving it down the road until it dies." We had no idea whether his assumptions were correct, but it was a belief widely held by lawyers who followed the case.

Ray was expected to take the stand and begin his testimony the next day.

"The defense calls Ray Buckey." At long last, the main event. After six years of silence, Ray was sworn in and sat down at the witness stand. He looked very dapper in his blue suit and, like his father, spoke with a deep, resonant voice. His hair was trimmed. He had a clean-cut, wholesome look. It would be difficult to find a more presentable witness. The courtroom was packed with media reporters, lawyers, spectators, and the familiar mob, watching Ray Buckey with harsh faces and hard eyes. Davis began by covering the times when Ray was not at the preschool, corroborating the other testimony that he was not even in Manhattan Beach at the time several of the accusing children attended.

Like all of the other defendants, Ray testified that at no time, since his first arrest in 1983, had he ever been questioned by anyone in law enforcement. They did not want any exculpatory information. As far as they were concerned, the case was closed.

Ray said he had an agreement with his parents that he would either go to college, at their expense, or get a job, but that he frequently skipped classes.

Davis asked him, "When you dropped out of class, did you . . . drop by the preschool?"

"No. I didn't want my parents to know that I wasn't attending classes."

"During the time that you were at the McMartin Preschool, did you ever reach an agreement of any kind with other teachers . . . that you would attempt to conceal children being molested at the preschool?"

"No."

"You heard Arthur describe your mother as being in her bra at the preschool. . . . Did you ever see anything like that at the preschool?"

"No."

"From what you know of your mother, is she the type of person who would do that at the preschool?"

"She would not even do it at home," Ray answered.

"Objection."

"Sustained. The answer is stricken."

"You heard suggestions that your mother was naked at the preschool. Is that something you ever saw at the preschool?"

"No."

"Have you ever been in St. Cross Church?"

"Never in my life."

"Have you ever touched a child to arouse or obtain sexual gratification?"

"No."

"Have you ever knowingly exposed your penis to a child?"

"No."

"Did you ever hurt Peter?"

"No."

"Did you ever molest Peter in any way?"

"No."

"Did you ever sodomize Peter?"

"No."

"Did you ever sodomize anybody?"

"No."

Ray testified that he had never even touched the boy.

When Ray was asked about the counts pertaining to several children he said that he had never even seen them until they testified at the preliminary hearing in 1984 and 1985.

"Have you ever been a member of any type of network of child molesters or involved in the sale or production of kiddie porn?"

"No."

"Have you ever seen kiddie porn?"

"No."
"Did you ever put your finger into the vaginal opening of a child?"
"No."
"Did you ever kill a horse with a baseball bat?"
"No." Ray laughed involuntarily, trying to control himself.
"Were you ever there when Cathy [one of the child witnesses] was at the preschool?"
"No."
"Have you ever been in the men's room at the Red Carpet Car Wash?"
"No."
"Have you ever been inside the women's room at the Red Carpet Car Wash?"
"No."

Again, Ray tried, unsuccessfully, to suppress his laughter.

Ray testified that during the times he stayed at the preschool in the afternoon there was almost always another teacher there with him, usually Betty Raidor. He said that the only time he came into contact with children's genitals was when he wiped them with toilet paper or a washcloth after an "accident" in which the child had soiled himself. He also stated that the first time he ever heard of the "naked movie star" game was when he was watching a Wayne Satz newscast on Channel 7.

Davis addressed each of the counts in minute detail, asking Ray if he had ever molested any of the children, which he denied.

"Did George Freeman ever talk to you about sex?"

"His sex. He told me about his ex-wives. He told me about the women he had sex with and the men he had sex with."

Buckey's gentle, wholesome character strikingly contrasted with the prosecutors' portrayal of him as a brutal fiend with depraved desires and weird cravings who butchered animals and drank blood and threatened children with death to terrify them into silence.

Ray denied playing a sexual game called "tickle," alleged by some of the children, but said he did occasionally tickle children. When he was asked why, he simply responded, "I don't know. Why do you tickle anybody? To make them laugh."

A friend who had not been in the McMartin courtroom for over a year sat next to us and whispered, during a sidebar conference, that she saw a remarkable change in the appearance of the jurors.

"How have they changed?"

"They're burned out!" she said.

During recess, as the lawyers, reporters, and spectators swarmed in the hallway, we saw Ray among the crowd, standing inconspicuously with his back to the wall, alone. We went over and greeted him.

"You've spent more time in the courtroom than most lawyers. After all this comes down, why don't you just go to law school and get your bar ticket and be a lawyer? After all this, it would be a snap."

"I don't know," he said. "It's a game with no rules. Anything goes. I don't know if I could play in a game like that."

At the end of the day, Ray was confronted by the television cameras as he came out of the courtroom, and he was asked by a reporter if he was worried about the coming cross-examination.

"Questions are questions," he said. "And I have the truth behind me so I'm not worried about any question anybody asks me."

When Deputy District Attorney Lael Rubin came out of the courtroom and faced the cameras and microphones, she said, "It is very, very clear that he has spent the last five and a half years practicing for his first day in court, and I think that being so well-rehearsed will be more underscored as he continues his testimony." She also said that there was not a "shred of truth" to anything he had said. If anything, Buckey was noticeably unprepared. He did not have the slick, facile answers that well-rehearsed witnesses gave. He seemed to be simply answering the questions from his memory of the events described, in simple, straightforward language.

Ray's attorney, Davis, told the reporters, when they shoved their microphones to his face, "It's one thing for my client to say he didn't molest that little girl, but it's another thing to begin to realize he wasn't even there."

We sat with Peggy on a bench in the hallway as she waited for Ray and her driver. She chastened us, as she frequently did, for not having our cat sterilized. Davis came over and Peggy asked him how Ray was holding up. Davis said he was okay and told her that he had ordered him to stop drinking coffee. Then he left.

"Lawyers. They think they're little gods," she said.

The next day, the *Los Angeles Times* published a story in which Peggy was quoted as having described her son as a "misfit." Seething with anger she showed it to us and said, "I'm going over and ask Lois Timnick why she did that!" Peggy asked us to accompany her. We followed her as she walked to the press box and said to Timnick, "Why did you call my son a misfit? I never . . ."

Timnick began talking over Peggy without allowing her to finish her question, speaking rapidly: "You said he was uncomfortable with adults and more comfortable with . . ."

"I did not!" Peggy said angrily. "I said . . ."

"Well, it's in your testimony." Avoiding eye contact with Peggy, Timnick continued to talk over her, drowning her out.

"Well, I'm just tired of hearing the word, 'misfit'! I am his mother and I have never said he was a misfit. How would you like it as a mother, to hear your son called a misfit?" Peggy asked angrily. Timnick continued to talk over her, turned her back to Peggy, gathered up her bag and notepad and walked away. Most of the media have now moved to a more neutral reportage of McMartin, with the exception of the *Los Angeles Times,* whose stories on the case read like handouts from the district attorney's office.

Back in the courtroom Davis resumed asking his questions. Buckey denied each of the fifty-two charges against him and at one point, with a tone of anger in his voice, said, "Nothing improper ever happened at the preschool." Asked about his encounter with George Freeman, he said that when Freeman was placed in his cell Freeman knew everything about him and about the case. Asked about the *Playboy* magazines found in the police search of his room, he explained that he used them "for sexual gratification." He said he tried to hide them from the police because "I believed Jane Hoag would make a big issue about my having adult pornography. I didn't think she needed any help in fabricating a case against me." Ray said he had never taken sexually explicit magazines to the preschool or displayed them to anyone. Again, Davis went over the written records to show that Buckey had no opportunity to molest children. He was never alone with Melinda.

When Davis asked him about the propriety of a male working as a preschool teacher, Buckey responded, "I don't see anything inappropriate about a male working with children." It is interesting to note that in the eighteenth and nineteenth centuries, almost all teachers were males and all students were boys.

Buckey also verified records that showed he never worked at the school when four of the alleged victims attended and was seldom alone with children on afternoons when parents were coming to pick up their children. During a recess, Davis told reporters, "Aren't we looking for a time and place when Ray could have done these things? These records weren't made up. The police seized them."

After recess, before the jury was brought in, Judge Pounders expressed concern and indignation over the fact that one television station had been careless enough to show the face of one of the jurors on its tape. Rubin obliquely suggested that the media be excluded from the trial.

Predictably, Rubin's cross-examination of Ray Buckey was filled with pornography and underwear. As we listened to it hour upon hour, we watched the jurors to get some sense of how all this was playing with them. One of them was laughing. They must have been wondering, as we had been, if Gunson's and Rubin's personal lives had been so chaste and pristine that they felt they had a right to stigmatize another for enjoying sexual images in a magazine of general circulation.

After six years no child pornography was found that could in any way be connected to the preschool or to the Buckeys, but Lael Rubin tried a new, innovative approach: she asked Ray if he had ever pasted pictures of the faces of preschool children on the photographs in the adult magazines. The spectators gasped in astonishment.

"I know I never did that," Buckey answered.

"How do you know that?" Rubin demanded.

"Because I know what I do and I know what I don't do."

The dialogue progressively heated up until Ray finally said, "Miss Rubin, I spent five years in jail for something I never did!"

That weekend we attended Virginia McMartin's eightieth birthday party and had a long, interesting conversation with her. We told her we had an assignment to write an article about baseball and needed some help. Virginia had an encyclopedic knowledge of the game. Smiling with enthusiasm she proffered us two beautiful coffee table books on the history of baseball and asked us to promise that we give her a copy of the story when it was published. We would be less than honest if we did not confess that we liked Virginia very much. She had guts and a generous spirit. Unlike most people she was not angered by the successes and good fortune of others but seemed to share their pleasure with enthusiasm and great interest.

Monday, July 31, 1989. Rubin resumed her cross-examination of Ray Buckey with hour after hour of endless questions about "pornography" and the missing underwear. Rubin liked to use rowdy language and frequently used the word "fuck" and "hard on" when she could as easily have said "erection." At one point, Davis said, "Your honor, I would protest Miss Rubin's language." The judge shrugged.

The cross-examination went on and on with the word "pornography" in almost every question. There had never been any evidence of child pornography and the questions about *Playboy* really did not connect with the charges in any way. They were pictures of adult women designed for a heterosexual, male audience. But the judge continued to allow the testimony to go in, based on the principle that it somehow rebutted the defense position that Ray did not and does not have any affinity for "unusual sex."

We did not understand why Davis and Gits did not raise their voices in protest, frequently and vociferously. The jury needed to understand that this was nothing more than a smear. But Davis and Gits sat there, silently, and listened. Most lawyers are intimidated by this kind of cross-examination. It is a crippling deficiency stemming from the ignorant belief that there is something shameful about sexual images in art and literature. There is also the fact that most defense lawyers are not offended by this conduct because it goes with the territory.

"Did you tell George Freeman that you screwed Peter in the ass?" Rubin asked.

"No, and I don't use your kind of language, Miss Rubin," Ray answered.

Asked about the girl who allegedly grabbed his genitalia through his trousers, Ray said that he had been told by the child's mother that the girl was in the habit of doing this with her father, who tolerated it, and that the mother had apologized and told her daughter not to do it again. But Ray was cut off, each time, by Rubin's objection, which was sustained. So the jurors never heard the whole story. In response to Rubin's question Ray said that he had told the girl in a stern tone not to do that.

Rubin asked Ray to reenact the tone of voice he had used with the girl. He said, "Miss Rubin, I am not an actor." Later, Rubin asked him to reenact the tone of voice he used when he first learned of the police investigation of him. Davis loudly objected, saying, "I object to asking him to perform. He is not an actor, dancer, or singer."

At the end of the day, Ray's anger flared up when he acknowledged that he had made a small inaccuracy in his testimony: "Miss Rubin, I'm very nervous. I probably said some things that are not quite correct, I'll grant it." Rubin moved in for the kill: "Including, Mr. Buckey, whether or not you molested children in this case?" her voice rang out sharply. "No, Miss Rubin," Buckey glared. "I know that I did not molest children, *ever*. I'm certain about that."

The small inaccuracy in Ray's testimony concerned reviewing photocopies of Virginia McMartin's diaries. But Rubin never missed an opportunity to hurl accusations at Ray.

A CBS television reporter asked Rubin, "What does it show that he didn't wear underwear? What does it show that he had some pornography? Isn't there still the crime that you have to prove?"

"Well, of course," she said, "but in most cases where there is not an adult eyewitness the case is put together with strong corroborating medical evidence as it is in this case, and a composite of circumstantial evidence which we believe a jury can do nothing but convict this defendant."

In the morning Rubin began with a long series of questions about Ray's occasional use of marijuana, strongly suggesting that it was more than just occasional. Her tactic was of questionable efficacy because if pot smoking in America is as prevalent as studies indicate, there might be some pot smokers on the jury. Nevertheless, Rubin was trying to paint Ray as a drug-crazed hippie pervert.

During a recess Peggy ran into further difficulties. The judge in the adjacent courtroom where the celebrated Harvey Rader multiple murder case was being tried came into Pounders' courtroom to tell Pounders that one of the jurors had overheard Peggy discussing the case in an elevator. Peggy was called into the Rader courtroom, where she explained that all she had said was, "My heart goes out to all of them."

"I am a friendly person," Peggy explained. "I speak to everyone." In the Los Angeles Criminal Courts Building it is extremely imprudent to speak to anyone at all. Peggy was severely admonished for this act of friendliness.

Then the real craziness began.

Before the jury was brought in, the prosecution argued that it be allowed to ask Ray about his interest in pyramids. They knew that he slept with a large, steel pyramid over his bed and their investigators learned that in 1982 he attended a health food and pyramid convention in Reno and was photographed wearing a wire pyramid hat. The judge looked unimpressed with this request and somewhat dubious. Turning to Gits and Davis, he asked, "Anything from the defense?"

"What does it have to do with the charges?" Davis asked, sounding tired and exasperated.

Gunson, raising his thin, harsh voice, hotly asserted that it was evidence of satanism. The prosecutors now wanted to paint Buckey as a deranged fanatic, and to resurrect the discarded allegations of Supermarket Billy, who said Buckey engaged in satanic rituals and molested him in a church and in a supermarket—with "atomically radiated mutants."

The plot thickened. The prosecutors had a written report from an investigator employed by the D.A.'s office that stated that after attending the pyramid convention Ray went to Pyramid Lake, in California, with a young woman, where the two were baptized, naked, by a wandering clergyman.

Realistically, pyramids, along with alfalfa sprouts, transcendental meditation, EST, and apricot pits, were simply a part of the "holistic" health and spiritual self-improvement fad of the seventies. There is also, however, a small coterie who believe that the pyramid is Satan's trademark, revered by secret societies committed to the worship of the devil. Gunson, apparently, had learned of this and wanted to use it to undermine Buckey in the eyes of the jurors. As Rubin told the media, she intended to dissolve the picture of Ray Buckey as an all-American boy.

We had expected that the judge would summarily deny this absurd offer, but instead, he said he would allow the jury to hear the testimony because it could rebut Peggy Buckey's assertion that she would never employ someone who would jeopardize the preschool's superb reputation.

"Why would she let somebody who . . . flies off to conventions like this, wearing a wire pyramid over his head [teach at the preschool?] . . . How is that person capable of serving the community in the capacity of a preschool teacher?" Judge Pounders said. In other words, a man with an interest in new ideas should not be allowed to teach.

During a recess, Rubin told reporters outside the courtroom that the pyramids may have been a link to child molestation.

Sitting in the courthouse cafeteria with a group of lawyers and paralegals, we commented, "Those prosecutors certainly play a dirty game. It's 'no holds barred.'"

"They're just doing their job," one of the lawyers said.

"I thought we settled that at Nuremberg," we answered sullenly.

Leaning forward like a bird of prey, Rubin faced Ray, strong in the knowledge that she had the upper hand. She knew all the lawyer tricks and was preparing to disembowel him in front of the assembled jurors, lawyers, and media reporters. But when she questioned Ray about the pyramid convention in Reno and showed a photograph of Buckey with a wire pyramid hat on his head, she was met with an outburst of uproarious laughter. Even the judge laughed uncontrollably. Rubin and Gunson waited for the laughter to subside, with the limp, disconsolate look of a couple of football team managers whose team had just been thoroughly trounced.

In response to Rubin's questions, Ray said he had met a young woman named Barbara at the convention, and that they had left early on a Saturday night and had driven to Lake Tahoe, where they spent the night at a motel.

In the hallway during recess, Davis was laughing. It appeared that he had scored some big points, but the scoreboard remained inscrutable; we had watched the jurors for over two years, seen them smiling, frowning, sleeping, laughing, and just staring off into space. It was impossible to tell what they would do with all of this, when it came time for them to make their collective decision.

After hours of harping on Ray's underwear, or more correctly, the absence of his underwear, Rubin got back to the pyramid convention and Barbara. Ray said that he had gone to the Fantasy Motel at Lake Tahoe with Barbara, that they had taken a bath in a heart-shaped tub, and slept together in a bedroom walled with mirrors. "It was *quite* a fantasy," he said.

"Did you have sexual intercourse with Barbara?" Rubin asked.

"Yes, we did," he smiled, with a look of joyful nostalgia.

"Mr. Buckey, did you see that portion of a [D.A.] report that states that Barbara said that she did not have sexual intercourse with you that night?"

"Yes."

"Would you describe your sexual relationship with Barbara?"

"In which location?"

"The Fantasy Motel."

"Sexual intercourse."

"Is there any reason that Barbara would say that you did not have sexual intercourse with her?"

"I'm sure she has her reasons. I'd like to hear them."

"Now, you're aware of the fact that Barbara told the district attorney investigator that she . . ."

"Objection! Hearsay."

"Overruled. It's not offered for the truth of the matter."

"Are you aware of the fact, Mr. Buckey, that Barbara has told district attorney investigators that she tried to seduce you but that you wouldn't be seduced?"

"I believe the report says that," Ray replied. "I don't know her reasons."

When Rubin asked if there were other times he had had sex with Barbara, he said, "The first time was in the Holiday Inn. She came down and stayed with me in my apartment . . . and we had sexual intercourse there."

"Did you and Barbara sleep under your pyramid?" Rubin asked. The jurors were grinning.

"Yes."

Rubin asked him how long he had intercourse with Barbara at the Fantasy Inn and he answered, "I wasn't timing it."

"Mr. Buckey, have you talked with any of your friends about your relationship with Barbara?"

"Objection. Vague as to time. Otherwise irrelevant."

"Sustained."

Rubin rephrased the question and Ray answered, "My friend, Steve, and my sister walked in on us once."

"Did Barbara get along with your mother?"

"I don't remember."

"Mr. Buckey, isn't it true that your mother told you to get rid of Barbara?"

"I know she wasn't happy that I had a woman living in my apartment with me. The whole family wasn't too happy about it."

"Why is that?"

"Objection. Calls for speculation."

"Overruled."

"It was their morals. I didn't think it was immoral." Ray also stated that "I was very much in love with Barbara."

Rubin and Gunson looked at Buckey with hard eyes. This was not what they wanted the jury to hear.

"Mr. Buckey," Rubin asked. "Do you have a belief that child molesters do not have relationships with adult females?"

"It's common sense. If you have a perversion for children you wouldn't have a desire for female adults."

"Is that your belief based on your experience?"

"What experience?"

"Having a perverted interest in children and therefore not having an interest in women?"

"... I can't imagine it.... It's like mixing apples and oranges. It's like homosexuality. You wouldn't have an interest in females."

"Have you met or heard about individuals who are bisexual?"

"I've heard of it but I can't imagine it."

"Now, isn't it true, Mr. Buckey, that in order to counter a claim that you had a sexual interest in children, you came up with and fabricated this account of sexual intercourse with Barbara?"

"I have no sexual desire for children, never had and never will," Ray said.

Asking about testimony of some of the children who said that he molested them, Rubin asked Ray if they were lying. He answered, "That is not the truth. I don't know if they were aware that they were lying." Rubin went over all of the allegations, all of which Ray denied.

In the morning there were arguments about the district attorney's investigator's report, which quoted Barbara as saying that Ray did not have sex with her. According to Gunson, the report stated that Barbara told the investigator that Ray wanted to wait until he was married before he had sex.

"Just because he wanted a monogamous relationship doesn't prove he was a molester," Davis argued.

The prosecutors said they would bring Barbara in as a rebuttal witness in a few days, since there was to be only one more defense witness, a medical expert. Peggy told us in the hallway during recess that Barbara was being outrageously harassed and intimidated at her home by law enforcement in order to ensure her testimony in support of the prosecution. She also told us, "They're trying to make Ray look like a mama's boy. I wish he had been more of a mama's boy and listened to me. Then we wouldn't have gotten into all this trouble."

The next day, Friday, Rubin ended her cross-examination of Ray Buckey. We had expected that she would press on for weeks, but everything the prosecutors tried backfired and they apparently decided to cut their losses and end it. On the same day there was another allegation that Peggy had talked within earshot of a juror. It was not a juror in this case, but the judge threatened to fine or jail Peggy if it happened again. There was a crowd of lawyers, paralegals, and reporters outside the courtroom. All seemed to agree that the prosecutors had instigated the incident and then brought it to the attention of the judge.

"They're losing it and they'll do anything to make Peggy look bad," one of them was saying.

Peggy was sobbing and Ray was holding her in his arms.

Tuesday, August 8, 1989. On this day the defense's medical expert witness began his testimony. There had been a lot of speculation as to who the witness would be, but those who knew would not talk. We saw him sitting on a bench outside the courtroom with a paralegal just before the bailiff unlocked the courtroom at 9 A.M. He was about sixty. We had never seen him before and hadn't the slightest idea who he was. He would be the last witness for the defense.

He was sworn in and gave his name—Dr. David M. Paul, the Queen's Coroner for the City of London and also a physician with the Department of Forensic Medicine at Guy's Hospital in London. The man's titles and credentials were many and impressive. He had examined over two thousand children for sexual assault, far more than all of the prosecution doctors added together.

Early in his testimony Paul told the court: "Here in America you call it sexual abuse. In the United Kingdom we call it 'buggery.' " The jurors laughed. "It is the same act," he said.

Paul was an immensely erudite and learned man and yet he had an easy, diffident humor in his testimony. At one point during the direct examination by Gits he answered a question from the judge, saying, "Yes, my lord." Gits explained to him that in this country it is not necessary to address the judge as "my lord." He laughed and said, "Very well."

We wondered why they had found it necessary to bring a doctor all the way from London when there were several excellent candidates in California. Then we found the answer. According to several newspaper stories, the medical profession had actually conspired to prevent medical experts in child abuse from testifying for defense in this case. The defense attorneys had indicated that they would call Dr. Robert tenBensel of Minneapolis as their expert witness, but tenBensel refused to come and testify for the defense because, he said, in a statment made to reporters that was subsequently published in several newspapers, "The pressures brought on me were more than the price I was willing to pay. The ante was too high. I received calls from every level of person I do business with. I have to work with other groups. Being involved in the McMartin case was destructive of my relationships with these professional groups."

Dr. tenBensel said that the Los Angeles District Attorney's office had called the chairman of his department. "Other people at the national level refused to tell me who talked to them." A doctor who was personally acquainted with him told us that tenBensel had even been called by the attorney general. Judge Pounders acknowledged that tenBensel's fear of losing federal funding if he testified in the McMartin trial could be construed as intimidation by the D.A.'s office.

Another doctor who had recently published a highly respected study on child sexual abuse that refuted the prosecution's "solid medical evidence" also was unwilling to testify for the defense, for the same reasons.

Just before going to the witness stand, Dr. Paul told a reporter, "I came here because I was ashamed for my profession." Ironically, almost all of the prosecution doctors cited Paul as the authority they had studied in reaching their conclusions. He told the newsman, "I was horrified at what was being done in my name. I wish they had read me more carefully."

There was a slide projector and a large screen set up in the courtroom. We are going to get another anal slide show. In color.

The defense attorney's inability to get an American doctor as an expert witness turned out to be a blessing in disguise. Paul was extremely impressive witness. His medical erudition, his eloquent use of language, and his wit combined to hold everyone's attention. And he did something the other witnesses did not do: when he answered the questions he turned and looked at the jurors as he spoke. He had a splendid voice and sounded like the late George Sanders, or Richard Burton.

Gits began by asking the doctor questions about Peter, the son of Judy

Johnson. The doctor had nothing to assist him but the written reports of two examinations by two physicians, one on August 12, 1983, and the other five days later. There were no slides or photographs. The mother was dead, and the defense had not been allowed to call the child as a witness. The mother had refused to permit any examination or any questions that could reveal the identity of the perpetrator. The written reports were inconsistent. According to one, the child had been circumcised; the other stated he was not. According to the first report, the physician saw nothing more than "erythema," a redness of the skin such as one might see in sunburn or blushing. The second report indicated the presence of anal fissures. Nothing was known about the medical history of the child. The written report of the second doctor indicated injury to the anal area, but it noted that the injury could have resulted from any number of causes, including constipation or diarrhea. Sodomy was far down the list of possible causes, Paul said, far less likely than other causes. As for the redness, he said, "I would dearly like to know whether the child wore nappies, or diapers. . . there are natural causes." One of these natural causes, he said, was female larvae causing itching and causing the child to scratch. "I do not believe he had a fissure. If he had, it would be very difficult to penetrate the child at that stage." The child would have had acute signs of bruising around the anal verge, he said.

"Given those physical observations, are they diagnostic of sodomy?" Gits asked the doctor.

"No, sir."

"Of all the variables I have put before you on August 17, including fissures, does that assist you in diagnosing sodomy?"

"No, sir. The presence of the fissure could be consistent but it could be inconsistent. . . ."

Dr. Paul's testimony suggested that, if the written reports were accurate, the child's condition was consistent with some form of injury or abuse. But why did the mother forbid any examination or questions that could reveal the identity of the perpetrator? Certainly not to protect Ray, since she was the first to accuse him.

Next, Gits projected a slide of Cathy's vagina on the screen. The doctor said that it was an abnormal vagina, larger than normal for a child of her age, and that the condition was consistent with digital penetration. But Cathy was one of the "Ray was not there" kids. And her photographic slides were taken nearly five years after she last attended the preschool.

A slide of Alice's vagina was projected on the screen. Dr. Paul said he could see no abnormalities consistent with sexual abuse. The slide of Billy's anus was next, the one that was taken several years after he had last attended the preschool. Dr. Paul said that it was consistent with injury, not sexual abuse; there was a fistula, not on the anus, but to the side of it. The injury, he said, was recent, probably within a week or two prior to the taking of the photograph. Dr. Paul had Astrid Heger's report before him, which said that the boy's physical examination, in 1984, was within normal limits. There was no mention of acute injury.

The next slide was that of the boy who said he was molested, along with a group of other children, in the public lavatory at the Red Carpet Car Wash. Dr. Paul said he could see nothing abnormal or consistent with sexual abuse, but that, like some of the other children, the boy had extremely poor hygiene. Prosecutor Rubin stared with enraged, distended eyes.

On Veronica, the youngest child, Dr. Paul could find nothing other than some scratches on the buttocks, nor did he see anything abnormal on the slide of the next girl, the one who never testified.

Surprisingly, Dr. Paul stated that in the slides and written reports on Melinda, the child with the most counts—approximately one-third of the case—he could see no evidence of sexual abuse. He said that her hymenal opening was exceptionally small. He testified that, in all the children in the case, except for Peter and Cathy, there was no hard evidence consistent with sexual abuse. These were the children who, the prosecution doctors said, were molested "to a medical certainty."

Davis asked Dr. Paul whether it was possible for a physician to look at the anus or genitals of a child and say, with certainty, that the child was molested "in the distant past."

"There are those who say that they can, but the honest ones will tell you that they cannot," he answered.

"Objection."

"Sustained."

The judge instructed the jurors to disregard the doctor's statement.

Dr. Paul noted that none of the family pediatricians who had seen the children before the case began observed anything that raised suspicion of sexual abuse. He also stated that the findings of sexual assault by Heger and the others probably resulted from misinterpretation of what they saw when the anuses and vaginas were greatly enlarged.

"You've got to be jolly careful when you magnify things up," Dr. Paul said. He also noted that tears and fissures identified by the prosecution doctors as signs of sodomy were more likely to be caused by nonsinister things like constipation and diarrhea. Sexual assualt, he said, was at the bottom of the list, "far behind constipation and diarrhea."

Gunson's cross-examination of Dr. Paul was a disaster. The doctor's vastly superior medical knowledge and infinitely superior use of language contrasted with Gunson's inept, fumbling questions, and the disparity between the two men was accentuated by the doctor's large physical stature, deep, resounding voice, and lordly bearing, juxtaposed with Gunson's diminutive size and thin, flat timbre.

Gunson appeared to be deliberately misquoting Dr. Paul in his questions, and the doctor was visibly angered. He responded with "Your words, not mine, sir," and "That's the opposite of what I said," and "You're taking it out of context, sir," and "No. That's not what I said."

After listening to hours of this, we sat with Dr. Paul in the hallway during recess and said, "Gunson seemed to be deliberately misquoting you in order to make you appear to be untruthful."

"Oh, yes. No doubt about it. But I straightened him out, didn't I?" he smiled.

"I'm sure you know that's a very standard ploy in the lawyer's bag of dirty tricks," Paul said to Dr. Paul. "If they can't find a flaw in your testimony, they invent one."

"Oh, yes. All lawyers do that."

Dr. Paul was a man of absolutely first-rate mind with a vast knowledge not only of medicine, but of law, history, literature, and science. He had passed the bar exams in England, although he did not practice law. He knew more about American history than most Americans and could give the history of the various regions of the United States in great detail.

"I still don't understand why they brought me all the way over from London when they could have found a homegrown, American doctor."

We talked about the strange phenomenon of government and elements of the medical profession applying such great pressure, behind the scenes, to prevent the defense from getting a qualified medical expert witness. What this said about the honor of the medical profession hardly needed to be explained. But why did the government find it so urgently necessary to obtain a conviction in this case when the allegations were so insubstantial? And if persons at the highest levels of power would bring sufficient pressure to make it impossible for the defense to get a qualified American doctor to testify as an expert witness for the defense, one cannot but wonder what pressures may have been applied to other players in this game: the judge, the lawyers, jurors, witnesses.

Monday, August 21, brought an even greater surprise. Barbara Dusky, who the prosecution had said they would call as a rebuttal witness, appeared as a defense witness. After watching and hearing Dusky for only a minute or two, it was not difficult to understand why Ray had fallen in love with her. She was thirty-seven, extremely pretty, blonde, and had a provocatively charming, sassy smile. When the prosecutors and their investigator came to her home in Montana, she told them that she had indeed had a sexual relationship with Ray Buckey, but she had lied to investigators because she was about to be married and feared the effect it would have upon her impending marriage. When the prosecutors realized their rebuttal was about to go up in a puff of steam, they cancelled her airline and hotel reservations. Ray's defense attorney then stepped in, picked up the tab for her flight and hotel accommodations and brought her in to testify for the defense.

Dusky was remarkable. She faced what would have been a crushingly humiliating experience for most women and answered the lawyers' questions, laughing, smiling at Ray, and occasionally giggling. Most women would have turned their backs on Ray and kept the sexual encounters with him a secret—especially if they were married. But Dusky recounted the visit to the Fantasy Inn exactly as Buckey had told it and described it as "very beautiful."

"Was there anything unhealthy or bizarre about your relations with Ray Buckey?" Davis asked her.

"No," she answered.

"Was there anything that would indicate he would prefer to have sex with little children?"

"No."

Asked whether she saw anything that would lead her to believe Ray was capable of molesting children, she said, "No possibility!"

Dusky also said that when she came to Manhattan Beach to be with Ray, "I observed Ray walk into the room and these children came running with outstretched arms. I was so amazed at the love that was exchanged."

Then came the cross-examination and Rubin's predictably abusive questions, suggesting that Dusky was a sexually promiscuous woman and that she had a history of drug abuse, which she denied.

Tears flowed from Dusky's eyes as she said that the prosecutors had harassed her for three weeks! She testified that they were rude and "pushy" and that they had gone to her home while she was away on a business trip and questioned her children and her husband.

At recess, reporters surrounded Ray and he told them, "This is a very brave thing for her to do." Rubin was then confronted by the reporters and made the same reply she had made about all of the defense witnesses: "She is lying." Rubin's statement was published by the media. Ray's was not.

After Dusky was excused the defense was permitted to briefly call the father of Peter, the child whose mother launched the marathon case. The man was flawlessly dressed in a tweed suit. He had black hair and a moustache.

Asked "What is your profession?" he said he was a real estate appraiser. His answers were careful and somewhat guarded. He told the court that on August 12, 1983, the day Judy Johnson made the police complaint, he had observed on his son a red, inflamed anus which, he believed, was the result of a long bout with diarrhea. He treated the condition with zinc oxide, he said.

Peter's father also related his observation that the boy, after being in the custody of his mother, had bruises on his arms and in other places, which led him to suspect that the boy had been physically abused or battered by his mother or someone else. He testified that one of the doctors who examined Peter stated in his report that the boy was circumcised and the other doctor who examined him wrote in his report that he was uncircumcised.

But the most interesting piece of information Peter's father gave was that when he attended one of the many mass meetings organized in Manhattan Beach in 1983, when mob hysteria first broke out, there was a professional public relations expert there, telling the parents how to work the media and get their version of the story to the public. We wondered whose money paid for all this, since public relations firms command substantial fees.

One final defense witness, Anthony Brunetti, was called again. Brunetti was the D.A.'s chief investigator during the first two years of the case. He was called by the defense for the purpose of telling the jury that, after a worldwide search for child pornography absolutely nothing was found that could be connected to the defendants. On cross-examination, Rubin led Brunetti into a lengthy discussion of child pornographers and how they operate, over the vociferous objections of the defense. Another smear, raising again the subtle deception that the Buckeys really were somehow involved in child pornography.

Finally, on Wednesday, August 23, 1989, after Brunetti was excused, Davis announced, "On behalf of Mr. Buckey we rest our case in chief."

"On behalf of Mrs. Buckey we rest our case in chief," Gits said.

Out in the hallway Ray told the waiting reporters that he believed the jurors' "common sense will let us prevail." Davis told them, "After the judge cut forty-five of our witnesses I hardly call this resting. It's more like being sent to bed."

Peggy was next. With the microphones thrust to her face she said, "I'm numb. I've been numb through this whole thing. I don't know if I can explain it to you. Even when it's over I think I will still be numb."

Rubin stridently told the reporters, "The defense has done nothing to discredit the children and the medical evidence. . . . The defense case has been extraordinarily helpful to the prosecution." Asked how the defense had been helpful, Rubin declined to explain.

The next day, the prosecutors called their first rebuttal witness. They told the judge that they would present about three weeks of rebuttal testimony, which would be followed by a few days of defense rebuttal. Then, there would be closing arguments and instructions to the jury.

The first rebuttal witness was William Guidas, an investigator for the D.A.'s office who, along with others, followed and surveilled Ray prior to his arrest in 1984. There were four cars following him everywhere he went. Guidas testified that at one time, Buckey was observed on the campus of Orange Coast College, sitting on the grass near a day care center, watching the children. Guidas told the court that although several extremely attractive young college women passed by, Buckey paid little or no attention to them and continued to watch the children at play. Apparently Rubin and Gunson believed they had at last demolished Ray's image as a wholesome, normal young man. But, like the rest of the prosecution's "evidence" it proved nothing.

Most young men are taught that to stare at strangers, particularly women, shows poor manners, and that to accost a woman who is a total stranger is ungentlemanly unless it is done with great delicacy and finesse. But the insinuation was being made that because Ray did not gawk at the young women or approach them he was therefore, conclusively, a child molester. Even the most obtuse juror would understand that this was not a rebuttal, but nothing more than a smear. It went on and on. Buckey, sitting at the defense table, laughed silently, grinning and shaking slightly, but making no sound.

Guidas testifed that he saw Ray wearing a wire pyramid hat while driving his van. On cross-examination Davis put the wire pyramid hat on his own head, getting another burst of laughter from the jurors. It was very effective, because it defused the solemn, pious tone of the prosecution's presentation. Davis also elicited from the investigator the fact that he was positioned behind Ray during the surveillance near the day care center and could not possibly have seen in which direction Buckey's eyes were turned.

A very large photograph of Ray was entered into evidence and shown to the jurors. Guidas was asked to identify it to establish that he recognized Ray as he looked in 1983. It was probably the worst picture ever taken of him and it showed him wearing thick, steel-rimmed glasses with an unhappy, querulous expression on his face.

The prosecution brought in two more investigators from the D.A.'s office who briefly reiterated the allegations that Ray did not gawk at the attractive, young women on the college campus and seemed to be watching the children at play. They also called a young lawyer who, several years before, lived in an apartment across the alley from Ray's apartment. The man testified that he was able to see into Ray's room and that he had observed him masturbating. Ray was now on trial for the high crime of onanism. How this related to the charges of molestation was not explained.

Virginia told us, during a telephone conversation the next day, that she had gone over to the apartment this witness once occupied, and found that it would have been "utterly impossible" for him to see into Ray's bedroom and observe this spectacle.

Monday, August 28, 1989. We arrived late at the Criminal Courts Building, prepared to tiptoe quietly into the courtroom because we expected that the trial would already be in progress. Instead, we saw Ray and Peggy standing in front of the building waving to us.

"There's no court today," Peggy said.

"Why?"

"The Doeppels didn't show up," Ray said.

"Did they resist the subpoena?" we asked.

"No," Peggy told us. "They just didn't come in."

"We knew Rubin wanted to bring them in to get them to say they saw

Ray masturbating, but we thought they had already publicly disavowed making any such statements.

"Well," Peggy said sadly, "they want to prove that Ray masturbated."

"But just about everyone who ever lived has masturbated!" we protested.

"Not Billy," Ray smiled.

"Billy who?" I asked.

"Billy Pounders," he answered.

Dean Gits pulled up in his shiny, new Mercedes Benz. Ray and Peggy got in and they drove away.

The next morning, John Doeppel took the stand and said that he had nothing to offer in support of the prosecutor's allegations that Ray masturbated. He testified that a number of statements in the D.A.'s report were untruthful. "I don't know where they got that from." He further stated that, "A lot of things have been changed and there's a lot of hearsay."

"Do you remember saying that Ray Buckey displayed sexually explicit material in his windows?" Rubin asked.

"I never said that," he answered.

Doeppel would not be called as a witness, we were told.

But there was no jury in the jury box. One of the jurors was hospitalized for a serious but unknown condition. It was, according to the judge, some kind of blood disease, but pathology reports so far had failed to diagnose it. The trial was recessed until September 11. That meant the courtroom would be dark for two weeks while we waited for the diagnosis. The juror was one who, nearly everybody believed, was one of those most likely to vote for acquittal. If he proved unable to continue to serve as a juror, there would be only one alternate left to replace him.

But there was still another juror whose ability to continue was in doubt. Attorneys had been ordered by the judge not to disclose the fact to anyone, and discussions about this matter, in the judge's chambers, were sealed.

If one or both of these jurors were able to return, the trial would continue, with brief rebuttal and closing arguments. But if both were unable to continue, the judge would be forced to declare a mistrial. If both sides agreed, they could conclude the trial with eleven jurors, but that was extremely unlikely. At least one of the lawyers had publicly stated that he would not under any circumstance be willing to continue with less than twelve jurors.

And so, until Monday, September 11, we had to wait for the news.

Monday, September 11, 1989. Juror number four is gone and the last alternate is sitting in his place. "We are a heartbeat away from mistrial," the judge said. "I think it's highly unusual that with eighteen jurors, five dropped out because of medical problems. I think it's due in part to the pressure."

In spite of this circumstance, the judge surprisingly ruled to allow the prosecution to call former neighbors who, according to a police report, once allegedly saw Ray masturbating with *Playboy* magazines in his bedroom. The offer, from the prosecution, was to show that Ray exposed himself. Saying he was terrified of the prospect of a mistrial due to juror attrition, the judge had cut forty-five defense witnesses but was now going to continue to allow days, perhaps weeks, of testimony that Ray masturbated, carrying with it the insinuation that he was somehow exposing himself to public view. It had been about a month since we had heard any testimony about the actual charges of molestation.

Charlotte Doeppel, the first of the former neighbors to testify, said she once caught a glimpse of a "*Playboy*-type magazine" in Ray's apartment, but said that he was not in the room. She also stated that the police report attributing statements about Ray to her was grossly inaccurate and not based on fact. She said that when two policewomen came to interview her and other neighbors, they were angered and glared at her when she told them that she had seen nothing unusual going on inside Ray's apartment.

The next day, the jurors sat and waited in the jury room for almost three hours while the judge and lawyers argued over the question of whether Ray masturbated. None of it had anything to do with the issue before the court: whether he molested children. After that we heard ten minutes of testimony from a woman who said that she had observed Ray when he was coaching her daughter's soccer team. He was not wearing underwear, she said. The prosecution was asserting that he "exposed himself," and that not wearing underwear showed that he had an interest in exposing himself to children.

Davis rose to cross-examine. He was wearing a conservative dark litigation suit. The lawyers were almost too impeccably groomed. They looked as though they had just stepped out of the window of an expensive department store. The jurors, on the other hand, were becoming increasingly casual in their attire. One of them, a young woman, occasionally came to court wearing a t-shirt with the likeness of Mickey Mouse emblazoned on the front. We wondered if this was a statement of her view of the proceedings.

The next rebuttal witness was John Doeppel, husband of Charlotte, who had testified the day before. Although he was technically a prosecution witness, he denied having made the statements attributed to him in the police report. Like his wife, he said the report contained statements that were never made during the interview. He said that, during the police interview, nobody stated that Ray was exhibiting himself or that they saw "pornography." He also said that there was no factual basis for the statement in the report that neighbors had said they saw him masturbating naked in his room. Doeppel also testified that in order to see all the way into Ray's room, one would have to be eight feet tall. He refuted virtually everything in the police report that Gunson read while questioning him.

In the elevator during recess, Davis turned to us and asked, "Well, what do you think of this?"

"They seem to be putting on defense witnesses," we said. "Why are they doing that?"

"Because if they didn't, they wouldn't have any witnesses!" he grinned. "They don't have any witnesses!"

"Then why don't they rest?" we asked.

"They would never do that," he answered.

The prosecution called Det. Patricia Picker, the police officer who interviewed Ray's neighbors and was, apparently, the author of the police report about the Doeppels, who said it was grossly inaccurate. She was one of the police officers involved in the abortive Michael Ruby molestation case of 1985–86, in which a majority of the jurors voted to acquit. Picker testified that the Doeppels did make the statements she attributed to them in her report. Asked where her original notes were, the notes from which the report was written, she said she did not know, that she had not seen them since she turned them over to a typist.

On cross-examination Davis asked Picker about the propriety of interviewing three people together, if there wasn't a danger that their answers would influence each other. He suggested that her interview was "incompetent" and asked, "Isn't it better to separate them?"

Picker replied that she had read a considerable amount of research and many books on the subject of conducting police interrogations and that some supported his viewpoint and some concluded the opposite. When Davis asked her what books she read, she was unable to come up with a title. When he asked her what research materials she had reviewed, she was again unable to give any titles. Picker also admitted that she had changed her answers to some of the questions she had been asked the previous week, during a hearing.

During a recess, a woman in the spectator section engaged us in conversation and asked what we were doing there. We told her about the book. She was expensively dressed in a two-piece outfit with and extremely short skirt and frosted hair. She had an attaché case. She told us that she was a psychologist, employed by the county.

"How much of it is true?" she asked.

"None of it," we answered.

"How could that be? Why would they be here if they hadn't done something?"

"Cops and D.A.s are human beings. They make mistakes, just like the rest of us. Those people never molested anybody."

"I don't believe that," she said.

"Haven't you ever been bumrapped?" we asked. "Hasn't anybody ever said something about you that wasn't true?"

"Everything I have ever done has been above reproach," she said. We wondered about that.

Before the jury was brought in, Rubin and Gunson asked the court's permission to bring in, as rebuttal witnesses, two sheriff's officers who took the confession of an organist at the Episcopal Church who allegedly touched a young girl on the leg while sitting at the organ. Their purpose in doing this was to rebut testimony that molestation could not have occurred at the church without somebody seeing or hearing it. Judge Pounders denied their request on the ground that it was too prejudicial. "Mr. Buckey is being punished for [the organist's] misdeeds." It was another attempt to undermine Buckey by insinuation.

Dr. Gene Abel was the next prosecution rebuttal witness. Since Rubin's attempt to show that Ray was not a normal, heterosexual male was shot down by Barbara Dusky, the prosecution was now presenting an expert witness to say that pedophiles *do* have heterosexual relationships with adult women. Abel was a psychiatrist from Emory University in Georgia. He testified that most pedophiles are married heterosexuals, according to his unpublished studies. He said he had received six major federal grants for his studies, predominantly on child molestation. Surprisingly, he said he had identified perpetrators as "heterosexual" on the basis of self-evaluation, meaning that perpetrators had told him that they were heterosexual.

"Most of the people you deal with are liars, aren't they?" Davis asked on cross.

"Yes," Abel answered.

"Then how do you know, when they say they are 100 percent heterosexual, that they're telling the truth?"

The doctor said that, at his facility, they used the "penile plathismograph." Numerous wires were attached to the subject's penis and then he was shown slides of nude people of various ages and of both genders; any enlargement of the penis was monitored.

"A porn show!" one of the reporters whispered, laughing.

Defense lawyers jokingly called this contraption "the peter meter." It was not generally accepted in the scientific community nor in the legal system. Davis also elicited from Abel the fact that he had not separated those who molested two- and three-year-olds from those who molested thirteen and fourteen-year-olds.

"Isn't that a defect?" Davis asked.

"No."

That evening we attended a banquet at one of L.A.'s large hotels. While we were having dinner a woman said, "Shirley, I hear you're writing a book about McMartin. They really did some bad stuff, didn't they?"

"No."

"You mean you think they're innocent?"

"There's no evidence against them at all."

"I can't believe that!"

"Do the words, 'lynch mob hysteria' mean anything to you?" we asked.

"They sure do," she answered. The woman was black.

As we began to explain McMartin to her the woman clapped her hands over her ears to shut us out, then turned and walked away. She found a group of friends and quickly engaged them in a lively conversation. It was extremely difficult to dislodge these beliefs with evidence because people don't acquire them with evidence.

That week, one of the local newspapers published a long letter to the editor, complaining of Rubin's "graphic and disgusting vocabulary" in the courtroom, terming it "objectionable and inexcusable."

The next rebuttal witness was Det. Augusta "Gusty" Bell, a veteran police detective, now employed by the district attorney's office, who accompanied Lael Rubin on her visits to the children before they testified. She presented us with a replay of the prosecution's version of the Barbara Dusky story, which had been very convincingly refuted by Dusky herself at the cost of considerable discomfort.

On cross-examination Bell testified that she and Rubin had not coached or rehearsed the children before they testified. But if not, then for what purpose did they visit the children six times, staying for hours? Another child received five visits just prior to testifying.

Gunson brought in two large stacks of manila folders containing transcripts of testimony. Davis grinned and said, "That's really intimidating, Roger."

Defense attorneys also elicited from Bell the fact that she had stopped taking notes, which they would have been required to turn over to the defense.

Another witness, the father of a girl who was not involved in the case, was brought in to tell the jurors, once again, that Ray did not wear underwear. On cross-examination, however, he testified that he did not recall saying that Buckey never wore underwear and that he had no recollection of seeing Ray's genitalia. Nevertheless, he was asked endless questions about Ray not wearing underwear.

The next and final prosecution rebuttal witness was Virginia McMartin! When we arrived she was sitting out in the hallway in her wheelchair. We greeted each other warmly. She told us she hoped to stay around until the thing is over "but I'll probably be a hundred years old." She showed us a pocket-sized copy of the U.S. Constitution, which she intended to brandish at the judge while giving him a piece of her mind. We knew this was going to be a boisterous shouting match between Virginia and the judge.

But first, a physician was called to the witness stand to tell the court whether Virginia would be able to testify. He said that although Virginia took a dim view of doctors and medicines, he was able to visit her "after I got past all the animals."

"I checked her blood pressure," he said, "and it was 214 over 106." He had persuaded her, he said, to ingest a beta blocker, an adrenalin-reducing agent that was "very good for this kind of situation in which stress will zap it up." He said that with blood pressure that high there was a 35 percent chance that, under the stress of being put on the witness stand, "something might pop," but that it was not likely to be catastrophic. He said that, as her physician, he had advised her not to testify, but finally stated that, "I think she'll do fine. God is good. She hasn't popped anything yet. We'll just cross our fingers." Virginia was brought into the courtroom in her wheelchair. We whispered to a reporter sitting next to us, "This is not going to be the tranquil, dignified examination the judge hoped for." She shook with laughter and nodded.

"Mrs. McMartin," the judge said, "my intention is to get you on and off today so you won't have to come back. If you can assist us . . . and just answer the questions we can do it today. If you want to fight . . . and we've had some difficulties before . . . if you just go to the issues that are presented to you, we can get it done today."

Then, Virginia spoke, "I just want to let all of you know that I'm a great believer in the Constitution. The Constitution says I have the right to talk all I want and to criticize public officials. It also says I am entitled to my privacy. . . . Therefore those diaries should be returned to me as my personal property, and you have no right to them."

"They will be returned to you at the conclusion of the case," Judge Pounders said.

"But you have no right to use them!"

"I understand. All I can say is they have become very significant evidence in this case."

"They're my personal property!"

"And that's why you're here, and that's all we need from you."

"You have no right to them at all!"

"There, we have a disagreement, and if you want to go into that in front of the jury, the jury's going to assess your credibility because you're aligned with the defense. . . . I'm going to plead with you in advance to simply answer the questions and I will get you out of here by four-thirty. If you go through a long fight here you're going to be here tomorrow and maybe beyond that time. It's to the benefit of everyone that we get to the issues that have to be explored and we can do that in one day with your cooperation. Anything else before we bring the jury in?"

Virginia was sworn in and Rubin, facing her at the lectern, asked, "Mrs. McMartin, what I want to talk about today are some of your diaries, okay?"

"No, it isn't okay. They're my private property."

Rubin asked Virginia if she had cut out the missing page in her diary and she replied, "No, I have never cut out a page in my diary."

"You would agree that it would be highly unusual that that half page was cut out of your diary, wouldn't you?"

"No. Because the police took my diaries and . . ."

"Your honor!" Rubin protested.

". . . and you people have had them for years."

"Would it be helpful if I showed you some of your testimony?"

"No. It wouldn't be helpful."

"Why not?"

"Because I don't trust any of you."

As the antagonism escalated, Judge Pounders finally interrupted and said, "Mrs. McMartin, if you want to go into a long narrative . . ."

Virginia said that the insurance company took something out of it "and that's all I know."

Rubin continued to pursue her inquiry about the diary, and, predictably, Virginia's loathing for Rubin built to an explosive crescendo. Asked when she had last seen the diary, Virginia said, "I was forced to move eight times!"

"Excuse me," Rubin cut in, "but there's no question pending."

"I'm allowed to talk because it's in the Constitution! I have freedom of speech."

"That's not exactly true, Mrs. McMartin," the judge interceded, explaining that she was required to obey the orders and rules of the court. There followed a heated exchange between the judge and Virginia that was impossible to decipher because both were speaking at the same time. Judge Pounders ordered the jurors removed from the courtroom. As they filed out, she roared at the judge, "You think you're above the Constitution!"

"I find you in contempt of court," the judge said. His voice loudly shattered the dialogue. "What I want to know from you is if you're going to comply with the court's orders. . . . The alternative is that you're going to spend the next two days in jail. If that's what you like."

"That's fine! And God help your conscience, if you've got one!"

"Mrs. McMartin, I have no ill feeling about you personally. . . ."

"Oh yes you have! You've been prejudiced against us from the beginning of this trial."

As they shouted at each other, Gits intervened and asked for a brief recess. The judge angrily told the lawyers, "She's going to go to jail. And if she comes back and still refuses to comply with orders of the court, the same result will obtain."

He did not order her taken to jail, but he ordered three female deputies, armed and uniformed, to "take her into custody if she attempts to leave the courtroom." Peggy pleaded with her, sobbing, and Ray held her hand. Virginia still looked enraged.

"She's probably unavailable to testify," Pounders told the lawyers, "because we're going to kill her if we continue this."

After the recess, Pounders asked her, "Are you willing to comply?"

"For my family's sake, I am."

The questions about the diary went on and on, but there was nothing very illuminating. After court was recessed, several reporters surrounded Gunson and one of them asked, "Why are you making such a big thing about the missing page in her diary?"

"What was on that page was so incriminating it had to be destroyed," he said, smiling blandly with an air of authoritative certainty.

Out in the hallway, Virginia sat in her wheelchair and told me, "I've seen their lousy jail. It doesn't scare me. We've got the rottenest legal system in the world. Don't tell me about South Africa!"

Virginia was the last witness. All that remained was closing arguments and then jury instructions. Then it would be in the hands of the jurors.

Jury selection is one of the defects in the legal system. A complicated case like this required jurors intelligent enough not to believe everything told to them by authority figures, people bright enough and strong enough to sort it all out—the logical from the clearly nonsense or, at best, dubious. Such people are almost invariably excused from jury service, and if they do not ask to be excused, prosecutors use their preemptory challenges to get rid of them. (Each side in a criminal court case is given a specific number of opportunities to excuse a prospective juror from being impaneled without showing cause for the person's unacceptability. After the maximum number of preemptory challenges has been reached, defense or prosecution counsel must offer compelling reasons why a given prospective juror should not be sworn in.)

The extraordinary lack of evidence and stunning disclosures of prosecutorial misconduct had had no effect. The machinery of the legal system was inexorably in motion, hungry for human sacrifice. Having already taken all of the defendants' possessions and six years of their lives, it was now preparing to devour what little remained: their freedom, their loved ones, their meager belongings, and their future.

In the crowded hallway Ray stood alone against the wall. We walked over and stood facing him.

"You know," we said, "now that it's about over you need to start thinking about the opportunities."

"What opportunities?" Buckey said.

"Well, an awful lot of famous people have a line of clothing or jewelry they sell by using their fame to make the product more attractive. Elizabeth Taylor has her line of perfume. Jane Fonda has her exercise video. You could do a line of expensive underwear and buy ads in men's magazines like *GQ*: 'For the man who cares! Buy the best! Buckey Boxer Briefs!' "

"Yeah," he smiled. " 'The kind he didn't wear.' "

We saw our old friend, Walter Hurst, a world-class attorney who had argued landmark cases before the Supreme Court. We greeted each other.

"Well, what did you think of this?" we asked.

Walter smiled sadly. "Psychologists and dogs will do whatever satisfies those who feed them. The same is true of doctors." He went on to explain what most people did not understand about the case—that the "experts" were not merely impartial scientists giving their objective opinions but stipendiaries of the district attorney's office. Their continuing flow of fees and grants turned on their providing testimony supportive of the prosecution. The "experts" were a part of the "child abuse industry," a phrase describing all those who benefited from the enormous funding provided by the new child abuse legislation.

"Do they really expect a jury to believe that Buckey and a bunch of elderly grandmothers raped babies?" someone asked.

"What they did," Walter said, "they arrested all the defense witnesses, like in the Minnesota case and a lot of the others. Because they had no case. They brought in witnesses they knew were lying. They concealed exculpatory evidence. It's not about justice. It's about winning."

In the Scott County case in Minnesota in 1984 two people, a husband and wife, were accused of child sexual abuse. All of their friends and neighbors held a town meeting to protest the arrests. These people who protested were promptly arrested and charged with child sexual abuse. After a lengthy investigation, all of the allegations were shown to be false and that the prosecutor had used an informer, similar to George Freeman, to testify against twenty-two defendants. But when the informant took the witness stand he could not even identify the defendants. The defendants were subsequently acquitted and the prosecutor was not reelected the following year. All of this is contained in a report by Minnesota Attorney General Hubert Humphrey III.

In this case, children were taken away from their families and interrogated over a period of months; some of them were subjected to hours of questioning every day until they broke down. Many were told that unless they "disclosed" they would never see their parents again. Some of the children recanted later.

Certainly the child witnesses were a surprise to nearly everybody who observed them testifying in the courtroom. After the sensational media reports that the children had been "ripped and scarred" and damaged beyond repair, many spectators said they had expected to see them brought into the courtroom in wheelchairs, attended by special duty nurses, staring starkly at the memory of some unspeakable act too hideous to verbalize. Instead, they came in smiling and sat there, fashionably dressed, basking in the attention and praise showered upon them by the prosecutor, her colleagues, and their supporters. Some looked as though they had just been chosen to play the leading role in the school play. And they related the lurid tales of being raped and violated in satanic, blood-drinking animal sacrifices with no emotion, in very much the same tone as a child reciting the Pledge of Allegiance or a multiplication table. And there was no corroboration whatsoever.

Three

The Closing Arguments

Prosecutor Roger Gunson began his closing argument by addressing one of the big questions at the center of the case: if, as the prosecution claimed, hundreds of children were being sexually assaulted at the preschool for years, why did none of them tell anyone, and why did not one person ever raise the slightest suspicion of sexual abuse at McMartin Preschool until the children were taken to CII and interviewed there?

Gunson suggested that the children were silent "because of an affection for the perpetrator." This was a new departure. Until now, the prosecutors had been saying that the children were silent because Ray terrified them by slaughtering small animals and killing horses with a baseball bat. Now, we were being told that it was because of their affection for Buckey, and, in another new departure, because they received attention or gifts.

Gunson also suggested that the children were silent because they felt blame, a third new departure. A fourth new explanation offered by Gunson was that the molestation began slowly and escalated.

The problem with all these explanations was that they contradicted each other.

Eventually Gunson resurrected the allegation that Ray terrorized them by killing animals. Gunson made the remarkable assertion that children would not have had nightmares unless something "monstrous" had happened to them. According to current psychiatric literature, nearly everybody has nightmares.

Gunson told the jurors that a child "cannot be brainwashed or programmed to believe something happened."

"Raymond Buckey exposed his genitals to children," he asserted, an allegation that had never been proven. There was testimony that he did not wear underwear, which Ray never denied, but Gunson took it a step farther and accused him of deliberately exposing himself. Could Ray have done that without it being observed by his mother, the teachers, and others?

Instead of skirting around the undeniable fact that the children's stories changed every time they testified, with some telling as many as five different stories, Gunson cited the discrepancies as proof that the children were not coached and rehearsed. If they had been coached and rehearsed, he said, they would have told the same story each time. This, of course, was a very questionable theory.

"Just because two statements are inconsistent, that doesn't mean they shouldn't be believed," Gunson said. But which one was to be believed?

Gunson urged the jurors to "believe the children." But which of their statements were jurors to believe? The denials or the "disclosures" made after the children were put through a kind of Pavlovian conditioning process?

Instead of distancing himself from George Freeman and Supermarket Billy, who told the most grossly unbelievable stories, Gunson asked us to buy the whole package. Although George Freeman was an admitted perjurer, he should be believed, Gunson said.

As for the bizarre stories the children told, Gunson explained that Ray created these bizarre events so that the children would not be believed.

As the hours passed, Gunson's tone became progressively more listless and perfunctory. He began talking faster and more softly. One of the jurors began nodding off. Another occasionally opened his eyes, yawned, and then closed them again. Gunson had a large stack of manila folders before him, and each time he finished reading from one, he paused for a surprisingly long time before beginning with the next one. At one point he got lost and was silent for several minutes; as he thumbed through his transcripts, the jurors stared blankly and looked at the clock.

Gunson was doing something extremely clever, aside from putting the jury to sleep. The prosecution's entire case was built on insinuation. Gunson knew that the defense was going to talk about insinuation, and so he was taking the wind out of their sails by repeatedly accusing the defense of insinuation. He told the jurors solemnly: "Insinuation is not evidence."

Gunson was doing another very clever thing—taking all of the uncertainties in the case and weaving them into a picture of Ray lurking in the school yard when he was actually in San Diego. But Gunson spoke so softly that it required some effort to understand him, and the jurors did not appear to be even trying to follow Gunson's exposition of his charts and graphs showing when each of the children was there and when Ray was there.

When Gunson talked about the counts pertaining to the car wash, two of the jurors were smiling. But they did not appear to be greatly moved by Gunson's recitation. Some of them definitely were not listening.

Gunson reiterated one mother's testimony that when the police told her of the investigation, and she subsequently called Peggy to find out what was going on, she heard Peggy say, "Oh, my God, Ray!" It was an unsubstantiated piece of hearsay that Peggy denied, and the words attributed to her could be construed to mean almost anything, but Gunson asked, accusingly, "Does that sound like someone who doesn't know what's going on?"

After recess, the slide projector and screen were in place and Gunson projected written portions of the children's accusing testimony, and then the anuses. He began with the girl with the twenty-seven spectacular counts of four-way sexual assault. Davis, sitting at the defense table, was laughing.

Although her testimony appeared to be memorized and had a rote, mechanical quality, Gunson explained that, "It was traumatic and this is how she handled it."

He put great emphasis on the fact that the defense's medical expert, Dr. Paul, was contradicted by seven—not one but seven—prosecution doctors. But Gunson failed to mention that the defense was allowed only one medical expert witness. The implication, of course, was that a majority was more credible that a minority. This, of course, is not necessarily true.

Addressing the fact that the children initially denied, at CII, that they had been molested, Gunson told the jurors, "Denial is a defense mechanism."

He raised, with considerable emphasis, the allegations of Ray's involvement with drugs and alcohol which, clearly, was minimal.

After talking for three days, Gunson told the weary jurors that the evidence formed "a ring around Raymond and Peggy Buckey that comes closer and closer and tighter and tighter to the extent that you should find them guilty." And with that he left the lectern and sat down.

The jurors did not appear to be greatly impressed. If anything, the "ring around Raymond and Peggy Buckey" rather than becoming "closer and closer" seemed to be getting more and more remote.

"We will be in recess until tomorrow morning at nine-thirty," Judge Pounders announced. Tomorrow, Gits would do his dance.

In the morning, when everybody was ready, Gits began by writing two phrases in large letters on a chalkboard facing the jurors:

COMMON SENSE

REASONABLE DOUBT

"These are the two tools I need you to use in assessing this case," he told the jurors. "Put them in your pocket and carry them with you today and bring them back tomorrow. When the prosecution responds, use them."

Gits told the jurors that the case resulted from incompetence. "There's something terribly wrong with this case." He also told them that he intended to complete his closing argument in one day. The jurors appeared grateful and relieved.

Gits erected a huge poster. At the top were photographs of the nine children who had testified in the trial, under the heading:

WITNESSES WHO HAVE SEEN MOLESTATION

Beneath these were forty-three photographs of teachers, postal workers, various inspectors, neighbors and parents, under the heading:

WITNESSES WHO CLAIM THEY DIDN'T SEE ANY MOLESTATIONS

Gits displayed another chart listing the names of twenty-four teachers employed at the preschool during the six-year period covered by the charges, all of whom testified they never saw anything that raised the slightest suspicion of molestation.

"What is the prosecution's theory—that all the teachers are lying? So if the teachers are lying, what about the neighbors? Are they a bunch of liars? If so, what about the parents who came and went on a regular basis? If they saw something, where are they?" Gits said.

Gits went on to retell the story of the police search of the school during which they took files and records for the previous three years and subsequently used the addresses in them to send out the form letter to two hundred families, creating pandemonium in the community. "This is why you're here today."

"Kee MacFarlane wasn't qualified to conduct the evaluations," he said, and Astrid Heger, who conducted the medical evaluations, was also unqualified, he asserted. "The worst part about Heger's exams was their effect on the parents. If you were a parent and you heard a medical doctor tell you she found signs consistent with sexual abuse, you'd believe her," he said. "So the contagion spread."

Gits said that because parents were told at CII to be supportive, the allegations were reinforced and children became convinced that they had been molested. Parents felt compelled to "believe the children."

Gits was not endowed with a magnificent voice, but he used what little vocal equipment he had with considerable effect, rising to full volume and then dropping down to a whisper for maximum emphasis, and to hold the jurors' attention. It seemed to be working. Pacing back and forth in front of the jury, Gits kept things moving, almost without missing a beat, and compressed the salient facts of the massive case into one day.

Gits pointed out that two of the child witnesses said, in the preliminary hearing, that they were molested during their first year at the preschool, and then, during the trial, they testified that it occurred during their last year at the school, bringing it back within the statute of limitations. "Someone had to get to them!" Gits asserted.

Attacking the medical "findings" of the prosecution doctors, Gits explained that there was no body of scientific medical knowledge that could enable them to examine a child and say, with certainty, that the child had been abused years before. "Think of the horrors that have resulted from doctors testifying about signs of abuse that proved not to be true!" For years, he told the jurors, prosecutors and their medical expert witnesses relied on the Cantwell study. Until a few years ago the Cantwell Study was used by prosecution doctors as authority for their assessments that children were sexually penetrated. The study concluded that a hymenal opening of more than four millimeters was evidence of sexual molestation. Since then this study has been thoroughly discredited and proven to be false.

Then Gits discussed the bizarre allegations: the chopping up of horses; groups of children being undressed and molested in a public lavatory while Ray's van was going through the car wash; molestation in a supermarket; the secret room. All of these, he said, were "beyond the realm of common sense."

"Those of you who have children . . . you know how long it takes to put clothes on two or ten or maybe twelve kids. . . .How could you put clothes on that many children before a parent discovered you?"

Ray was not at the school when four of the child witnesses attended it, Gits noted. "Is that beyond reasonable doubt?" he asked.

"Would Peggy Buckey operate a school for years and then suddenly become the kind of person who takes clothes off children and molests them? Why? Is it reasonable? Does it meet the standard of common sense?" Gits asked.

And if these alleged marathon molestations really occurred, ranging from the school to the car wash, the supermarket, and the farm, "Why didn't somebody see it?" There was a tone of urgency in Gits's voice that contrasted with Gunson's low-energy, monotonous presentation of the day before.

Gits described the genesis of the case as the product of "insanity," and "incompetence."

"Innuendo and 'believe the children.' That will be the prosecution's rebuttal in this case."

The prosecution doctors, Gits reminded the jurors, said that Dr. Paul was a recognized expert and that they relied on his work and publications. But now the prosecutors were saying that Paul was a fraud. They had not known that he would testify as a witness for the defense.

Gits concluded with a rousing statement about Peggy, "a lady who for twenty-eight years had . . . friends, a preschool she was proud of, standing in the community. Now, she has none of these things. She lost it little by little. First, the allegations. Then attendance dropped. Then friends turned against her with hatred." Gits's voice rose in loud indignation: "And they made vile allegations against her. And she now wants your verdict."

Court was recessed for the day and Lael Rubin, approached by a television newsperson outside the courtroom, called Gits's argument "predictable rhetoric." She said she believed the jurors would "believe the children," whom she described as "the people who were present when these events occurred."

In the hallway outside the courtroom, Davis called Gits's closing "boring" and said he would be more forceful when presenting his closing argument in the morning. A jury selection expert told reporters, "The jurors have decided this case a long time ago. The mind seeks closure." This was reported in the *Los Angeles Daily Journal.*

Davis was next.

* * *

"All of the jurors are present. You may begin your argument, Mr. Davis," Judge Pounders said.

Davis started out in a casual and chatty fashion, like a man standing in his living room talking to guests. His style was loose and less pompous than Gits's.

"I'm going to talk about the evidence. There was something very, very wrong. . . . It's not just a nightmare circus of mistakes. It's a very important case.

"If you believe all the insinuations, you're not talking about Ray Buckey, criminal defendant. You're talking about the most superhuman child molester of all time." Davis told the jurors with great emphasis that he was not ridiculing or denigrating the children, because he knew that Rubin would bludgeon him with the accusation that he was doing just that when she rose to give her final rebuttal.

"What's wrong with this trial is that we brought children into this courtroom under the pretense of caring for children. But can you say you care about children if you don't care about the truth?"

First, Davis digressed and gave us a brief lecture on the history of witch hunts. He said that McMartin, the Salem witch trials, and the McCarthy era were harbingers of progress and positive change. They were nothing of the kind. All were the products of ignorance, mob hysteria, and malignant backlash against new ideas and heterodoxy, plus a generous admixture of greed, ruthless ambition, fraud, malice, and incompetence.

We were more comfortable when Davis abandoned his exegesis of history and returned to the issues before the court.

"It's almost as though the prosecution is suggesting doubts about my client's innocence because he didn't wear underwear and because he experimented with pyramid power and marijuana.

"Are we going to end up saying that if enough noxious stuff with Raymond Buckey's name on it was thrown on the wall, and that it stuck, and because you think that his personality is something that you don't totally approve of, that we'll go with the insinuation and say that he must have molested a little boy in '78 or '79 when the proof shows that he wasn't even there? Are we going to make leaps to create a man bounding over the fence at the preschool when all the teachers, grandmothers, and mothers were in session, because he took a trip to Lake Tahoe, or because he had dirty pictures that might offend other people?"

Davis reached into a box and took out the pyramid hat, the undergarments with the humorous slogans printed on them, the *Playboy* magazines and adult "pornography," and the rubber duck, items that were taken in a search of Ray's apartment.

"When you get bits of evidence like a rubber duck, ask yourself, what does it say about the charges against Raymond Buckey? What do you get when a medical expert corroborates a crime that didn't happen?"

Davis characterized the medical evidence as "molestation by medicine."

"Do you think you can render a verdict in this case, and that you don't have to consider its impact on you morally in the future—that it's just a quick shot that you don't have to worry about afterward?"

Referring to the prosecutors' allegation that because Ray had photographs of nude adults and also had snapshots of clothed children, Davis said, "the prosecution is making the inference that he superimposed kids on adult porn. Is that reasonable? I don't think that is a reasonable inference. It is a bizarre insinuation. And bizarre insinuations are the stock of the McMartin case."

Davis picked up an abstract painting and placed it on an easel. Then he took out one of the anus photographs and placed it over the painting on the easel. The judge looked puzzled. Everybody looked puzzled. "Why did they show it so many times when there was no count?" Davis asked.

Davis went over all of the counts and all of the prosecution testimony thoroughly. "You have to consider each count and the elements of each count separately." He showed the jurors the check stubs, which contained very few checks made out to Ray Buckey before 1981, just a few small payments for maintenance and menial tasks.

"They did not say, 'for mass molestation,' or 'sneak attack,'" Davis said.

Davis then asked the jurors to "Look at the diaries and find anything that suggests that Ray Buckey was molesting children!"

Addressing the medical evidence, Davis said, "I'm really bothered by the medical evidence, and if you think I'm bothered by it because it affects my client's fate, you're right. You've got to look at that medical evidence. . . . You're going to see that something's real wrong! Two doctors examined Peter. One said he was uncircumcised. The other said he was circumcised. One sees fissures. One sees no fissures. If you don't believe George Freeman, that count's gone. If you don't believe the medical, that count's gone."

Davis asserted again that "Ray was not there!" during the times when four of the children—plus the doctors—said molestation happened. Davis spoke of the nonexistent "secret room" one child had said he was molested in. "We had to bring in people from the car wash to prove that it couldn't have happened." The children, when asked about oral copulation, described urine, not semen, he said. And he recalled the little girl who said, "Peggy put her vagina inside my vagina," an impossible act for a large, adult woman to perform upon a two-year-old child.

Davis spoke about the girl who told, in flat, emotionless tones, of being penetrated both digitally and genitally in both orifices. Davis described the allegation as the "four-way crazy," and said, "She couldn't remember what position her body was in."

Davis recalled the testimony of three children who said, in the preliminary hearing, that they were molested during their first year at the preschool, but at the trial, testified that it happened during their final year at the school, in order to bring these alleged acts back within the statute of limitations. "A little too much adult influence," he commented.

Davis noted that prosecutor Rubin and Det. Bell visited the children as many as five times during the weeks preceding the trial, coaching and rehearsing them at great length, right up to the time they testified in the trial.

"It's not unusual for an attorney to ask witnesses what they're going to say before calling them to the witness stand," he said. But Davis strongly suggested that the prosecutors did not merely ask but in fact *told* the children what to say. "My argument is [that] the children were focused on Raymond Buckey through rehearsing, coaching, and cueing."

"What the prosecution is really afraid of is a close study of two things, the accounts the children presented, and the process the children were put through before coming into the courtroom," Davis said. "Rather than the children's memories fading, they were enhanced." That, he said, "defies reality."

"Medicine goes through fashions," he said. He recalled a time when it was fashionable for doctors to prescribe thalidomide for pregnant women, until the deformed babies were born; when it was fashionable for doctors to use leeches in the treatment of common diseases; when the government approved the Dalkon Shield. "The kind of medicine in this case . . . it's really not medicine at all," Davis said.

"I hope you will look at the medical evidence in the context of medical fashions and realize you may be caught in a fashionable medical event— that what we believed in 1984 is wrong." Davis told the jury that recent studies had concluded that physical "signs" previously defined as solid evidence of molestation were found in "normal" children who had not been molested, and that at the time Astrid Heger examined the McMartin children, there was no body of medical knowledge to support her findings. Davis characterized the medical findings as "endless speculation," and referred to one of the prosecution doctors as a "hit man," brought in to "fix" one of the counts.

"The parents," Davis said, "must conclude that 'either my child was molested or I participated in the biggest sham of the 1980s.' " He asserted that people were unwittingly drawn into the case by a "handful of ambitious carpetbaggers," that is, the interviewers at CII, "trying to win at all costs," and overly ambitious prosecutors "trying to fulfill their career ambitions."

Davis talked about the little girl who was unable to identify Ray in the courtroom, but was able to identify him when the prosecutors brought her back, after a weekend recess. The same girl also told of being taken by Buckey on an airplane ride. She had four counts against the defendants. "Evidence that defies reality," he called it.

Davis spoke of the children who graduated from the preschool before

Ray began teaching there as "the fraudulent four." Only one of the child witnesses was in Buckey's class.

"Where there's smoke, there's fire," he said. "How could the prosecution bring this many counts if there wasn't some fire? Well, there's another explanation. Where there's smoke, there's smoke."

Then, something happened that troubled us a great deal. When Davis said, "I may take another day or two," he saw the sudden anger in the jurors' faces. Not all of them, but several were visibly angered. And the hard anger remained in their faces throughout his closing argument. We did not see that anger and hardness when Gits and Gunson were speaking. During a brief recess we learned that we were not the only spectators who had observed this. We had thought—and certainly hoped—that we might be mistaken. And Davis did not merely talk for another day: he talked for six days. And his voice was flat and monotonous.

Stranger still, a newspaper story appeared the next day, beginning with an interview of Davis in which he told the reporter that one of his professors in law school had told him, "Davis, there's something wrong with you. You won, but we don't like you. And when you go out into the real world other judges aren't going to like you." Davis then chronicled a series of incidents throughout his life in which it had been evident that people didn't like him.

"I don't buy the idea that there is something wrong with me," Davis was quoted as saying. "But I accept the fact that others react to me that way."

This frightened us because trials are won and lost because of the irrelevant but elemental fact that the jurors did not like one of the lawyers. We hesitate to say it, and do so only with great reluctance, because we know lawyers who are gifted and honorable men and women, but the general public's perception of lawyers is that they are evil.

We think the jurors failed to understand what a massive body of allegations Davis had to meet. All of the spectators we had spoken with believed that the jurors had made up their minds and wanted to go home, after giving two and a half years of their lives to serve as jurors in this record-breaking trial.

Nevertheless, Davis did his best to address the charges. He got down on his hands and knees to demonstrate how difficult, if not impossible, it would have been for Ray Buckey to molest children while they were riding on his back, as alleged by some of the child witnesses. He said that Ray was "a goner" once the Manhattan Beach police sent out the form letter to two hundred parents about the investigation and Ray's arrest. The CII interrogations focused on Ray and the doctors tailored their findings to correspond with the CII interviewers' pronouncements. Davis described them as "the most coached of any children in the history of American law."

"The truth never had a chance," he said.

During the mid-afternoon recess we spoke with a woman who was the daughter of one of the former defendants in the preliminary hearing. She was about thirty-five, and a very friendly, likable woman. We had met before.

"I used to believe in our government," she told us. "I used to salute the flag. Now, I don't know what to tell my children. I no longer believe in the government."

When the jurors filed in and were seated, Davis continued to go over testimony in which children admitted to having rehearsed and practiced with Rubin before coming in to testify in the trial. One small girl who was a complaining witness against Ray, when asked if she knew what "penis" meant, said she didn't know.

Occasionally, when Rubin said, "Objection!" Davis smiled at the jurors and said, "We're getting a little heat."

"Three neighbors were brought in . . . to suggest that he [Ray Buckey] was exhibiting himself. None of them said that. If he masturbated, does that prove beyond a reasonable doubt that he did something with children? I would hate to think that every man who ever masturbated molested children," Davis said.

"Mr. Ray Buckey does not have to prove that because he didn't wear underwear, that he's innocent. He doesn't have to prove that because he was a man with a child on his lap, that this isn't a crime." Generally, Davis's message was that the prosecution's evidence did not begin to prove beyond a reasonable doubt that he was guilty of molesting children. Davis urged the jurors not to use "the standards of a witch hunt."

"What happened to Ray Buckey could happen—without molesting children—to anybody."

That evening we received several telephone calls from other states that brought shocking news. We were told that CBS television was going to broadcast a film, based on McMartin, with all the elements of the McMartin case, showing the defendants to be guilty!

"They were able to get it aired just four days before the McMartin case goes to the jury!" a woman from Connecticut told us. "Who has that kind of clout? It had to come from the highest levels of power in America. They know the judge will tell them not to watch it. They wanted the judge to tell them about it!"

We watched "Do You Know the Muffin Man" on CBS. It did indeed bear a shocking resemblance to McMartin. A middle-aged woman who was a pillar of the community, allegations of satanic rituals and animal mutilations, a rabbit killed with a knife, a van, and defense arguments similar to those in McMartin! And, the next day, we were told that it would be aired again on CBS in a few days!

Davis played parts of the CII-videotaped interviews for the jurors to show the shaping process. Children were told that every other child had told of the "secrets," and, he explained, any child who did not "disclose" was made to feel isolated, to feel that he was the only one who was "out of sync" with the community. Denials were met with harsh disapproval. "Disclosures," no matter how tentative, were met with boisterous praise. Ray was identified as the culprit, even though some children didn't know who he was. The children were told that Ray was being watched, twenty-four hours a day, by a "secret policeman." They were told to beat up the Ray doll. Davis described it as "hate therapy."

"If a kid said he wasn't molested, he was alone," Davis explained.

Going back to the girl who described the "four-way crazy," Davis described her "singsong" testimony of sex acts. She had twenty-one counts against Ray and six against Peggy.

"All the adults would have to have known," he said. "All the teachers! That number of counts defies reason . . . unless you can prove that Ray Buckey was somehow there. There are real-life impossibilities. Ray wasn't there, and there is not one person who has put him there." Davis also stated that the girl's vaginitis, which the prosecution offered as evidence of molestation, was diagnosed by her pediatrician as infection caused by improper hygiene.

Davis told, as an analogy, a story of being taken on a raccoon hunt in Texas. Dogs were used, he said, and the older, more experienced dogs avoided the tree where the raccoons were hiding because they knew that raccoons can be very vicious if trapped or wounded. So the older, smarter dogs barked up at the tree where there were no raccoons, and the younger dogs barked up at the tree where there really were raccoons.

"The first tree, that's the medical evidence. There's nothing there. They're still trying to prove something, although there's nothing up the tree. A lot of noise but nothing up there." The other tree, Davis said, was the CII interviews: a "smokescreen" he called it. "What the prosecution is really afraid of is that you're going to look at the other tree. The Children's Institute," Davis said. "Even one of the doctors said that, at that time, there was no such thing as an expert in child sexual abuse."

Davis said the real game was "the CII game." He likened the CII interviewers to car salesmen who ask you, "Do you want to buy the red car or the yellow car?" failing to offer you the alternative that you might not want to buy a car at all. The CII interviewers, he asserted, did not entertain the possibility that molestation did not occur.

"The truth never had a chance."

"The doctors did not know what they were doing. It's not their fault. None of them did."

"The medical evidence was in ignorance."

Rubin and Gunson were scribbling intermittently as Davis spoke. Rubin would say the last words the jury would hear before they began deliberations. It was generally expected that Rubin would attack the defense ferociously.

After two and a half years in this trial it seemed as though time had stopped. The past two months seemed like a year. The past ten minutes seemed like an hour. Rubin would begin her final rebuttal in another day. The trial would end, appropriately, on Halloween.

After covering all of the prosecution's counts, witnesses, and testimony, Davis described the allegations as "impossible, unreal occurrences" and charged that the doctors who examined the children were determined to find signs of molestation because their colleagues, the therapists at CII, had declared that the children had been molested. "Are you confounded that the medical evidence is not only unreliable in this case but it may have been fabricated, it may have been false?"

Angrily, Davis reminded the jurors that the district attorney's office had to grant George Freeman immunity from perjury prosecution because he had lied in the McMartin preliminary hearing and in other proceedings. "That sort of thing went on in this trial! Nothing short of dealing with the devil! The heart of George Freeman is nothing less than the heart of the integrity of the prosecution's case."

Asking the jurors to evaluate the credibility of George Freeman as compared to that of Ray Buckey, Davis recounted the nine felony convictions and Freeman's history of perjury. The evidence against Ray Buckey, he said, included "two counts of pyramid, two counts of masturbation, one count of rubber duck, one count of marijuana. Match that record against that of George Freeman.

"We need him desperately in this case. Because if we find out that it was diarrhea, and Manhattan Beach went berserk after a stupid letter, the horror that this case is a sham is numbing! Absolutely numbing.

"So we call in the badge of integrity. We call in George Freeman. George Freeman himself, on the witness stand, said, 'I have no credibility.' He testified that Ray Buckey's attorney intimidated him, and the result of that was that he . . . was let out early, given money to move, and given money from the district attorney."

Davis reminded the jury that the district attorney had an open murder charge on Freeman, which would give Freeman a powerful motivation to lie and give whatever testimony the prosecution desired.

"How can you sanction that? And if it doesn't make you sick, try this count alone. And it hinges on the credibility of George Freeman. Whom do you believe? And if George Freeman doesn't find himself credible, should you?"

Davis said, "You should give an individual opinion. . . . You should not change your independent opinion simply because someone else disagrees with you. It should be something about the quality of the evidence. . . . Look deeper and look closer.

"The case lost its integrity. George Freeman has to be the standard of that problem. The destruction of the sources of truth by the shaping of little children, so different from their first comments that no one would rely on what they're saying by the time they come to trial. Advocates were brought in. . . . They had some ambition and they had a purpose—part of the McMartin problem. You'll hear it when I sit down. Excuses. Insinuations. Irrational suggestions dealing with impossible, incredible accounts.

"We're not going to learn if you address that McMartin problem by rewarding people who bring in perjurers, and shaped children, to pretend they care about children. Because what has to endure is a standard of law. . . . But if you lighten the standard for a burden of proof, consider this. These children are your legatees. If you say they've proved any of these counts beyond a reasonable doubt, you are confirming and ratifying the base absence of integrity in this case. Perjurers facing a possible murder! Not five but nine prior felonies. That's the standard at the heart of the McMartin problem.

"I have a little different view of what moral evidence is. And if it's amoral, if it's intolerable, reject it! The moral obligation you have does last over time. The standard of integrity and the requirement that there be a consistent proof beyond a reasonable doubt, or acquittal, is the legacy of your verdict."

Davis asked for an acquittal by indirection. He displayed a photograph of Muhammad Ali standing, victorious, over the battered, comatose body of Sonny Liston and said, "The people with the burden in a court of law have a haymaker coming. If it's insinuation, if it's excuses, if it's lame rationales, if it doesn't answer the base problem with integrity, *you* figure out who had the burden in this case! *You* figure out if Ray Buckey had any different burden than Muhammad Ali. Prove his innocence! Because the evidence we looked for to prove otherwise isn't there. Maybe there'll be parents, parents who haven't been here during the defense. Maybe you'll recognize some of them as witnesses. Maybe you'll have a little jolt, that your verdict may affect their feelings. Well, Ray Buckey's been hidden for five years behind this case and he's entitled to the benefit of the doubt, no matter how this courtroom's packed, no matter how the evidence is loaded. Bottom line, it's a question of integrity. Not a badge anyone can wear but yourselves. So I'd thank you. . . . Please keep your health. And keep your head. Keep on the case. And please give both sides your fair, objective and independent verdict. Thank you."

In the morning, when all the jurors were in their seats, Deputy District Attorney Lael Rubin began her final closing argument. The courtroom was packed with the hard-faced mob that had come early and filled all of the front rows.

Facing the jurors, Rubin began by saying that, although this is called "argument," she preferred to call it "an appeal to your reason." She said she would try to address the questions jurors might ask if they were able to sit down together for an informal conversation. She wrote in large chalk letters on a blackboard:

338   The Abuse of Innocence

DON'T BE FOOLED.

Rubin urged the jurors not to disbelieve the children's stories because their statements seemed unbelievable. "These stories were simply less painful ways of dealing with the truth," she said, asserting that the children told the "bottled up" truth when they told the bizarre stories, sublimating the emotional pain of being molested into preposterous tales.

Rubin said the children had repressed memories of their sexual abuse until they were evaluated at CII. But that was where they told of being taken for rides in airplanes and hot air balloons, and even more remarkable adventures.

"Children are as suggestible as adults or, putting it another way, no more suggestible than adults," Rubin asserted. She dismissed as "tricks to fool you" defense claims that hysteria and suggestive, biased interviewing techniques had led children to say they were molested.

Rubin harshly contradicted Davis's statement that he was not ridiculing the children, and accused Davis of threatening George Freeman, citing as proof of this allegation the fact that Davis had interviewed Freeman alone, without a witness present. She made the accusation that Davis, realizing that Ray had confessed to Freeman, visited Freeman and threatened to have him killed.

Rubin accused defense attorneys of insinuation and trickery and of harassing child witnesses.

Responding to the question of how hundreds of children could have been molested at the preschool without any of them telling anyone until the investigation began, Rubin said, "My response to that is [that] many of those kids tried to talk in their own way and nobody listened.

"Behind the facade of what supposedly was this loving, caring, wonderful preschool was a place that was really, truly horrible because there were children who were abused at that preschool," Rubin charged.

"What these teachers did to these children is really unfathomable," Rubin said. As evidence to support this, she cited what she called the "unusual behavior" of the children at the time they attended the McMartin Preschool: aggressiveness, bedwetting, masturbation, staying too long in the bathtub, resistance to going to school.

During a brief recess, when we were all standing in the hallway, Ray said, "I'd hate to be convicted on a bunch of nonsense like that."

"They're not attacking you. They're attacking me!" Davis laughed.

"Yeah, but I'm the one who gets to go to jail," Ray responded.

"You're not going to jail," Davis reassured him.

After the recess, Rubin continued. She characterized as "nonsense" Gits's assertion that medical knowledge of molestation was "primitive" in 1984. She accused the defense attorneys of intimidating, embarrassing, and confusing child witnesses so that others would be discouraged from coming in and testifying.

One newspaper described Rubin's speech as "attorney bashing."

Rubin read lengthy portions of the testimony of the children, the parents, and other witnesses. There was not much substance to it, though. Two of the jurors were sleeping, another was yawning, and Gunson, as usual, was looking at the clock. We have seen a lot of lawyering during our careers as journalists, good, bad, and mediocre. Once we saw a true world-class lawyer at work. He was a short, elderly Jewish man, but when he rose and began speaking to the jury he was suddenly ten feet tall. His statements had the hard clarity of cut glass, but in addition to his powerful presence there was an aura of generosity and compassion. The jurors were spellbound. There was nothing like that happening here. The jurors looked tired, resentful, and bored.

"The horror of horrors in this case is that these children were molested and they have been attacked all over again in this courtroom right in front of your eyes," Rubin continued. "Are we going to let people who molest kids get away with it? I hope not." She said that she would comment on "what I feel to be some of the more outrageous and egregious misstatements of the evidence made to you by the defense.

"You will see, loud and clear, that there were some pretty awful things that went on in that preschool at the hands of Ray and Peggy Buckey."

Rubin said it was unreasonable to believe that Kee MacFarlane, CII, and the prosecution engaged in a "Svengali-like conspiracy." She suggested that Barbara Dusky lied on the witness stand to help Ray. She asserted that if there were nothing incriminating in the missing page of Virginia's diary, somebody would have brought it in. She brought up, once again, Betty Raidor's mysterious hand signals to a mother when discussing Ray Buckey, insinuating that Raidor had knowledge of some dark depraved sexual secret.

Like Gunson, Rubin was bringing up all of the uncertainties, all of the events and statements that could be seen as ambiguous, and offering them as evidence of molestation and conspiracy. One of these was the testimony of a mother who said that she had received a telephone call from the police informing her of the investigation, and said that when she called Peggy and asked, "What is going on?" she heard Peggy say, "Oh my God! Ray!" It was an uncorroborated piece of hearsay and the words she attributed to Peggy Buckey were ambiguous and could be construed to mean almost anything. Nevertheless, it was being offered as proof that Ray was a molester and that Peggy knew it.

Rubin spent almost an hour on the encounters between Davis and George Freeman at the county jail, arguing that Freeman should be believed and Davis should not be believed.

Rubin attacked Gits's assertion that Peggy did what innocent people do: she called the police. Rubin suggested that Peggy called the police because she was guilty and wanted to find out how much the police knew. Rubin went on and on, reading testimony of children, doctors, parents, and other witnesses, raising small ambiguities and transforming them into damning evidence against Ray and Peggy.

During the mid-afternoon recess, as we all gathered in the hallway with Ray and Peggy, one of the paralegals said, "I'm having trouble staying awake. She isn't saying anything." Everyone agreed that Rubin seemed to be just filling time. Former prosecutor Glenn Stevens walked over and said excitedly, "No! She's taking all the little inconsistencies and asking you to adopt the most sinister explanation."

Back in the courtroom, after recess, Rubin continued to read portions of the testimony of many witnesses. She talked too fast, in a monotone; she seemed to be rushing to get it over with. The jurors seemed to be having difficulty keeping focused on her.

Rubin ended her speech by quoting the testimony of the father of one of the child witnesses, who had said, "This has not been something that all of us wanted to do. It's something that we all decided was the right thing to do."

Rubin concluded, "Mr. Gunson and I and the children hope that you will do the right thing as well." As she returned to her seat at the prosecution table, the judge said, "That does it. That's the end of the trial."

The next day, Judge Pounders read thirty-two pages of instructions to the jury, one of which was that, "You should not discount or distrust the testimony of a child solely because he or she is a child, nor should you believe such testimony solely because he or she is a child."

When he had finished reading the instructions and the jurors had adjourned to the jury room to elect a foreman and begin deliberations, the judge said, "It seems like a historic moment but I'm too tired to enjoy it."

And so, after two and a half years, 124 witnesses, and nearly a thousand exhibits, the jurors had to reach a verdict on each of 65 counts.

But the jurors did not get full and complete information. They got a very stripped-down version of the case.

The jurors were not told that the prosecution's "expert," Dr. Gordon, had reportedly been banned from examining children for sexual abuse in San Luis Obispo County, nor that he was reprimanded by a judge for destroying exculpatory evidence to keep it from falling into the hands of the defense, and that even prosecutors complained that Gordon's bias was so flagrant and conspicuous that he was "blowing" their cases.

They were not told of Dr. Woodling's role in the Bakersfield cases, in which Woodling, along with Gordon and Heger, provided the prosecution's "solid medical evidence." In one of the Bakersfield "mass molestation" cases Dr. Woodling stated that a child's anus was "totally destroyed." The judge was skeptical and brought in another physician for a second opinion. The second doctor said there was nothing wrong with the anus at all.

They were not told of the copious monetary gain and career advancement received by those who perpetrated the myth of mass molestation at McMartin and all over America.

They did not learn—nor, apparently, did the attorneys and the reporters—that McMartin was only a piece of a much larger, extremely sinister agenda that included a nationwide witch hunt fueled by federal funding and put into effect by people who had no expertise to offer and no hesitation about destroying the lives of people who had committed no crimes, some of these innocent people would spend the rest of their lives in prison.

Had the jurors received the full story they might well have risen up and demanded that the prosecutors be indicted. However, the tunnel vision imposed on them precluded any real insight into the case.

Since they were not permitted to read or hear about the case outside the courtroom, the jury did not learn of the D.A.'s snitch scandal, or the prosecutors' practice of trading leniency for perjury in cases where the evidence was tenuous. Such knowledge would have enabled the jurors to evaluate the quality of George Freeman's testimony.

The jurors were not told of the study by Duke University statisticians of the grossly unrealistic reporting of the case, which created a mass hallucination generated by sensational electronic and print media.

They did not hear from Glenn Stevens, who gave up his job in the D.A.'s office rather than build his career on the ruin of innocent people. He could have provided extremely detailed and compelling testimony as to how he came to form the belief that the case was built on nonsense and devoid of evidence.

The jurors were not told that the supermarket kid also told of being molested by "atomic mutants."

They were not told of the recantations presented in the preliminary hearing: the kids who admitted, on cross-examination, that they had not been molested.

The jurors were not told that the prosecution had not just one but seven jailhouse snitches on their witness list, including the notorious Leslie White.

The jurors did not get to hear the full testimony of Virginia McMartin, the only witness who had the fortitude to look Lael Rubin straight in the eyes and call her a liar.

They did not get to hear the defense's second expert witness, Elizabeth Loftus, Ph.D., a professor at the University of Washington at Seattle, who would have provided an extremely important piece in the puzzle, showing that the allegations were, at best, extremely questionable. She published articles and studies on "false memory" and memory distortion and has testified as an expert witness in many criminal trials.

They were not told about the immunity shield that opened the floodgates to a tidal wave of false and malicious accusations of child abuse, built into the child abuse statutes by authors of the molestation witch hunt.

And the jurors probably did not understand that the prosecution was permitted to go on for fifteen months, bashing the defense for the unseemly length of the trial, then Judge Pounders simply shut the defense down by disallowing their last forty-five witnesses.

The trial ended leaving a number of questions unanswered, questions to which we may never get answers. One of the paradoxes of the American legal system is that witnesses are required to swear to tell "the whole truth." But those attempting to tell the whole truth, are often quickly cut off and told to answer the questions with a simple yes or no, to refrain from volunteering additional information. Attempts to tell "the whole truth" a second or third time can reap a citation for contempt and a guest pass to one of America's jails. The American legal system is often built on not telling the whole truth. The whole truth is not necessarily admissible in an American court of law.

But after sitting through five years of McMartin proceedings, seeing and hearing all of the evidence, and getting to know the defendants, we believe, beyond a reasonable doubt and to a moral certainty, that the Buckeys never abused a child. Neither of us would ever be afraid to leave a child with them and, in fact, would feel secure in the knowledge that the child was in the hands of exceptionally good and caring people.

When prosecutor Lael Rubin began her opening statement in this trial, she stated that this was a case of "betrayal of trust." She was correct. But it is now clear that the betrayal of trust was perpetrated not by the preschool teachers but by the prosecutors, the police, the self-anointed "experts," the doctors, and all of those who worked in the service of the prosecution and did their best to consign innocent people to prison for the rest of their lives in order to score points toward a promotion and pay raise, career advancement, or a federal grant. It is abundantly clear that these people undermined the process of justice. It is also extremely unlikely that any action will ever be taken against them for these actions.

What is profoundly troubling about all this is the fact that the prosecutors and all those who worked in the service of the prosecution, if they did not know at the beginning, could not have been unaware, long before the conclusion of the trial, that the allegations were unfounded and based on hysteria. Yet, as it became increasingly clear with each day that there was insufficient evidence to hold the defendants, the prosecutors and those in their service redoubled their efforts to convict them and used every weapon, every deception in the lawyer's bag of tricks, to win their case and move on to greater fame and fortune.

As the evidence unfolded, it became increasingly clear that the Buckeys were kind, gentle people who loved children and animals and would be incapable of harming either. Yet they were deprived of everything they owned, and Peggy spent two years in jail, Ray five, on allegations that were demonstrably ridiculous. The Buckeys operated what was probably one of the best nursery schools in the country. They were friendly, trusting people who did not believe in the existence of evil, until they were overtaken by it.

We moved slowly with the crowd toward the elevators. We felt like those O.S.S. officers in World War II who lived behind enemy lines for years. Finally it was over and we were leaving the Los Angeles Criminal Courts Building for the last time, except for the day the jury would return and render its verdicts. But with sixty-five counts to consider, that could be a long time.

We attended the national conference of Victims of Child Abuse Law (VOCAL). There have been so many cases in virtually every county in the United States that this nationwide organization formed almost overnight. As with most conventions there was the first-evening's "get-acquainted" cocktail hour. There were many noted lawyers, psychologists, psychiatrists, and other experts present to analyze the current avalanche of child abuse prosecutions. The hotel was packed with people who had been accused or whose family members had been accused and were seeking help, advice, and insight into their predicament.

One of the first things we learned was that many of the day-care cases were so much like McMartin that they were clearly played from the same script with only the names and minor details changed. In nearly all instances there were the familiar allegations of witchcraft, satanic rituals, and the butchering of animals and infants. In most of these cases there was virtually no evidence, and stunning prosecutorial misconduct. Yet, there were hundreds—perhaps thousands—of people in jails and prisons in the wake of trumped-up prosecutions.

In the celebrated Scott County case in Minnesota, children were removed from their parents for months and grilled for hundreds of hours. Those who refused to acquiesce and say that they had been molested were told that unless they "disclosed" they would never see their parents again. This happened in many of the other, similar cases we read. As in the seventeenth-century witch trials, it has become a national pathology.

Tom Roehr, an attorney who successfully defended a group of young men accused of child molestation in California said, "In the fifties we were told that there were five hundred Communists hiding behind every shrub. Now I'm not saying that molestation doesn't exist but they've gone crazy. They've blown it out of all proportion into a massive witch hunt."

We heard and read of endless day-care cases like McMartin and we were told that the prosecutors were winning almost all of them. As we stood in the crowded room filled with cocktail-sipping men and women, a psychologist told us of cases in which juries had found defendants guilty on the most absurd, unfounded allegations.

"The problem is how do you maintain a democracy," she said, "when there are so many millions of people who are stupid enough to believe anything."

Allen McMahon, a distinguished California lawyer who has defended many people accused in similar cases, told us about the genesis of the strange phenomenon. "In 1974 the Federal Child Abuse Act was passed by Congress and this law provided that huge federal grants to states would be paid if they passed mandatory reporting laws. So they passed these mandatory reporting laws in order to get this money. But in order to get the money they had to generate cases! They are fabricating these cases! One child abuse clinic that you and I have knowledge of got a two million dollar grant because they created a big case with lots of victims, lots of suspects. None of the kids said they were molested until they were put through the process with the interviewers.... And that's how we got the child abuse industry. It's money. And money fuels the system. And that's what makes the social workers so anxious to open new cases. It's their job that's on the line. So they send the child to one of their favorite agencies or doctors who have a reputation as being professional child abuse finders. They will find sexual abuse even if they have to keep working on the kid and break him down and put words in his mouth. And these agencies make a lot of money. They not only get paid per case, but they get grants! One of these agencies of which you and I have knowledge is run by a lady whose only license is a New York State welder's license. That agency, I am informed, also received a two-million-dollar grant. Every city has one or more of these child sexual abuse agencies. They are creating these cases!

"I said earlier to look for the profit motive if you really want to know what this thing is all about. Most of these schools carry liability insurance of one million dollars per kid, and all these parents are pushing and pressuring the D.A.'s office to convict these people so they can sue for millions.... But people are bankrupted by the expense of fighting this. Families are destroyed. And 70 percent of the cases are unfounded. Now any system that produces 70 percent error is faulty or deficient."

During the conference there was much discussion of Dr. Roland Summit, whose article, "The Child Sexual Abuse Accommodation Syndrome," is unanimously embraced by the prosecution faction, those referred to as the child abuse industry, as gospel. The divine word. It has been a powerful weapon in the hands of prosecutors because it posits the premise that children never lie when they say they have been sexually abused and that when they say they have not been molested they are "in denial," meaning that they are concealing molestation. The problem with this theory is that it leaves no room for the possibility that no molestation has occurred.

There was much discussion about the way the children are interrogated at the child abuse clinics. One psychologist told us, "This afternoon, you're going to see several hours of the videotaped interviews these people did with the kids in these McMartin-type cases, and a psychiatrist is going to explain exactly what's going on. You will see how they break the kid down, using precisely the same techniques the Chinese used to brainwash the American prisoners in the Korean War."

One of the speakers, Douglas Besharov, was the first director of the National Center For Child Abuse. "Now, all the pressure is toward reporting," he said. "If you report, you have total immunity. . . . The situation is getting so bad—junk cases flooding the system so seriously that the system's ability to function is seriously weakened. A lot of junk is being accepted. And you know what the newspapers are saying: 'CHILD ABUSE GETTING MORE SEVERE!' While the number of reports has increased phenomenally, the number of kids actually getting help has gone down!"

Dr. Lee Coleman, M.D., a psychiatrist who had testified as an expert witness in about two hundred of these cases, discussed the medical evidence used by prosecutors in these molestation trials and preliminary hearings.

"There is not a single study in the entire world literature which can tell us what is the range of normal of the genitals and anus of little girls and boys. . . .There is absolutely nothing to stop any doctor from claiming that 'This child has been molested.' They look at the child and claim that [he or she] has been molested. And that's what has been going on!

"Now, I want to keep going with how they're doing this, in two different ways. And if you study the cases you'll see that there are two different ways that they do it. One is that they examine the child, and even with their incredible bias and zealotry to find abuse, they still say, 'The child is normal.' That happens. You see a lot of that in the McMartin case in Los Angeles. . . . There were normal physical examinations. So how do they support an allegation of molestation with that kind of examination? Well, they do it! The first way they do it is they say, 'History of sexual abuse.' To equate the claim of sexual abuse with what is normally considered the history of medicine is a total outrage, a total fraud. It's a misuse of medicine to promote an allegation by confusing lay people into thinking this is a medical finding when it is nothing more than a doctor repeating an allegation. An allegation has become 'medical evidence.'

"The next way they do it is write down, 'Medical examination is consistent with sexual abuse.' I don't know of a more vicious kind of language than that! 'Consistent with child sexual abuse'! Now, what is the thinking behind that? The thinking behind that is that a lot of kids who get sexually abused won't show any findings. Most of them do not show anything. Is that justification for using language like 'consistent with child sexual abuse'? You'd better believe that it is not. That is a total fraud because the lay person who reads that is likely to read that as meaning there is some kind of support for an allegation of sexual abuse.

"So what I would typically say if I were asked on the stand, 'Doctor, does the statement, "consistent with sexual abuse," teach the court anything?' I would say, 'It doesn't teach the court anything about whether the child has been abused, but it teaches the court a lot about the bias of the person who wrote it that way. It teaches us that the person seems to have a desire to promote the possibility that the child was molested when he could have equally written, 'Physical examination consistent with not being molested.'

"They are claiming to see things that are not even there. . . . Are the people who get the child to believe these things child abusers or aren't they?

"What have we got here? I'll put it in the politest terms I can use that are suitable for television. *This is an unadulterated medical fraud!* It is a medical fraud because it is false! It is holding out to the lay community that doesn't have the fortitude to look into this and speak up about it.

"Advertising to the lay community and to the rest of the medical community that they have the tools and skills they do not have! Is that any different than if I go out and advertise a snake oil to cure cancer? It's no different. It's an unadulterated medical fraud.

"Is there anything we can do? Well, if you do not let yourself get intimidated and if you do not let your lawyer get intimidated, you can fight this. The other thing we have to do is we have to take the medical community by the collar and tell them, 'We are not going to let you be spineless. We are going to create so many problems for you because you are not speaking up—because you are letting fraud be perpetrated in the name of your profession—that you are going to have to speak up about it.' . . . And that's what's really going to turn the tide. If we can get the medical community to live up to their responsibility and not let fraud be perpetrated in their profession."

The other central dispute in the current epidemic of child molestation cases is the issue of how the children are being interrogated. A psychiatrist addressed the conference and stated that what was being done in McMartin was part of a nationwide system being used in precisely the same fashion across the country. "It is not therapy," he said. "It is interrogation which, like all interrogation, assumes the truth of a given hypothesis and sets out to support the hypothesis." The interrogators, he said, ignore any exonerating statements and pursue only statements of the suspect's guilt. The denials are ignored and the "therapy" is invariably in the service of the prosecution.

Dr. William McIver, a noted clinical psychologist, described a study he had done on the use of "anatomically correct" dolls in interrogating the children, as was done in McMartin. He concluded that, "The data show that the dolls are of no use as diagnostic instruments for discriminating between children who have or have not been abused."

A New York attorney said, "The outcome of all this, in addition to entrapping innocent people, is to teach children that sex is tainted with evil and guilt. And all this fraudulent hysteria about child abuse, created by agents of our government, diverts our attention from society's failure to provide adequate food, housing, and education for its children."

A lobbyist and former state senator who is active in electoral politics said that legislation had been introduced in several state legislatures that would require chemical castration for convicted child molesters, a chilling presentiment since so many convictions have been based on such questionable evidence. A woman in the audience raised her hand and spoke: "There have been several judges and some deputy attorneys general and some deputy D.A.'s, and some members of state legislatures who have been found to be child molesters. Are they going to be chemically castrated, too?"

"Oh no!" he said. "It's just for the little people."

In the evening there was the obligatory social hour with wine, beer, and refreshments. A woman whose husband was involved in a California case said, "I can't believe this is happening in America. I used to believe in America and the government."

A lawyer from one of our larger cities who had defended a group of people in a molestation case sat in the bar and spoke with a group of attorneys. He was an extremely large man with a leathery face and a deep, bass voice. He talked about McMartin and some of the other cases.

"A lot of these people here are getting their first taste of reality," he said. "You wonder where they've been for the last twenty years. Let me tell you about the county where I live and practice law.

"The county is run by a tight little club. They are the power brokers. They decide who will be the D.A. They decide who will be the judge, the city councilman, police commissioner. They control all the political offices. They run the county.

"You want to know what they do for amusement? They take thirteen-year-old boys out of the county juvenile detention center and take them home under the pretext of providing them with the opportunity for respectable, gainful employment, as house boys. What they're actually doing is sodomizing them and turning them into boy prostitutes. They provide them with money, wheels, cocaine, clothes, and that's the up side. The down side is they tell them, 'Look. You're facing five years in the slams if you don't do what I say.'

"Some of the boys have been killed because they talked too much. And one of them went crazy and stabbed his keeper thirty-seven times. He's in prison. They got him out of the county.

"These politicians are the most respected men in the community. They are judges, D.A.s, city councilmen, state senators, deacons of their churches. These are the guys who go on television and say, 'We've got to put child molesters behind bars,' and 'I believe the children,' and all the prosecution stuff about witchcraft and satanic ritual molestation and chopping up babies and roasting them. This is what we have for leaders in America. And once you understand what the quality of our leadership is, it's not too surprising that a thing like this could happen.

"There are a few good judges scattered sparsely across the country and a few good prosecutors like Glenn Stevens in California who refused to build his career on the ruin of innocent people. But the system did not honor Stevens for his courage. They spat him out and threatened to ruin him by stripping him of the right to practice his profession."

There was the obligatory Saturday night party with too many people crowded into the available space. We heard endless stories of the most hideous injustices, stunning prosecutorial misconduct, and the destruction of families and innocent people's lives by the child abuse industry.

Two men from Montana, dressed in work clothes, said, "We were just having dinner with our wives and kids when the police came in and busted us. They wouldn't tell us why or anything. When we got to court they told us we was charged with molesting our kids and the cop said we were drinking blood and eating feenal [sic] matter."

There was much discussion of the new mandatory reporting laws and the guarantee of immunity and anonymity to anyone making an accusation of child abuse. "Pathological liars and lunatics are shielded from view," a lawyer said. "They have created an ideology to use as a smokescreen to hide what they're doing. One of their first principles is 'Children never lie.' If you think this is the raving of an inmate at some psychiatric facility, read the literature of the child abuse industry." (See the bibliography for lists of that literature.)

There is a general belief among the VOCAL people that the child abuse witch hunt is only a small component of a larger agenda to separate children from their parents and indoctrinate them. Private nursery schools are being shut down everywhere and replaced by federally funded day-care centers operated by the child abuse industry, we were told.

One young woman, about twenty-five years old, told us that she and her husband had moved to New Jersey, where the husband had taken a new job. The wife was lonely, had no friends or relatives in the community, and became depressed. A neighbor gave her a telephone number to call and was told, "They can help you." It happened to be the number of child protective services. They came and took away her children, stating that they were not properly cared for. Later, allegations of sexual abuse were added. The young woman wept as she told us that she had not been allowed to see her children since then and that all efforts to find them had failed.

A former child protective services worker told us that the social workers, backed by police, were removing children from their homes by the thousands. They had lobbied for laws that were so broad that almost any family in the world could be accused of child abuse, and although it is strictly illegal, judges have generally supported the "child savers."

They can remove your child because (1) you are too strict or (2) you are too lenient.

They can remove your child because (1) there is no religious training or (2) because you are excessively preoccupied with religion.

They can remove your child because (1) you allow the child to watch too much television or (2) the child is allowed to watch no television at all.

One of the most interesting of the rules that exist in some states is that your child can be removed if the family holds beliefs that conflict with society.

Most of the children are being removed for reasons that have to do with nothing more than poverty, even though they have responsible, loving parents.

"Once they get your kid," the former child protective services worker said, "you will probably never see him again. They will prohibit communication by telephone or mail and they will have him adopted and change his name so that you can't find him. Kids are being taken away from their natural parents for no good reason and placed in the chaotic foster care system where many of them have been beaten, raped, and murdered. It is a fact not generally known, but a child is far more likely to be abused in foster care than by its natural parents."

"Why are they doing this?" we asked.

"They have to create a national pandemonium about child abuse and child saving in order to keep the enormous federal funding for their jobs. It's just money. And careers. Most social workers are not mental giants. Most of the people in the child abuse industry were flunkouts until they found the child abuse bandwagon and climbed aboard. All of this is a demonstration of what happens when great power is given to people of low mentality. You would think that they would have some contrition, some difficulty reconciling this with their conscience, but I'm afraid there are an awful lot of people in the child abuse industry who came off the genetic assembly line with a few parts missing.

"To lose your natural parents in early childhood is just about the most damaging experience that can happen to anybody. I've followed up on a lot of the kids [who] were taken away from their families and thrown among strangers and reared by the state. A lot of them are in the prison system. Some are in the nut house. Most of them just grow up to be inconspicuously dysfunctional cases of arrested development.

"The justification they uniformly use is the familiar aphorism: 'We must always err on the side of the child.' That means always remove the kid from the home and put [him or her] in foster care. But it costs about five times as much to maintain a kid in foster care as it would to simply give some assistance to the family and keep the family together. The state makes a lousy parent. We are not going to have a lot of Thomas Edisons or Henry Fords. Just a great harvest of basket cases. What these people are doing is monstrous. I cannot think of any punishment cruel enough to atone for what they're doing."

The woman went on to say that this was a reflection of the utter bankruptcy of our leadership.

"Don't any of the parents resist this violation of their constitutional rights?" we asked.

"Some resist when the social workers come to take their kids away, but the cops slam them up against the wall and handcuff them. The smartest parents just take their kids and their stuff and disappear. I know of several cases in which the mother told the kid to run away and where to meet her so she could hide him from the child savers. There was one small mountain community up near the Canadian border. I can't tell you where. The people up there were tough loggers and their kids wore rough work clothes. Their homes did not look like Beverly Hills. The social workers were going to take the kids because they said the homes were untidy and they told the parents that their kids would be returned only if they 'admitted' sexually abusing them. But the social workers ran into a little difficulty this time."

"What happened?" we asked.

"Nobody ever saw them again," she smiled.

"We're surprised the public hasn't risen up in outrage about this," we said.

"The public hasn't been told," she said. "In all the cases the media report only the government's point of view. The national and state conferences of VOCAL have been almost entirely blanked out in the media."

"You'd think people would question the credibility of this circus."

"Most people don't want to ask questions. Once you start asking questions everything you've been told and believed falls apart."

Most of the more cerebral members of VOCAL believed that the current child abuse witch hunt is only a small part of a larger agenda to (1) establish, once and for all, the government rather than the family as having ultimate authority over children; (2) establish greater government control over the individual; and (3) remove children from their families at an early age and indoctrinate them. Mind control.

On the airplane returning to L.A. we thought about Henry Miller's statement that fascism is perfectly normal human behavior.

There is also an organization of people who are solidly in support of the prosecution and want tougher laws. It is called CLOUT. They want to get rid of the rule against hearsay and the Sixth Amendment right to be confronted by one's accuser. The meeting was held in a very large hall near Long Beach, and the buffet was an opulent spread with prime rib, lobster, caviar, and other delicacies in great quantity, and liquid refreshments of every variety. One of the guests looked at us and said, "Somebody took a large piece of money out of his pocket for this. It isn't hors d'oeuvres; it's dinner!"

There were some speakers, a state senator and two members of the lower house, making their bid for votes, proclaiming their solidarity with CLOUT. One of them, a black woman, ended her speech by saying that child abuse was one of the most terrible crimes "but we have to look at the other side, too. There's nothing worse than being falsely accused of child molestation.

I feel terribly sorry for anybody [who's] falsely accused of child abuse." This statement was received with a cold, dead silence.

There were a number of unescorted women slouching seductively about the room. One of them, a young lady about thirty, confided to her companions that these people had found a new social life and several unmarried women had found new lovers and husbands in this club. She said that not only do they party at night, but that they also have picnics.

"A molestation picnic," someone quipped. The others were not amused.

There were a number of psychologists, "therapists," lawyers, and others involved in one form or another with the prosecution, and the familiar, militant parents' clique from Manhattan Beach.

A middle-aged couple introduced themselves to us and we stood talking among the child abuse revelers. The woman told us that recently at a feminist group therapy session she had suddenly remembered her father, whom she had idolized, sexually abusing her when she was an infant. She went on to say that she was attending meetings of the women's group regularly, "working on my anger." Then she left to go to the ladies' room. Shirley went with her.

"That's really horrible," Paul said to her husband. "I cannot imagine anyone wanting to do a thing like that."

"The problem is," the man told me sadly, looking at me with troubled eyes, "her father died when she was less than a year old, shortly after she was born."

We had gone to the meeting of CLOUT to gather what information we could, to get their side of the story. But we found that these people, although they asked many questions of us, told us very little in response to our questions except for the familiar eerie tales of satanic ritual molestation and blood-drinking demons.

There is also the National Center For the Prosecution of Child Abuse. They hold frequent conferences and seminars instructing prosecutors in new strategies to discredit defense attorneys and their expert witnesses—particularly on the volatile issue of how the children are questioned. A young prosecutor from California asked the speakers on the panel, "If a child was overly pressured and coached, wouldn't you want to know that?" Her question was met with a long, cold silence.

During the first five weeks of deliberations the McMartin jury sent out only two sealed verdicts. The judge told reporters he planned to read the verdicts piecemeal because it could take months before all sixty-five were reached. The jurors reacted with shock and told the judge they feared possible harassment or assault from neighbors, coworkers, and the public if the verdicts were announced. The massive media coverage of the defendants had created a general belief that they were guilty, and the fact that the jurors were so shaken by the judge's plan to open and disclose the verdicts while they were still deliberating strongly suggested that they were leaning toward an acquittal, that announcing the verdicts would put great pressure on the jury to convict. Judge Pounders agreed to withhold the verdicts until the jurors returned from their Christmas vacation. We waited.

Shortly after the jury began deliberations, CBS television broadcast a film titled *Unspeakable Acts*. Like "Do You Know the Muffin Man?" it was about preschool teachers accused of child sexual abuse, sending the clear and unmistakable message that the defendants were guilty. The many lawyers and others who discussed it with us over the telephone unanimously agreed that it was definitely an attempt to influence the jury, and that only persons at the highest levels of power would have been able to get these films broadcast at such a critical time. But why was it so important to them to win this case at any cost and by any means?

The *Los Angeles Daily Journal* and other newspapers reported that prosecutor Lael Rubin was engaged to be married to *Los Angeles Times* managing editor David Rosenzweig, who supervised the *Times*'s coverage of the case for five years. A senior editor at the *Times* stated that, "The liaison has in no way affected the McMartin coverage."

But a reporter who had been with the *Times* for twenty years conducted a six-month investigation of the case which, the reporter said, indicated the defendants may have been wrongly accused. His editors not only refused to publish his piece but also rewarded him with a two-day suspension without pay for questioning the credibility of Lois Timnick, the reporter who had covered McMartin almost from its inception. According to one newspaper story, the reporter resigned, saying, "I cannot work for a newspaper that will not tell the truth."

On the twenty-fifth day of their deliberations, just before the Christmas vacation, the jurors returned twenty-four more verdicts. Only thirty-nine remained. After Christmas, on January 3, 1990, they returned another six verdicts. On January 11, they delivered thirteen more. Finally, it was announced that the jury had reached verdicts on fifty-two counts and were deadlocked on the remaining thirteen counts, and that the verdicts would be read in court the following day, Thursday, January 18, 1990.

When we got out of the elevator, the fifteenth floor was packed with television camera crews, newspeople, lawyers—the precision briefcase drill team—and an amorphous mass of men and women, young and old, waiting. We were told that the judge had reserved seats for us in the courtroom but we were unable to get past the phalanx of uniformed sheriff's deputies. So we watched the proceeding on the large television monitor of one of the local stations, squatting under the camera and microphone boom.

First, the judge read off the counts on which the jurors had deadlocked and said, "I declare those counts a mistrial." Then, he said, "There's no point in reading the remaining fifty-two counts because they're all the same."

Something inside us jumped and our hearts began pounding. We were fairly sure we knew what the news would be. Everybody exchanged glances in silence. A feverish tension gripped the crowd. Then, the clerk of the court began reading: "We the jurors find the very defendants . . . not guilty."

The shock wave went out through the crowd and across the nation with a tremendous impact. There were shouts of joy mixed with the raucous screams. Lael Rubin sat at the prosecution table, looking down, eyelids lowered, with the dejected face of someone who had just lost everything in a poker game, or had just lost a fight she thought she could win. Ray's face radiated with the elation of a man who had just risen from the dead and ascended into heaven. Gunson was, as always, expressionless. Davis threw his arm around Ray, giving him a squeeze and a pat on the back. Peggy removed her glasses and dabbed at tears with a handkerchief. A newsman held his microphone to her face and asked her something and she answered tearfully, "I just think what they've done to us is the most horrible thing they could do to anybody."

We spoke with a group of young lawyers and one of them commented, "I noticed the judge's face got very red when he opened the fifty-two not guilty verdicts."

"Yeah," another responded. "If there had been no jury and it had been up to that judge, he would have sent them to prison for life."

The media went quickly into action. They moved in on the mob with their cameras and lights, recording their ravings on videotape. Newspeople coldly turned their backs on anyone aligned with the defense. A paralegal approached a woman who was in charge of one of the television crews, pointed to one of the defense attorneys and asked her if she would like to interview him. "Oh no!" she said, quickly turning her back. Another woman spoke to one of the television newsmen and pointed us out. "That's Paul and Shirley Eberle. They sat in the courtroom for five years and wrote two books about this." The newsman coldly said, "No. We wouldn't want to do that," and turned his back.

But the press followed the angry mob everywhere and even pursued them into the lavatory! One attorney associated with the defense was allowed to stand before the camera and speak for a minute or so, but when the tape was broadcast on the five o'clock news, we only saw his lips moving. The sound was turned off.

"They're doing it again!" Paul exclaimed.

"What did you expect from those pea-brains?" a paralegal said. "Those aren't writers. They're just clerks."

Peggy and Ray quickly left through the rear exit, but when they reached the parking lot, there were the familiar, mean faces of the lynch mob, shouting, "We're gonna kill you!" "You're gonna die!"

Paul did get interviewed by one radio station, only because the producer was an old friend. But the woman who was his assistant asked afterwards, "What makes you so sure those people are innocent?"

"What makes you so sure they're guilty?" Paul asked. "Are you sure they're guilty? Absolutely certain?"

"Yeah, I'm sure," she answered.

"You must have spent a great deal of the time studying the evidence," Paul said. "Which of the witnesses do you think was the most convincing? Which of the counts did you think was most convincing?"

"I don't know anything about the case," she said.

"Do you feel there is any qualitative difference," Paul asked, "between the jurors' judgment, based on almost three years' scrutiny of the evidence, and your judgment, based on knowing nothing about the case?"

"There is no difference," she said. "They have their opinion and I have mine."

We went home and turned on all three television sets in the hope of not missing anything. For the next several days both the network and local television stations pumped out one of the most massive propaganda campaigns of all time. Once again Ray was tried, convicted, and hanged in the media. Nationwide television talk shows presented only the mob spokespersons and packed the audience section with their followers, allowing a few words of input from the defense in a pretense of "balance." The defense people were generally drowned out by the howling vigilantes. Could all of the people in the mass media have been that uniformly stupid? Paul found that difficult to believe. It seemed more likely that they were just obeying orders. But in whose name were the orders given?

After the verdicts were read and court was adjourned, the reporters were allowed to interview the jurors. One of them, when asked why he didn't believe the children, said, "One of the kids said that Ray Buckey killed a horse with a baseball bat. I just figured that to do that, and get rid of the carcass, he would have to be a genius."

What saved Ray and Peggy was the presence, on the jury, of several exceptionally intelligent people. One of them was a Ph.D. Another was a scientist who apparently knew something about logic. Another was the black woman who laughed at the prosecutors and their witnesses. Apparently they were able to convince the others that the evidence required to find the defendants guilty beyond a reasonable doubt did not exist. The media generally ignored these jurors and focused on the minority, the two who voted to convict Ray, even though, on the thirteen deadlocked counts, the overwhelming majority of the jurors voted to acquit him. But one of the jurors, a young woman, said "I'm sorry if the world isn't happy with the verdict, but they weren't there. That was me in there for two and a half years, and I can live with it."

One reporter was told by some of the jurors that if they had known of the insanity of Judy Johnson, the woman who launched the case, they would almost certainly have voted "not guilty" on all counts.

We watched the "Geraldo" show and Paul saw Bob Currie saying, "This was a Satan-worship, devil-worship case." At the bottom of the screen, throughout the program, there was a caption which strongly proclaimed the guilt of Ray and Peggy:

THE McMARTIN OUTRAGE
WHAT WENT WRONG?

The audience was packed with the Manhattan Beach mob. In another pretense of "balance," Peggy Ann was allowed to say a few words on the show. She said that if the jurors had been allowed to hear the whole story, "they would have been out for two hours and come back with all not guilty verdicts." She was drowned out by the howling spectators who shouted insults at her. In fairness to Geraldo Rivera, it must be said that Oprah Winfrey and Sally Jessy Raphael were far worse in terms of one-sided, proprosecution bias.

Not all of the print media were as irresponsible as the television carnivals. Even the *New York Times* denounced Lael Rubin's "graceless, unprofessional" remarks after the verdicts were read, and D.A. Ira Reiner's comment on NBC's "Today" show that "It is very clear to us that these defendants are guilty."

On local television we were shown a demonstration in Manhattan Beach in which large numbers of people marched with picket signs demanding that Ray be retried. But that kind of event does not occur without leaders. Who instigated the march?

We were also shown, on television, a large stack of boxes that the district attorney's office purported to be five thousand letters demanding that Ray be retried, but an acquaintance who is employed by the D.A.'s office privately told us that the boxes were stuffed.

The following evening we were invited to a conference of psychologists and other mental health professionals. They had read our book and wanted us to speak. When we had finished speaking and returned to our table, several people asked us the familiar question: "You don't really think those people are innocent, do you?" Once again we went over the case, trying to explain it to them. A blonde woman who is a noted psychologist spoke.

"Paul. Shirley. I have an idea." Her eyes were wide with enthusiasm. "After your book is published, why don't you write another book that says they're guilty?"

Four

The Retrial

After the case had consumed over six years, nearly sixteen million dollars, started with over two hundred counts and concluded without one guilty verdict, one would think that any sane, civilized community would end it and let the defendants get what's left of their lives back together. But it was not to be. Too many people had too much to lose and they were not willing to accept defeat. On January 31, 1990, the prosecutors announced that they would go forward on the thirteen deadlocked counts and retry Buckey.

Ray was interviewed on the Larry King television talk show and when King made the comment that, "You're thirty-one. By the time this is over you'll probably be thirty-three or thirty-four," Ray replied, "I think I'll probably be forty before it all comes down." He recalled that jury selection alone, in this last trial, took six months, and that the trial was expected to last for a year. He observed that all of the proceedings had lasted far longer than the lawyers predicted. An article in the *Los Angeles Times* stated that the case "will stretch out for years to come." By that time the the children would be adults.

The media continued to pump out proprosecution propaganda, conveying the message that the guilty had gone unpunished. No mention was made of the fact that everything possible was done to tip the balance in favor of a guilty verdict.

Certainly the police letter of September 8, 1983, was a shining example of reckless, malicious incompetence, and the CII "evaluations" were equally irresponsible and unprofessional. But a large share of the responsibility for this atrocity must be laid at the door of the media reporters whose desire to surpass their competitors motivated them to fabricate even more lurid, revolting horror stories. It was as though they were all working under the direction of the same editor: the prosecutor. A truly competent journalist would have seen that the real scoop was in debunking the whole absurd story. A journalist of first-rate mind could have blown this thing apart in less than a month. American journalism has had some very gifted virtuosos among its ranks: Edward R. Murrow, who broke the power of Joe McCarthy, and I. F. Stone, who questioned everything and shed light where there had been dangerous ignorance. But they are gone.

It was not that the truth was inaccessible. Defense lawyers Forrest Latiner and Walter Urban shared their knowledge generously, as did Dr. Lee Coleman and other defense experts.

But sin sells, and the yuppie reporters wanted stories of blood-drinking demons raping and butchering babies. The fact that they just might be consigning innocent, gentle people to prison for the rest of their lives was of no interest.

A study of the media coverage of the case conducted by the professors from Duke University disclosed that the *Los Angeles Times* reported the prosecution's point of view over the defense's by a ratio of about 14 to 1. Television was far more lopsided. The television newspeople commented on the case as though there was not the remotest doubt of the defendants' guilt. One of the most disgusting examples of uncritical prejudgment was broadcast on ABC's "20/20" program, in which one host asked, "How deeply marked are these children? Will they ever recover from it?" The reporter replied, "Psychologically, perhaps never."

The Buckeys' chances of getting a fair trial were dismal, almost nonexistent.

"I cannot believe that nearly everybody could be so feeble-minded as to buy into those spectacular horror stories without some doubts or questions," Paul told one of the defense attorneys from another, similar case who had come to see and hear the big climactic event.

"Most of those people out there are like algae," he said. "Those little tiny green organisms that grow in stale water. They just go with the flow. They don't ask questions. They don't swim upstream. Americans are not taught to think."

As the media pumped out their revolting stories in a tone that said there was no doubt of their authenticity, Walter Urban prepared a full-page newspaper advertisement characterizing the McMartin case as a recrudescence of the seventeenth-century witch trials. The *Los Angeles Times* refused to publish the ad.

Immediately after hearing the verdicts and witnessing the massive media propaganda campaign telling the world that the wicked had gone unpunished, Los Angeles County Supervisor Mike Antonovich publicly proclaimed that the children had been denied justice and demanded that the D.A.'s office refile the thirteen deadlocked counts. Other local politicians similarly began posturing for votes by riding the tide of public indignation over the acquittals. Lael Rubin told Judge Pounders, a few days later, that the prosecution would go forward with the unresolved counts. It was Reiner's decision.

It was purely a political decision. There was no reason to believe that the D.A.'s office would be more successful in a second trial. Some of the parents indicated they would not be willing to have their children testify again. Even on the thirteen undecided counts, the overwhelming majority of the jurors voted to acquit. But Reiner was running for election as state attorney general, and Attorney General John Van De Camp was running for governor. There was really no other plausible explanation for the retrial than the fact that Reiner was running for election and the public still believed Buckey was guilty—even though most of the people in Los Angeles County knew little or nothing about the case.

Senior deputies in the district attorney's office advised Reiner against putting Ray through a second trial after failing to win a single guilty verdict out of one hundred counts in the longest, costliest trial in history. But if they could get just one conviction on one count, it would take the heat off Reiner and the entire judicial system, and vitiate the massive lawsuits filed by former defendants. It would permanently brand Ray as a convicted child molester and somewhat vindicate the child abuse industry, the obsessive fanatics who saw molesters hiding under every bedspread, the nationwide community of child sexual abuse racketeers whose ambition and greed were out of control and whose intelligence and abilities were not equal to the difficult, complicated task of child protection: the new child abuse units that had sprung up everywhere, seeded by copious federal funding.

The massive, saturation campaign, followed by the refiling of the thirteen deadlocked counts, reminded us of the civil war in the Dominican Republic in the early 1960s when, under pressure from the United States, the military dictatorship agreed to hold elections but announced, later, that if the democratic opposition party won, they would not be allowed to take office. It also reminded us of the time Paul played poker with some small-time, New York thugs and won, but when he rose to leave he was told he would not be allowed to leave until he lost the money he had won. Asked about his motives for refiling the counts, Reiner hotly denied any political motivation. "We don't want to get involved in that," he snapped. But the media reported that a day or two before Reiner had dropped several points in the polls against his closest opponent, Arlo Smith. What were Reiner and Van De Kamp to do? They could have taken the risky step of facing the public and telling them the simple truth that there was not enough evidence to convict Ray. But they would have run the risk of sacrificing their careers. They preferred to sacrifice Ray.

Lael Rubin and Roger Gunson were taken off the case. Rubin was transferred to Santa Monica, hardly a step up the ladder of career advancement. Judge Pounders was replaced by Judge Stanley M. Weisberg, who was a deputy district attorney for eighteen years and who prosecuted Marvin Pancoast for the murder of Vicki Morgan, mistress of Alfred Bloomingdale, another case that left in its wake a lot of unanswered questions. A deputy county counsel described Weisberg as a judge who was "willing to listen to kids and give them credibility."

Two new prosecutors were picked for McMartin II: Pam Ferraro and Joe Martinez. Martinez was a twenty-three-year veteran of the district attorney's office, a former child abuse social worker with Catholic Charities of New York, and a former military officer. He had a reputation for winning cases characterized as "sure losers" by other prosecutors. Martinez told a reporter, "Lael Rubin and Roger Gunson wanted out." Ferraro was a Wellesley graduate who had majored in philosophy and was regarded by other attorneys as an accomplished trial lawyer.

What saved the Buckeys in the first trial was the fact that, even though the jurors felt the pressure of ignorant public opinion everywhere they went, they were given a long, long look at the evidence, which forced them to conclude that the evidence just wasn't there. The system was not going to let that happen again. The supervising judge of the Los Angeles Superior Court announced that the second trial would go much faster. A crucial piece of evidence was the jury's viewing of the preschool and seeing how physically impossible the allegations were. That too would not happen again. The school was being demolished. And the prosecution dropped the most transparently untruthful witnesses, making it a less palpable deception. They wanted to dispatch Ray to prison as quickly and unceremoniously as possible, hoping it would soon be forgotten. And after the massive, pro-prosecution propaganda campaign in the media it would be extremely difficult if not impossible to assemble an impartial jury. Defense attorneys Davis and Gits announced that they would file complaints against prosecutor Lael Rubin with the California State Bar Association alleging that she knew George Freeman was lying and had a long history of committing perjury when she put him on the stand as a witness, and also that she unfairly blocked the release on bail of Ray and Peggy Buckey.

On Wednesday, March 6, 1990, five of the remaining counts against Ray were dismissed. Ray's attorney argued against dismissing the counts because doing so would preclude the defense from presenting to the jury the full story of how the case began and the insanity of the mother who had launched the marathon case.

On March 26, the U.S. Supreme Court refused to hear the appeal of a lawsuit by Virginia and Peggy Ann contending that CII and the prosecutors conspired to fabricate evidence against them. Other appellate courts had held that those who reported or prosecuted any person for child abuse had total immunity from both civil and criminal liability—even if the report was made in malice, with full knowledge that it was false.

In a television interview Ray said that the three children on the prosecution's witness list were the weakest witnesses in the case. He said he still feared the instinctive reaction of "where there's smoke, there's fire." "But," he said, "you fight because you have to." Kee MacFarlane was not on the prosecution's witness list, but there is very little doubt that she would be called by the defense. Astrid Heger was slated to be a prosecution witness. Jurors in the first trial stated, after the verdict, that they were not impressed with her. One of the children who would testify was Veronica. The first jury acquitted Buckey on a charge that he put a pencil in her anus.

Peggy Buckey and two other family members filed a lawsuit against Bob Currie, who appeared on innumerable television talk shows during the week after the acquittals, for making "false, malicious and slanderous statements." He had accused Peggy and Virginia of exposing themselves to him.

Jury selection began on April 8 and after two weeks, twelve jurors and six alternates were impaneled. Of the twelve jurors, three were black, one Asian, half college graduates. Seven were parents.

Arlo Smith, Reiner's opponent in the California Primary election for the Democratic nomination for attorney general, called for a grand jury investigation into Reiner's decision to retry Buckey, saying that the decision was purely political. The retrial had not helped Reiner's campaign. He was now being bashed by both sides. The mob was calling the retrial a "sham," and a "charade." Reiner had been far ahead of Smith only a few weeks before, but he had now fallen behind him in the polls.

The militant parents began an investigation of their own. They were digging up the McMartin school yard again, looking for secret tunnels and satanic caverns. They hired former FBI investigator Ted Gunderson and a contractor with a backhoe to dig up the yard. They found a plastic bag with some Walt Disney characters printed on it.

Monday, May 7, 1990. The trial began with opening statements. In violation of the California rules of court, Judge Weisberg forbade tape recorders in the courtroom. Martinez gave a brief opening statement. He confused the names of two of the principal witnesses and told the jurors that the preschool was in Redondo Beach. He also told the jurors that a certain symptom defined by prosecution doctors as a sign of sexual abuse was found in one of the children's vagina. This particular symptom is found only in the anus. Martinez was definitely not "up to speed," not prepared for trial. He did not know the case.

Martinez said in his opening statement that the McMartin Preschool had enjoyed a good reputation but that, "Things began to change when Ray Buckey came into the picture." He stated that parents of the child witnesses began to notice changes in their children's behavior such as nightmares, reluctance to go to school, diaper rashes. These he defined as symptoms of molestation. He said the prosecution would prove its case with the testimony of three girls, their parents, the physicians who examined them, and the videotaped interviews at CII. He said that witnesses would testify that Ray did not wear underwear and that he read *Playboy* magazine.

Davis began by correcting Martinez's misstatement of the names of key witnesses and told the jury that the preschool was in Manhattan Beach, not Redondo Beach. He said that the three girls were so brainwashed by CII, "therapists," and parents into believing they had been molested that "the truth never had a chance." He said that the letter sent out to two hundred parents by the police identifying Ray Buckey as a molestation suspect eradicated all opportunity to get to the truth of the matter. He went on to say that the doctor who examined the children at CII, Astrid Heger, was unqualified in the area of child abuse evaluation and grossly biased, and used examination techniques that have since been proven faulty.

Davis stated that the woman in charge of interviewing the McMartin children had nothing more than a welder's license and experience in writing grant proposals.

"These women were giving therapy to children who were saying it didn't happen!" Davis said. He said the CII interviewers confirmed the parents' worst fears by telling them, "Your child was a victim of molestation." He said the children were manipulated and coerced into implicating Ray and "we aim to prove everything that followed CII was so tainted with the processes of the puppet lady that even today it is impossible to separate fact from fiction."

During Davis's opening statement Martinez was working on a crossword puzzle. Opening statements were surprisingly brief. During the mid-morning recess, John Wagner, Davis's co-counsel, came over, greeted us, and shook our hands.

"I'm really glad that you're in this case!" Paul told him. "It'll give the trial some class." He was an extremely eloquent lawyer.

"Don't sell Davis short," he said. "He's a very smart lawyer."

"I know that," Paul answered. "But the two of you have very different styles, and you are stronger together than one of you would be alone."

"What do you think of this so far?" he asked.

"It's unreal. It's a rerun."

"Well," he said. "You and I both know that if Reiner wasn't running for election we wouldn't even be here."

In an interview with reporters during recess, Davis called the prosecution's case "a kamikaze run." "They've bolted them in. There's no gas for a return trip." Martinez was quoted as calling Davis's remark "racist."

The mother of the first child witness scheduled to testify for the prosecution was sworn in. She told the court that her daughter never complained about the school or Ray until the investigation and the attendant publicity began. Before that, the girl seemed to like Ray, the mother said. She said she saw rashes in her child's anal and vaginal area during the time she attended the preschool, not before or after. This statement was inconsistent with her testimony in the preliminary hearing.

Asked if she was informed of Kee MacFarlane's credentials, or her lack of credentials, the woman simply stated that she was told by a friend that this was "the place to go." She acknowledged that she attended the mass meetings led by the prosecutors. She also testified that Kee MacFarlane told her, after the CII interview, that her daughter had been sodomized and raped. She said that Astrid Heger told her there was physical evidence of rape. She said she was told to support the child and not question the truthfulness of these allegations, and was proffered a list of therapists for her child. When Davis asked her, "Did you get a second opinion?" the woman said she had not.

Asked if her daughter appeared on a television show about the case, she stated that, "Lael asked her to go on TV," and got them on television.

In the afternoon, a videocassette recorder and television monitors were set up for the showing of the girl's CII interview. There were no spontaneous disclosures. In the interview, the child said she liked Ray the best of the teachers and denied witnessing any improper sexual conduct by him. The interviewer, using a doll with a vagina, continued to narrow the focus to the doll's genital area. The girl put the Ray doll's hand on the female doll's chest, nose, face, and back. "All the kids told us," the interviewer told her, repeatedly directing her to the genitals until she understood what was being required of her, finally complying by pointing to the genital area. "Your mom and dad are going to be so proud that you helped us figure out the secrets!" the interviewer exclaimed.

The child, sitting in the courtroom watching this, was laughing. On the television screen, the interviewer continued to prod the child: "I was hoping you could help us figure out this stuff. Maybe you can show us what touched [you]. What went in there? That would be a great secret gone in the secret machine." The interviewer kept asking leading sexual questions, but was getting little out of the child. She repeatedly denied being molested or witnessing any such act at the preschool, and when asked if she heard Ray threaten the children, she said, "No, my dad just told me that."

Wednesday, May 9, 1990. Defense attorneys Davis and Wagner asked the judge to issue an order prohibiting the demolition of the McMartin Preschool by the new owners. The judge said he was not sure he had jurisdiction to issue such an order. The new owners had been served subpoenas for the hearing but did not show up.

The first child witness whose CII video was shown the day before denied the two specific acts that were her two counts against Buckey! Ray was charged with putting his penis into her vagina and rectum. It would seem reasonable to assume that those two counts would be dismissed, but prosecutor Martinez asserted that he would present medical evidence to rehabilitate the charge that the girl was raped. The girl also denied other accusations she had made. During the preliminary hearing she accused all seven defendants of molesting her, but now she said she did not remember the women teachers doing this. She said she believed Ray molested all of the children at the preschool, but never saw saw him abuse a single child.

This child was on the stand for the rest of the day. Most of her answers were "I don't know," and "I don't remember." She was asked, during cross-examination, "Do you believe he took naked pictures of all the children at the preschool?"

"Yes . . . I know they were molested."

"How do you know?"

"I was at the school."

"Did you see children molested?"

"No."

"Six years ago at the preliminary hearing you said nothing happened to the turtle. Today you say it was stabbed. Which is the truth?"

"Today I believe it."

There was a fifteen-minute break. After the break, at three o'clock, the judge announced that the child was too tired to continue. Court was recessed until the following morning.

The angry band of parents were still digging up the McMartin school yard. They found part of a broken milk bottle but no tunnels. A neighbor who lived next to the preschool told reporters that Gunderson, the former FBI agent bossing the dig, had come to the door to search his home and go through his closets. "What do they do if you say no?" the neighbor asked. "Do you become a suspect?"

In the morning, the girl repeatedly answered, "I can't remember" to questions about previous statements she had made accusing Buckey of molesting her. Fifteen minutes after Davis's cross-examination had begun she suddenly asked, "May I be excused? I have a stomach ache." The girl had told her parents and prosecutors that she did not want to return the second day. There was a lengthy recess. Defense attorney Davis demanded that the prosecutor remove the distressed child from the stand, and return her to the security of her parents, which he refused to do. Apparently the prosecution wanted the jurors to see the girl in that condition. She was persuaded to return to the stand and, again, most of her answers were "I can't remember." Davis asked about her meeting with prosecutor Pam Ferraro prior to testifying.

"They told you that Ray touched all the children, didn't they?"

"I don't remember."

This was the witness the prosecution had touted as powerful, new evidence that would greatly bolster its case. Davis, outside the courtroom, told reporters, "Why she's here is a mystery."

At two forty-five, a videotape of the second girl slated to testify was played. It began with MacFarlane and the girl sitting on a sofa with the dolls. Kee drew a line drawing of a human body and then focused on the sexual parts.

"Do you know anyone who doesn't wear panties?" she asked.

"Sometimes I don't."

"Anyone else?"

"Daddy when he takes a shower."

"Haven't you seen anyone naked at the school?"

"No."

"MacFarlane stripped a doll naked and asked, "Who's that?"

"That's Barbie."

The girl was shown a large doll with a vagina and asked if anything ever went in her vagina. She repeatedly denied that anything went in her vagina.

"Did anything happen to other kids?"
"No."
The screen went white. The show was over. We were in recess until morning. Some of the jurors were laughing as they departed.

The next witness, a young woman who asked that her name not be published, testified briefly that she had worked at the preschool when she was seventeen years old, and that she had never seen any evidence of molestation. Prosecutor Ferraro asked, "What did he wear?" She replied that he usually wore shorts and that she had once seen his penis, but that he never intentionally exposed his genitals. "I was embarrassed for Ray," she said. She also testified that she had never seen any "naked pictures" taken at the school.

After this witness was excused, the prosecution played a CII videotape of Veronica, the girl slated to testify next, after her parents. It was short. MacFarlane brought out a bunch of dolls, designated as Peggy and Ray.

Veronica: "This is me and dad and mom."

MacFarlane: "No, this is Ray and Peggy. . . . Did Ray put his penis in you?"

Veronica: "No."

MacFarlane: "Did you see Ray do it to other kids?"

Veronica: "No."

When the tape ended it was still mid-morning, but the prosecution did not have another witness available and the judge recessed the court until Monday, May 21. Ferraro asked the court's permission to take a videotape out of the building to show the witness. The judge said it was okay but there would have to be a witness to the viewing, other than a parent or someone from the D.A.'s office. Davis said, "The only problem I have with that is that in the past, [Det.] Gusty Bell went to the child witnesses' homes for hours and intentionally did not take notes."

The next week Davis told the *Los Angeles Daily Journal* that Ray had rejected a plea bargain offer from Reiner's office, "in rather colorful language." Previously, both sides had denied that a plea bargain had been discussed, but Davis told the *Daily Journal* that he had decided to publicly disclose the discussion out of anger at the way the prosecution was handling the case. Davis provided the *Daily Journal* with a surreptitiously recorded audio tape of the meeting. Reiner's opponent in the June 5 primary, Arlo Smith, seized upon this incident and said, "Do the voters of California want a liar or a lawyer as attorney general of California?"

According to another newspaper, Davis asked the prosecutors which counts they wanted Buckey to plead "no contest" to, and Ferraro answered, "You can pick whatever sex act you feel most comfortable with." In a televised debate with Smith, Reiner had said, "There has never been any offer whatsoever made in any form, directly or indirectly to Mr. Buckey's attorney."

Davis said, "I made an agreement to lie to the public and I'm ashamed of it.... I should have known it would turn into another hokey McMartin D.A. move.... Raymond Buckey is the only person who hasn't lied about this." Davis said he asked that Ray's charges be dismissed and that he be issued a public apology. He demanded that Reiner resign his candidacy for attorney general. When Ray had disclosed the plea bargain offer earlier, Martinez had called him "a liar."

"I'm not pleading guilty to something I didn't do," Buckey said. When Martinez became aware of the tape-recorded conversations he said, "This is getting really, really nasty."

On Monday, May 21, Judge Weisberg, before the jury was brought in, began by stating that a district attorney's investigator had called him while he was in New York and tried to set up a call between him and Ira Reiner. Weisberg was visibly angry and said the caller "stated that Ira Reiner wanted to talk with me the next morning and wanted to know if I would make myself available to receive a call. I personally cannot conceive of any reason why Mr. Reiner attempted to communicate with me *ex parte* (outside the presence of lawyers for the opposing side)." Weisberg said he refused to talk with Reiner.

Davis said, "For prosecutors or Mr. Reiner to conspire to have an *ex parte* communication about a pending case with the judge is not only unethical, [but] intolerable. To his credit the judge made a record of it. Somebody has to answer now why that was attempted.... If he's trying to mess with our judge then I want to know what he's up to."

A district attorney's spokesman offered the explanation that Reiner wanted to make a conference call with attorneys for both sides. But the media gave extensive coverage to the story, and Reiner was severely criticized. He had definitely gotten himself into a wringer.

The prosceution called Astrid Heger, the physician who examined the McMartin children, to the stand. Once again, she recited her curriculum vitae. She looked at the jurors and smiled.

"Are you a qualified child abuse expert?" Martinez asked.

"Yes." Heger said she had testified in seventy to eighty cases. She testified that she examined Veronica in 1984 at the request of the district attorney with the assistance of Dr. Bruce Woodling. Kee MacFarlane was present, she said, and she spoke with the mother, got the "history," and spoke with the child. Heger went off on a long discourse about the girl's interest in eyes and was cut off by objections. She said that Veronica had a 0.7 centimeter hymen. "There appears to be disruption or scarring ... transsection of the hymen at three o'clock, five o'clock and seven o'clock." She said the hymen was "rolled back."

There were no slides on this child. Heger said her physical findings were "consistent with blunt force trauma" and also "consistent" with sexual abuse.

Heger said she had also examined the next child slated to appear in the trial and that the exam revealed normal labia, neovascularization, a one-centimeter scar on the forchette, disruption of the hymen, and an anal scar seen microscopically. Heger said that her findings on this girl were "blunt force trauma," and that her diagnosis was "consistent with sexual abuse."

On the third girl Heger testified that she had examined her and that her hymenal opening was 0.6 to 0.7 centimeters, rounded, pushed back, and that she observed a linear scar of 0.6 centimeters, a six o'clock scar across the vagina and an anal scar of one-half centimeter. Her conclusion, Heger said, was "blunt force trauma consistent with sexual abuse."

"No further questions," Martinez concluded.

Davis began his cross-examination, "Assuming Linda was sodomized, when did the sodomy occur?"

"I have no idea."

"Did it happen at the McMartin Preschool?"

"I can't fix the exact time."

"Assuming the anal examination was four or five years later, when did this occur?"

"I can't time the injury."

"In 1984 did it tell you how old the scar was?"

"No. It depends on the fissure laceration."

"Did she have fissures?"

"No."

"Isn't it true that there were no standards of diagnosis in 1984?"

"Yes."

"Did you see any blood?"

"No."

Heger said she did not get any medical records from private physicians, just the "history" from the parents. She also said that the photographic slide of one of the girls was normal, and that she did not see any evidence of molestation on this child. Yet her diagnosis was also "consistent with sexual abuse."

"When you provide a measurement in centimeters, is it an important finding?" Davis asked.

"In my mind sexual abuse occurred," Heger replied. "I don't find hymenal openings important in sexual abuse."

Davis showed Heger a photograph of the genital area of one of the three girls and asked, "Was it a diagnostic finding?"

"I don't see anything indicating sexual abuse," Heger answered.

Davis asked Heger about measuring the vagina and about stretching and traction by the physician. "Is there a precise accuracy?"

"There's an error factor," Heger said. "I don't think it could be relied on." But Heger noted the diameters to the grand jury in 1984; it was her view then that a hymenal opening in excess of 0.4 centimeters was a finding of sexual abuse.

"Is it possible that your finding was consistent with normal?"

"Possible."

Ray looked worried. The jurors looked bewildered.

"Tell the jury what 'acute trauma' is," Davis asked.

"Within seventy-two hours."

"In your opinion are these acute?"

"Old," Heger answered. She stated that if a person had sodomy with a child the acute injury would heal and become an old injury within two to three weeks.

"Would you see signs after the event?"

"Depends on the injury." As the questions and answers went on it became apparent that Heger had relied more on the statements of the parents ("history") than anything else.

"Can children be mistaken about sexual abuse and say it happened when it really didn't happen?"

"Every study I've seen says that children don't fantasize about sex with an adult."

"After the exam, did you tell the parent that the child was molested?"

Heger's answer was equivocal and not responsive to the question.

"Do you rely on the history of the child when there's no physical findings?"

"Yes."

"Did any other doctors give a second opinion?"

"No."

"By and large, you testify for the D.A.?" Davis asked.

Heger's answer was, again, not responsive. She said that she testified "for the court." Davis asked her if there was anything in her past that would cause bias.

"Have you been a victim of molest[ation]?"

This time Heger answered, "No."

The next witness was the mother of Veronica, the youngest child in this case. During a brief direct examination by Martinez, she said she had received calls from the police department in 1983, and that when she visited the preschool there was "total chaos" in the room where Ray Buckey was teaching. "Children climbing on him! He was reading a *Playboy* magazine!"

The woman said she believed it was a "giant witch hunt" until she visited CII and was told that her child had been molested. On cross-examination she acknowledged that before the police communicated their accusation to her she had seen nothing that raised any suspicion of sexual misconduct at the school. She said, "The kids did love Ray," and that the school enjoyed a good reputation. She didn't like the way Ray was dressed, she said, and, "He didn't wear underwear!"

The woman admitted she had attended meetings in the community where the prosecutors and others were actively stirring up hysteria. She said she recalled that Kee MacFarlane was there. Asked if she got a second opinion about her daughter's alleged abuse, she answered, "I don't think so."

Davis asked her, "Did Kee tell you your daughter was molested?" The woman's answer was vague: "I think she felt something happened." There was a sense of unreality to the trial. It had all been said before. But all the players had polished up their dance to some degree, except for the prosecutors, who were new to the case and apparently had not been able to absorb the massive body of evidence and nonevidence.

Davis asked the mother, "Did you see [the CII videotape] in its entirety or just parts?"

"I can't answer that."

"Do you have any recollection what it was you saw that led you to believe your daughter was molested?"

"I don't remember."

The woman gave that answer over and over again in response to Davis's questions. He showed her the transcript of her preliminary hearing testimony. The answers did not match up with what she was saying in this trial.

Veronica was the next witness. She answered, "I don't remember" to almost all the questions. She did not remember who was present at the "naked movie star" game, what Ray Buckey was doing, whether or not he had a camera, what he said. She testified that she had learned of the "naked movie star" from her sister. She did not remember if she was required to take off her clothes; she did not remember whether she had ever told her mother; she did not remember whether Buckey was naked or clothed. She answered, "I don't remember" so many times we lost count. She said that when she played "horsey" with Ray, sometimes he was the rider.

Davis asked Veronica on cross-examination, "When he was [riding] on your back . . . did his body weight crush you to the floor?" Veronica made no reply.

Veronica stated that the man who molested her had a beard and a moustache. Davis asked her, "Any man who touched you in your private parts who did not have a beard or moustache?"

"No."

"There's no doubt in your mind?"

"No," she answered.

Virtually all of the witnesses had been asked whether they ever saw Ray Buckey at any time in his life with a beard or moustache. All of them answered in the negative. This would seem to be a serious problem for the prosecution, and it would suggest that the counts pertaining to Veronica would have to be dismissed, but deputy D.A. Martinez told reporters during a recess that Ray might have worn a beard for just a day or two and then shaved it off.

The problem with that is that fact that human hair grows only about an inch in two months and it takes several months to grow a full beard.

The girl told of being flown away on an airplane and taken to a "costume shop" where there were seven bathtubs, and where children took bubble baths and Ray wore a witch costume. Then, Veronica said, they were flown back to the preschool—all of this in three hours.

"You must have been pretty excited," Davis said. "Did you tell your mom and dad about the airplane ride?"

"No."

Davis read from the transcript of Veronica's CII interview, in which she denied experiencing any of the acts alleged in her counts against Ray. In her CII interview MacFarlane asked Veronica whose finger went into her bottom and she said, "You."

"And Kee told you what to say in court?" Davis asked.

"Yes."

"And you were going to say what Lael Rubin told you to say?"

"Yes."

"And you don't know if all those things are true?"

"No," Veronica answered.

The prosecution quickly called for a bench conference to block the line of questioning.

When they had finished with the girl, Martinez briefly recalled Veronica's mother to the stand and asked her what her child had said to her on the way home from CII. The woman put her hands over her face and sobbed, "She told me it went in her mouth." Minutes later, when the woman stood and left the stand, she was composed and her eyes were dry. Over the years, it has been our perception that people who are experiencing genuine grief do not quickly turn it on and off.

The next witness to be called by the prosecution was the father of the third and final child witness. Asked if he ever saw anything that led him to believe children were being molested at McMartin, he said no. Davis asked him, "You filed a lawsuit against McMartin . . . against Ray Buckey as well. . . . Would it be your hope to get money in that lawsuit?"

"No. Just to make sure he gets put in jail."

The man's wife was called to the stand and told of being called by the police and told of the "investigation." The woman said that her daughter had rashes in her vaginal area and that she had been told by a pediatrician that they were probably caused by bubble baths, her underwear, or by rubbing. The woman said she had had no belief that her daughter was molested before going to CII and being told that her daughter had been sexually abused. She said that the rashes appeared only while her child was attending the preschool. However, in the last trial the woman had said the rashes were present before the girl attended the school.

Asked if she observed any suspicious "sexualized behavior" by her daughter, the woman said she had observed the girl with her sister in the "sixty-nine" position, that they were touching and licking each other, and that, another time, she saw the girl putting a tinkertoy inside her vagina. She said that her pediatrician told her it was within the range of normal behavior and that she should just "tell her not to do it."

"Do you believe all the teachers were molesting children?" Davis asked the woman.

"I know it was a fact."

Asked if she had ever seen the entire tape of her daughter's CII interview, the woman said no, she didn't want to see it. She, too, had attended the party to celebrate the arrest of Ray Buckey.

After the witness was excused the prosecution showed the videotape of her daughter's CII interview. It followed the same script as the others: "We thought you could help us because we know that you know the secrets." The girl replied: "I don't remember anything that happened there." She was shown photographs and asked to "point to the people" who scared her.

"I've been talking to all the kids and they told us all the secrets," the interviewer, Sandra Krebs, said. "Mr. Ray has a secret policeman that watches him all the time.... What about the 'naked movie star'?"

"No, I never played that."

"You know all about this stuff, Mr. Pickle. We're getting rid of so many yucky secrets . . . we're so proud of [you]!" Krebs said.

There were dolls all over the place and the interviewer put the Ray doll on top of the others in a position suggesting pederasty or vaginal intercourse. She kept asking the same questions over and over. "What parts did Miss Peggy touch? Right on the vagina? Did that hurt? What a stinker! Let's punch her."

"Can you pick up the Ray doll and show us what it looked like when Ray hurt [you]?" The child twirled the doll with her hand. She did not understand what was being required of her. Krebs kept prodding her to put the two dolls together, then heaped praise on her and told her she had gotten rid of a secret. When the tape ended we were put in recess until morning.

For weeks the militant band of parents had been digging up the McMartin school yard in a last-ditch effort to find the labyrinthine network of tunnels some of the children described at CII and the preliminary hearing. The diggers' said they found veins of debris. The head of the operation said the veins of debris were evidence of a network of tunnels that had existed under the school and been filled in. But how would the perpetrators have removed tons of soil and then replaced it without being seen? Paul Barron, a private investigator, said, tentatively, that what they had unearthed were really "old shitholes." The preschool was situated on what was once a farm with horse stables. The *Los Angeles Times* did not interview anyone from the defense and repeatedly referred to the site as "the infamous McMartin Preschool."

374 The Abuse of Innocence

No evidence was found. But the media reported the story, implying that something very sinister had been discovered, so much so that we received many telephone calls from people asking if it was true. A woman sitting next to us in the courtroom spoke during a recess and said, "Did you hear? They found the tunnels! It was in the papers!"

"Tunnels!" Paul snorted. "You can be sure that if they had found any substantive, credible evidence, there would have been banner headlines on all the newspapers. Every TV program would have been interrupted with an abrasive news bulletin, the prosecution would have reopened and brought in the evidence, and the jury would have been bussed down to the preschool to see it for themselves!"

"I never thought about that," she said.

We saw some of these vigilantes sitting in the back of the courtroom watching us darkly and felt the chilling presence of evil.

On Tuesday a bulldozer arrived and crushed Virginia McMartin's beautiful nursery school to rubble, along with the gifted Charles Buckey's artifacts and toys, made with his own hands and tools. It was a house filled with love and beauty, to which the family had given their entire adult lives. It was cleared away for the construction of an office building.

Neighbors were interviewed by the media. They said they were greatly relieved by the demolition of the preschool. It had stood for seven years as a silent testament to their guilt, their silence, their cowardice, their failure to come to the aid of a neighbor falsely accused and persecuted.

Thursday morning, May 31, 1990. The third and final child witness took the stand. By this time she was thirteen, almost fourteen years old. In a dramatic cross-examination she recanted her sexual abuse accusations against Peggy Buckey. In the last trial she had testified that Peggy sexually assaulted her. From the stand she said, with considerable force, that Peggy never molested her! Her statements differed radically from her testimony in prior proceedings.

The girl's three counts alleged that Ray molested her while she was sitting on his lap. Now she said that Ray had been lying on his back. "Ray was on the floor and I got on top of him." She also said that Ray had been naked. Previously she had said he was clothed. She said that Ray cut off the ears of a rabbit with scissors. In the first trial she said he did it with a large knife. There were many inconsistencies. She did not remember the color of the rabbit, nor did she remember anything about the preschool.

In the preliminary hearing the girl had testified that nobody put anything into her vagina, her mouth, or her "bottom." Davis scored some big points when he asked, "You talked to us about his touching your vagina with his penis. Are you saying it went inside?"

"Yes," the girl answered. The hymenal opening of a three-year-old is so tiny that if an erect, adult penis had been put through it she would have been ripped to shreds, bleeding profusely, and screaming.

The girl also testified that Ray undressed and took off his underwear—the underwear that countless hours of testimony had darkly established he never wore.

After the child was excused, the prosecution briefly recalled the mother, in an attempt to rehabilitate her credibility. The mother began weeping and screamed at Ray, "I'm so angry at you I could kill you right now!" Court was recessed for the day.

Friday, the prosecution rested after only thirteen days of testimony. This brought cries of outrage from the militant parents.

On Tuesday, June 5, 1990, the district attorney, Ira Reiner, lost his bid for the Democratic nomination for attorney general in the California primary election, and Attorney General John Van De Kamp lost by a considerable margin to San Francisco Mayor Diane Feinstein for the party's nomination for governor. At the outset, Reiner had been running far ahead of his opponent. Spokespersons for both sides, including Reiner, said they believed the McMartin case was Reiner's undoing. It is not unreasonable to suppose that if Reiner and Van De Kamp had been more forthright about the case, they might have finished stronger.

On the same day, Judge Weisberg refused to dismiss five counts against Ray after attorney Davis argued that they were not supported by testimony from the two girls. The judge ruled that the inconsistencies in the testimony were not sufficient cause to dismiss the charges. However, he noted that Davis could use the discrepancies to attack the prosecution's credibility in his closing arguments.

The first defense witness to be called was Virginia McMartin, now eighty-two. On the stand she was as defiant and outspoken as ever. When Davis asked her about the "naked movie star" game she said, "Until this witch hunt started, I had never heard of it." She answered, "Never!" and "Heavens no!" when asked about alleged sexual improprieties at the preschool. She said she had never seen Ray taking nude photographs of children. As the questions and answers progressed she began offering her own thoughts about the case, and the judge cut her off.

"Oh, so you're not allowing freedom of speech in this courtroom, either. I'm so glad to know there's no First Amendment." The judge did not respond. When Davis had no further questions, Virginia asked if she could ask questions. The judge said no.

"I just wanted to know when the Angels game starts," she said cheerily. When the lawyers gathered at sidebar for a bench conference, Virginia began talking to the jurors about baseball. The judge tersely told her to be quiet.

On cross-examination prosecutor Martinez asked Virginia if she thought it was appropriate for her grandson to wear shorts without underwear, allowing his genitals to be seen. She said, "With modern bathing suits I don't know how the kids could help but see everything." Martinez had a formidable stack of documents to refer to in his cross-examination, but after only a few minutes he ended his cross-examination. Outside the courtroom he told reporters he had shown Virginia to be a "biased, prejudiced witness" who was trying to protect her grandson. "Why go on?" he shrugged. At least Virginia got the jurors' attention and started the defense presentation with a lively day.

The next court day began with the lawyers arguing before the jury was brought in. The argument was over whether the defense should be required to disclose to the prosecution the identity of defense witnesses in advance. Davis did not object to disclosing names of regular witnesses but did not intend to reveal the names of expert witnesses because "during the last trial, our expert witnesses were threatened with loss of funding and the loss of their chairs."

The defense called Charles Buckey, Ray's father. Davis went over the various parts and measurements of the school in minute detail, boring but necessary material needed to lay a foundation for questions to follow. Charles Buckey was involved in the construction of the school and drew the plans. He also designed and built his own home. A videotape was shown of the school as it looked in 1983, with children and teachers there. Chuck Buckey built the wooden toys. There was indeed one tunnel at the school—a wooden tunnel he had built, a play tunnel. Asked if any animals had died at the school, he said there were two dead turtles. "They hibernated in the winter." He said that they had not been injured or damaged in any way. He put one of the dead turtles up on the roof, he said, hoping that the soft tissue would disintegrate and they would have an intact turtle shell for the children to see in the school.

"To frighten children?" Davis asked.

"No."

"Any birds at the school?"

"I built a big aviary for the school in 1970, but somebody broke in and stole all the birds so we gave the aviary away." Buckey also said that there were no locks on the bathroom doors.

"I have no further questions," Davis concluded.

Martinez cross-examined. He asked Buckey where he was employed. The witness replied that he had been employed at Hughes Aircraft for forty years.

"What do you do there?"

"I'm an experimental test engineer."

"What does that mean?"

"Hughes builds many components and systems for the government. I see that they function."

"Any for aircraft?"

"Yes."

"Do you go out and see these things fly?"
"I never left the building to see these things fly."
"Were you acquainted with the pilots who flew them?"
"No. I knew who they were but I was not acquainted with them."

An investigator from the D.A.'s office brought into the room a large box and took out something that looked like an old, primitive cash register with lots of buttons and lights. It was red. "Have you ever seen this before?" Martinez asked.

"I made it."
"What is it?"
"A problem toy."

Buckey explained that you have to press the right combination of buttons, or switches, to make all the lights go off.

"Does it require adults?"
"No. Children catch on quicker than adults."

Davis, on recross, asked: "Was this an instrument of torture, to torture children?" The jurors broke into boisterous laughter.

"Is it possible that while you were working at Hughes, you and Ray flew a bunch of children away in an airplane?"

"I'm not a pilot. Ray is not a pilot. It was a private airport."

The next witness was Babette Spitler. She taught at McMartin from September 1973 to June 1976 and then again from July 1980 to January 1984. She had three children, Wendy, nineteen, and Chad, fourteen, and one, who was much younger. She said Ray was there when Chad was at the preschool. Chad started in 1981 and quit in 1983. She said Ray started as an aide, or helper, and later had his own class. She said she never saw children molested at the preschool or photographed while naked.

"Did you permit others to molest children?"
"Never."
"Ever see Ray Buckey dressed as a witch?"
"No. The teachers didn't dress up for the Hallowe'en parade."
"Did Ray Buckey ever come in and take Linda out of the class?"
"No."
"Veronica?"
"No."
"Could he have spirited them away?"
"No. Children were watched very carefully."
"Ever see Ray Buckey with a beard or a moustache?"
"No."

Spitler said she could hear what was going on in Ray's room, which was adjacent to hers. "You could hear through the heater."

"Ever hear screams?"
"No."

"Noise?"
"Yes."
"Ever go in the next room?"
"Yes. I asked them to quiet down. Kids were running around and laughing. Betty's class was very disciplined. Ray's was not."
"Ever see anybody mistreat children?"
"No. There was just not enough control."
"Were games ever played where adults crawled around on all fours on the floor?"
"Yes."
"Did you?"
"Yes."
"Was Veronica in the class?"
"Yes."
"Without her clothes on?"
"No." Spitler said that she often assisted children in the bathroom when she had the youngest class.
"Would that involve some contact with private parts?"
"When they had bowel movements, yes."
"Ever hear the 'naked movie star' chant at McMartin Preschool?"
"No."
"Did you ever see Peggy Buckey in her bra and panties? In a state of undress?"
"No."
"Ever see children crying?"
"Yes."
"Did you associate that with mistreatment of children?"
"No."
"What was done to punish unruly children?"
"They were 'benched' for five minutes."
"Ever see Ray Buckey tied to a door?"
"No."
"Were there any rope games at the preschool?"
"Yes."

Spitler told of games played where the children stood in a circle holding a rope. She went on to describe various games played with music where children hopped and imitated animals. She was extremely gentle and charming, precisely the kind of person one would want to care for their children! Like Chuck Buckey, she had a kind of radiant wholesomeness and her answers were short, direct, and forthright. She was a very good witness. Spitler went on to say that her children were videotaped at CII, and that her daughter refused to be examined by Astrid Heger. Spitler has a degree in early childhood education.

"Did you ever see Ray Buckey harm [the three girls] in any way?"

"No."
"Was there a game played called the 'alligator game'?"
"No."
"Did children engage in sexual acts with Ray Buckey?"
"No."
"Did you ever see Ray Buckey tied to any part of the preschool while naked?"
"No."
"I have no further questions."

Pam Ferraro began her cross-examination by asking, "How was it you became affiliated with McMartin Preschool?" Spitler explained that she was looking for a school to put her daughter in. She said that she had taken courses in psychology, seminars in child abuse, and worked at a well-known child abuse clinic where she counseled and worked with abused children.

"Including sexual abuse?" Ferraro asked.
"Yes."
"Were you taught to recognize the signs of sexual abuse?"
"Yes."

Spitler said that her eldest daughter came and worked as a helper with Peggy and Ray and that she worked in close proximity to Ray. There were many questions to ascertain whether she could see Ray and his group at all times, the position and height of the windows.

Thursday morning, June 7, 1990. Before the jury was brought in there were arguments over the issue of whether the videotape f the CII interview of Chad Spitler, Babette's fourteen-year-old son, could be shown to the jury. Davis said the tape showed that Spitler's children were pressured to accuse their own parents. He said that the interview with Chad was different because CII was really out to "get" his mother. "Chad comes out of this interview with mixed feelings. He's told, after the interview, that not only his sister but he, too, was molested. . . . These people are trying to crush the recollections of these children. . . . [Kee MacFarlane] is going to have to be confronted with what she did."

Ferraro protested, "We're going to be trying CII instead of the defendant." It seemed reasonable to assume that CII's credibility was in question.

Ferraro continued her cross-examination after the jurors were herded back into the courtroom. The questions focused on whether or not Ray could be observed at all times.

"Did you ever see Ray Buckey having organized activity?"
"Yes. Art, collage, painting, music . . ."
"Alligator?"
"No."
"Games accompanied by music and songs?"

"Yes."

Spitler said she had never heard of the "naked movie star" game from her children or anybody else at the time. She said that parents often came in and picked up their children early, adding further doubt to the possibility that teachers could have molested children at the preschool without being detected.

Then Ferraro walked into a devastating haymaker. She asked Spitler about being arrested and held in jail. Spitler said it was the worst experience of her life. Ferraro then asked her if it wasn't true that she was angry at the D.A.'s office.

"Anger, no," she answered. "Hurt."

Ferraro suggested that if Ray was found not guilty Spitler would then have a "better position in the community," and ended her cross-examination.

Davis, on redirect, was quick to take advantage of this opening "You said you were hurt by the D.A.'s office. How?"

Spitler replied sadly, "If they'd really investigated this case, it would never have gone to court. I would never have lost my children for two years; lost my home, job, income; my picture in the papers." The jurors were riveted by the words of this gentle, charming woman telling of the horrors she experienced as a defendant in this case. She did not mention the fact that she was held in jail for two months without bail.

"If you had seen anything at McMartin—molestation, child abuse—would you have reported it?"

"I would have reported it."

"If you saw Ray Buckey molesting little children, would you have come into court twice and lied about it so he could get an acquittal?"

"No, I would have reported it."

The next witness was Babette's daughter, Wendy Spitler. She was now nineteen years old. She testified briefly that she attended McMartin as a preschooler and then came back with her mother, when she was older, to work as an assistant. She read to the children, helped them color, poured fruit juice and served crackers. She told the court she had never seen Ray Buckey with a moustache or a beard, that she had never seen him molest children or touch them in any improper way. She said the children liked Ray Buckey.

"Did you ever see him interact with animals?" Davis asked.

"He would hold the animals and show them to the kids," Wendy said.

"Ever see teachers in a state of undress?"

"No."

"Were children afraid of Ray Buckey?"

"No."

Wendy denied all of the prosecution's allegations. On cross-examination she said that the 'naked movie star' game was just a taunt, a form of "teasing," not connected with any activity. After the prosecution was finished with her there was a brief recess, and Wendy walked out into the hallway, found her mother, and began to weep. Babette held her in her arms as the jurors walked by and looked.

Chad was next. He was extraordinarily animated and expressive. He sat at the witness stand grinning, wide-eyed, with his teeth showing, and appeared to be amused. His candid, spontaneous answers brought a chorus of laughter from the jurors several times. He appeared to be bursting with energy and good humor. He, too, said he saw no naked children at the preschool.

"You know that Ray Buckey is charged with molestation. If you saw something like that happen to a child, what would you do?"

"Go tell someone."

"Did you ever see Ray Buckey do something like that?"

"No."

"Ever see that done to other kids?"

"No."

"If there were naked kids, you think you'd remember that today?"

"Yes."

"Was there a rhyme? The 'naked movie star'?"

"Yes."

"When did you hear that?"

"On my [CII] video."

"Was that rhyme part of a naked game?"

"No."

"What was it part of ?"

"Just a way of putting someone down."

"Did you ever say that rhyme at the preschool?"

"Yes," he grinned. "There was no 'naked movie star' game. If somebody made fun of you, you'd say, 'What you see is what you are. You're a naked movie star.' "

"Did you have your clothes on?"

"Yes."

"Ever sit on a teacher's lap?"

"Yes. Virginia."

"How do you remember benching?"

"I always got benched!" he smiled broadly.

"Did you ever see Ray Buckey with a beard or a moustache?"

"No." Chad said it was the boys, not the girls, who chanted the "naked movie star" chant.

"When your mother brought Michelle . . ." Davis began.

"Who's Michelle?" the boy asked. Davis clapped his hand to his forehead and said, "I'm sorry. I don't know where that came from."

The judge spoke: "Mr. Davis, perhaps you'd like to tell us who Michelle is." This brought another outburst of laughter from the jury.

"Would you like to play detective?" Davis asked.
"No."
"Do you have any yucky secrets?"
"No."

There were only about forty-five minutes left to the day, but the defense called Betty Raidor to the stand and began direct examination. Davis asked her, "How old are you now?" She was seventy, blind in one eye, and had an infection in the other stemming from a corneal transplant.

"You have children and grandchildren?"
"Yes."

Raidor first taught at McMartin in 1970. After going over the names of teachers who were there at the preschool and the times they taught there, Davis asked, "Did it appear that children were frightened of Ray Buckey?"

"Hardly! The children were extremely fond of him and loved him. They loved to sit on him and hang on him."

Asked if she ever saw an animal killed at the school, she said that Peggy, Ray's mother, kept a number of birds in her office and that once, a child slammed the door and crushed Peggy's parakeet, killing it.

"What was Peggy's reaction?" Davis asked.
"She picked it up and took it into her office. She was in tears."
"Did you get to know Ray at the school?"
"I knew him since he was a baby."
"Was there ever anything about his conduct that may inform the jury that he was a sex molester?"
"Never."
"Did you like him?"
"Yes."
"Would you have reported sexual molestation if you believed it had occurred?" Davis asked.
"Yes."
"Have you ever reported it?"
"Yes."

Ferraro began her cross-examination by somewhat bullying Raidor, making it appear that Raidor was interrupting her when, in fact, it was the other way around. Ferraro's questions suggested that Raidor was untrained, incompetent, and would not have recognized sexual abuse if she saw it.

Davis, on redirect asked, "Can you imagine . . . a grown man having sexual intercourse with a three- or four-year-old child?"

"Yes, I guess I can. I never saw that. I can imagine hearing the rape of a four-year-old. I never heard that."

Raidor said she had never seen anything suggesting molestation at the preschool.

We heard the lawyers saying something about serving Kee MacFarlane and Sandra Krebs with subpoenas to testify the next week. The medical expert witness for the defense was also coming soon.

On Sunday the two of us were invited to speak at another dinner meeting of an organization of psychologists and other mental health professionals. They wanted to hear about McMartin. At the buffet table a woman asked, "You don't really believe those people are innocent, do you?"

"Do you believe Buckey molested those kids?" we asked.

"Yeah. I think he's guilty."

"It's a very complicated case," we said. "You must have spent a lot of time studying the evidence. Which of the witnesses did you think was the most convincing?"

"All of them."

"But more than half of the witnesses said it didn't happen. And others said it did. How can you believe all of them?"

"I believe the ones that said it happened."

"Okay, we're narrowing it down. Half of the kids who said it happened were at the school when Ray was living one hundred miles away in San Diego. The other half all told conflicting stories. And each kid changed his story every time he testified. Which witness did you think was most convincing? Which of the counts do you think was the strongest?"

The woman stared blankly.

"Do you know who any of the witnesses were and the specifics of what they said?"

Again she stared blankly.

"You've formed a belief that he's guilty without knowing anything about the case," we said. "That's lynch mob mentality!"

The woman began babbling incoherently. We turned and walked away. Another woman asked, "If they didn't do anything, why would the government have them sitting there for six years?"

"Because [the government people] want to keep their jobs."

Monday, June 11, 1990. The defense called Kee MacFarlane to the stand. At the beginning of the case, her videotaped interviews were the heart of the prosecution's case and she was one of their principal witnesses in the first trial. Now, her videotapes appeared to become the core of the defense case and she was being called as a defense witness. The prosecution did not call her.

It was the position of the defense that MacFarlane was not a child abuse expert but a prolific grant writer. It was also their position that she and her colleagues at CII were ambitious careerists rather than caring child advocates, and that her videotaped interviews began—and ended—with a presumption of guilt, strongly communicated to the children right from the start. This, the defense claimed, could clearly be seen on the tapes.

The judge ruled that the jurors could hear about MacFarlane's romance with former ABC television newsman Wayne Satz, but that it could not be explored in detail. Judge Weisberg also ruled that the defense could inquire as to whether MacFarlane tried to enhance her career by becoming part of, and exaggerating the severity of, a high-publicity child sexual abuse case.

MacFarlane was generally evasive and ambiguous in her answers.

"You directed your questions with Ray as the perpetrator," Davis. began.

"My questions were directed to what happened to children. . . ."

"After the interview of Veronica did you assess child abuse or molest[ation]?" Davis asked.

According to the defense and media reports, MacFarlane interviewed hundreds of children and in almost every case told the parents that their child had been molested.

"What I did was pass along information to the D.A. and parents," MacFarlane said.

MacFarlane went on to say that there was a strong suspicion of sexual abuse in the three children in this case.

"Did the children show fear on the tape?"

"To some extent," MacFarlane answered. On all the CII tapes we have seen, the children were laughing and playful.

"Did [Veronica] say she was raped, sodomized, and fellatioed?"

"I videotaped her and I don't recall."

"Was Linda hit, drugged, and tied?"

"I don't remember."

MacFarlane's reports stated that the three alleged victims in the case claimed to have been hit, drugged, and tied up while naked. The three girls testified under oath that it did not happen.

Asked about the big federal grants, MacFarlane's answers were vague and evasive.

MacFarlane said that the use of dolls did not lead to false allegations.

When Davis asked her about the celebrated welder's license, she said it was a "certificate, not a license. You and other people have been saying that."

When asked if she had appeared at meetings organized by the district attorney to whip up public hysteria, MacFarlane said, "I may have," and "I don't know."

"Did you make statements about McMartin being part of an international conspiracy of child molesters?" Davis asked.

Martinez objected on the grounds that the question was irrelevant. His objection was sustained. Davis launched into a long series of questions about the fact that before the McMartin case MacFarlane had had no public recognition for evaluating children, but that after the case broke, she made many appearances on television.

"In 1985 did you have a close personal relationship with Wayne Satz?"

"Yes."

When asked if she practiced questions and answers with the children before the grand jury hearing, MacFarlane answered, "I don't recall," and "I don't know."

"In a class photo of Veronica and her friends you said everyone interviewed was molested."

"Objection."

"Sustained."

"Does 'contamination in interviewing' have any meaning to you?"

"This came out of the defense witnesses . . . there is no legitimate research on this."

Asked if she advised the D.A. as to which children would make the best witnesses, MacFarlane answered, "I thought I told them about the emotionally strong children."

Throughout the case defense attorneys had tried to demonstrate that MacFarlane was an integral part of the prosecution rather than an impartial fact-finder. MacFarlane had countered that she was doing it "for the children." But this time, Davis put her in a corner. He asked her why she had waited for ten months to make a report of suspicion of child abuse, instead of reporting it within thirty-six hours, as required by law.

"Did you comply with the law?" Davis asked. "Were you aware of the criminal penalties for not reporting in thirty-six hours?"

MacFarlane was forced to defend herself by stating that she had been working closely with the D.A.'s office and law enforcement.

"You were a direct arm of law enforcement," Davis said.

"No, I was not a direct arm of law enforcement."

Then MacFarlane said something very revealing.

"I helped draft that law. . . . I worked at the National Center on Child Abuse," she said. MacFarlane had been one of the authors of the new child abuse legislation that makes every doctor and teacher an agent of the government and a police informant, and gave total immunity to anyone who reported a suspicion of child abuse, even when the report was malicious.

Wednesday, June 13, 1990. The defense called Sandra Krebs, Kee MacFarlane's understudy in the interviews. Davis asked her, "What is your occupation?" She answered, "I am a counselor. I work in the field of child abuse." Krebs said she worked at CII, for the Torrance Police Department, for an organization called "Child Health U.S.A.," and for the Richstone Family Center. She said that at CII she was "developing training materials for law enforcement." She said she was "a clinician in child abuse." She had interviewed one of the girls in the current trial.

"Did you have an operating procedure, a standard format in interviewing her?" Davis asked.

"I don't understand the question," Krebs answered.

She went on to tell of the many conferences she had attended on child molestation.

"Did you make the statement to [the girl's] parents that their child had been molested?"

"No," Krebs answered.

Davis then referred Krebs to her testimony in the preliminary hearing. "Do you remember testifying in the preliminary hearing that you did tell the parents of five children that their children were molested?"

"No, I did not," Krebs answered.

Davis then read from the transcript of her preliminary hearing testimony in which Krebs said that she did tell the parents that their children were molested.

"Was that your testimony?" Davis asked.

"It was the testimony I was pressured into giving. . . . I changed it the next day. . . . You're leaving out the pressure part. . . . Kind of what I did was show them portions of the videotape."

How Krebs was "pressured" and by whom was never explained.

"You recommended they go to the police and make a report?"

"I don't remember."

"Was the interview with [the child] a therapeutic interview?"

"Yes, it was."

"You weren't a therapist."

"No."

"A licensed social worker?"

"No."

"Did you ever indicate to McMartin parents that to get compensation it was necessary to file a police report?"

"No."

Again, Davis read from Krebs's preliminary hearing testimony, which contradicted that statement. Davis asked Krebs if she told the parents that filing a police report might help them to obtain funds to pay the therapists she recommended. There was a long silence. Finally Krebs said she was aware that the state victim-witness fund would help pay for "treatment." Davis again read from Krebs's prior testimony, which was at odds with what she was now saying. Davis asked Krebs if she had made the statement that every child at McMartin over a period of ten years had been molested. She denied it.

Davis asked Krebs if there had been anything in the child's interview, any indication, that she or anyone was engaged in anything that could be described as fellatio or cunnilingus.

Krebs testified that she filed about two hundred reports of suspicion of child abuse.

"For children who did not disclose?" Davis asked.

"Yes."

"Why?"

"Because the original suspicion came from outside, from the D.A.'s office."

"What do you mean by that?"

"I'm not sure."

Davis read from the transcript of the child's CII interview in which she was saying "no" to all the questions about having been sexually abused. "Do you think that's disclosing molestation? Wouldn't you agree that she's saying no?"

"She may be retracting at this point," Krebs answered. "Showing fear. ... In my experience children don't say it happened when it didn't."

"Any degrees before CII?"

"Yes, a B.A. in theater and journalism."

Asked what Krebs did when she was behind the camera assisting in the interview of the child, she said she made notes of portions of the tape to be shown to the parents "so they wouldn't have to watch the entire tape."

"Did [the girl's] behavior indicate molestation?"

"Yes, I think her fear."

"Did you conduct a series of seminars, speeches training people to evaluate molestation?"

"I don't know."

At 3:00 P.M. the defense called Dr. Michael Maloney, the psychologist who had testified in the last trial. The judge sent the jury home because of a dispute about Maloney's appearance. Maloney was sitting next to us. We asked him, "What's going on? Are they trying to limit the scope of your testimony?"

"No," he said. "They don't want to let me testify at all. They tried to do that in the last trial." The hearing began and prosecutor Martinez argued fiercely against allowing Maloney to testify. "We feel he is unqualified to offer an opinion. . . . We question an opinion from any expert as to what would be a proper way to evaluate children." Davis offered, "He will not proffer [an] opinion as to whether children were molested."

Judge Weisberg inquired, "Is it the opinion of the prosecution that no human being can criticize the CII techniques?" Martinez began again, arguing ferociously, "He is not qualified to offer an opinion!"

Maloney explained that his purpose was not to offer any conclusion as to whether any child was or was not molested, nor whether any child was or was not telling the truth, but simply to assist the jury in evaluating the CII techniques and their reliability. He further explained that there was a model accepted by virtually all mental health professionals that consists of (1) "getting the child to talk"; (2) "keep[ing] the child talking"; (3) "getting the child to say in [his/her] own words what happened"; and (4) "resolving inconsistencies, getting explanations."

"If you start out asking these questions, you bias the child. There's a script there. It presents all the pieces to the puzzle. If you want a noncontaminated report from a child, this is a very different way to do it. It is a logical model of how to get information."

Martinez again tore into Maloney: "Are there any empirical studies that support your model? Is there any literature? Does anybody endorse your model?" Maloney replied that "it's just common sense." Martinez argued relentlessly to have Maloney disqualified as an expert witness, which would have crippled the defense because the CII videotapes were at the heart of the case, and Maloney would almost certainly dismantle their credibility, as he did in the first trial. When the lawyers stopped arguing, Judge Weisberg asked, "Is the matter submitted?"

"Yes," the lawyers answered.

"It seems to be the position of the prosecution that these CII interviews are the Holy Grail. I don't find that to be the case. The prosecution has proferred a model of its own. That opens the door to a critical evaluation of the tapes."

In the morning, we saw Joe Martinez walking down the hallway behind Maloney. He overtook him, put his hand on Maloney's back, affectionately, and with a friendly grin, began speaking to him. It was just a game! An innocent man's life hangs in the balance, but that issue appears to be so remote as to be almost nonexistent to these prosecution lawyers.

The jury was brought in and Maloney was called to the stand. Davis spent about an hour going over his credentials and professional accomplishments to solidify his credibility. He was a clinical psychologist. For years, he had been evaluating allegedly abused children for the courts, hundreds of children over the previous seventeen years, and had published three books on interviewing techniques. He said that he had studied the videotapes of the three children in this trial. He said that it was important to ask nondirective questions, to get the child to tell, in his own words, about his experience, instead of providing the child with the information. "If the examiner presents an opinion, information, a desire, the child can pick up on that. . . . If we present information, the child can mimic that."

The next step, Maloney said, was "facilitation." "Keep them talking, making every effort not to provide information about what you want." Showing the child photographs of suspects, he said, contaminates the evaluation. Introducing dolls starts to focus the child on areas the interviewer wants him to talk about. Focusing on sexuality should not be done at the beginning, he explained, because the child will acquiesce to questions; the interviewer needs to give children the opportunity to talk spontaneously. "Your job is to make sure you're not creating contamination."

Davis read from the transcript of a CII interview in which Sandra Krebs laid a doll on the floor and said, "The kids sat on him . . . just like that on that penis? We just got rid of a secret, didn't we?" Maloney explained that this was "stage setting," and that Ray was presented to the child as a nude doll. "The rest of the questioning goes around that situation."

"Direct questioning comes at the end," Maloney said. "If you do it the other way around, you're telling the child what you want." The pattern in these interviews, he said, could be broken down into subparts: talk about Ray being surveilled by policemen or "yucky secrets." The interviews were tailored to this case. "I can't tell whether the child had been molested or not," he said.

Some of the subparts Maloney named were (1) drawing a person; (2) naming parts; (3) presenting sexually accurate dolls; (4) naming parts on dolls; (5) offering "sexual education"; (6) "dolls help us figure it out"; (7) class photographs; (8) introduction of kids; (9) the secret machine; (10) younger kids–older kids (the older ones are told they have a duty to "disclose" in order to help the younger, less verbal ones); (11) secret police; (12) games introduced; (13) secret games; (14) "stuff out of Ray's penis"; (15) kids have been scared.

"This is unlike an interview that is child-directed. It is predetermined. What it does is present all the parts of the puzzle to the kid." Maloney also stated that a strong motivation is provided for certain answers when the interviewer tells a child, "Your parents will be proud." He said that with this approach you are giving the child all the pieces of the puzzle and it would be very difficult to get a spontaneous answer.

" 'Dolls help us figure it out,' " he said, "presents a pressure, that there's something that needed to be figured out. Most of the kids didn't say anything happened. It's very difficult to sift out. . . . It also reduces personal responsibility. 'The puppets tell the secrets and you don't have to say anything.' You have to weigh how much of what you're getting is game-playing."

Telling a child that other kids have come in and told stories already runs the risk of social pressure. "Kids have been scared," he explained, presents a statement that something has happened. "The secret machine . . . is confusing the issues. . . . Second, it's not true. It isn't gone. . . ." And as for "Younger kids–older kids,' . . . they say, 'You can help us. . . . If you're good you're going to give us something.' " Maloney testified that "telling children that something happened can affect their memory."

Davis asked about the legal requirement to report suspicion of child abuse within thirty-six hours to law enforcement. "Do you do that if the child has not said that there was molestation?"

"No. There must be reasonable suspicion."

"With these three complainants," Davis asked, "would you report abuse, based on the interviews?"

"I wouldn't have done those interviews, but I wouldn't have reported on them either." Referring to the CII interviews, Maloney said that, "It is inappropriate in that most of the talk is by the interviewer and the interviewer does not accept the child's report and take it further. . . . There was a lot of stage setting, social pressure . . . to make these children say things that may not have happened."

"How do you determine by empirical study if [children] can be led to believe they were molested when in fact they were not?" Davis asked.

"You would have to mimic whatever happened in this case. Feasibly and ethically you couldn't do that."

Martinez's cross-examination was uneventful, and some jurors appeared to be laughing at him.

Monday, June 18, 1990. Dr. David Paul was back on the stand. We witnessed the anal slide show once again, and, along with it, a two-day seminar of questions and answers about the anatomy of the anus and the vagina. Paul's resume was explained—Her Majesty's Coroner for the City of London, professor at the University of London in clinical forensic medicine, member of the Royal College of Physicians and the Royal College of Surgeons. Paul said he examined both the living and the dead. He said that he had examined about 1,500 children for sexual abuse.

Once again, Dr. Paul literally demolished the prosecution's case. After going over the slides, the photographs, Astrid Heger's written reports, Paul said that there was no evidence of any tactile sexual abuse in any of the children. No "blunt force trauma," nothing "consistent with child sexual abuse."

"Are you licensed in distant past sexual abuse?" Davis asked.

"The whole field of sexual abuse," Paul answered.

"Can you tell, after four years?"

"No. Of course you can't!"

During a discussion of "patulent" (open, gaping) anuses, Davis pronounced it "flatulent," which brought a few giggles from the audience. Paul has a sharp, subtle wit that, several times, got the jurors laughing. At one point during the direct examination, he told Davis, "Your anatomy is atrocious." He also noted that pictures of tissue magnified to 15-power, as is done with the colposcope, present great danger of misinterpretation and distortion.

Predictably, the media were absent. The *Los Angeles Times* and the electronic media always showed up for the prosecution's heavy hitters, but when crucial defense witnesses like Maloney and Paul testified, they were gone.

Paul testified that the size of the hymenal opening was of no significance, and that the "anal skin tags" the prosecution doctors identified as proof of molestation were often seen on newborn infants. He said that measuring with a paper tape, as Heger had done, is extremely inaccurate.

"Can normal girls have a perforated hymen?"

"Yes."

"Is rounding of the hymen indicative of molest[ation]?"

"No."

"Is diaper rash indicative of molest[ation]?"

"Good heavens, no! If it were, all of the parents in this room would be suspects!" This brought another chorus of laughter from the jurors.

The doctor said that white areas identified as "scars" by the prosecution doctors were, in some cases, mucus, and in others, merely reflected light.

"Is neovascularization [the presence of new blood vessels] diagnostic of sexual abuse?"

"No."

"Do you see a scar that transsects the hymen?"

"No."

"Looking at this slide, is it evidence of blunt force trauma?"

"No."

Ferraro was no match for Dr. Paul, on cross-examination. As she, herself, admitted, "I don't know anything about anatomy." But as the questions and answers progressed, Ferraro seemed to become increasingly angry. During a discussion about the average size of the adult penis, she asked him, "How many men have you slept with?"

"Not my style," he answered calmly. Paul had been doing this for years and he knew all the prosecutors' tricks and how to parry them. After trying all afternoon to poke holes in the doctor's testimony and getting nowhere, Ferraro was visibly angered.

"Do you mean to say that there is no scar on this picture?" she asked with a tone of outrage.

"That's correct," he answered.

Then Ferraro suddenly blurted out shrilly, "How much are you being paid to say this?"

"That is an offensive question and I will not answer it," Paul replied. Then he said that he was not being paid anything for his testimony.

"You're being paid for your expenses, aren't you? Your airfare?"

"Madam, I live in London. How else could I get here?" More laughter. Then the doctor raised his voice slightly and said, "May I ask what your salary is?" Ferraro made no reply. Her harsh manner in questioning a man who was probably older than her father did not play well with the jurors.

Toward the end Dr. Paul stated that nightmares, sleep disturbances, masturbation, and children getting into bed with their parents were all perfectly normal behaviors. As for the allegation that one of the girls was seen putting a tinkertoy into her vagina, he said he believed that was motivated more by curiosity than masturbation. Asked if he had attended lectures on sexual abuse, he answered, "I give them."

"Are you aware that Drs. Heger and Woodling have cited you as a source of their knowledge?" Davis asked.

"I'm afraid so," he said sadly.

During the cross-examination, Ferraro began pointing and jabbing her finger at Paul in a menacing manner and Davis protested to the judge.

"She can point all she wants," the doctor smiled. "She doesn't frighten me." As laughter erupted from the audience, coprosecutor Martinez looked back angrily, his eyes sweeping the room to find out who was laughing.

After Paul was excused, the defense called Janie Friedkin, who had also testified in the first trial. She had a radiantly sunny smile and good humor. She was a good witness. She taught at the preschool for years and was there in 1982 and 1983. She testified that she spent about 80 percent of her time at the school with Ray Buckey, and that when she was not working with him, he was generally out in the play yard with his group of children. Friedkin said that she had never seen him with a beard or a moustache at any time, that Ray was very much loved by the children. When Davis asked her if she had ever observed anything suggesting sexual misconduct, she replied, "Not at any time!" She denied all of the allegations against Ray.

On cross-examination, Martinez asked her, "Wasn't your purpose in going to the school to socialize with Peggy, and not to help?"

"No, that is not true," Friedkin answered. Martinez asked a number of questions to suggest that Friedkin was not always able to observe Ray, but it went nowhere.

On redirect, Davis asked her, "Did you feel that Peggy was covering up some kind of mass molestation?"

"No."

"Did you ever see Ray Buckey undressed?"

"Oh, no!"

Friedkin went on to say that the children loved Ray and that he was their favorite teacher. She stated that for years she lived in terror of being arrested as a suspect.

Other women, benign grandmothers, told us they had returned home from work to find that their homes had been entered, ransacked, and that they had discovered monitoring devices in their telephones.

A turtle doctor was called again as a witness for the defense, a veterinary pathologist who specialized in tortoises. He was asked if it would be possible for a person to stab a tortoise to death with a knife.

"Absolutely not," he laughed. He explained that a tortoise's shell is so strong that when a motorcycle runs over a tortoise, it is often the motorcyclist, not the tortoise, who is killed. He also testified that in some states tortoises are a protected species and that "it is a crime to kill or molest them."

On Friday, June 22, 1990, the defense called three doctors who were the family pediatricians of the three girls in the trial. All of them said they had examined the girls thoroughly during the time frame of the purported sexual assaults and found no signs of sexual abuse. They were very much aware of the mandatory reporting laws. One of them said that masturbation is not uncommon in children of preschool age and that nightmares were not, "in themselves," a sign of molestation.

Deputy D.A. Anthony Brunetti testified briefly about the worldwide search for child pornography related to McMartin that consumed a year and one million dollars and in which nothing was found.

Det. Augusta "Gusty" Bell was called by the defense. They wanted to know the content of the lengthy conversations she and Lael Rubin had had with the child witnesses before they testified in the first trial. Children had testified that Bell took notes during the sessions. Bell had testified that notes were not taken during the later visits. Since the defense is entitled to all evidence in the case, they wanted to know where the notes were, if they existed. Bell testified that during one girl's interviews in December 1989, she did not prepare reports and took very few notes. She said she did not destroy them. She said she did not recall taking notes during the interview with the second girl.

"Did anyone tell you not to take notes?" Davis asked Bell.

"No. The decision was made on the fact that there was no conflict. The decision was made on the determination of Rubin and I."

Davis asked whether the other children the three girls identified as also participating in the naked games had ever been asked about their participation. Bell answered, "I did not ask any of them. To my knowledge it was never done."

Davis asked Bell about one girl's description of the "horsey game." She answered that, "To the best of my ability to recall, Ray would lie down and she would sit on his back."

"Then what happened?" Davis asked.

"That was it."

We now have at least three different versions of the "horsey game" from one witness alone.

Bell testified that it was her belief that MacFarlane was working with the district attorney's office during the investigation. She also stated that no leading questions were asked of the children. It was our perception that Bell was visibly uncomfortable with her testimony.

Monday, June 25, 1990. The defense brought in a psychologist who was prepared to testify about studies she had conducted that show that making statements to a child long after an experience makes the child vulnerable to distortion of memory. The judge granted the prosecutors' motion to exclude this witness. While we sat and waited through a long bench conference and a brief recess, a corpulent woman with a large stack of spiral notebooks began speaking to us. Smiling with excitement, she told us, "This is a case of satanic ritual molestation!"

"Do you really believe that?" we laughed.

"Children never lie! Didn't you know that?"

"But why is it that in all these hundreds of cases all over the country, not one single piece of evidence has been presented to back up those stories of satanic molestation?" we asked.

"There are reasons. Those D.A.s know what they're doing."

"If you were the judge, and there were no jury, and the decision was yours and yours alone to make, would you send Ray to prison for the rest of his life?" we asked.

"Yes."

"Would you have him put to death?"

"Yes."

"And would you be at all troubled by the possibility that you made a mistake and destroyed an innocent young man?" we asked.

"No."

The woman looked troubled by our skepticism as she left the room. She returned later and told me that she had discussed the matter with some cops on the fifth floor and that they agreed with her.

"Well, I guess that settles it," we laughed.

The woman frowned. She told us that she was a graduate student and would soon be teaching at the college level.

Defense attorney Davis asked that under sections 1101 and 1102 in the evidence code, the prosecution be precluded from asking, before the jury, questions about Ray Buckey's: drinking; use of marijuana; masturbation; interest in crystals and pyramids; heterosexual experience or relationships with adult females; designation by law enforcement as a suicide risk; or possession of adult pornography or the book *Sexual Secrets*. Also asked to be precluded were the missing page in Virginia McMartin's diary; the details of a quarrel Ray allegedly had with his mother while drinking; and allegations that he once shouted at a child. All were insinuations and smear tactics the prosecution would almost certainly use in cross-examination, since the state didn't really have anything else.

Prosecutor Ferraro asserted that Ray's drinking and marijuana use might become relevant but that she intended to "steer clear" of George Freeman's testimony.

Ray was sworn in and Davis began by asking if he had ever engaged in any sexual conduct with the children. He answered the questions with "No," and "Never." Then there was a surprise. Ray said that during the entire time since he was first accused, including the five years he spent in jail, he was never asked by any law enforcement officers whether he had molested a child. Their minds were already made up.

"Did you ever do anything that might be construed as an act of molestation of Veronica?"

"No."

"Did you ever place your finger in the anus of Veronica?"
"No."

Asked whether he helped children "go to the bathroom," Ray said he had done so infrequently, but that the door was always open. "That was the rule." One by one, Ray denied all of the allegations.

"Did you penetrate the anus of Linda?"
"No."

"Did you penetrate the vagina of Linda?"
"No."

Ray testified that he had taken pictures of the children once or twice when asked to do so by his mother, and that they were fully dressed.

"Have you ever had a beard or a moustache?"
"No."

Ray explained that his trip to South Dakota had been planned in June, long before the first allegations were made, and was not an attempt to conceal evidence. Ray said he didn't want his sister to drive back to California alone.

"Did you ever take off your clothes at the preschool?"
"No."

"Did you ever do anything to a child that was some intent to arouse yourself sexually?"
"No."

"Didn't you think there was something improper about not wearing underwear at the preschool?"
"Not then. I do now."

"Did you ever see your mother without clothing at the preschool?"
"Not *my* mother!"

Ferraro began her cross-examination by asking, "You're not going to say you molested [the children], right?"
"I'm not going to because I didn't."

"And you're not going to say you're a child molester."
"I'm not going to because I'm not."

"What attracted you to [teaching children]?"
"I did volunteer work. It was nice. Easy."

"Easy job. That's it, wasn't it?"
"I wanted to be a preschool teacher."

"At the preschool in San Diego did you take photographs of children?"
"Yes."

"Why?"
"For my scrapbook."

"You worked as a parking lot attendant?"
"Yes."

"Did you take pictures of the parking lot?"
"No."

Ferraro repeatedly asked Ray if he had ever talked to the children about sex. He answered that he had not. To one of Ferraro's questions Ray answered, "You're trying to twist it." Predictably, Ferraro focused at great length on the underwear.

"When did you decide not to wear underwear?" she asked.

Ray answered that he had made that decision gradually, that when you play volleyball on the beach and get wet, underwear don't dry as quickly as outer garments "and you get rashes."

"Did you ever sit at the preschool with your knees apart?"

"Probably. I don't remember."

The saga of the underwear went on and on. Ray said that when the police first began calling parents in the community he believed that because his mother was a very prominent citizen, she would be able to get to the bottom of it and exonerate him.

"So you thought your mother could fix it!" Ferraro charged.

"Did you ever take a child to Old Town Mall?" she asked. Ray explained that he, his mother, and his grandmother had taken a small girl there because her mother had just died and they were trying to cheer her up.

On redirect, Davis asked, "I want to talk some more about shorts and no underwear. . . . Did you dress to molest?"

"No," Buckey laughed.

"Were you dressing in any fashion to expose yourself?"

"No."

Ray also said that no parent or teacher had ever commented about the way he was dressed.

Davis asked if the children's parents were aware that Ray photographed them on one occasion. He replied that they were standing right behind him. On recross the prosecutor spoke of the "danger" of children seeing Ray's genitals.

"On behalf of Mr. Buckey we rest our case-in-chief with the understanding that we may need to reopen for limited purposes only," Davis concluded. The prosecution called Peggy Buckey as its first rebuttal witness.

Martinez asked her, "During any time, did you ever see a child sitting on Ray's lap?"

"Yes."

"Did you ever check [Ray] to see if he had an erection?" Martinez asked.

"Yes, one time," Peggy answered.

"Why?" Martinez asked.

"As the director I had to think the way parents think." She explained that this was after the first accusations were made, the burgeoning hysteria arose, and there was a parent who didn't like having a male teacher there.

"You checked because you thought he might have an erection!"

"No!"

Davis, on cross-examination, asked, "Did you see an erection?"

"No!"
"Any kind of misconduct?"
"No."
"Were you accused in the last trial?"
"Yes."
"And did you listen to testimony from adults and children that you molested them?"
"Yes."
"Were you ever convicted of molestation?"
"No."
"Have you ever been falsely accused?"
"Yes."
"I have no further questions."

After the judge recessed the court for the day, Ray and Peggy were confronted by several television camera crews with their hot, white lights and microphones, and a crowd of reporters. One of them asked Ray about the celebrated underwear. "I'm not the only person in the South Bay who doesn't wear underwear," he said, "but I was probably the dumbest, not to have worn it at the preschool. I'm wearing it now."

"What brand do you wear?" a young reporter asked.

Another reporter asked what he thought of the cross-examination.

"They don't have anything!" Ray said, smiling sadly. "They don't have a case. They're saying I didn't wear underwear and asking you to take a giant leap across the Grand Canyon and say that because I didn't wear underwear I must be a child molester."

The prosecution called William Guidas, an investigator employed by the district attorney's office and assigned to surveil Ray in 1984. He said that at that time he was assigned to the Organized Crime Intelligence Unit, and that he and sixteen other officers and four police cars were allocated, full time, to surveillance of Ray Buckey about sixteen hours a day, from the time he awoke in the morning till the time he went to bed at night. "It was a large-scale molestation case. We were watching him to see that he didn't molest children or try to leave the country."

Guidas said that he had observed Buckey sitting on the grass, after leaving a classroom at Orange Coast College, and watching children at play in a day care center adjacent to his classroom. The main purpose of this testimony was to suggest that Buckey apparently was a pedophile. On cross-examination, Davis elicited from Guidas the fact that he could see only the back of Buckey's head.

"You don't know what he was looking at, do you?"
"I couldn't see his eyes."
"You don't even know if his eyes were closed, do you?"
"I couldn't tell."

"You saw some good-looking girls go by?"
"Yes."
"Isn't it true that they drew your attention?"
"I didn't take my eyes off Mr. Buckey."
"Not for one second?" Davis stood with his back to the witness and asked, "You can't tell whether my eyes are open now, can you?"
"No, I can't."
"Your eyesight doesn't go through heads, does it?"

During this time, the witness acknowledged, Buckey ate an orange, took a nap, read a magazine and a book, and went roaming around the campus.

The prosecution called a final rebuttal witness, Cynthia Cesena, a director of the day care center at San Diego State University. She testified that at the time Ray volunteered to work at the university nursery school there were no male volunteers there and that the staff thought it was "kinda neat" that a male was going to assist at the day care center. She testified that when he applied for the job he stated that his family operated a preschool and that he missed the preschool environment of his home and family. She said she observed no misconduct on the Ray's part and had issued him a "Certificate of Outstanding Participation."

Court was recessed early because the prosecution had no more witnesses. The brief testimony they put on was negligible in value. That night the news media was filled with horror stories about child abuse that segued into McMartin, another attempt to influence the jury, timed to coincide with the end of the trial. They were doing it again. This was the last chance to save the credibility of the child abuse industry.

It was almost over. There would be two days of closing arguments, Monday and Tuesday, and then it would go to the jury.

Monday morning, July 2, 1990. It was the next-to-last day of the trial. Closing arguments were about to begin. The courtroom was packed and the television stations had their gear piled up in the hallway After lengthy and tedious arguments between the lawyers, Deputy D.A. Pam Ferraro went to the lectern and began her summation. She began by explaining the elements of section 288, concerned with lewd and lascivious acts with a child under the age of fourteen, and told the jurors that it must be proven beyond a reasonable doubt that "such act was committed with the intent to arouse, sexually, Mr. Buckey or the child."

This case, Ferraro said, "revolves around who you believe." She said she would not ask the jury to convict Ray Buckey solely on the testimony of the children, but asserted that "the children's testimony is corroborated by circumstantial evidence." She went on to explain that circumstantial evidence is inference that may be drawn from a fact or a group of facts, and that a finding of guilt on circumstantial evidence cannot be had unless there is no other reasonable explanation.

But the circumstantial evidence Ferraro cited was nightmares, rashes, fear of being alone, and not wanting to go to school! Incredibly, Ferraro also cited sexualized behavior by the children as circumstantial evidence of molestation, based on the mistaken belief that children are asexual unless corrupted by an adult.

"How could children fantasize about sex if they hadn't experienced sex?" she asked.

Since the "evidence" against Buckey was so flawed and insubstantial, the prosecutors were in the position of going into their closing arguments unarmed, and we had suspected that they would offer some extremely complicated verbiage to impress and confound the jurors. Instead, they resorted to ridicule and insult directed at the defense witnesses.

Ferraro scornfully referred to Peggy Buckey as "a real work of art" and said she could understand why a person would not want to work for her. In her assault on Maloney Ferraro ridiculed his partial blindness and the fact that he wore a patch over one eye. She made much of the fact that he was paid for his expert testimony, implying that this corrupted him and invalidated his statements. But Ferraro did not bother to mention that the prosecution doctors were also paid. Ferraro called his assessment of the CII interviews "absurd."

As for Dr. David Paul, Ferraro asked, "How much money would it take to sell your soul? Dr. Paul took seven hundred dollars a day to come here." She failed to mention that Paul was paid far less than prosecution doctors like Bruce Woodling, who testified that his fee was $2,500 a day. As for the zoologist who testified that the turtles died naturally and were not slaughtered, Ferraro said he "even looked like a turtle." She also harshly berated Ray as "a young man who worked for his mommy." Even the octogenarian, Virginia, did not escape Ferraro's loathsome insults.

Pam Ferraro is a visually attractive young woman but her demeanor is harsh and severe. We never saw her smile except when she made a thin, perfunctory smile while talking to a lawyer or a witness in a formal situation. We never saw her open up and laugh. Ferraro's voice is thin, cold, and monotonous and she talked at an incredible speed, so fast that it was sometimes difficult to understand what she was saying.

Ferraro continued to batter Dr. Paul, saying that he failed to see that which "any reasonable person would see." She made the highly questionable statement that the accusing parents were not people who were involved in a witch hunt, but "rational people." She explained away the contradictions and inconsistencies in the children's testimony by saying that they "tried to forget." She said that all of the defense witnesses "had an ax to grind."

"There are things in the CII tapes that cannot be explained away," Ferraro asserted, "things that could not be the result of coaching or brainwashing." But she did not say what these "things" were. "You have to ask, 'Would all these children come into court and say it happened?' " But what about the children who came into court and said it did not happen? And the hundreds of children who went to CII but did not come into court?

As for the puppet ladies' lack of credentials, Ferraro said that one job that required no credentials was the presidency of the United States (not a very impressive argument). She continued to assert that the girls had vaginal scarring and asked the jury to accept Heger's explanation and reject Paul's. "Linda is a victim of child molestation!" she proclaimed.

As for the circumstantial evidence, Ferraro said that Ray had ample opportunity to molest children; animals were killed; Ray didn't stare at attractive women on that day in San Diego; he didn't wear underwear; he took pictures of children but didn't take photographs of the parking lot. And he read *Playboy* magazine!

"This is a young man who, when accused, leaves town," she said. But the defense provided very solid evidence that Ray planned the trip to South Dakota long before the first accusations were made, so that his sister would not have to drive from South Dakota to Los Angeles alone. And Ray did not flee but returned to California to face the accusations.

Ferraro concluded her argument by saying that when all of the evidence was reviewed, "you [the jury] will not be able to come to any rational conclusion consistent with Mr. Buckey being innocent," and "All the evidence . . . leads to the irrefutable conclusion that Mr. Buckey committed these crimes."

It was noon. Court was recessed until one-thirty.

At one-thirty, Davis began. He told the jurors, "The truth simply never had a chance. . . . The truth was changed. We never really heard from the children. If you don't think the change is going on from the minute the child got in CII, look at the videotapes. These little kids are being told that all the other kids said it happened. The truth never really had a chance."

Davis recalled that one of the three girls accused Peggy Buckey of several counts in the first trial and then admitted, in the second trial, that it didn't happen. He said it was equally possible that children who originally accused all seven teachers, then testified that it was only Ray and Peggy who molested them and then said that it was just Ray, that they would also recant in the future. "Are we going to wait twenty years and then look back and say, 'What we did to Ray Buckey was wrong'?"

Davis quoted one girl, who changed her story each time she testified and, when confronted with her untruthfulness, casually said, "That was then. This is now."

Reviewing the evidence, Davis said, "I began to wonder what the burden of proof might be in a court of law. *Playboy!* Photographs of children in a day care center. . . . For what? Is there anything you see indicating that a male who has a *Playboy* magazine has an interest in children? How does that square with *Playboy* magazine? Is this the kind of stuff that says Mr. Buckey was molesting children? Could you say in any objective sense . . . that's a molester? *Playboy?* We're doing it in this case. They have the burden of proof!

"But where are the items that tie Mr. Buckey to molestation? Is it the photographs or the *Playboy* magazine? If you look at [the evidence] you'll see how it can happen to anyone. You'll see Peggy Buckey and all the teachers, all arrested in this case. Where is the burden of proof? The burden of proof is on the prosecution."

Davis explained that the charges were not evidence, and that, under the law, there was a presumption of innocence. "This is not a roll of the dice."

Davis erected large charts on posterboard and spoke of the "blunderous letter that eradicated any chance of the truth in this case," the letter that contained descriptions of sexual acts, "and introduced Ray Buckey to the parents in a very bad light, with no evidence." The parents, he said, were told not to talk, but the police were calling parents even before the letter went out. "The truth never had a chance. What stopped the process? Parents asked but the children said nothing. There is an initial focus on Ray Buckey."

Davis mentioned that the three family pediatricians came in and said they never saw any evidence of sodomy. One family, he said, when they filled out the intake form at CII, mentioned their child's monster dreams. "You can decide if monster dreams have anything to do with molestation."

"The videotaped interviews began to change the truth so that the truth never had a chance. Take the video logs and ask yourself if you don't find a remarkable inconsistency. . . . When the child says, 'No, nothing happened,' . . . ask yourself, 'What were the puppet ladies doing?' What chance did Ray Buckey have?" The investigation, he said, was turned over to people who had no experience whatsoever.

Davis spoke of the girl who said the man who molested her had a beard and a moustache and reminded the jurors that in the first trial she could not even identify Ray Buckey as he sat before her in the courtroom. Davis described the CII as "a bunch of carpetbaggers and overnight experts."

Once again Davis gave his analogy of the raccoons in the trees, brought out the Russian abstract painting, and began losing the jurors' attention. He described the findings of Heger and her colleagues as another passing fashion in medicine and likened it to other disastrous medical fashions of the past, such as the use of thalidomide. He talked about the new McCann study, which showed that much of what prosecution doctors had been identifying as signs of molestation were also found in normal children. He brought out another large sheet of posterboard with a diagram showing the flow of witnesses between the district attorney's office and CII and the payments from the California victim's aid fund for therapists referred by CII. He explained that once the parents had been bought into that system there was no way to get a second opinion. "Why was there no second opinion. . . . Why did they get no medical opinion other than Dr. Heger's?"

Referring to the third girl to testify, Davis said, "She didn't feel uncomfortable when presented with the fact that in the last trial she made allegations against Peggy Buckey and now she says it didn't happen. What does it say about what she said about Ray Buckey? She changed! It wasn't true any more. . . . We already know she can change her story." As for the girl who testified that she was flown away in an airplane to a "costume house" full of bathtubs, Davis said that not one of the girl's classmates recounted such an excursion. He noted the child accusers in this trial were among the children who had originally accused all seven teachers.

"Where is the evidence? Where is the fear? It's just not there! If you want to find out where the fear is, go to the CII tapes. The fear is in the language of the puppet lady. If somebody penetrated both orifices of your body, would you sit there and play? Is that the kind of thing you can believe?

"Do men without underwear molest children? Do all men who read *Playboy* molest children?" Davis spoke of the worldwide search for "pornography," which came up with nothing. "Where is the pornography? When you look at those videotapes you'll see where it's coming from," he said. "The burden is on the [prosecution] of proving beyond a reasonable doubt. . . . It's a system of law that presumes innocence. The burden is on the People and the reasonable doubt is the defendant's. . . . You cannot jump from *Playboy* and gazing to sexual acts."

Davis explained the law pertaining to circumstantial evidence and said in a situation with two reasonable inferences, you must adopt the one that points to innocence. "If a girl had nightmares about spiders does that point to molestation?" he asked

Davis spoke of the girl who denied the specific acts that were the substance of her two counts against Ray, and who answered, "I don't know" and "I don't remember" to most of the questions put to her.

"I want to talk about Dr. Paul," Davis said, knowing that Martinez would inflict a thoroughgoing smear on Paul during final rebuttal. Davis recited Paul's impressive credentials and accomplishments and stated that, "He has to answer for his opinions. Contrast that to Dr. Heger and it's alarming. . . . A perfectly normal finding, in her view, was consistent with sexual abuse! Think of the danger of a doctor looking at a perfectly normal child and saying, 'I find your [child's condition] consistent with sexual abuse'! 'I don't find any findings but in my opinion she is consistent with sexual abuse'!" Astrid Heger, Davis said, used criteria that were no longer accepted. "She didn't know what she was doing." The CII phenomenon, he said, was a case of "medical molestation."

Davis told the jurors that the accusation of child molestation, even when it is false, is so inflammatory and evokes a response so violent that "all of the forces that define what happened operate to presume guilt." He listed some of the dynamics that operated to spread the belief that Buckey was guilty: the police letter implicating Ray without any evidence to support it; Heger's pronouncement that even physically normal children were "consistent with sexual abuse"; shaping; peer pressure; contamination; "other parents and children"; distortion; sibling rivalry; cross-germination; submission to authority; reward and punishment; brainwashing; mass hysteria; group acceptance; the witch hunt atmosphere and scapegoatism; coercive and suggestive techniques; the arrest party.

"It didn't happen. People believed it happened," Davis said.

"What happened to the children over time? The letter, the meetings, the CII, the attempt to treat the child[ren] as victims . . . leaving parents with no other opinion than that their child was molested. . . . Going to the home of a child before trial. How long, how many times do you have to prepare? . . . Nobody knows what might have happened when the truth might have had a chance. Look for that proof . . . that didn't come out of the puppet lady's mouth. . . . Look at those videotapes and see what they were doing to children."

Davis cited as sources of reasonable doubt the impossibility of the acts alleged, misidentification, incompetent investigation, incredible witnesses, and the incredible fact that the prosecution was trying to put Ray at the school "when he wasn't there."

"Look at the sexual abuse reports of Kee MacFarlane. They all say 'drugged.' The children didn't say that!" Davis said.

"Counts are not the crime," he said. "They are not the proof. Ask yourself if what you are hearing is raw emotionality or real evidence in a court of law," he said.

"And so I leave the balance of argument to the prosecution, the people who have the burden of proof. Maybe you will hear about how you should sympathize with the child. But as he talks, ask yourself about the burden of proof. What we do in law is eliminate salesmanship. So assist this process. Test all the arguments in this case, but test one: what is being said that is beyond reasonable doubt? And if it is not there, reject it!

"Honestly bring [in] what you believe is a just verdict."

Davis was interviewed by the media outside the courtroom and asked what he expected Martinez would say in his final rebuttal. He said, "I expect a pitch man relying on emotionality and asking the jury to do what the law prohibits."

After lunch the jurors, spectators, and reporters filled the courtroom and waited. The mob was there, filling their empty lives with the exhilaration of burning a witch. Like the furies of Aeschylus and Virgil their faces were formed in an expression of perpetual hate and loathing. They had come to punish and torment their victim to the end of the earth and into the underworld.

Deputy D.A. Joe Martinez began his closing argument. His was the most remarkable of all the closing summations. He began by doing something we found so offensive that the revulsion will remain with us for the rest of our lives. He used the words of Charles Dickens as a weapon to urge conviction. The sentence he quoted was, "In the little world in which children have their existence there is nothing so finely perceived or finely felt as injustice." Dickens was not writing about child abuse. In the real world of the prosecutor, the problem is that children often do not perceive an injustice, particularly after they have been put through seven years of merciless indoctrination and are exploited to help disguise an injustice.

Martinez urged that the children be believed and asserted that their inconsistencies and self-contradictions were of no significance, but rather the result of repressing traumatic events. He stated that the children were no match for a "slick lawyer"—his repeated way of referring to Davis and a popular strategy in the lawyer's repertoire. Martinez likened Davis to a "used car salesman" and told the jury that intelligent people did not believe the lies of used car salesmen. We could not believe that the jurors did not recognize Martinez as the quintessential used car salesman himself, but maybe they didn't. Addressing the fact that none of the witnesses had heard any animals screaming in pain, Martinez came up with an absolutely astounding hypothesis. He posited that Ray killed the animals twice! He told the jurors that the reason the animals didn't scream or cry out in pain is that they were already dead and that Ray Buckey "simulated" killing them to terrify the children, who were too young to perceive that they were already dead!

Like Ferraro, Martinez reserved his most vicious assault for Dr. Paul, the man who demolished the prosecution's case. He repeatedly characterized Paul as "a comedian," and asserted that Heger was "a more professional expert," disregarding the fact that Heger was a beginner when she examined the McMartin children and that Paul had been examining children when Heger was eight years old. Of course, Martinez also disregarded the fact that Heger and other prosecution doctors cited Paul as their mentor before they learned that he would be coming in as a defense witness. Martinez appealed to bigotry and xenophobia by telling the jurors that Paul said the British usage of the word "coroner" was more correct then the American usage. It was a misstatement of what Paul had said and an appeal to the natural, gut-level resentment people feel when they are told that Americans are somehow inferior to people of another nationality. It was a cheap trick, but it was the stuff this case had been built on, the appeal to mindless emotion rather than logic and reason.

Martinez made much of the fact that the defense found it necessary to go nine thousand miles to find an expert medical witness, suggesting that they would go to any length to find a doctor who would make false statements. He did not mention the fact that pressure and intimidation by the prosecution and the child abuse industry made it impossible for the defense to get a qualified American doctor to testify.

"The nature of these crimes," Martinez said darkly, "is that they are done in ultra secrecy so that nobody is going to believe [the children]." After claiming that Ray threatened and terrified the children, he then said, "These children loved Ray," and "That is the nature of sexual abuse . . . the children gravitated to him!"

That really did not compute. If the children were terrified of Ray, why would they "gravitate" to him?

Referring to the bizarre statements of the prosecution witnesses, Martinez said that, "We brought the parents and children to court so you could see [that] these people were not brainwashed. . . . This is evidence! This is a catharsis!"

Martinez continued, "Mr. Davis infers that some of the parents may have molested them [their own children]. That is preposterous! In a trial the accused often becomes the accuser. That is what Mr. Davis has done. He has accused Dr. Heger of being a quack!"

The two women who interviewed the children at CII had "great rapport" he told the jury. "They may not have Ph.D.s, but when you review the videotapes you will see. . . ." Martinez heaped praise upon CII, ridiculing the notion that children were brainwashed there.

Addressing the fact that the defense had brought in a man who had conducted a survey of the city that showed how many cars passed by the preschool on an average day, Martinez said it would be just as reasonable to call in an air traffic controller to tell us how many airplanes passed over the McMartin Preschool. The problem with that is that jets fly about seven miles above the earth and the cars passed only a few feet away from the gate. The cars' occupants could definitely see into the school.

Naturally Martinez did not fail to mention the misleading and inflammatory allegation that Ray's mother once checked him for an erection. But he did fail to mention the exculpatory fact that nobody ever saw him with an erection. "Peggy Buckey checked him for an erection! Why? She knew her son!"

Martinez told the jurors, "You can acquit Buckey and he can start another preschool," another transparent ploy to strike fear in the jury.

Martinez also appealed to the prevalent sexual hysteria and fanaticism that remains as a vestige of the Dark Ages and asked the jurors, "What would you do if you took your children to school and saw the teacher reading *Playboy* magazine? You would have a fit!"

"The predator is always close to his prey," he said ominously. "And that is why Buckey has got to be close to children." Martinez was pleading for the condemnation and ruin of Ray Buckey, a young man he knew little or nothing about. It was just theater—for everybody but Ray Buckey.

At the conclusion of a very unimpressive speech, Martinez told the jurors, "This Ray Buckey is a sick man. He stole these children's dreams. He is a sick man! We have proved this case beyond a reasonable doubt."

"These children were molested," he said. "These children have felt injustice for so long that they've come to you for help. Ray Buckey did this thing to them. Don't reject them."

That was it. The trial was over. The jurors would receive instructions and begin deliberations Monday. Faced by the television cameras and microphones, Ray told the media, "I think [Martinez] should be a comedian instead of a lawyer."

Many people speculated as to how long the jury would be out and what the verdicts would be, but the jurors were inscrutable and unpredictible. Nobody really knew. We would just have to wait.

Judge Weisberg ordered Ray to remain in the Criminal Courts Building while the jury deliberated. He sat there, alone, and waited.

Meanwhile, the system had responded quickly to the acquittals in the first trial. The California Supreme Court ruled on Thursday, June 28, 1990, in *California* v. *Jones,* that it was not necessary for a child witness to provide the time, place, and other specific details of his alleged molestation, in order for his testimony to be admissible and sufficient for a conviction. This virtually annihilated any possibility of defense against false allegations of child sexual abuse. How could you impeach a witness's testimony if he is not required to be specific as to time, place, and other details, even if the alleged act would be physically impossible depending on those details?

A day earlier, in an astounding abrogation of the Sixth Amendment confrontation clause, the U.S. Supreme Court upheld the constitutionality of state statutes that permit child witnesses in child abuse trials to testify outside of the courtroom over one-way, closed-circuit television, outside the presence of the defendant. Justice Sandra Day O'Connor, delivering the majority opinion of the court in *Maryland* v. *Craig,* wrote that the "state's interest in the physical and psychological well-being of child abuse victims may be sufficiently important to outweigh . . . a defendant's right to face his or her accusers in court." She went on to state that "the right to confront and cross-examine is not absolute." She cautioned that there had to be a finding of necessity, a finding that the child would be traumatized by the presence of the defendant. This could be accomplished with the testimony of "expert" witnesses called by the prosecution. O'Connor did not address the fact that these "expert" witnesses were invariably psychologists and other "mental health professionals" paid through the district attorney's office and well known to the district attorney as persons who could be relied upon to give testimony to support the prosecution.

What is even more egregious is the fact that the use of closed-circuit television strongly communicates to the jury a presumption of guilt.

In a scathing and eloquent dissenting opinion, Justice Antonin Scalia wrote, "Seldom has the court failed so conspicuously to sustain a categorical guarantee of the Constitution against the tide of current opinion ... and because the Constitution is meant to protect against, rather than conform to, current widespread belief, I respectfully dissent." He recounted in considerable detail the infamous *Scott County* case in Minnesota and the outrageous prosecutorial misconduct in which children's testimony was distorted and coerced by malevolent adults. Apparently, Scalia was the only justice who did his homework. He wrote in conclusion, "I have no need to defend the value of confrontation because the court has no authority to question it."

In both of these appellate rulings the majority opinions were filled with the rhetoric of the child abuse hysteria: children do not lie; children are not suggestible; children would be psychologically damaged by having to confront the accused.

On June 5, 1990, California voters approved by a 52 percent plurality a ballot initiative known as Proposition 115, which, according to defense attorneys, abolished at least thirty constitutional rights of defendants in criminal proceedings. It eliminated the right to a preliminary hearing; it allowed police officers to give hearsay testimony; and, most importantly, it greatly speeded up the entire process of criminal prosecution. What saved the Buckeys in the first trial was that the attorneys were given enough time to "get this case back from Salem to Los Angeles." Defense attorneys would be precluded from doing that in the future. Also under Proposition 115, the judge, rather than the lawyers, would conduct the examination of jurors during jury selection. Proposition 115 was sold to the voters by packaging it as the "Crime Victims Justice Reform Act," and the "Speedy Trial Act," and the "Night Stalker Initiative." It was clearly unconstitutional and would probably be struck down eventually, but in the meantime, how many innocent people will be rushed into the state's prisons?

These three radical changes in the law were targeted at precisely the constitutional guarantees that made it possible for Ray and Peggy Buckey to win fifty-two acquittals in the first trial. The establishment was going to make sure that that didn't happen again.

Meanwhile, the child abuse witch hunt has not abated. Clearly, it hasn't even peaked yet. In virtually every county in every state, new cases are popping up. Some of these are big, McMartin-type circuses with multiple defendants and hundreds of counts. Some are based on allegations too ludicrous to believe. In Oregon (in *People* v. *Gallup*), a sixty-two-year-old woman was sentenced to a long prison term for touching a four-year-old child on the chest! Many current cases are equally ridiculous, but some of them result in convictions and long prison terms. In 1989-90, California recorded a total of over 440,000 reports of child abuse. All but 16 percent were shown to be unfounded, and of that 16 percent, 8,448 (or 12 percent) were defined as sexual abuse. Many of these allegations were of such high crimes as touching a baby's chest and others equally remote in terms of "sexual abuse."

Recently, we became aware of something even more shocking. The authorities are arresting eight- and nine-year-old children, charging them with "molesting" other children of approximately the same age group, putting them through court proceedings and permanently stigmatizing them as "sex criminals." In the cases we have been able to research there was no evidence of assaultive or abusive behavior, just children "playing doctor." It has been generally understood for the past half century that sex play among children is perfectly normal, healthy behavior but apparently the child abuse industry is so hungry for new cases that it is reaching even into the eight- and nine-year-old age groups for new "suspects." In Los Angeles County recently an eight-year-old boy was taken into custody and charged with molesting an eight-year-old girl. We have received letters and newspaper clippings of similar cases all over the United States about the arrests of small children for nonabusive sexual contact with their contemporaries. In Oregon, an eight-year-old boy was arrested for allegedly engaging in some sex play with another child. The authorities did not go to the boy's home; they preferred to go into his classroom and subject him to the humiliation of being arrested before the eyes of all of his schoolmates.

In Los Angeles County, a supervisor in the Department of Children's Services wrote a letter to the DCS newsletter, and several letters to a member of the county board of supervisors, in which he strongly challenged the views and activities of DCS and its "child abuse experts." In one of the letters, he wrote, "Responding to reports of nonviolent sexual behavior among children just because there is a vague suspicion that such behavior may be abusive does not meet a reasonable test of probable cause. We have no mandate for that. We waste ourselves and violate standards of privacy and meaningful definitions of child abuse through such intrusions. We need to carefully maintain a social work role and not participate in guiding our sexual children gratuitously from a role of ignored nonclient to that of the most rigorously stigmatized of outcasts in our society, that of the child molester."

The county supervisor did not respond to the man's letters, but the government responded by arresting him and charging him with twenty-three counts of child molestation. The district attorney had some problems with the case. The man had worked with children for twenty-eight years and no one had ever had the slightest suspicion that he was a pedophile or a molester. If he were one, would it have been possible for him to conceal it for that long? The man was being held on $500,000 bail. His attorney put on no defense whatever. He was convicted and nobody has been allowed to communicate with him.

Social workers from all over the country have told us that there are so many people reporting each other for child sexual abuse that it is impossible to process all of the reports. The child abuse industry has spun out of control and become a voracious monster, hungry for human sacrifice, devouring everything in its path.

Several state legislatures are considering legislation for the construction of special prisons for those accused of sexual "offenses," and for the use of chemical castration as a punishment. A West Coast doctor who asked that his name not be published was convicted on transparently false allegations of child molestation and sentenced to spend the next eighteen years in state prison. In a letter to VOCAL he offered the following advice to anyone living in America today: "Keep your assets liquid and keep a current passport for all members of the family, and have a contingency plan, and at the first sign of interest from the child abuse people, leave the country. Whatever hardships are involved are not likely to be as bad as what they will do to you."

On June 26, 1990, a federal advisory panel told the U.S. Congress that child abuse had increased at an "astronomical" rate in recent years. Clearly, this was nonsense, but the average American ingests these "facts" as uncritically as he swallows junk food. The report states that the sudden, "astronomical" increase in child abuse constituted a "moral disaster" and a "national emergency so compelling that it dictates an immediate response." The report proposed that the existing system be replaced by a new, greatly expanded one, "child centered" and "neighborhood based." It was a transparent demand for money, but the language of the report strongly implied that the new system would be one that motivated people to inform on their neighbors, providing more cases for the system to process, more bodies for the meat grinder, more families to destroy, more clients for the penal system, more career opportunities for the child abuse racketeers.

The report conveyed a strong message that there was a need for the government to forcibly intrude into the sanctity of our homes, our families, our private lives.

Defense attorneys, expert witnesses for the defense, and social workers who express skepticism about the dogma of the child abuse, industry have been arrested and jailed. Curators of museums that exhibit photographs of nude families have been arrested, as have musicians whose songs contain sexual images. Approximately every thirty years, a wave of irrationality washes over us. We are riding one of these waves. Like the witch hunts of the past, it is a manifestation of an agenda to compel mindless conformity and blind obedience. It is also an excellent demonstration of what happens when great power is given to persons who are ill equipped to use it wisely.

As the jury deliberated, the media continued to poison the atmosphere with horror stories of child abuse leading into McMartin, communicating the powerful implication that Ray and the others were guilty. The very worst offenders were PBS television and National Public Radio.

On Friday, July 20, 1990, the jury brought out one sealed verdict. The judge did not announce whether he would unseal and read it before the jurors reached verdicts on the remaining seven counts. On Monday, July 23, the jurors sent out a second verdict and a note to the judge saying, "We appear to be hung on the remaining six counts." Judge Weisberg asked them to "go back in the jury room and continue your discussions." During the next three days the jurors asked to see some of the medical testimony, but there was no indication which way they were going with it.

Then, on Friday morning, July 27, we received a call from a friend, a reporter, who said, "The jurors are all dressed up today. They're going to have a hearing at one-thirty. I think this is it." The man also told us that the jurors had asked that the two sealed verdicts be returned to them because one juror had changed his mind. We hurriedly drove to the courthouse and arrived just in time. The eleventh floor was packed with television crews and reporters. We were able to get one of the few remaining seats in the courtroom. The jurors were summoned and filed into the jury box.

The judge asked the jury foreman, a young engineer, if there had been any progress toward unanimous verdicts. The foreman told the judge that the jurors were now hopelessly deadlocked on all counts, and that with each successive vote they were moving farther apart rather than closer to agreement. He told the judge that he believed each of the jurors had reached his final decision, from which he would not be moved. The judge asked each of the twelve jurors, individually, if he or she believed there was any possibility of their coming to a unanimous agreement. Each of them answered very emphatically that there was not. The judge asked the foreman how the jurors had split on each of the counts. The foreman told him that they had split 11-1 on three counts, in favor of acquittal; on the other five counts, the votes were 8-4, 9-3, 7-5, 8-4, and 6-6.

"It is clear," Judge Weisberg said, "that the jury will not reach a verdict in this case on any of the counts, and therefore there is legal necessity to declare a mistrial and I do so at this time. The court does declare a mistrial in this case."

Shortly after that, the jurors took seats in a row facing the audience, which was composed mostly of reporters. There were questions from the *Boston Globe*, the *Washington Post*, and newspeople from all over the world, most of whom knew little or nothing about the case. Paul stood and asked the jurors, "How has this changed your perception of the legal system?" Their eyes lit up. They really wanted to talk about that! A woman with a friendly, smiling face, a UCLA medical technician, said, "For the Buckeys to go through this for so many years. . . . It's criminal!" She went on to say that "We just got half a deck and we had to play like we had a whole deck." An extremely bright young musician said, "There were too many gaping holes . . . too many unanswered questions. We weren't even told how this thing started." A lean, dark-haired man with a slight European accent said, "Before they waste the taxpayers' money like this, they should make sure they have a case!" A woman said, "To me, they were not guilty." Someone asked the jurors if they would favor a third trial. All of them loudly answered, "No!"

All of the jurors who spoke reserved their severest criticism for the CII-videotaped interviews of the children. "They were terrible," the foreman said. Another juror, Lloyd Isaacson, an employee of the U.S. Treasury Department, commented, "If a child is pressured to say that those yucky things happened, they are going to go along with the adult. . . . They said, 'All your friends . . . have told us their yucky secrets and we want to hear this from you.' "

We were told that there was going to be a press conference in the district attorney's office in about two minutes. We went up to the eighteenth floor and walked in. Prosecutor Joe Martinez was asked whether there would be another trial.

"No," he answered. Ira Reiner announced that there would be no third trial. "It would be reasonable and fair to say, 'Enough' at this point," Reiner said. But Martinez zealously asserted that "Ray Buckey is not an innocent man!" Reiner stated that the district attorney's office would move to have the case dismissed Wednesday morning. The word spread quickly through the packed criminal courts building: "It's over!" A man with a little brown moustache confronted us and told us that we would have to leave the district attorney's office immediately. Someone had recognized our names and faces.

"We don't understand. We have more credentials than anyone here. We write for newspapers and we also write books. You have let people in there who don't even have a business card!"

"We are not going to discuss it," he said, "You will have to leave. Right now." Two other thugs moved forward, communicating to us the message that they were prepared to assist us if we did not leave quickly. A lawyer who had watched this laughed and said, "Maybe they didn't like your book."

Down on the eleventh floor there was pandemonium. "It's over!" was the repeated refrain. We embraced and said, "It's over!" The television newsmen asked Ray Buckey their robot questions. "What are you going to do now?" Ray said that he might go to Oregon and plant trees "or maybe teach people how to survive a witch hunt." He said that he would probably have to go and get a job. "I don't want to be a lawyer and I don't want to be a reporter," he smiled. "And I don't like wearing ties." Asked how he would spend his first evening of freedom, he said, "I'll probably go watch myself on TV and see if my tie is straight."

"I'm very relieved," Ray told another reporter. "I don't know if people can understand the feeling of waiting seven years for people who don't know you to decide your fate." Asked if he planned to file a lawsuit, he said he didn't know, that he would like his family to be settled in their own home, which they lost because of the enormous cost of defending themselves in these proceedings. "They can never give us back the seven years they took from us," he said. "I've been through anger, I've gone through fear, and even a feeling of revenge for the people who have done this to my family. I'm glad it's over. I would just like to be left alone."

On the way to dinner we listened to a radio talk show on which a caller was angrily proclaiming Ray's guilt. The talk show host asked him, "If you were presented with solid, irrefutable evidence of Ray Buckey's innocence, would you be willing to apologize to him?"

"No!" the man growled.

We don't know what other journalists and historians will say about this. But after sitting through six years of McMartin proceedings what troubles us most is the certainly that everybody involved in the case knew the Buckeys did not molest children, or at the very least, knew that there was no credible evidence to support a belief that they did. It was not just the children who changed their stories every time they testified; the prosecution's adult witnesses changed their stories, too. We saw them in the courtroom, again and again. We did not see the anguished, pained faces of parents who believed their children had been raped and violated. Some were laughing. Others affected great indignation. Some sobbed, but not very convincingly.

We do not think there will ever be total agreement as to what happened in this case. There will always be those who will say, "Something must have happened." But the fundamental standard of law in criminal proceedings in America is that a defendant is presumed innocent until proven guilty beyond a reasonable doubt and to a moral certainty.

At home, we watched the late news on television. A high-ranking law enforcement officer was giving his views on the McMartin case. "I believe in protecting the rights of defendants," he said. "But the pendulum has swung too far in that direction."

Meanwhile, the prosecutors' practice of using jailhouse snitches as witnesses continues unabated. They have been criticized for this in the press, but no action has been taken against any prosecutor for using a witness he knows is lying.

No appellate judge has struck down the immunity and anonymity clause in the child abuse statutes, even though there are constitutional defects that would give them grounds to do so. Apparently it is their perception that it would be politically inexpedient.

It was generally recognized by people on both sides of the McMartin case that CII's videotaped interviews, more than anything else, were the prosecution's undoing. Legislation has been introduced in several states to prohibit the videotaping of these interrogations in child molestation cases.

At a VOCAL conference, a woman from one of the West Coast states told her listeners that the McMartin case was actually an anomaly—that there are hundreds of other cases in progress in virtually every county in the United States, based on equally absurd allegations, and that the prosecutors were winning almost all of them. She said that a number of people in her chapter were seriously planning to emigrate and renounce their United States citizenship. "Our government officialdom is so corrupt and so firmly entrenched in power that it's beyond fixing," she said. "In the nineteen thirties, the most intelligent people in Germany got out. We feel that is our only sensible option."

The woman went on to say that statistics from the federal government's Sentencing Project show that the United States now has more of its citizens in prisons and jails than any nation in the world. The United States now incarcerates 426 of every 100,000 citizens, far more than the former Soviet Union, South Africa, or China. Australia has only seventy-two out of every 100,000 of its citizens behind bars while the Netherlands imprisons only forty. Another study recently made public by the National Council on Crime and Delinquency showed that only 18 percent of the 1.1 million Americans behind bars are there for committing serious crimes such as murder, rape, grand theft, or aggravated assault. About 82 percent of America's prisoners are people who have harmed no one but are being punished for "offenses" pertaining to their beliefs and lifestyles. And poverty. The figure for black Americans behind bars is 3,109 per 100,000.

"What was once the freest nation in the world is now the least free," the woman said. "America is gradually becoming a prison camp."

As for the Buckeys, who believed in the government, in obedience to authority, in the basic goodness of their neighbors, they are trying to put what's left of their lives back together. It is almost certain that nothing will be done to compensate them for their ruin and the seven-year nightmare they endured. It is equally certain that no action will be taken against those who falsely accused, imprisoned, and prosecuted them, and those who gave false witness against them.

We don't know if anybody cares. But it's not going to go away. As long as there is abuse of power, abuse of innocence, what happened to Ray and Peggy could as easily happen to you.

Bibliography

Alexander, David. "Giving the Devil More Than His Due." *The Humanist,* March/April (1990).
Barnhart, Keith. *Guilty Until Proven Innocent.* Hannibal, Mo.: Hannibal Books, 1990.
Baroja, Julio Caro. *The World of Witches.* Chicago: The University of Chicago Press, 1961.
Bernard, Fritz. *Pedophilia.* Rotterdam, The Netherlands: Enclave Books, 1985.
Best, Joel. *Threatened Children.* Chicago: The University of Chicago Press, 1990.
Cirino, Robert. *Power to Persuade: Mass Media and the News.* New York: Bantam, 1974.
Coleman, Lee, M.D. "False Allegations of Child Abuse: Have the Experts Been Caught with Their Pants Down?" (34-p ge paper available from the author).
Cory, Donald Webster, and R. E. L. Masters. *Violation Taboo.* New York: Julian Press, 1963.
Eberle, Paul, and Shirley Eberle. *The Politics of Child A! use.* New York: Lyle Stuart, Inc., 1986.
Eliade, Mircea. *Rites and Symbols of Initiation.* New York: Harper and Row, 1985.
Goldstein, Michael, and Harold Sanford Kant. *Pornography and Sexual Deviance.* Berkeley: University of California Press, 1973.
Hansen, Chadwick. *Witchcraft at Salem.* New York: George Brazilier, 1969.
Humphrey, Hubert H., Jr. "Report on the Scott County Investigations." Minnesota Attorney General's Office, 1985.
Huxley, Aldous. *The Devils of Loudun.* New York: Harper & Brothers, 1952.

Lawless, Joseph F., Jr. *Prosecutorial Misconduct.* New York: Kluwer Law Book Publishers, 1985.

Lewinsohn, Richard. *A History of Sexual Customs.* New York: Harper & Brothers, 1958.

Lyons, Arthur. *Satan Wants You: The Cult of Devil Worship in America.* New York: Warner Books, 1988.

Marwick, Max, ed. *Witchcraft and Sorcery.* Middlesex, England: Penguin Books, Ltd., 1970.

Nobile, Philip, and Eric Nadler. *United States of America v. Sex.* Minotaur Press, Ltd., 1986.

Paul, David M., MRCS, LRCP, D. (obst.) RCOG, D, DJM (Clin.). "What Really Did Happen to Baby Jane?: The Medical Aspects of the Investigation of Alleged Sexual Abuse of Children," *Medicine, Science and the Law* 26, no. 2 (1986).

Pride, Mary. *The Child Abuse Industry.* Westchester, Ill.: Crossway Publishers, 1986.

Rigert, J., D. Peterson, and J. Marcotti. "The Scott County Case: How It Grew, Why It Died," *Minneapolis Star & Tribune,* May 26, 1985, p. 1A.

Starkey, Marion L., with an introduction by Aldous Huxley. *The Devil in Massachusetts.* New York: Time, Inc., 1949.

Stanley, Lawrence A. "The Child Porn Myth." *Cardozo Arts and Entertainment Law Journal* 7, no. 2 (1989): 295–358.

———. "The Child Pornography Myth." *Playboy,* September 1988 (follow-ups in January and February 1989 issues).

Summers, Montague. *The History of Witchcraft.* New York: Lyle Stuart, 1956.

Ullerstam, Lars, M.D. *The Erotic Minorities.* New York: Grove Press, 1966.

Wexler, Richard. *Wounded Innocents.* Buffalo, N.Y.: Prometheus Books, 1991.